Groping *for* Ethics *in Journalism*

Groping *for*

Drawings by Fran Goodwin

in

Iowa State University Press / Ames

Ethics

Journalism THIRD EDITION

Gene Goodwin AND Ron F. Smith

The authors and the publisher gratefully acknowledge permissions to reprint the following:
The Society of Professional Journalists Code of Ethics.
The Radio-Television News Directors Association Code of Ethics.
The American Society of Newspaper Editors Statement of Principles.
The Associated Press Managing Editors Code of Ethics.

⊗ Printed on acid-free paper in the United States of America

First edition, 1983
Second edition, 1987
    Second printing, 1990
    Third printing, 1993
    Fourth printing, 1993
Third edition, 1994

Library of Congress Cataloging-in-Publication Data

Goodwin, H. Eugene,
    Groping for ethics in journalism / Gene Goodwin and Ron F. Smith. — 3rd ed.
        p.   cm.
    Includes bibliographical references and index.
    ISBN 0-8138-0847-2
    1. Journalistic ethics — United States.   I. Smith, Ron F.
    II. Title.
    PN4888.E8G66   1994
    174′.9097 — dc20
                                                    93-50737

CONTENTS

PREFACE

This third edition brings up

to date the groping for ethics by 20th century journalists, particularly those practicing in the United States and Canada. We wish we could report that the ethics of journalists have improved since the first and second editions of this book were published in 1983 and 1987, but we cannot. Whether you agree or disagree with our judgment about this lack of progress, we hope you will be interested in and stimulated by the supporting data we have gathered.

The new edition differs from the first two. It now has two authors, and many more cartoons. It is also more judgmental and prescriptive than the first two editions. This time we argue for a system of ethics in journalism based on principles we believe every thinking journalist can accept. We take a more prescriptive tack because of our strong suspicion that journalists, particularly younger ones, need more guidance in ethical decision making in an age in which narcissism and moral illiteracy and confusion seem to be dangerously on the rise.

We are not happy with our mostly negative conclusions about the state of ethics in journalism. Both of us worked for many years in journalism with an assortment of news organizations including The Associated Press, the Baltimore *Sun,* the old *Washington Star,* the *Cedar Rapids Gazette, The Daily Iowan,* the old *Pennsylvania Mirror, The Muncie (Ind.) Star,* the Greenville, Ohio, *Daily Advocate* and the *Fort Pierce (Fla.) Tribune.* And we have taught journalism at three American universities for an accumulated 45 years. So we know and like many people who were and are active in the profession we now criticize.

Journalists are easy to like. They do interesting things and tell interesting stories. Many are delightfully irreverent and skeptical. Most are plainspoken and able to cut through to the core of things in a world that prefers obfuscation and beating around bushes. But, with all their virtues, journalists still have problems distinguishing right from wrong. And that's what this book is all about. We sincerely hope that our evidence and arguments will help journalists and journalism students be more ethical.

Scores of working journalists helped by allowing us to interview them. Many are quoted in this book. We are grateful — both to those who are and those who are not quoted — for sharing their knowledge and views with us. We learned from all of them.

We owe a special thanks to Fran Goodwin, wife of the senior author, for her marvelous cartoons that have helped make our points more tellingly than our words could do. She also contributed her editing and library research skills, for which we are deeply grateful.

We are aided by valuable criticism and suggestions from journalism faculty colleagues at Penn State University and the University of Central Florida, namely, Tom Berner, Bill Dulaney, Fred Fedler, Mike Meeske, John Nichols, Vince Norris, Dan Pfaff, John Rippey, Don Smith and from working journalists Rene Stutzman and Loraine O'Connell.

Students in our journalism ethics classes have helped us through their discussions of and reactions to the ethical problems dealt with in this book. A few have made a more direct contribution through research papers, some of which are quoted in this edition and all of which expanded our knowledge of journalism ethics. We particularly acknowledge the research done by Deborah Bennedetti, Charles Brewer, Neil Genzlinger, Sally Heffentreyer, Robert W. Hollis, Robert King, Robert LaBarre, Patrick McFadden, George Osgood, Kathleen Pavelko, Laura Rehrmann, Michael Salwen, Donna Shaub, Donald Sneed and Jack Tobias.

Our gratitude also extends to Iowa State University Press editors, Gretchen Van Houten, Jane Zaring and Bob Burdette, for their many suggestions and criticisms that helped us improve this third edition.

H. Eugene (Gene) Goodwin
Professor Emeritus of Journalism
Pennsylvania State University

Ron F. Smith
Associate Professor of Journalism
University of Central Florida

ABBREVIATIONS

ABC = American Broadcasting Company
AFL-CIO = American Federation of Labor–Congress of Industrial Organizations
AIM = Accuracy in Media
AP = Associated Press
APME = Associated Press Managing Editors association
APSE = Associated Press Sports Editors association
ASNE = American Society of Newspaper Editors
CBS = Columbia Broadcasting System
CNN = Cable News Network
FCC = Federal Communications Commission
IRE = Investigative Reporters and Editors association
NAA = Newspaper Association of America
NAB = National Association of Broadcasters
NBC = National Broadcasting Company
NCAA = National Collegiate Athletic Association
NCEW = National Conference of Editorial Writers
NLRB = National Labor Relations Board
NPPA = National Press Photographers Association
ONO = Organization of News Ombudsmen
PBS = Public Broadcasting System
RTNDA = Radio-Television News Directors Association
SND = Society of Newspaper Design
SPJ = Society of Professional Journalists
UPI = United Press International

Groping *for* Ethics *in Journalism*

The Search
for Principles

Many Americans think journalists are pretty foul.

A straw poll a few years back found that people considered the ethical standards of reporters below those of used-car salesmen. Scientific polls are not much more encouraging. A poll by the *Los Angeles Times* found that less than a fourth of the public believed journalists were essentially ethical and almost one in 10 thought journalism ethics needed a complete overhaul.[1] Although most reporters enjoy exposing the foibles and chicanery of politicians, the public is convinced that politicians are more ethical than journalists.[2]

Some public perceptions of journalists are undoubtedly shaped by movies and television shows. Journalists are second only to police officers in how often they appear as characters on prime-time TV, but these portrayals are rarely flattering. Only 14 percent of fictional newspaper reporters and 24 percent of their TV brethren are shown favorably, according to one study. Most reporters are depicted as unethical, sloppy, insensitive and foolish.[3] They go about their day lying, stealing, eavesdropping, trespassing and seducing. They diligently avoid letting the facts get in the way of good stories and then run back to their newsrooms to tell gleeful editors about their big scoops.

Things are no better in the movies. After viewing more than 1,000 films depicting journalists, one researcher said that only a few showed journalists as the least bit competent,[4] and rarely do journalists come across as great humanitarians. In one movie popular a few years ago, a reporter, played by Kirk Douglas, was so desperate to write a series of front-page stories that he bribed rescuers to slow their efforts to free a man trapped in a cave. When the reporter found a way to free the man, he didn't tell anyone. Instead, he let the miner die a slow death so he could continue to write front-page stories.[5]

In a *New York Times* story headlined "Movies Blast Media, Viewers Cheer," Glenn Garelik pointed out that in the 1930s, reporters were often depicted in screwball comedies as fun-loving "blue-collar, salt-of-the-earth types," but today the image has changed. The wisecracking of earlier reporters has become arrogance, and reporters who had been shown as the working-class enemies of pretension are now seen as pretentious themselves.[6]

Oh wad some Power the giftie gie us
To see oursels as ithers see us!

—ROBERT BURNS

It's easy for journalists to write off these fictional depictions as exaggerations, but many Americans find the actions of real journalists equally distasteful. They've seen stories about a TV news crew in Alabama that filmed a man as he doused himself in gasoline and set himself afire but did little to stop him. They've heard about reporters at some of our most prestigious newspapers who have had to give back major journalism awards because they made up their winning stories or plagiarized them. They've watched TV camera crews pushing one another out of the way to get shots of mourning families. They've read accounts of journalists prying into people's private lives, even paying women to divulge the secrets of their affairs with presidential candidates. And they've questioned the patriotism of reporters who badger military leaders during wars. These incidents have led many Americans to wonder if journalists think about ethics at all.

Lots of Talk, Little Agreement

But American journalists do a lot of thinking, writing and talking about ethics these days. Workshops and panel discussions about ethics are fixtures at nearly every journalism conference, and trade magazines like *Quill, American Journalism Review* and *Columbia Journalism Review* frequently print stories analyzing journalists' conduct. A great many news organizations now have printed codes of ethics. The increased consciousness of ethics, however, has not led to substantial agreement. American journalists have some major problems coming to grips with their ethics.

One problem is the strong feeling throughout American journalism that First Amendment freedom is paramount, even it if means protecting bad journalism. Many journalists believe that to ensure freedom of the press, they must protect the legal rights of any reporter or editor, no matter how reprehensible they consider the person's conduct. These journalists are aware of the important distinction between news media laws and news media ethics, but they probably don't do a good job explaining that difference to the public. Laws determine what journalists are allowed to do. In our country, the courts have ruled that the First Amendment gives journalists much latitude, even to be unfair and in some cases inaccurate. Ethics, on the other hand, deals with what journalists ought to do as responsible members of a free society. Clearly, some actions of journalists may be legal but ethically offensive.

Another problem for journalists in groping for answers to ethical questions is a tendency to think of ethics as a list of prohibitions. In fact, many codes of ethics primarily spell out what a journalist should not do: Do not accept freebies. Do not engage in activities that may create a conflict of interest. Do not plagiarize. But ethics can also be thought of as a set of principles that journalists live by and as obligations to society.

A third problem relates to the difficulty in dealing with the contrasting and often conflicting pulls of journalism, the profession, and journalism, the business. Unlike most lawyers and doctors, people we think of as journalists—reporters, writers, photographers, editors, news directors and news producers—are mostly hired hands, not completely in

6

"I said they had a right to publish — but that doesn't mean I want you to read it!"

control of their own methods and products. (This problem will be dealt with more fully in Chapter 3.)

GENERAL AND PROFESSIONAL ETHICS

Some ethical theorists write about two kinds of ethics. The first consists of the demands placed on all members of the community. In American society, for instance, we are taught that in most cases we should tell the truth, help those in need, and not do things that harm others. We expect all members of our society to abide by these rules. The second consists of obligations placed on members of a community because of their special roles in that community. Physicians are obliged to heal patients. Priests and psychologists are obliged not to repeat what they are told during confession or counseling.

Journalists, too, accept certain obligations. The special role that journalists play in every society is to provide information to the public. In a free society, journalists are obliged to gather information as well as they can and to tell the truth as they find it. Journalists have an obligation to truth-telling.

However, it does journalists little good to strive for the truth if many people do not believe what they read in the papers or hear and see in newscasts because they do not respect the honesty of the news media. Journalists will have a hard time claiming to be the "eyes and ears of the public" if the public has no respect for them and offers them no support in their efforts to obtain access to information and question political leaders. Therefore, to satisfy their obligation to truth-telling, journalists are faced with a second fundamental obligation: to treat people — those in the audience and those who are making news — with fairness and compassion.

In a democratic society, the press has a third obligation. If the people are to govern themselves, they must be informed about the issues and the actions of their leaders. Journalists provide an important link between the affairs of government and the public. Fulfilling this role is the third obligation of journalists.

Truth-Telling and Objectivity

That journalists have an ethical obligation to tell the truth may seem perfectly obvious. "Accuracy, accuracy, accuracy" is preached in every news reporting class and demanded in every newsroom. But problems begin to arise when you try to decide what "accuracy" means and how "truth" relates to the daily rigors of the newsroom.

Until rather recently, most journalists believed they had an adequate definition of truth-telling. Truth-telling meant getting information from sources in appropriate positions of authority and relaying that information with as few personal embellishments as possible.

Journalism historians offer many explanations of why objective news reporting developed. Some contend that the growth of wire services like the Associated Press required reporters to make their writings seem unbiased since they would appear in newspapers with differing political positions. Other historians trace the beginnings of objective reporting to criticism by community leaders of the excesses and sensationalism of "yellow journalists" like Hearst and Pulitzer during the late 19th century or the muckraking reporters in the early part of the 20th century who sometimes turned their stories into impassioned pleas for a cause. Some scholars contend that objectivity evolved from journalists imitating the scientific method during the first part of the 20th century.

The development of this philosophy has also been traced to an unlikely source: the "Penny Press" of the mid-1800s and its development of court reporting, police reporting, and other assignments that made the interview the chief way of gathering information.[7]

Early American papers had little "news" in them as we think of the term, and they employed no reporters. Instead, the editors filled their papers with lots of political essays and announcements about the availability of products and services at local businesses. What news they did report they injected with a strong dose of their own opinions. These early editors scoffed at the idea of presenting opposing viewpoints. One editor likened presenting the other side of an argument to preaching

Christianity in the morning and advocating paganism in the evening.[8] Most of these papers had small circulations, and many depended on contributions from political parties to stay afloat.

Then a major change in the orientation of American newspapers occurred. Low-cost, high-volume printing techniques were developed, and many editors discovered they could make lots of money printing inexpensive newspapers for the masses and selling advertising to merchants who were looking for ways of enlarging their markets. To attract readers, these early editors recognized they would have to broaden their definition of "news." Rather than rely on their opinions to sell papers, they hired full-time reporters. When they recognized that crime stories could sell papers, many assigned their first reporters to covering the courts, where juicy stories of murder and wrongdoing were readily available, and the police, who could give them shocking details of crimes and arrests.

Thus crime reporting provided an early training ground for reporters, some historians contend. A style of journalism developed in which reporters wrote stories based on facts they gathered in interviews or heard during court proceedings. Thus, gathering and recording facts became the prime duty of these early reporters.

At about the time the Penny Press was replacing opinion-based stories with more factual accounts of the day's news, the telegraph became a key instrument in the gathering of news, noted James Carey, former dean of the College of Communications at the University of Illinois. Telegraph offices charged by the word. "As the telegraph made words expensive, a language of spare fact became the norm," Carey contended. The telegraph "made prose lean and unadorned and led to a journalism without the luxury of detail and analysis." He argued that the Penny Press and the telegraph elevated "objectivity and facticity into cardinal principles" of reporting, principles that many still cherish today.[9]

HERE'S HOW IT WORKS

In practice, "strict objectivity" resulted in reporting that worked as follows: Police reporters covering a murder would interview the detective at the scene and then write their stories, trying to be faithful to the comments of the officer. They would trust the officer to give them the correct information. However, just in case the information was wrong, they would sprinkle their stories with attributions like "the officer said" and "according to police." If the story was later shown to be inaccurate, the journalists were not to be blamed since they had just reported what the detective said. Furthermore, these reporters would argue, if the officer gave them wrong information, another source—perhaps an eyewitness or another police officer—would tell the reporters about the inaccuracies. They could then write another story relaying what this second source said. It was not their job to judge the truth of the comments. Their job was to present the facts and leave it to the public to decide who was telling the truth. Their major occupational demand was to report accurately what important people said and did.

This method of reporting seems more likely to produce truth than the strident political pontificating of earlier papers. The problem was, as former University of Illinois communications dean Theodore Peterson pointed out, the press made a fetish of its commitment to objectivity.[10]

Michael J. O'Neill, a former editor of the *New York Daily News,* learned about this narrow definition of objectivity when he covered a meat packers' strike in Chicago for United Press International around 1950. The union claimed the company had scabs working in the plant, but management denied it. O'Neill climbed over the fence and discovered non-union workers living inside the plant and sleeping on 125 cots he counted. When O'Neill got back to his office, his editor told him he could not use what he had seen unless he could attribute it to some company official.[11]

"I hope I can find some authoritative source to tell me this is a bad storm."

Other journalists of that era told stories of calling their newspapers in the middle of hurricanes and having editors order them to get sources like fire chiefs or police officers to confirm that the wind was blowing hard.

FACTS OR TRUTH?

The philosophy of strict objectivity served reporters well on many types of stories. They were able to gather and relay information quickly, and they were not bogged down by ethical concerns. They didn't have to worry about such niceties as whether the facts they were reporting gave a truthful account of an event. Under the theory of strict objectivity, reporting became such a non-judgmental task that a *Washington Post* editor once said he would prefer to hire reporters who didn't think at all.

The press received a major lesson in the flaws of this kind of objectivity from a master of the art of managing the media — Sen. Joseph McCarthy of Wisconsin. McCarthy won election to the Senate at a time when many Americans believed that Communists were slowly taking over America by secretly infiltrating the leadership of our government, military, political parties and media. Once in the Senate, McCarthy wanted to make a name for himself, and the Washington press corps was unwittingly ready to help him. McCarthy learned that if he made a sensational charge, the papers would report what he said almost word for word. Armed with this knowledge, McCarthy began a campaign that made him one of the most feared men in Washington in the 1950s.

McCarthy would announce to reporters that through a diligent investigation he had learned that key people in the State Department were members of the Communist Party. The reporters, bound to the philosophy of strict objectivity, believed it was their obligation to report the statements of a U.S. senator. Even if the reporters doubted what he said, their stories the next day would report that a diligent junior senator from Wisconsin said he had discovered known Communists in the State Department. McCarthy was getting the publicity he craved. Before long, McCarthy claimed to have found Communists in most branches of government, the military, the entertainment business and the media, although he rarely named names.

The shallowness of such reporting angered many reporters. They knew they were being used, yet they felt trapped by the demands of strict objectivity. Some asked to be taken off the McCarthy beat. Others stayed on the beat and were totally frustrated. In *The Powers That Be,* David Halberstam described the plight of Phil Potter, a reporter for the Baltimore *Sun:*

> During the various McCarthy hearings, [Potter] would astonish admiring colleagues by coming back to the *Sun* bureau and writing a first draft of a story in which all his anger, all his rage at what McCarthy was doing would come forth: "Joseph R. McCarthy, the no good lying son of a bitch from Wisconsin . . ." Then, having vented his spleen and released his anger, he would tear up the story and sit down and go to work. Often when Potter had finished for the day he would go to the National Press Club, where he would find some of his colleagues and tell them that they had to start covering McCarthy, trying to explain what McCarthy was like, what he was

doing. It was, he thought, missionary work. Most of his colleagues thought he was simply too involved. A story was a story. If Joe said something, you reported it; that was all it took.[12]

Many of Potter's colleagues were wedded to the philosophy of strict objectivity and its lack of concern for the distinction between fact and truth. It was a fact that McCarthy had said there were Communists in high-ranking positions in the military. And since he was a U.S. senator, his statements were news. Whether his statements were likely to be true was not the responsibility of the reporters. If the information was not true, someone else should come forward and say the senator was lying.

But not all journalists of that era saw their jobs as repeating whatever charges McCarthy made. The biggest challenge to McCarthy's credibility came from a news medium that was then in its infancy — TV. CBS's Edward R. Murrow exposed some of McCarthy's tactics on his program *See It Now,* and soon McCarthy's bubble began to burst. After the Senate in 1954 voted 67 to 22 to censure him for his reckless and abusive conduct, many in the press took a hard look at how they had been used by this skillful abuser of truth.

THE IMPACT OF VIETNAM

The notion of strict objectivity took a further beating during the Vietnam War in the 1960s and early 1970s. Official sources in Washington tried to paint pictures of South Vietnamese leaders as patriots who were popular with the people and would soon lead their country to victory over the Communists. But the official government line often clashed dramatically with what reporters were seeing in the field and hearing from people in the cities and villages. In the early days of the war, many editors, accustomed to the friendly relationship that existed between the press and the military during World War II, discounted the stories from their reporters and played the official Washington versions of the war.

Even *New York Times* reporter David Halberstam, who eventually won a Pulitzer Prize for his Vietnam War coverage, said he felt pressure from editors who wished he would more closely follow the dictates of strict objectivity. "Some editors disliked what they felt was my lack of balance and wished my reporting were more conventional, with more articles directly quoting high-level officers about how well things were going."[13]

Another reporter, Seymour Hersh, became so dissatisfied with the dictates of his editors that he quit his job with a wire service and formed his own news service. His stories — some of which uncovered the massacre of hundreds of Vietnamese civilians, including old people, women and babies, by American soldiers in the village of My Lai — earned him a Pulitzer.[14]

The reliance on strict objectivity was so strong during the early part of the war that newspaper editors were forced to make some strange decisions. Journalism Professor Daniel Hallin recounted one occasion when the State Department in Washington gave its "official" version of an incident in Vietnam and the U.S. Embassy in Vietnam released its "official" statement about the same incident. The *New York Times* bureau in Washington dutifully filed a story quoting the State Department version, and at the same time the *Times* bureau in Saigon filed a story quoting embassy officials. The two "official" versions disagreed on many key points. *Times* editors in New York were at a loss to deal with two conflicting "objective" dispatches. The editors argued among themselves, then made a decision that would be inconceivable today. The paper ran the stories side by side with a note apologizing to its readers for the contradictions.[15]

Events like these led more and more reporters and editors to believe that truth-telling meant more than just compiling what officials said.

GETTING THE OTHER SIDE

For some time, many journalists have thought they could come closer to the truth if they made a point of "getting the other side." If a Democratic senator made a statement, reporters would track down a leader of the Republican Party to get the GOP's reaction. The reporter would then write a story quoting both sides, and the public would be left to decide what to believe. These stories seemed to satisfy the demands of objectivity since they gave equal weight to both political parties. Today, many journalists remain convinced that the process of getting the other side is as close to a truthful account as journalism can come.

Yet the process of getting the other side of arguments isn't as easy as it might seem. For one thing, when reporters try to get the other side, they often introduce elements of subjectivity because they have to choose whom to interview. Some contend that liberal reporters tend to be drawn to liberal sources.[16] Even when reporters honestly seek out sources from both sides, if they present a spokesperson for one side who is glib and quick-witted and a spokesperson for the other who is dry and dull, readers and viewers may get a lopsided understanding of the issue.

Selecting sources is made even more difficult because most stories don't have one easily identifiable "other side." Complex social issues like

"I need a few more pro-quotes to make this story ring true."

abortion or homelessness have an impact on many groups, and each group has its own point of view. Even such "simple" proposals as new roads or new schools can touch off reactions from widely divergent community groups. If reporters settle for stories that quote a city council member who is for a project and one who is opposed to it, their stories will probably be accurate and seemingly objective. Yet by reducing the complexity of the story to these two viewpoints, these reporters may be presenting a misleading and incomplete picture of what's really going on in the community. The problem is further compounded when some community groups are well-organized with public relations programs while other groups may have equally valid viewpoints but may not be savvy at dealing with the press. Reporters who are drawn to the easier sources may produce stories that are accurate but not complete.

The problem of tracking down divergent sources is made even more sticky because journalists want to quote people with some claim to credibility. Therefore, they seek out people with titles (Professor, Mayor, the Reverend, Attorney) or other signs of "authority." TV journalists have an even tougher time since they need to find sources who can speak well on the air and present their views quickly, preferably in 20-second sound bites.

Even when reporters have found sources to represent the various sides, they are faced with an even more perplexing problem: How do you deal with conflicting information from supposedly authoritative sources? For instance, during the 1950s and 1960s, scientists began to find striking evidence that smoking cigarettes was linked to several diseases. Reporters would quote from these scientific studies, then attempt to get the other side by calling the tobacco companies for their responses. Often a representative for an industry group would attempt to debunk the scientific research. Applying the standards of objectivity, reporters would give equal weight to both sides.[17] The reader was left with two conflicting claims and given little help in trying to sort out the truth.

Reporters are still accused of practicing this kind of "equality." In the fall of 1992, the Union of Concerned Scientists issued an environmental warning. Dr. Henry Kendall, chair of the scientific group and a Nobel laureate in physics, complained to a national conference of journalists that reporters often balanced the views of many top scientists with remarks from a public relations official for one of the fossil-fuel industries. Kendall said he understood the value of presenting opposing viewpoints but believed the news stories should have pointed out the "relative credibility of a document signed by about half the living Nobel laureates with that of a paid spokesperson."[18]

But establishing the relative credibility of sources is not a simple task. Journalists writing stories about major issues like global warming, new educational techniques, developments in medicine and science, or international trade treaties are making tough calls when they try to decide which experts and which groups to quote and which to leave out. Nearly 70 percent of the reporters in one poll said that one of the toughest things about covering environmental issues was trying to find unbiased experts.[19]

Today's journalists would quickly acknowledge that in their daily accounts of complex events they cannot be expected to discover "truth." Yet many want a definition of truth-telling that is more satisfying than the mindless reporting of statements by officials that strict objectivity required or the muddled reporting that often comes from defining truth as trying to present both sides objectively.

Social Responsibility

The idea that American journalists should do more than just pass along facts without concern for their truth or social significance is not new. Several years ago, a group of well-regarded intellectuals studied the news media and wrote a report that may have indirectly influenced the way many American journalists view their work.

The report grew out of a request Henry Luce, the founder of *Time* magazine, made of his friend Robert Hutchins, chancellor of the University of Chicago, in the 1940s. Luce offered to provide funds for a study of the American press. Hutchins assembled some of the best minds of the era, including philosophers, legal scholars, political scientists and a poet, but no one with a media background. After two years of study, Hutchins' Commission on Freedom of the Press issued a report that the press was in serious trouble. The commissioners objected to the growth of chains, feared the concentration of so much power into the hands of a few wealthy media owners, and complained about the poor quality of news coverage.

More important, one part of the commission's reports called on journalists to rethink their obligations to the truth. It said that newspapers were too concerned with "scoops and sensations" and suggested better ways for the press to inform the American citizenry. The report challenged the press to provide

1. A truthful, comprehensive and intelligent account of the day's events in a context which gives them meaning. . . . It is no longer enough to report the fact truthfully. It is now necessary to report the truth *about the fact.*

2. A forum for the exchange of comment and criticism.

3. The projection of a representative picture of the constituent groups in the society.

4. The presentation and clarification of the goals and values of the society.

5. Full access to the day's intelligence.[20]

The commission's report was lambasted by the press. Robert McCormick, publisher of the *Chicago Tribune,* railed against the report, claiming it would lead to government control of the press.[21] Journalism groups branded its members "eggheads" and said their ideas would destroy freedom of the press.

THE THEORY DEVELOPS

The work of the commission might not have had much impact on journalism if it had not been for Theodore Peterson, a journalism professor and former dean of the College of Communications at the University of Illinois. He wrote a chapter in *Four Theories of the Press* articulating the commission's concerns and giving the name "social responsibility theory" to its ideals.

Peterson wrote that the major premise of the social responsibility theory is that "freedom carries concomitant obligations; and the press, which enjoys a privileged position under our government, is obliged to be responsible to society for carrying out certain essential functions of mass communications in contemporary society."[22]

The social responsibility theory was seen by Peterson as replacing the traditional libertarian theory, which had guided those who established our press system when this country was founded. Libertarianism, a composite of the ideas of thinkers like John Milton, John Erskine, Thomas Jefferson and John Stuart Mill, holds that the press and other media should be privately owned and as free as possible from government so that they can pursue the truth as they see it and be a check on government. According to the libertarian theory, the press can be irresponsible as well as responsible, printing falsehoods as well as truth, because the citizens are rational and can separate one from the other. The rationale behind the libertarian theory is that in a free marketplace of ideas where all voices can be heard, the truth will surely emerge. "But somewhere along the way, faith diminished in the optimistic notion that virtually absolute freedom and the nature of man carried built-in correctives for the press," Peterson maintained.[23]

He argued that social responsibility for the press was born out of several changes. One was the technological and industrial revolution that changed "the American way of living"; added movies, radio and television to the media system; and encouraged concentration of media ownership in a few hands. Another change, Peterson wrote, "was the development of a professional spirit as journalism attracted people of principle and education, and as the communications industries reflected the growing sense of social responsibility assumed by American business and industry generally."

"This social responsibility stuff is no fun at all. I liked it better when we could let the chips fall where they may."

Peterson did not try to build a complete set of ethical standards. In fact, he cautioned his readers in 1956 to "remember that the social responsibility theory is still chiefly a theory. But, as a theory it is important because it suggests a direction in which thinking about freedom of the press is heading."

HUTCHINS' IDEAS ENDURE

The commission's guidelines offer an approach to truth-telling that has become widely accepted by many journalists. The commission's first suggestion—that the news media should provide comprehensive accounts of the day's events in a context that gives them meaning—would not seem alien to most modern journalists. Reporting the "truth about the facts" is now a common aim of most news organizations.

The commission did not define what it meant by "truth." Peterson suggested that the commission did not expect the press to discover absolute truth but did expect the press to discover "a number of lesser truths, tentative truths, working truths."

Today's journalists have broadened their definition of "news." At one time news of crime and politics dominated the papers. Now business, health and science, and changing lifestyles are important to papers and newscasts. Reporters have also expanded the kinds of sources they use, so they are no longer as dependent on official versions of the news. The best examples of modern journalism include in-depth stories on social issues like poverty, AIDS, and homelessness that contain comments not only from politicians, welfare agency officials, and sociologists but from lower-level staff in the agencies and the impoverished, sick and disenfranchised themselves.

Over the years newspapers in particular have made efforts to become forums for the exchange of ideas, the second of the commission's recommendations. In the past, many papers limited opinion to their own editorial writers and columnists. But today most papers have added additional editorial pages, called op-ed pages, featuring opinion articles and columnists with different political orientations from the papers' editorial positions. Most papers print letters to the editor, and many encourage readers to submit columns.

In its third suggestion, the commission demanded that the media make a better effort to portray the various groups in our society. Slowly, media managers are making some progress in this area. Until recently, most daily newspapers were produced primarily by white middle-class men. All too often, the news was covered in ways that reflected the social background of these journalists: It was filled with white middle-class male values.

But the news media have learned some tough lessons about the weaknesses caused by lack of cultural diversity in their newsrooms. Editors and news directors recognized that the media failed to anticipate and cover adequately the urban riots in the last half of the 20th century. They began to sense the distance between their news product and many people in the communities they hoped to serve.

Today many newsrooms have greater diversity in their staffs than ever before. The percentage of minority journalists has more than doubled in the past decade, although it is still far below their representation in society as a whole. Women make up more than a third of the journalism work force, about the same percentage as in the early 1980s.[24] Most news staffs today include gays and lesbians.[25]

Also, many news organizations now make efforts to reach out to divergent groups in their communities. Some writers have argued that these efforts are among the reasons for the decline of the African-American press in many major cities. Mainstream newspapers are now doing a better job of covering the black community than they once did, and African-Americans are now more frequently interviewed on TV newscasts. Also, the black press faces staffing problems because mainstream newspapers and TV news departments now hire many of the top African-American journalism graduates who earlier would have worked at black newspapers.[26]

But the media still have a long way to go in achieving sufficient diversity. James Lewis, publisher of an African-American newspaper in Birmingham, said that although blacks trust national white-owned media like CNN and *USA Today,* many do not trust their local newspapers.[27] Acceptance of minorities in the newsroom has not gone smoothly in some cases. One writer concluded that on many newspaper staffs "the average black reporter is having a hard time being accepted by his or her average white colleagues and being treated like anyone else by management."[28] A *Wall Street Journal* bureau chief wrote that the weak economic conditions of the early 1990s had slowed progress toward diversity. But, she said, "even in the best of times . . . newsroom managers tend to be largely cynical toward the concept of multicultural staff." She suggested that unconscious prejudice may influence the evaluations of some minority employees and cause others to be hired as trainees or kept as news clerks when whites with similar backgrounds would be given reporter status.[29]

The fourth commission objective for the media is one that many news organizations are still debating: the presentation and clarification of the goals and values of the society. The commission wrote, "We must recognize . . . that the agencies of mass communication are an educational instrument, perhaps the most powerful there is; and they must assume a responsibility like that of educators in stating and clarifying the ideals toward which the community should strive."

Although the notion of the press as an intellectual leader of the community was held by many Colonial editors who were just as likely to publish critiques of the community values as what we might consider news, modern editors are less sure if it is their role to be an observer of the community or a participant in it. (This issue is discussed further in Chapter 4.)

The fifth of the commission's suggestions called for newspapers to provide full access to the day's intelligence. The media have sought better access for citizens by getting public business conducted in public. Media companies have fought efforts by politicians and bureaucrats to close records from the public and hold secret meetings. News organizations hire attorneys to ensure that city councils and school boards comply with government-in-the-sunshine laws. The media have waged a long and reasonably successful campaign to get most of the states to adopt open-meetings and open-records laws and to get the federal government to enact the Freedom of Information Act. None of these laws has worked to the complete satisfaction of most journalists, but they have been useful in opening up more activities and records of government to the news media and the public.

The report of the Hutchins commission was controversial when it was issued a half century ago, and its critics are correct that the social responsibility theory it spawned is not an adequate basis for a thorough system of news media ethics because it does not address enough of the ethical concerns journalists face. But most modern reporters and editors would find little to quibble with in the commission's efforts to define goals for truth-telling by journalists. Today the commission's principles still challenge American journalists to commit themselves to complete and thorough reporting and to make their reports truthful and socially responsible.

OTHER AVENUES TO TRUTH

The Hutchins commission wanted reporters to worry about the truthfulness of their accounts, to examine events in light of their knowledge of the community, and to relate the news so that its social significance could be understood. These demands go far beyond those of traditional objective reporting.

Many newspapers have begun to encourage their reporters to "write with authority." They are expected to research their stories so that they can provide context and explain the significance of the developments. Their stories often provide the factual background without as much attribution as traditional journalistic writing requires.

Staffers at the *Portland* (*Maine*) *Press Herald* call the technique "expert reporting." Lou Ureneck, the paper's executive editor, told an ASNE conference, "Too many daily newspapers use only the eyes and the ears of their reporters and don't use their brains." When Eric Blom, a reporter at the *Press Herald,* was working on an investigation of the workers compensation system in Maine, Ureneck and other editors told Blom "to get beyond the whipsaw of competing quotes that are often put into a story for 'balance.' We told him to avoid bogging down in excessive attribution, weasel words and hedging phrases. We told him to support his conclusions with facts and to write forcefully in plain language."

Some critics have branded the *Press Herald*'s efforts as advocacy journalism and not honest reporting. But Ureneck said that reader response has been overwhelmingly positive and that the paper has no plans to change its approach. "These techniques," he told *American Journalism Review,* "can put some meaning back into journalism."[30]

Other editors, like Geneva Overholser of *The Des Moines Register,* argue that the shift away from objectivity is long overdue. "All too often, a story free of any taint of personal opinion is a story with all the juice sucked out," Overholser said in a speech at the University of Southern California. "A big piece of why so much news copy today is boring as hell is this objectivity god. Keeping opinion out of the story too often means being a fancy stenographer." Although she understands the concerns of editors who believe that moving away from objectivity "will open the floodgates of opinion writing," she argued that a greater danger is posed by the boredom of "wishy-washy, take-it-or-leave-it writing that is wholly objective."[31]

Someday "journalists will be seen as information experts, just as bankers are relied upon for financial expertise and jewelers for appraisals of gems," in the view of Carl Sessions Stepp, former *Charlotte Observer* reporter and editor who became a University of Maryland journalism professor. What sense does it make for "journalists to research subjects with increasing thoroughness and expertise and then hold back their conclusions, depriving readers of what may be the most trustworthy, studied assessments available anywhere?"[32]

These views of the role of the journalist are common in other Western countries. Unlike American journalists, who are often generalists trained in journalism schools, many British newspapers try to hire experts in various areas like economics or foreign affairs and then train them to be journalists. These reporters are then given much freedom to use their expertise in their stories. They see themselves as committed to truth, but they do not look upon themselves — nor do their readers — as neutral observers. They view themselves as knowledgeable writers trying to make sound observations about matters in which they have developed an expertise. Michael Kinsley, who worked as an editor for a British news magazine, explained that British reporters try to be "fair and accurate and balanced, but they're not afraid to express their own views."[33]

After comparing coverage of the 1991 Gulf War in London's *The Independent* and the *Los Angeles Times,* Katrin Schumann, a Boston radio journalist, praised the British paper for its "feisty skepticism," efforts to debunk government public relations statements, and occasional first-person writing. She concluded, "I came away with the feeling that the *Times'* news articles may have been factual, but they had none of the sense of reality that appeared in *The Independent.*"[34]

Often European papers allow their stories a distinct political slant. In London, readers of the *Guardian* expect the paper to give a liberal interpretation to the news and the *Times* of London and the *Sun* to provide conservative views. *The Independent,* a paper that began in the 1980s, hires reporters with both Labour Party and Conservative Party leanings. The French and German newspapers are even more overt in their blending of news and analysis and portray a much wider spectrum of political thought than American newspaper readers are used to. David Shaw of the *Los Angeles Times* noted that in Europe "seven different journalists might put seven different spins on a given story."[35]

Few American newspeople are willing to go as far as the Europeans in synthesizing and interpreting the news, but according to a national study, about half of today's journalists believe it is very important to analyze complex problems. Newsmagazine and newspaper journalists are more likely than television and radio reporters to believe this is their proper role.[36]

Although journalists may not often think about it in philosophic ways, their understanding of "truth" has a major role in determining how they go about the task of reporting the news.

The Need for Compassion and Fairness

CBS newsman George Crile was in court to answer a libel suit after a CBS documentary contended that Gen. William Westmoreland had deliberately overstated the success of the American military effort in

Vietnam. The trial, featuring charges of official misconduct by the military and questionable reporting techniques by CBS, was big news. When Crile left the courthouse, he was surrounded by packs of newsmen shouting questions and TV camera crews jockeying for the best angle. The veteran journalist later remarked, "I'm shocked at the way the media cover these things; they're like a bunch of hungry animals." To which another journalist responded: "George, you have met the enemy and he's in our business."[37]

His experience is not unique. Many journalists have learned of the ugliness of an uncompassionate press only when they have become the newsmakers.

Eleanor Randolph, who recounted Crile's story in her column in *The Washington Post,* recalled that the first time she read a story about herself, she "could not breathe properly for five minutes." She said her "first name was misspelled, and the salary increase I reportedly had received by going to a new job was double the real thing. Moreover, the reporter had not called to ask."[38]

Los Angeles Times writer David Shaw tracked down several journalists who had become subjects of news stories. When he asked them to describe what it was like to deal with reporters, he got responses like "a sobering experience," "a humbling experience," and even a "humiliating experience."[39]

Edward Kosner, editor of *New York* magazine, said being the subject of news stories has changed the way he edits his magazine. He learned how painful and unnecessary some negative writing can be. This realization "has made my pencil a little more attentive when it hovers over a cute line which is a throwaway line to the writer but in fact may wound somebody very much."

Pulitzer Prize–winning investigative reporter Seymour Hersh told Shaw: "It's terrific to be written about because then you get a real sense of what it's like for the victim you impale. It's a great tool for self-examination, self-criticism."

Opinion polls suggest that the public also perceives people in the news as victims impaled by ruthless reporters. Several surveys have been done by different groups. Consistently, they have found that

- Only a third of the public think reporters care anything about the people they report on.
- Fully 73 percent think the media do not respect people's privacy.
- Nearly half the public is unwilling to call journalists moral.[40]
- Almost two-thirds think the press looks out mainly for powerful people, not the ordinary citizen.

- More than half think reporters abuse their constitutional privileges.[41]
- About half don't think reporters get their facts straight, and more than half think the media cover up the mistakes reporters make.[42]

Even more alarming, the respect people have for journalists is declining. The number of people who told pollsters that they believe the media are doing a "very good job" has declined from 30 percent in 1985 to 17 percent in 1993, and the percentage who believe the media are doing a bad job has nearly tripled—from 4 percent to 11 percent.[43]

BEING COMPASSIONATE

In our society, most of us expect people to behave in ways that are fair and compassionate. Our level of respect drops when we see someone behave arrogantly or tromp on another person's feelings. We scorn those who use others or deceive them.

Since fairness and compassion are so much a part of our society's moral fiber, on first glance some might wonder why we need to include it as one of the three major obligations of the press. And many journalists will quarrel with the notion that compassion is an ethical obligation in the news business. They fear that the softness implied by that emotion might deter the primary mission of journalism—to get the news out.

But it is treated here as one of the important categories of ethical obligations because, in a way, a scarcity of compassion is at the base of many of the troubles journalists have with methods of gathering information, privacy and other ethical areas. Failure to feel sympathy for or empathize with the people involved in news—sources and subjects alike—produces a sterile sort of journalism.

There seems to be something in the way many journalists interpret their role as neutral observers that makes them come across as cold and uncaring. This impression is conveyed not just in a few clear-cut cases in which journalists turn their backs on human victims in the name of doing their job but in their often uncivil and snobbish treatment of news sources both on and off camera. The great journalists are people who excel at getting the news out but also never forget their humanity. Being sensitive and compassionate with other human beings in the news should be seen as a virtue in a news professional. But the history of journalism is filled with episodes in which reporters and editors did not show fairness and compassion, and the profession is worse off for it.

Some journalists are rather quick to dismiss these arguments. They point out that the job of the press is not to be popular and that too many

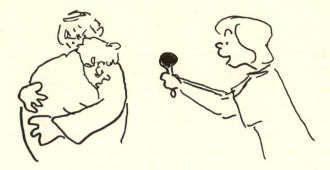

"And can you tell us, ma'am, how you feel about. . . ?"

people blame the messenger when they do not like the message. These observations have some validity. Nearly every news story, even the most lighthearted feature, has the potential of offending someone, and the public is ill-served if reporters back away from tough stories because they fear negative public reaction. Journalists must be tough-minded and must ask the tough questions.

The problem is deeper than not being able to please all the people all the time. If journalists cannot earn the respect and trust of the public, they will face increasing difficulties in gathering the news and being believed by the public. A poll by the *Los Angeles Times* found that a third of the public favors limits on news media access to government records and files. An even more discomforting finding was that a third of Americans believe that a government official should have the right to stop the media from reporting a story that the government official believes might be inaccurate.

Not only would many in the public like to limit journalists' access to news and allow some censorship; they want the media to suffer financially for their mistakes. Pollsters found that nearly half the people believe that expensive libel suits are a good way to keep the media in line, and more than half would allow the courts to fine the media for inaccurate stories.[44]

Perhaps the most damning indictment of the press was reported in a large-scale survey by journalism professor Robert O. Wyatt. American journalists take great pride in the First Amendment and the protection it gives them. Yet according to Wyatt's survey, Americans would probably not ratify the First Amendment if it was on the ballot today. Two-thirds would limit such media practices as endorsing candidates, criticizing the government and military, and reporting on politicians' past mistakes.

About a fourth said the media should not be involved in these kinds of activities at all.[45]

None of these findings proves that journalists are innately unfair or uncompassionate. But they are a strong indication that too many journalists do not understand the importance of dealing with the people they encounter and their readers in a fair and compassionate manner. Too many apparently believe that they must turn in their sense of humanity when they receive their press cards. (Compassion is discussed more fully in Chapter 12.)

BEING FAIR

In an earlier era, journalists thought their vows of objectivity protected them from the criticisms of bias or unfairness. They imagined their job to be much like those of research scientists who walk through laboratories coolly reading dials and jotting down findings. Reporters saw themselves attending meetings and press conferences and writing their stories with the same degree of neutrality and dispassion. They believed they could produce totally objective accounts if they adhered to the strict demands of traditional newswriting formulas like the inverted pyramid and watched their word choices to hide any personal reactions to the news.

But journalists make several subjective decisions when they process the news. Editors decide which stories get assigned and which do not, and they select the ones that will get major coverage. Writers decide which facts should be placed at the top of the story, which go near the bottom, and which get left out altogether. The problem is that journalists write about issues and events that often strike at the very basic tenets of our society. Their stories may be about major societal concerns like abortion and war or local issues like schools and taxes. These issues touch reporters' lives just as strongly as the public's. Likewise, journalists meet and often get to know many political and social leaders. They will like some of these leaders as people, and some they will not.

"It's stupid and dishonest for journalists to continue to insist that they are without gut feelings, values, politics, et cetera," said Robert Scheer, whose reporting and editing career has included stops at the rabble-rousing *Ramparts* and the mainstream *Los Angeles Times*. "And if they are, I want to know why and how did they get to be without those things and where have they been. . . . To me the more important question is not whether you can be neutral but how you do your job in a fair and honest way."[46]

Some argue that many see journalists' claims of objectivity as hypocritical. Gary Hoenig, editor of *News Inc.* magazine, noting that any hint of bias in news stories provokes "endless hand-wringing" among journalists, has asked:

> Why, then, if we are so painfully earnest [about objectivity], does the thinking, reading public insist there's an agenda behind every significant story? I think it's because people find our guise of objectivity stilted and self-righteous. Who would believe that people as aggressive and intelligent as today's reporters are not affected by what they see and hear, and who they meet, while on the job? [47]

Many journalists agree with Scheer and Hoenig. They believe the challenge for journalists is to be willing to acknowledge that they are making judgments when they write the news and to admit that some of these judgments may be influenced by their backgrounds, beliefs and opinions. Once reporters recognize these influences, they must strive to overcome them. Editors and news directors must do the same and then police their reporters' work to make sure that reporters' personal opinions are not unduly shaping the news. Compassion and fairness should be a consideration in nearly every ethical decision journalists make.

Democratic Principles

> Congress shall make no law respecting an establishment of religion, or prohibiting the free exercise thereof; or abridging the freedom of speech, or of the press; or the right of the people peaceably to assemble, and to petition the Government for a redress of grievances.

That guarantee of freedom in the First Amendment to the U.S. Constitution, along with similar guarantees in the constitutions of the 50 states, provides the legal basis for press freedom in this country. That freedom in turn has had a powerful influence on the ethics of journalists and the news media, principal beneficiaries of the First Amendment.

It must be understood that the First Amendment does not literally mean that no laws whatever can abridge freedom of the press. Like all provisions of the Constitution, the free press provision has been interpreted and reinterpreted by the courts over the years so that several restrictions on absolute freedom—libel and slander, for example—have been permitted. Paul Poorman, former editor of the *Akron Beacon Journal,* once counted 34 broad areas, including interstate commerce and labor-management relations, in which Congress has made laws limiting the freedom of the press.[48] Despite these restrictions, the interpretations that journalists give to the First Amendment shape their attitudes toward ethics and ethical standards.

Although scholars who have studied the Founding Fathers are not sure exactly what they had in mind regarding freedom of the press, Colonial newspaper editors seemed to have a pretty clear notion. Even though their newspapers were a far cry from the ones we read today, their comments seem very modern.[49] These editors saw it as their job to watch the activities of the political leaders and to comment on them. One South Carolina editor argued that as long as newspapers were keeping tabs on Congress, senators could not "betray their trust; convert serious matters into jokes; or transfer mountains into molehills." Another editor wrote, "Considerable Latitude must be allowed in the Discussion of Public Affairs, or the Liberty of the Press will be of no Benefit to Society."[50] To these Colonial journalists, freedom of the press was important if the American experiment in democracy was to work.

Modern journalists view their work in much the same way. For the past 20 years, four large-scale research projects have tried to find out what values are important to American journalists. Each time, a large majority of journalists said investigating government claims was among their top priorities.[51]

Although journalists agree that they should serve as watchdogs of the activities of government, they differ on how to handle this responsibility. David Weaver and G. Cleveland Wilhoit, two Indiana University journalism professors who have conducted three of the studies, said that journalists' attitudes fell into three groups. The largest group saw their role as interpretive, believing they should investigate claims by politicians, analyze complex problems, and discuss policy. A second group placed greater importance on getting the news out as quickly as possible; radio journalists in particular were likely to be in this group. The smallest group was journalists who believe they should take an adversarial relationship with government.[52] (The relationship between journalists and the government is discussed more thoroughly in Chapter 7.)

THE PUBLIC'S RIGHT TO KNOW

Journalists have been talking about their "watchdog role" since the early days of our republic. But another popular phrase used to define the role of journalists is relatively new. "The public's right to know" ("people's right to know" if you prefer) became a chant of American journalists after World War II, a slogan in their fight to expand their access to news of government, business and other areas of society that have found ways to hide from public scrutiny.

The phrase seems to have started with Kent Cooper, former top executive of the Associated Press. It became cemented into the conventional wisdom of journalism when Harold Cross used it as the title of a book he wrote for the American Society of Newspaper Editors in 1953. The general theme of his book and the doctrine the slogan represents is that the public has a legal right to know what its government is doing and that the press is the representative of the public in finding out. Thus "the public's right to know" became a flag for the many journalists who infer from the roots of press freedom a special responsibility to be watchdogs of government, to protect the people from abuses by government.

Journalists in recent years have tended to use the phrase less and less. Some shy away from the phrase because it seems to suggest a constitutional right, even though the courts have not supported that view. Other journalists are tired of seeing some of their colleagues turn the doctrine to their own ends, invoking it, for example, as a justification for questionable conduct such as stealing or lying to get a story.

Yet it remains a basic principle of journalism ethics that the press makes a vital contribution to our democracy when it monitors the activi-

"As soon as the mayor's kid gets home from the prom, I'll hit him with my 'public's right to know' pitch."

ties of politicians and provides citizens with information they need to know. The belief in this principle has stimulated journalists, somewhat arrogantly in some cases, to see themselves as representatives of the people. Many reporters have sensed a special responsibility when covering some important public meeting with no members of the public present except perhaps an observer for the League of Women Voters and a couple of lawyers representing some special interest. Reporters in that all too common circumstance usually make a special effort to report actions that might affect those absent citizens — not to sell more papers or increase the station's ratings but from a sense of duty. This same sense of representing the public at large has spurred journalists as they have tried to shed light on the less obvious activities of business and other areas of the private sector in which the public has an interest.

Beyond Situational Ethics

Journalists are neither first nor alone in their struggle to be ethical. It is a struggle that occupies all the professions and occupations to one degree or another. Some have found help in the ethical theories developed by philosophers and thinkers, past and present, to guide us in deciding moral questions. But ethical theory does not seem to interest most journalists. You don't see newsrooms cluttered with the works of Jeremy Bentham (1748–1832), the founder of utilitarianism, or Immanuel Kant (1724–1804), who professed among other things that the moral measure of an act is whether the maxim underlying it can be universalized — made a maxim for all persons, everywhere, for all time. It does not seem likely that journalists are going to turn to the classics for their ethical guidelines.

If journalists don't seem able or much interested in adapting classical ethical theories to their problems of right and wrong, does that mean they have no choice but to continue to rely on situational ethics without any guiding principles, calling each ethical shot as it comes? No.

We believe that American journalists are intelligent enough to develop and agree on a set of principles that will give them a basis for a system of ethics. And they can do this without endangering their freedom and independence, which, it must be conceded, is enjoyed by some journalists more than others.

To develop these principles, we can start with the role that has evolved for journalism as a major provider of information in modern America. Modern societies, communities and organizations need valid information to achieve knowledge and wisdom to survive and thrive. Note that we define the need as *valid* information. For information to be valid, it has to be as untainted as humanly possible.

Validity also requires that the carriers of the information — the news organizations and their journalists — be independent (not in the sense of how you register to vote if you don't want to affiliate with one of the major political parties but being free from outside control and undue influence). If journalists cannot resist those special and vested interests seeking to use the press for their own ends, they produce not information but propaganda. Journalism and propaganda are antithetical. Journalists must also resist unreasonable profit demands of media owners and pressures from political groups and the business community. Journalists must be independent searchers for facts and truth.

But achieving independence is not enough. Ethical journalists still must consider the impact of the information they have gathered, and sometimes they need to withhold or tone down stories because of the harm that might result from their publication or broadcast. The extreme view of some aggressive journalists — "letting the chips fall where they may" — is unacceptable to most thoughtful Americans.

Journalistic dispassion in the search for and presentation of news is often valuable, but it needs to be tempered with compassion for the other people who get caught up in the news. Too often, trying to be dispassionate, uninvolved observers of contemporary affairs creates an uncaring, "I'm above it all" attitude. The lack of compassion in the way so many contemporary journalists practice their craft is one of the principal reasons that journalists and the news media are neither understood nor supported by many in their audiences. This is particularly sad when men and women who are otherwise decent, caring and often compassionate people see their profession as demanding just the opposite kind of behavior. Journalists need to look hard at any discipline that teaches them to "walk through brick walls" and "kick ass and take names," to quote two pieces of advice from the folklore of American news work.

Fairness is an important virtue for all people, but it is essential for journalists. Treating everyone fairly and giving all elements of each news situation a fair hearing — that's the only sensible route for a profession that depends totally on the trust and respect of the public it serves. Fairness has to guide journalists in each step they take.

It almost goes without saying that journalists should strive for truth. That principle seems unarguable. Even when complete truth about some news event is so evasive as to be unachievable, journalists must keep hacking away at that goal in the hope that eventually truth will emerge. Because truth is so often unattainable instantly, journalists should sometimes resist their deadline and competitive pressures and delay their reports until a picture closer to the truth is possible.

Being truthful in the pursuit of facts and truth is also important for journalists, who sometimes seem too causal in their use of dishonorable means to achieve ends they see as honorable. The folklore of American journalism is full of journalists lying to or tricking news sources, pretending to be somebody they aren't, performing all manner of deceit to get the news. Maybe there are rare occasions when threats to life or society justify journalists lying to get at the truth, but usually ethics and decency demand that both means and ends be truthful and honorable, not just for journalists but everybody.

In summary, journalists could move away from dealing with their ethical problems case by case by building a system of ethics based on these principles:

1. Journalism should provide valid information, information that is truthful and untainted by vested and special interests. Journalists have to be independent searchers for truth.

2. As they gather and report the news, journalists must be fair and compassionate in their treatment of people and events.

3. Journalists are not exempt from the ethical principle that means are as important as ends, and both means and ends must be truthful and honorable.

4. Journalists have to be honest to themselves, their news sources and associates and, above all, the public. And a little humility wouldn't hurt. Arrogance has no place in a profession so dependent on credibility.

5. Journalists make a vital contribution to our democracy when they monitor the activities of politicians and provide citizens with information they need to know. Likewise, they are fulfilling a basic obligation to the public when they shed light on the less obvious activities of business and other areas of the private sector in which the public has a legitimate interest.

6. Although the news media are businesses, they should be much more than that. In payment for the special constitutionally protected privileges they enjoy in the American system, the news media must be socially responsible and strive to serve the public good. Profits are justifiable only if the public is served by the highest quality of journalism that such profits can afford.

7. Ethics need constant attention. Journalists should continue serious discussion of their ethical principles and problems not just among themselves but with the public. The guiding principles that emerge from such discussions should help journalism become a truly ethical profession. And isn't it about time?

Codes and Professional Status

Assume you are a doctor practicing general medicine in a medium-sized city.

You enter the doctors' lounge of the hospital just after checking on your patients and are greeted by a fellow general practitioner who says, "Now we know how you can afford that new house!" Then he shows you an article in that morning's local newspaper reporting on fees charged by various medical specialists in the area. Your name is listed at the top of a column of general practitioners. You look at the list, and the fee it says you charge is more than twice what you really charge.

Does this mistake upset you? It probably would.

You decide to call the paper and get them to print a correction. You leave your name and phone number with an editor you know. But he doesn't call you back. So you call the reporter whose byline is on the story. He's not in, but the city editor listens to you and tells you he'll get back to you. A week later, you still haven't heard from him. You call back, and he tells you he sees no reason to print a correction because the figures were based on Medicare records. After you exchange a few unpleasant words, he suggests you talk to the reporter.

Finally you get the reporter on the line. You explain how unreliable his sources were. You tell him you wish he had talked to you before the story appeared in the paper and suggest he should recheck his figures. His response floors you. He tells you (1) he didn't have time to check his figures and (2) even if he had checked with you, he wouldn't have changed anything in the article.[1]

If you were the doctor, what might you do? The first thing you might think of is suing the newspaper. But you are unsure if you could collect enough money to make it worth your while. Lawyers are expensive, and court cases often drag on for years.

You might wonder if there are rules that apply to journalists like those that apply to doctors. To become a doctor, you had to pass tests and meet standards set by state law and the medical societies. You swore an oath promising to abide by ethical codes. If you violate those codes, you can be called before a committee of the medical society, and in severe cases the committee can even take away your right to practice medicine. You know that lawyers, dentists, optometrists and other professionals have similar organizations that can judge a practitioner's ethics.

Do journalists face those kinds of standards? Are there codes of ethics for journalists like the codes for other professions? Are there ethics panels that will listen to your grievances against the media? What do you do, short of suing for libel, if you believe you have been wronged by the media? Some people joke that journalism is really a game in which the batter gets to call balls and strikes. Are they right?

Craft or Profession?

If the doctor wondered whether journalism is a profession with codes of ethics, he stumbled into a debate that has been raging for years at journalism conferences, in trade journals, and even in courts of law.

During the past 30 years, many journalists began to view themselves as members of a "profession." They had college degrees like other professionals and earned (at least those working on larger news organizations) middle-class salaries. They believed their jobs required intelligence, creativity and independent judgment and placed demands on them that required the same level of performance expected in traditional professions like the law. So, they argued, they should be looked upon as professionals and given the same kind of respect. This sentiment became so widespread among journalists that in 1987 they dropped the Greek letters from the name of their major trade group, which was begun in 1912 as Sigma Delta Chi, so it would be known as the Society of Professional Journalists.

But some journalists were not so sure it was wise to want professional status. They argued that professions like the law and medicine are regulated by the government. Doctors and lawyers must have licenses, and the government can take those licenses away. These journalists were afraid that efforts to make journalism a profession might encourage legislators to license them, setting up a First Amendment challenge.

Other journalists had less idealistic objections. They discovered that being part of a profession had an unwanted consequence: It lowered their pay. Some media companies began to label reporters, editors and news producers as professionals so they could avoid paying them over-time and giving them other benefits required by the Fair Labor Stand-ards Act. The act excludes employees who are in "learned" or "artistic" professions or professions that require "specialized intellectual training." Wanting to keep these benefits, many journalists sued their news organi-zations claiming that they were not really professionals but people en-gaged in work, as one NBC writer contended in his suit, that was "for-mulaic and mundane." The media companies, of course, rejected that argument. They said that journalists were bona fide professionals who, as *The Washington Post* contended, "exercise a great deal of judgment in their work."

The Labor Department has sided with the journalists. It has ruled the work of reporters, photographers and copy editors is not "original or creative" enough for them to be considered professional. Therefore they are covered by the Fair Labor Standards Act and must receive overtime pay. But the rules say that editorial writers, critics and columnists do "analytical, interpretive or highly individualized" writing, making them professional and not eligible to be covered by the act. Several news organizations, including *The Washington Post, Concord (N.H.) Moni-tor* and NBC, challenged these rules in court. In 1993 federal district judges rejected arguments by the *Monitor* and NBC and ordered them to pay journalists overtime. Other legal challenges were still pending in the early 1990s.[2]

Even if the courts continue to rule that journalism is not a profes-sion in a legal sense, many journalists will continue to believe they func-tion as professionals in a sociological sense. But even on that point there is disagreement. Most sociologists would not agree that journalism is a "profession" as they define the term.

Sociologists usually limit the term "professional" to occupations whose practitioners can meet three necessary standards: have specialized university educations that indicate mastery of a specific body of knowl-edge, be self-employed or work with little or no supervision, and abide by a uniform code of ethics that everyone in the profession follows. Obviously, doctors and lawyers usually meet these standards, and clearly journalists do not. Anyone, regardless of education, can be a journalist, and most journalists have direct supervision. And unlike the legal and medical professions, journalism has no binding uniform code of ethics.

Journalism professor Edmund Lambeth has proposed a compromise that many, including the authors of this book, have adopted. He called journalism a "craft with professional responsibilities."[3] Many journalists believe that one of those professional responsibilities is to create a code of ethics for journalism.

THE GROWTH OF CODES

The belief that journalists should be bound by a uniform code of ethics has been around for a long time. As a matter of fact, one of the first things the American Society of Newspaper Editors did when it was organized in 1923 was write a code of ethics.[4]

But the push for codes of ethics did not pick up momentum until the 1970s. The Society of Professional Journalists, which had endorsed the ASNE canons as its code of ethics in 1926, created its own code in 1973 and revised it in 1984 and 1987. During the 1970s, codes were either written or revised by the Radio-Television News Directors Association, the Associated Press Managing Editors association, the ASNE, and the national organizations of travel writers, sportswriters, editorial writers and business writers. (The ethics codes of the ASNE, SPJ, RTNDA and APME are reprinted at the end of this chapter.)

News organizations also began to write codes. In the mid-1970s fewer than 10 percent of daily newspapers had codes. A decade later, surveys found that as many as 75 percent did.[5] News organizations initially copied the national codes.[6] But now most of them write their own codes and constantly revise them as they encounter new problems and technology creates unanticipated ethical concerns. Forty percent of the daily papers and 33 percent of TV stations modified their codes between 1990 and 1993.[7] With each revision, many of the codes grow. The original codes could often be printed on one sheet of paper, but now codes fill entire chapters in stylebooks. ABC News's new code is 75 pages long.

CODES ARE CONTROVERSIAL

Not everybody is happy with development of the codes. Some, like Leslie H. Whitten, a senior investigator for the Jack Anderson column for 12 years, didn't see codes improving the behavior of journalists. "The few unethical journalists I've known are really flawed people," Whitten said. "It's not that they don't follow any codes—they're not interested in codes. They were poorly brought up and they did dishonest things."[8]

But syndicated columnist Ellen Goodman of *The Boston Globe* doesn't believe good breeding alone will make journalists ethical. In a TV interview she admitted that when trying to get a big story, she might consider using a less than ethical reporting technique. "Hot in the middle of the chase, I always think it's justified," she said.[9] Codes and discussions of ethics are needed to keep journalists true to their own values, she argued.

A more serious charge made against codes is that they deal primarily with cut-and-dried issues like forbidding reporters to accept freebies or moonlight as publicists for politicians. Too many of the codes, it is charged, don't come to grips with the realities of newsgathering or help reporters solve the ethical problems they frequently encounter.

Abe Rosenthal, who held most of the top editing positions at *The New York Times,* has criticized codes because they "aim at the lowest common denominator" and are "too easy." He noted that the codes apply only to journalists, not to media managers whose decisions often shape a news organization's ability to cover the news. (The ethical role of media owners is discussed in Chapter 3.) If journalism is going to have codes of ethics, they should be thorough and apply to all people involved in the news process, including management and owners, Rosenthal argued. "If you're going to have a code, it has to be tough and it has to deal with questions of how much news, how much profit and how much space." He said that if he drew up a code of ethics for the entire news business, "damned few would sign it."[10]

Other journalists argue that there are better ways to deal with ethical problems than codes of ethics. Andrew Barnes, former editor and president of the *St. Petersburg (Fla.) Times,* approved of written rules against freebies and conflicts of interest, but he preferred frequent staff meetings to discuss ethics and other newsroom problems. Barnes said he was bothered by the tendency in some shops to hang a code of ethics on the wall, declare themselves ethical, then go back to getting the paper out with no real change in behavior.[11]

Although the *Times* now has a detailed code of ethics, Barnes' concerns about codes being written and then forgotten worry other people too. Researchers have found that some reporters are unaware of their organization's codes and that editors sometimes allow reporters to violate the codes to keep up with the competition.[12] Other studies have raised questions whether journalists at newspapers with strong codes of ethics behave more ethically than those at papers that don't have codes.[13]

Regardless of whether codes improve ethical standards, some media attorneys recommend that news organizations not adopt them. They note that codes have been used as evidence against journalists in libel and privacy suits. By showing that the accused reporter did not follow

38

"That's our ethics code over the editor's desk. When anybody asks, he says, tell them that's our bible."

the code of ethics, plaintiffs' attorneys try to sway juries into awarding larger settlements against the media.

RULES OR IDEALS?

Within a year of the establishment of its first code of ethics, the ASNE was hit by a controversy that still rages in national journalism groups: What do you do with journalists who violate your code of ethics?

When the ASNE finished codifying its ethics in 1923, several of the 124 charter members of ASNE wanted their society to have powers similar to those of the legal and medical societies, which can punish unethical practitioners and even ban them from the profession.

Many ASNE members wanted to flex the muscles of their new code of ethics by expelling F. G. Bonfils, publisher of *The Denver Post,* from their organization. Bonfils had accepted $1 million in bribes to agree not to report stories about government oil reserves in Wyoming that were being sold illegally to private interests. At first, ASNE members voted to expel Bonfils. But then Bonfils threatened to sue the group and each of its directors for slander. He offered to drop the suits if the society would forget about expelling him. The directors agreed, and the debate about punishing him for apparently violating virtually all of its canons of ethics ended.[14] A few years later the society formally passed a motion stating that adherence to its code would be strictly voluntary.[15]

Inadvertently, these early code writers may have set a precedent. Since their vote more than 70 years ago, no national or state organization of journalists has adopted a code of ethics with machinery for enforcement. The codes of all the professional societies are statements of ideals about what constitutes ethical conduct by journalists.

The fear of litigation is still a major roadblock that keeps some of the professional societies from making their codes binding. In 1985 the SPJ board of directors voted against enforcing its code after being told that the society could be sued if it took punitive action against a member for violating the code. The board feared that paying lawyers to fight these lawsuits might bankrupt the society.[16]

A more surprising opponent of mandatory codes of ethics is the labor union that represents many journalists, The Newspaper Guild, AFL-CIO. Guild leaders said they had no problem with voluntary codes, but they believe codes that reduce the income of journalists should be subject to normal labor-management bargaining like any other wage issue. For instance, major league teams often paid baseball writers as much as $3,500 a season to be the official scorekeepers. But when newspapers adopted codes of ethics, the sportswriters were prohibited from making this money. When the Guild filed legal objections to clauses in mandatory codes at two newspapers, the complicated cases dragged through the federal system for nearly 12 years before the codes were ordered rescinded.

SOME CODES HAVE TEETH

Although the ASNE, SPJ and RTNDA codes are just voluntary statements of principles, that's not the case with the written codes in effect at most major daily newspapers and the ABC, NBC, CNN and CBS network news departments. These codes call for hearings for employees suspected of violating the codes and spell out penalties, ranging from verbal warnings to dismissal.[17]

An ASNE survey of the nation's 25 largest dailies found that newspapers with codes had dismissed or suspended more employees than papers without codes. The 14 with written codes had dismissed 11 news staffers and suspended six for code violations in the three years before the survey was taken. The 11 big dailies without written codes said they had dismissed three employees and suspended five in that same period. A survey of smaller dailies found a similar pattern.

The ASNE Ethics Committee said in its report on the survey:

> The reason most frequently cited by editors for the dismissal was lying. One editor said an employee was fired for falsely listing a college degree on the employment application. Three other employees were dismissed for fal-

sification of expense accounts or time sheets.

In another instance, a reporter used material obtained from a television interview without attribution. That act, the editor said, did not warrant dismissal. But the reporter insisted the material had been obtained independently, and subsequent investigation proved otherwise. "The person lied to us," the editor said, "and was dismissed."

Most of the other dismissals involved some form of outside employment that created a conflict of interest. For example, one reporter retained color transparencies and other materials that were received for the newspaper job and used them in free-lance work for other newspapers and industry publications.[18]

A newspaper that tries to enforce its tough ethics code is *The Philadelphia Inquirer,* where a sports reporter was once taken off the local college basketball beat when editors learned that his part-time journalism teaching contract had been renewed only because the college feared reprisals in his coverage of its basketball team. He was reassigned to cover horse racing, but then it came out that he owned a part interest in a race horse. He was forced to sell the horse. Shortly after that, when he was assigned to cover the NCAA basketball tournament, it was discovered that he had written material for an NCAA brochure. All these outside activities violated the conflict of interest section of the *Inquirer*'s "Standards of Professional Conduct." The erring reporter, according to the paper's managing editor, finally had to be told that "if one more conflict developed, he would be assigned to the only job left in the sports department — office clerk."[19]

"Well, of course you're right, dear. They are unethical. But think what beautiful codes they write."

The managing editor of *The Milwaukee Journal* suspended a reporter who took part in a political demonstration and a copy editor who surreptitiously produced campaign material for a political candidate, a close friend.[20] When he was managing editor of the *Democrat & Chronicle* in Rochester, N.Y., Richard B. Tuttle had to negotiate a resignation with a veteran copy editor who was clandestinely doing public relations work for several clients. "The guy's doing very well in PR now," Tuttle noted.[21]

Some Professional Codes

The written codes of ethics of the four largest organizations of American journalists present a commendable array of ideals. As statements of ideals, they are praiseworthy. If all American journalists lived up to these ideals, journalism would indeed be an ethical profession. But keep in mind as you read these codes that ideals are not the same as rules or even working principles. They may paint the way for journalists who truly want to be ethical, but unfortunately they can not stop journalists from behaving unethically.

RADIO-TV NEWS DIRECTORS ASSOCIATION
The responsibility of radio and television journalists is to gather and report information of importance and interest to the public accurately, honestly and impartially.

The members of the Radio-Television News Directors Association accept these standards and will:
1. Strive to present the source and nature of broadcast news material in a way that is balanced, accurate and fair.
   A. They will evaluate information solely on its merits as news, rejecting sensationalism or misleading emphasis in any form.
   B. They will guard against using audio or video material in a way that deceives the audience.
   C. They will not mislead the public by presenting as spontaneous news any material which is staged or rehearsed.
   D. They will identify people by race, creed, nationality or prior status only when it is relevant.
   E. They will clearly label opinion and commentary.
   F. They will promptly acknowledge and correct errors.
2. Strive to conduct themselves in a manner that protects them from conflicts of interest, real or perceived. They will decline gifts or favors which would influence or appear to influence their judgments.

3. Respect the dignity, privacy and well-being of people with whom they deal.
4. Recognize the need to protect confidential sources. They will promise confidentiality only with the intention of keeping that promise.
5. Respect everyone's right to a fair trial.
6. Broadcast the private transmissions of other broadcasters only with permission.
7. Actively encourage observance of this code by all journalists, whether members of the Radio-Television News Directors Association or not.

SOCIETY OF PROFESSIONAL JOURNALISTS

CODE OF ETHICS

The Society of Professional Journalists believes the duty of journalists is to serve the truth.

We believe the agencies of mass communication are carriers of public discussion and information, acting on their Constitutional mandate and freedom to learn and report the facts.

We believe in public enlightenment as the forerunner of justice, and in our Constitutional role to seek the truth as part of the public's right to know the truth.

We believe those responsibilities carry obligations that require journalists to perform with intelligence, objectivity, accuracy and fairness.

To these ends, we declare acceptance of the standards of practice here set forth:

I. RESPONSIBILITY: The public's right to know of events of public importance and interest is the overriding mission of the mass media. The purpose of distributing news and enlightened opinion is to serve the general welfare. Journalists who use their professional status as representatives of the public for selfish or other unworthy motives violate a high trust.

II. FREEDOM OF THE PRESS: Freedom of the press is to be guarded as an inalienable right of people in a free society. It carries with it the freedom and the responsibility to discuss, question, and challenge actions and utterances of our government and of our public and private institutions. Journalists uphold the right to speak unpopular opinions and the privilege to agree with the majority.

III. ETHICS: Journalists must be free of obligation to any interest other than the public's right to know the truth.

1. Gifts, favors, free travel, special treatment or privileges can compromise the integrity of journalists and their employers. Nothing of value should be accepted.

2. Secondary employment, political involvement, holding public office, and service in community organizations should be avoided if it compromises the integrity of journalists and their employers. Journalists and their employers should conduct their personal lives in a manner which protects them from conflict of interest, real or apparent. Their responsibilities to the public are paramount. This is the nature of their profession.

3. So-called news communications from private sources should not be published or broadcast without substantiation of their claims to news value.

4. Journalists will seek news that serves the public interest, despite the obstacles. They will make constant efforts to assure that the public's business is conducted in public and that public records are open to public inspection.

5. Journalists acknowledge the newsman's ethic of protecting confidential sources of information.

6. Plagiarism is dishonest and unacceptable.

IV. ACCURACY AND OBJECTIVITY: Good faith with the public is the foundation of all worthy journalism.

1. Truth is our ultimate goal.

2. Objectivity in reporting the news is another goal that serves as the mark of an experienced professional. It is a standard of performance toward which we strive. We honor those who achieve it.

3. There is no excuse for inaccuracies or lack of thoroughness.

4. Newspaper headlines should be fully warranted by the contents of the articles they accompany. Photographs and telecasts should give an accurate picture of an event and not highlight an incident out of context.

5. Sound practice makes clear distinction between news reports and expressions of opinion. News reports should be free of opinion or bias and represent all sides of an issue.

6. Partisanship in editorial comment which knowingly departs from the truth violates the spirit of American journalism.

7. Journalists recognize their responsibility for offering informed analysis, comment, and editorial opinion on public events and issues. They accept the obligation to present such material by individuals whose competence, experience and judgment qualify them for it.

8. Special articles or presentations devoted to advocacy or the writer's own conclusions and interpretations should be labeled as such.

V. FAIR PLAY: Journalists at all times will show respect for the dignity, privacy, rights, and well-being of people encountered in the course of gathering and presenting the news.

1. The news media should not communicate unofficial charges affecting reputation or moral character without giving the accused a chance to reply.

2. The news media must guard against invading a person's right to privacy.

3. The media should not pander to morbid curiosity about details of vice and crime.

4. It is the duty of news media to make prompt and complete correction of their errors.

5. Journalists should be accountable to the public for their reports and the public should be encouraged to voice its grievances against the media. Open dialogue with our readers, viewers, and listeners should be fostered.

MUTUAL TRUST. Adherence to this code is intended to preserve and strengthen the bond of mutual trust and respect between American journalists and the American people.

The society shall—by programs of education and other means—encourage individual journalists to adhere to these tenets, and shall encourage journalistic publications and broadcasters to recognize their responsibility to frame codes of ethics in concert with their employees to serve as guidelines in furthering these goals.

(Adopted 1926; revised 1973, 1984, 1987)

AMERICAN SOCIETY OF NEWSPAPER EDITORS

A STATEMENT OF PRINCIPLES

PREAMBLE. The First Amendment, protecting freedom of expression from abridgment by any law, guarantees to the people through their press a constitutional right, and thereby places on newspaper people a particular responsibility.

Thus journalism demands of its practitioners not only industry and knowledge but also the pursuit of a standard of integrity proportionate to the journalist's singular obligation.

To this end the American Society of Newspaper Editors sets forth this Statement of Principles as a standard encouraging the highest ethical and professional performance.

ARTICLE I—*Responsibility.* The primary purpose of gathering and distributing news and opinion is to serve the general welfare by informing the people and enabling them to make judgments on the issues of the time. Newspapermen and women who abuse the power of their professional role for selfish motives or unworthy purposes are faithless to that public trust.

The American press was made free not just to inform or just to serve as a forum for debate but also to bring an independent scrutiny to bear on the forces of power in the society, including the conduct of official power at all levels of government.

ARTICLE II—*Freedom of the Press.* Freedom of the press belongs to the people. It must be defended against encroachment or assault from any quarter, public or private.

Journalists must be constantly alert to see that the public's business is conducted in public. They must be vigilant against all who would exploit the press for selfish purposes.

ARTICLE III—*Independence.* Journalists must avoid impropriety and the appearance of impropriety as well as any conflict of interest or the appearance of conflict. They should neither accept anything nor pursue any activity that might compromise or seem to compromise their integrity.

ARTICLE IV—*Truth and Accuracy.* Good faith with the reader is the foundation of good journalism. Every effort must be made to assure that the news content is accurate, free from bias and in context, and that all sides are presented fairly. Editorials, analytical articles and commentary should be held to the same standards of accuracy with respect to facts as news reports.

Significant errors of fact, as well as errors of omission, should be corrected promptly and prominently.

ARTICLE V—*Impartiality.* To be impartial does not require the press to be unquestioning or to refrain from editorial expression. Sound practice, however, demands a clear distinction for the reader between news reports and opinion. Articles that contain opinion or personal interpretation should be clearly identified.

ARTICLE VI—*Fair Play.* Journalists should respect the rights of people involved in the news, observe the common standards of decency and stand accountable to the public for the fairness and accuracy of their news reports.

Persons publicly accused should be given the earliest opportunity to respond.

Pledges of confidentiality to news sources must be honored at all costs, and therefore should not be given lightly. Unless there is clear and pressing need to maintain confidences, sources of information should be identified.

These principles are intended to preserve, protect and strengthen the bond of trust and respect between American journalists and the American people, a bond that is essential to sustain the grant of freedom entrusted to both by the nation's founders.

(Adopted as the "Canons of Journalism" in 1922; revised and renamed "Statement of Principles" in 1975.)

ASSOCIATED PRESS MANAGING EDITORS

MODEL CODE OF ETHICS

This code is a model against which newspaper men and women can measure their performance. It is meant to apply to news and editorial staff members and others who are involved in, or who influence, news coverage and editorial policy. It has been formulated in the belief that newspapers and the people who produce them should adhere to the highest standards of ethical and professional conduct.

RESPONSIBILITY. A good newspaper is fair, accurate, honest, responsible, independent and decent. Truth is its guiding principle.

It avoids practices that would conflict with the ability to report and present news in a fair and unbiased manner.

The newspaper should serve as a constructive critic of all segments of society. It should vigorously expose wrongdoing or misuse of power, public or private. Editorially, it should advocate needed reform or innovations in the public interest.

News sources should be disclosed unless there is clear reason not to do so. When it is necessary to protect the confidentiality of a source, the reason should be explained.

The newspaper should background, with the facts, public statements that it knows to be inaccurate or misleading. It should uphold the right of free speech and freedom of the press and should respect the individual's right of privacy.

The public's right to know about matters of importance is paramount, and the newspaper should fight vigorously for public access to news of government through open meetings and open records.

ACCURACY. The newspaper should guard against inaccuracies, carelessness, bias or distortion through either emphasis or omission.

It should admit all substantive errors and correct them promptly and prominently.

INTEGRITY. The newspaper should strive for impartial treatment of issues and dispassionate handling of controversial subjects. It should provide a forum for the exchange of comment and criticism, especially when such comment is opposed to its editorial positions. Editorials and other expressions of opinion by reporters and editors should be clearly labeled.

The newspaper should report the news without regard for its own interests. It should not give favored news treatment to advertisers or special-interest groups. It should report matters regarding itself or its personnel with the same vigor and candor as it would other institutions or individuals.

Concern for community, business or personal interests should not cause a newspaper to distort or misrepresent the facts.

CONFLICTS OF INTEREST. The newspaper and its staff should be free of obligations to news sources and special interests. Even the appearance of obligation or conflict of interest should be avoided.

Newspapers should accept nothing of value from news sources or others outside the profession. Gifts and free or reduced-rate travel, entertainment, products and lodging should not be accepted. Expenses in connection with news reporting should be paid by the newspaper. Special favors and special treatment for members of the press should be avoided.

Involvement in such things as politics, community affairs, demonstrations and social causes that could cause a conflict of interest, or the appearance of such conflict, should be avoided.

Outside employment by news sources is an obvious conflict of interest, and employment by potential news sources also should be avoided.

Financial investments by staff members or other outside business interests that could conflict with the newspaper's ability to report the news or that would create the impression of such conflict should be avoided.

Stories should not be written or edited primarily for the purpose of winning awards and prizes. Blatantly commercial journalism contests, or others that reflect unfavorably on the newspaper or the profession, should be avoided.

No code of ethics can prejudge every situation. Common sense and good judgment are required in applying ethical principles to newspaper realities. Individual newspapers are encouraged to augment these APME guidelines with locally produced codes that apply more specifically to their own situations.

(Adopted by the APME Board of Directors, April 1975.)

3

The News
Business

When we make decisions on ethical problems, most of us are guided by our consciences, our personal needs, and concerns about our families, friends and communities.

But when journalists confront ethical decisions, other forces also influence how they behave. Most work for news organizations owned by profit-seeking corporations. The business considerations of these corporations inevitably play a part, either directly or indirectly, in gathering and presenting news. Corporate decisions made hundreds of miles from the newsroom may have as much to do with how well journalists perform as decisions made in the newsroom. Decisions by media owners can encourage quality journalism or undermine the ethics of reporters and editors.

Greed and Idealism

Major media corporations have made lots of money for their investors. Many corporations, like Gannett and the Tribune Co. of Chicago, own both newspapers and TV stations, two of the most profitable industries in America. Gannett's newspapers and TV stations are so lucrative that the company was able to post quarterly profit reports, each report showing higher profits than the one before, for 22 straight years.[1] Gannett's former president Al Neuharth was once asked whether he pronounced the company's name "GAN-nett" or "gan-NETT." He said he pronounced it "MON-ey."

Even during the recession of the early 1990s, the newspaper industry reported pretax profits of 17 percent. Although that figure was down from 24 percent five years earlier, "there are lots of industries that do not see 15 percent margins in the midst of their biggest booms in history," a financial analyst noted.[2]

Television stations, particularly network affiliates, have traditionally made even more money than newspapers, although competition from cable has begun to put a damper on their profit growth. Profit margins of 40 percent were not uncommon before the recession in the early 1990s, and big-city stations often made more than $50 million in pretax profits. Even during the recession, the larger stations with network affiliations had average profit margins of 26 percent and average profits of $33 million. Jon Katz, a former producer at *CBS Morning News,* quipped that "nobody but Colombian drug lords makes as much money" as station owners.[3]

Since the news media are big businesses, they are influenced by the same forces as those that bear on all American business enterprises. There is nothing intrinsically wrong or illegal about the media following the same economic Pied Pipers that motivate K mart, Mobil, United Technologies, IBM and Crazy Joe's Used Cars, but news businesses differ from other businesses in one important way. Their constitutionally protected freedom is interpreted by most people to mean that they are semipublic services as well as private profit-seeking businesses.

This dual role of serving the public and making profits for the owners can create ethical problems for journalists. James C. Thomson Jr., former curator of the Nieman Foundation, has noted that this duality creates tension "between greed and idealism." Thomson believes every news organization has "two cultures, or at least outlooks, that are often at odds with each other: on the one hand, reporters and editors, who traditionally see their role as uncovering and disseminating the truth (or some approximation thereof); and on the other hand, owners, pub-lishers, 'management,' who seek to stay in business and make a tidy profit."[4]

Robert P. Clark, former executive editor of the Louisville *Courier-Journal,* wrote that he fears greed may be taking a bigger role now than ever before. "We in journalism are facing a new ethics problem not addressed in any of our codes: bottom-line journalism." Too many cor-porations are buying media just to make a buck.[5]

THE CHANGING NATURE OF OWNERSHIP

At the beginning of this century more than 98 percent of American newspapers were independently owned, often by local families.[6] Some families owned newspapers to make money; others wanted the power and prestige of newpaper ownership.

Many newspapers flourished under local publishers whose roots in the community and commitment to the family-owned business pushed them to produce quality papers. Often these families took such pride in their papers that they willingly poured a large part of their profits back in the newsroom to improve the newspaper.

For example, although *The Washington Post* is today one of Ameri-ca's best newspapers, that has not always been the case. Donald Gra-ham, publisher of the *Post,* recalled a time when it was struggling. "In the early 1950s, the *Post* aspired to be a world-class newspaper; its heart was in the right place, but it just didn't have enough money. There's an old joke around the *Post* that in those days we could cover any interna-tional conference as long as it was in the first taxi zone." He noted with pride that although the *Post* had no foreign correspondents before 1960, it had bureaus all over the world by the early 1980s.[7] Today the paper has about 25 reporters overseas.

With a publisher who spent money to improve news coverage, the *Post* hired top-notch journalists and gave them the time and resources they needed to produce responsible and complete stories. They readily met the ethical demands of their profession and by doing so made the paper one of the most influential in the country.

The Louisville papers also gained national respect under the Bingham family. "The Binghams published distinguished newspapers," former *Courier-Journal* executive editor Clark said. "The motive was not primarily money, but public service."[8]

However, not all family-owned newspapers encouraged their staffs in ethical journalism. Some of these papers suffered under narrow-minded owners who pushed the paper toward one-sided reports and political favoritism. Journalism Professor John Hulteng cites several classic cases of activist publishers, such as conservatives Eugene Pulliam of *The Indianapolis Star* and William Loeb of *The Union Leader* in Manchester, N.H. When Loeb decided to back a candidate in one election, his paper began a crusade that included front-page editorials with misleading quotes from other papers. *The Union Leader* devoted twice as much space to Loeb's choice (not considered a serious candidate by most observers) as to all the front-runners combined. Similarly, when Robert Kennedy was running for president in the Indiana primary, Pulliam's *Star* heaped negative coverage on Kennedy while writing many favorable stories about a favorite-son candidate who was running only to keep Kennedy from winning the primary.[9]

While not all family-owned papers were used this blatantly to promote the political philosophies of owners, many were hopelessly co-opted by "sacred cows," the publisher's friends and favored institutions that were to receive preferential treatment. Others engaged in hometown boosterism that required reporters to paint rosy pictures of the city's economy and government.

THE RISE OF CHAINS

The number of family-owned newspapers has declined dramatically since the turn of the century when nearly all papers were owned by people who lived in the community. Today four out of five daily newspapers are group-owned.

Many journalists bemoan the loss of truly local papers. Former *Washington Post* ombudsman and journalism dean Ben Bagdikian worries that the growth of group ownership of the American media will result in less individuality in American papers and the loss of distinct editorial voices.[10] Other journalists believe newspapers may lose their sense of purpose under chain management. C.K. McClatchy, a newspaper editor and owner, once said: "I fear the day when newspaper people are no longer in charge of newspapers. . . . To make a gross generalization, one can say that good newspapers are almost always run by good newspaper people; they are almost never run by good bankers and good accountants."[11]

Some publishers have even taken steps to keep their papers from being bought by chains. Nelson Poynter gave all the controlling stock in his highly respected *St. Petersburg (Fla.) Times* to the Poynter Institute for Media Studies, which uses its share of the profits from the *Times* to fund studies of journalism and conduct workshops for journalists. In Peoria, Ill., Henry Slade set up an employee stock ownership plan in an effort to keep the *Journal Star* in local hands.[12]

But most families decided to sell their papers. Estate taxes caused some to sell. At one time these taxes were as high as 70 percent. If the paper had an appraised value of $100,000, the children had to pay the government $70,000 to inherit it. Many decided to sell the paper rather than scramble to find that much cash. Sometimes the children did not want to be newspaper publishers and sold the paper so that they could follow other careers. Occasionally, a family sold because a chain had made an offer that was just too good to turn down. Only on rare occasions did a family have to sell the newspaper because the paper was losing money.[13]

The trend toward group ownership accelerated in the 1980s, a decade when corporate raiders fueled by "junk bonds" took over many major corporations. Media properties were highly prized by investors because they had "been able to generate rivers of cash decade after decade," as the national business magazine *Forbes* put it.[14]

There was frenzied buying of newspapers and TV stations on a level that few other industries had experienced. Many investors were willing to pay whatever it took. Newspapers and TV stations sold for what *Forbes* called "preposterously high prices."[15] Financial observers watched in awe as newspapers sold for prices two or three times what businesses with similar earnings in other industries would bring. When the McClatchy Newspapers chain paid $74 million for three small papers in South Carolina, *The New York Times* headline read, "Sale Price Arouses Wonder Over Deal in South Carolina." Scripps-Howard set what may have been a record in price per subscriber when it paid $160 million for the independently owned *Naples (Fla.) Daily News,* a paper with a circulation of only 34,380 but located in fast-growing South Florida.[16] Larger papers, of course, have sold for much more. Gannett paid the Bingham family of Louisville $307 million for the *Louisville Times* and *The Courier-Journal;* Hearst paid $375 million for the *Houston Chronicle;* Times Mirror paid $450 million for *The Sun* of Baltimore; and the New York Times Co. paid $1.1 billion for *The Boston Globe.*[17]

Today there are so few independent papers that chains are left with no way to grow except by buying other chains. This they are doing with enough regularity that an investment banker has predicted that all American mass media may eventually be owned by six conglomerates.[18]

FCC CHANGES TV OWNERSHIP RULES

Television ownership in the 1980s was in even greater disarray than newspaper ownership. Unlike newspapers, TV and radio stations are regulated by the federal government. Until the early 1980s, the Federal Communications Commission limited to seven the number of TV stations one company could own. Then, in the midst of an already heated market for TV stations, the FCC decided to allow companies to own up to 12 TV stations.[19]

Many media companies saw this as a chance to own more stations in bigger markets. They borrowed heavily and entered into bidding wars that pushed prices of stations to record levels. For example, just three years after WCVB, a Boston TV station, was sold for $220 million, it was purchased by Hearst for $450 million.

The desire to own American media led Rupert Murdoch, an Australian press baron who owned media properties around the world, to become a naturalized U.S. citizen to meet FCC regulations that require station owners to be Americans. Murdoch now owns enough TV stations to reach 21 percent of the nation's TV viewers, and he started the Fox network with affiliates in most large markets. In 1993 the FCC gave him special permission to own a New York TV station and the *New York Post* despite its rules that one company can't own a TV station and a newspaper in the same town.

All three commercial TV networks changed owners during the 1980s. General Electric bought RCA, the owner of NBC, for $6.28 billion. Capital Cities Communication, which already owned seven TV stations and 17 newspapers, bought ABC for $3.5 billion. Both Ted Turner, owner of TBS and CNN, and conservative Sen. Jesse Helms made efforts to acquire CBS until Laurence Tisch of Loew's International bought a controlling interest in the network.

By the late 1980s, however, competition from cable and a drop in advertising sales brought down the prices of TV stations. Taft Broadcasting had to settle for $240 million for five big-city independents, about half what the company had expected.

OWNERSHIP AFFECTS QUALITY

What happens to the quality of journalism at newspapers that have been purchased by investors who sometimes have borrowed heavily to buy their media properties? Are journalists allowed to meet the ethical demands of their profession, or do the business needs of the new owners intrude to the point that journalistic principles must be bent to ensure profits?

Researchers have studied these questions, and there seems to be no clear answer.[20] It seems to depend on what paper is being discussed and what chain bought it. Some chains, like Knight-Ridder and Times Mir-

"The vote is overwhelmingly against hiring more reporters. So now let's discuss whether to put our profits into that billboard company or another sports franchise."

ror, have willingly spent money in newsrooms to pump new life into mediocre newspapers. For instance, Knight-Ridder turned *The Philadelphia Inquirer,* once a disreputable newspaper, into a well-regarded publication that has filled its trophy cases with Pulitzer Prizes and other top journalism awards. Eugene L. Roberts Jr., executive editor of the paper during the turnaround, said that although Knight-Ridder "doesn't understand losing money" and "goes berserk with red ink," the group wanted "the *Inquirer* to be accurate, reliable, fair, and aggressive."[21]

During Roberts' editorship, the *Inquirer* opened foreign bureaus, added to its news hole, and encouraged reporters "to go off for months—even years—on massive investigative projects," a journalism review reported.[22] Roberts said that in general, his experience with Knight-Ridder and the *Inquirer* showed that "good journalism is amicable with good business."[23] Roberts retired in 1990, however, after a series of fights with management over the *Inquirer's* budget.[24]

The Gannett chain has been credited with improving some of the small-city papers it purchased, but the chain also is well-known for its concern for the bottom line. It has purchased some papers and doubled the profits they generate in a couple of years, often by tighter management, volume buying, and considerably higher advertising rates. The chain owned more than 80 daily papers, including *USA Today,* and had the largest circulation of any newspaper group in America in the early 1990s.[25] Gannett also owned about 35 weekly newspapers, 10 TV stations, and radio stations in nine cities (see Table 3.1).

Table 3.1   *Largest U.S. newspaper companies*

	Daily Circulation	Daily Papers	Sunday Circulation	Sunday Papers
Gannett Co. Inc.	5,882,595	81	6,070,256	66
Knight-Ridder Inc.	3,701,479	28	5,193,557	24
Newhouse Newspapers	3,038,360	26	3,889,713	21
Times Mirror Co.	2,760,334	9	3,468,786	8
Dow Jones & Co. Inc.	2,360,256	23	531,547	14
Thomson Newspapers	2,148,135	120	1,930,561	78
The New York Times Co.	1,964,681	24	2,557,634	16
Tribune Co.	1,425,359	7	2,029,971	7
Scripps Howard	1,330,367	21	1,314,351	13
Cox Enterprises Inc.	1,322,207	18	1,761,092	16
Hearst Newspapers	1,209,664	12	1,795,829	10
MediaNews Group	1,138,761	18	1,349,964	15
Freedom Newspapers	932,883	27	985,979	19
The Washington Post Co.	854,346	2	1,205,014	2
Central Newspapers	818,845	1	999,577	4
McClatchy Newspapers	803,939	12	946,970	9
Donrey Media Group	790,235	55	810,372	48
Capital Cities/ABC Inc.	749,331	8	991,169	6
Coply Newspapers	746,957	11	811,005	7
The Chronicle Publishing	734,854	6	903,560	3

Source: *Facts About Newspapers, 1993.*

Robert H. Giles edited the two Gannett dailies in Rochester, N.Y., before he became executive editor of Gannett's *The Detroit News.* He said that although Gannett gave him a free hand to make news decisions in Rochester, it influenced his job in other ways. "The bottom-line requirements limit what we want to do." He explained:

> The Gannett Company has very aggressive and ambitious profit goals. Anybody who wants to work for Gannett and be comfortable ought to understand that Al Neuharth [then chairman and president of Gannett] clearly sets the pace, and the standard is that our profits will be 15 percent better this year than they were last year. Everybody in the group, for the most part, is expected to contribute to that, which means that the kind of news hole I think we require here to put out absolutely first-rate newspapers is not available to me. That's a frustration because of my own standards for good newspapers and the standards of many of the people I've hired or promoted here.

Giles said that Gannett has taken over many family-owned newspapers and improved them enormously, but on a very good independent newspaper like the *St. Petersburg Times* "the resources made available" to the editor by the owning family "are superior to what I have to work with in Rochester." Giles contended that Gannett wants it both ways: "Put out good newspapers and continue to make a lot of money, and you can't always do that."[26]

Some journalists are even less fortunate. They work for publishers who are concerned more about making money than producing quality newspapers. These publishers may keep the size of the news staff small to save money and keep profits high. They require their staffs to work long hours churning out stories to fill the paper. To these reporters, some journalistic principles may seem to be luxuries they can't afford. They don't have time to check several sources or provide a social context. And to add insult to these injurious conditions, these journalists are often among the lowest-paid people in the business, barely making a living wage.

Thomson Newspapers Inc. is often cited as a company that puts profits ahead of news. Some journalists who have worked for Thomson sarcastically cite a statement by the chain's founder, Roy Thomson: "The news is the stuff that separates the ads."

This Canadian company owns more American papers than any other chain, although its total circulation of more than 2 million is far below those of Gannett and Knight-Ridder. In the early 1990s, its possessions included more than 120 dailies and 25 weeklies in the United States, more than 40 dailies and about 20 weeklies in Canada, and publications in Great Britain and Australia. It has a reputation for buying papers in small cities, where profit margins are typically higher than those of papers in major cities and competition is less intense.[27] Thomson turns these small-city dailies and weeklies into cash cows that make profits as high as 40 percent.[28] Norman Isaacs, who edited daily papers in Indianapolis, Louisville and St. Louis, refused to label Thomson a newspaper chain, preferring to call it a "commercial printer."[29] A Canadian government commission that examined chain-owned papers in that country concluded that Thomson's "small-town monopoly papers are, almost without exception, a lacklustre aggregation of cash boxes."[30]

It is clear that the quality of newspapers is shaped by their owners' concern for the bottom line, and *Columbia Journalism Review* contributing editor Karen Rothmyer wrote that the 1980s were "a time when any remaining illusions about journalism as an enterprise different from other businesses were finally put to rest."[31]

MONEY AND THE NEWSROOM

When owners decide how much of a newspaper's or TV station's income should be spent on gathering news, their decisions will have a direct impact on the quality of work that journalists can do. If these business executives do not hire enough reporters and editors or allow a big enough news hole, news that editors believe the public should know cannot be covered. In understaffed newsrooms, editors may struggle to fill the paper by deadline and may trade ethical concerns for expediency. To meet deadlines, they hastily scan the first couple of paragraphs of stories from the AP or another news service. If the first few paragraphs look good and the story will fill the space, the story may appear without having been read in its entirety by anyone in the newsroom. Stories aren't edited; they're shoveled into the paper. Similarly, press releases may get only minor editing before they are put in the newspaper to fill space.

"Hurry! More! More! We still have three pages to fill before deadline."

An even more pernicious effect of having an underfunded newsroom is the over-reliance on story quotas. In an effort to fill the paper each day, many editors set formal or informal quotas requiring reporters to write a minimum number of stories each week. If the newsroom is shorthanded, the editors may increase the quota. This practice may lead to ethical problems for reporters. To meet the quota, some may feel pressured to turn in stories before they have had time to gather all the information they need or check with additional sources to provide balance and ensure accuracy. They may produce stories with only one source, often a government official, and bypass important but time-consuming stories altogether. The papers are filled with "quick hits" that reporters can knock out in an afternoon. Norman Pearlstine, managing editor of *The Wall Street Journal,* fears that newspapers will do less investigative reporting in the future partly because newspaper groups may cut newsroom budgets to the point that editors will not be able to afford it.[32]

At wealthy papers, reporters are still given the resources and time they need. In addition to giving a reporting team several weeks to work on one investigative project, the *Los Angeles Times* spent $10,000 photocopying records reporters needed and $30,000 to hire people to enter data into their computers so they could analyze it. But many editors would have trouble freeing a reporter for even a few days. Michael Pride, editor of the *Concord (N.H.) Monitor,* said the recession in the early 1990s had that effect on his paper. "I have 14 reporters, down three or four from a year ago, with the same news load. I just can't back off and give someone time to do an investigative report."[33]

It is not that newspaper companies have been unwilling to spend money. Many point with pride to the new equipment they have purchased. But often this equipment allowed them to reduce the number of production employees and did little to improve the quality of the news in the paper. As newspaper stock analyst John Morton has pointed out, "Newspaper managers never skimped on reinvesting in their own businesses when there was a clear payoff in sight. . . . Where newspapers *did* skimp was in investment that offered no clear payoff, indeed, investments that would have lowered profitability in the short run." Morton argued that newspapers need to make what he called "strategic investments" in "higher pay, bigger staffs, bigger news holes, more and better journalism, more and better market research and promotion." If newspapers in the past had invested more in journalistic quality, they might have strengthened their hold on readers instead of experiencing readership declines, Morton maintained.[34]

There is some evidence that Morton is right. One study found a strong connection between the quality of a newspaper and its circulation. Journalism professors Stephen Lacy and Frederick Fico concluded, "Papers that cut quality as a short-run cost-saving device may end up paying in future circulation."[35]

BROADCAST NEWS ALSO SUFFERS

Television newsrooms have also felt the sting of budget cuts. Some station owners were hit with a double whammy. They bought stations during the economic boom of the early 1980s by borrowing heavily, then had to repay that debt. They had expected revenues to continue to climb as they did in the 1970s and early 1980s. However, by the early 1990s, most Americans had hooked up to cable TV, and VCRs reigned supreme in two-thirds of their living rooms. Revenue at many broadcast stations did not grow as much as the new owners had predicted, and then the recession slowed advertising sales even more.

These owners were desperately looking for ways to cut their expenses, and news department became prime targets. They got an unexpected assist in these efforts from the federal government. The FCC had required local stations to devote 10 percent of their time to public affairs programming and 5 percent to local programming. News departments were responsible for filling much of that time. Then in 1984 the FCC dropped this requirement. A media critic noted, "Broadcasters no longer have any motivation to do public service unless there's a direct relationship to profitability."[36] Some independent stations stopped broadcasting local news altogether because they could make more money with other kinds of programming.[37]

Not all stations cut their news efforts. WCVB in Boston has 100 reporters, producers and technicians in its news department. Other stations—like WFAA in Dallas, KCRA in Sacramento, WBBM in Chicago, WSMV in Nashville, WPLG in Miami and WCCO in Minneapolis—were cited in an article in *Columbia Journalism Review* as stations whose owners have made financial commitments to better newscasts.[38]

But budget cuts and underfunded news departments are commonplace. "With the old profit margins a memory, cutting costs became the industry's imperative," former Chicago television journalist Dillon Smith wrote in *Washington Journalism Review*. "If *Wheel of Fortune* could produce a bigger profit than local news, the *Wheel* won. If paid 'infomercials' violated broadcast standards, the standards were eliminated along with those who enforced them."[39] One news director, responding to an ethics survey, wrote that he "was concerned about shrinking staff due to budget cuts." He was "worried about compromising our quality standards and ability to gather and edit the news."[40]

As his fears suggest, the effects of underfunding the station's news department can be devastating. TV stations often hire fewer than a tenth as many reporters as newspapers in similar-size cities. Assignment editors, trying to fill the local newscast with too few reporters, may elect to send them only to events that are sure to provide good video, a necessity at most stations. Crime news is often emphasized because it is readily accessible.

Public relations people and promoters know that they can get their message on the air by staging media events that offer the promise of good pictures. The harried reporter, who probably has other assignments on his schedule that day, may lack the time to research the issue and provide balance and depth. The result is that some news segments are shaped largely by the sources, not the journalists. One study suggests that as much as 70 percent of some TV newscasts are reports of pseudo-events, events created by individuals or groups to draw attention to their activities or positions.[41]

At understaffed stations, the news director may use video news releases to fill time. Video news releases are newslike segments that public relations firms develop to promote the interests of their clients. For instance, James Beam Distilling Company can't advertise its whiskeys on TV, but many stations used a VNR about the patriotism of the company and its promise to use only American-grown grains. Political candidates also offer VNRs to local TV newsrooms, and nearly two-thirds of the stations are willing to make use of them.[42]

The viewer may not be able to tell VNRs from news stories the station has obtained from regular news services. Some VNRs are designed so that the station's reporters can appear in the segment, further giving viewers the impression that they are watching locally produced news. A company that distributes VNRs to TV stations via satellite claims that at least one release is used each week at 78 percent of the stations it surveyed.[43] Randall Rothenberg, who covers advertising for *The New York Times,* said he expects the use of VNRs to continue to grow as TV stations cut back on the number of reporters they hire while expanding the length of their newscasts.[44]

Perhaps the most public haggling between journalists and management over the size of the news budget occurred in 1987 when the new owners of CBS decided to slash $36 million from CBS News — about 10 percent of its budget — and to fire 215 employees. Many of CBS's most influential journalists openly attacked their employer. They believed the cuts would reduce the quality of CBS News, which had a proud history, beginning with legendary newsman Edward R. Murrow.[45] Anchor Dan Rather wrote an op-ed piece in *The New York Times,* titled "From Murrow to Mediocrity?" in which he said:

> Our new chief executive officer, Laurence Tisch, told us when he arrived that he wanted us to be the best. We want nothing more than to fulfill that mandate. Ironically, he has now made the task seem something between difficult and impossible.
>
> I have said before that I have no intention of participating in the demise of CBS. But do the owners and officers of the new CBS see news as a trust . . . or only as a business venture?[46]

SALARIES OFTEN LOW

Cost-conscious newspaper and station owners also keep journalists' salaries below those of similar occupations. Their salaries are almost directly proportional to the size of the paper's circulation or the TV station's market. Reporters and editors at metro-size papers and television stations in large markets make decent salaries. For example, *The New York Times'* minimum salary for a reporter with seven years of experience was about $60,000 in the early 1990s. At midrange papers like *The Modesto Bee, The Indianapolis Star* and the *Portland (Maine) Press Herald,* reporters and copy editors averaged more than $35,000, which was about the median salary for newspaper journalists.

Newspaper journalists at papers that had contracts with The Newspaper Guild, a labor union for journalists, made about $8,000 more a year than those at nonunion papers. Papers with unions are often in bigger Northeastern and Midwestern cities.[47] The average TV journalist earned about $25,000 in 1992.[48] Salaries at most smaller papers and radio and television stations are unconscionably low, often below those of beginning teachers and postal clerks. Journalism graduates' starting pay ranked dead last among 28 academic majors in one study.[49]After surveying salaries paid entry-level journalists in Virginia, Steve Nash, a journalism professor, concluded they had better be prepared to drive a very used car and eat lots of peanut butter sandwiches.[50]

*"This is a great place to work as a reporter —
if your dad can afford to send you."*

Even worse, salaries at small papers often remain low despite the quality of work done by the journalist. When Betty Gray won a Pulitzer Prize in 1989, her small-town paper, the *Washington Daily News* in North Carolina, gave her a $25-a-week raise, pushing her salary to $15,000 a year. Starting salaries at her paper were about $12,000 a year.[51]

These low salaries contribute to the poor quality of journalism in many small cities and towns. The salaries are unlikely to attract the best minds among college and university graduates. Worse, beginning journalists who accept the low salaries often plan to stay at the newspaper or TV station only long enough to get enough experience to move to a bigger, better-paying newspaper or station. If they can't find jobs at bigger papers or TV markets, many good young journalists leave the profession altogether. This constant turnover in reporting staffs results in inconsistent coverage and less than thoughtful accounts of the day's news as each new batch of reporters tries to learn the workings of the community and develop reliable sources.

The Search for Readers

Weekday newspaper circulation figures have remained amazingly consistent for the past 30 years, hovering around the 60 million mark almost every year. And that's the problem. While the adult population of the country grew from about 116 million in 1960 to more than 186 million in 1990, weekday newspaper circulation hardly grew at all.[52] (See Table 3.2.)

Table 3.2   *Readership trails growth in adult population*

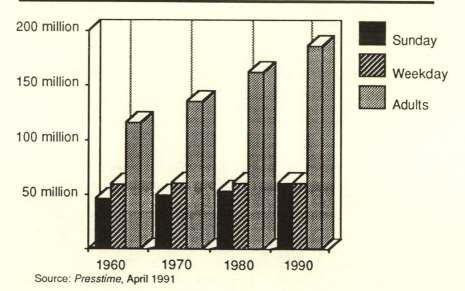

Source: *Presstime*, April 1991

The plain truth is that newspaper reading is not as popular today as it has been. For several years researchers have asked people if they read a paper yesterday. In 1946, 73 percent of the population said yes.[53] By 1990, only 43 percent said they had.[54] Researcher John P. Robinson found that "this decline in newspaper reading is evident in almost every consumer segment regardless of age, education, family type, or employment status."[55]

The biggest concern for many in the newspaper industry is the dramatic decline in the use of print media by young adults. Several studies have focused on this age group, each asking slightly different questions and getting slightly different answers. But the trend is clear: Young adults are no longer getting the newspaper habit. One study found that in 1965, 67 percent of those under 35 said they had read a paper yesterday; in 1990, only 29 percent had.[56] While about two-thirds of people over 50 told Times Mirror pollsters they considered themselves regular newspaper readers, only a third of those between 18 and 30 said they were.

A knee-jerk reaction to statistics like these is that people are watching the news on TV and not buying newspapers. But that's not the case. Although news junkies have made CNN successful and programs like *60 Minutes* get high ratings, the number of people who regularly watch TV news is also going down. According to Nielsen researchers, the percentage of people watching evening network news shows has dropped from 56 percent to 31 percent in the past 25 years.[57] And as with newspapers, young adults are less likely to watch TV news. About 62 percent of adults under 30 say they regularly watch, but 83 percent of those over 50 consider TV news part of their daily routine.[58]

Researchers have even more bad news. Another Times Mirror study found that today's young adults "know less and care less about news and public affairs than any other generation of Americans in the past 50 years."[59] After reading this research, Robert Haiman, president of The Poynter Institute for Media Studies, concluded, "Whether you look like a phone book or *USA Today* doesn't make any difference to this group."[59]

None of this bodes well for journalists and the news media. If young adults continue not to care about the news, they are unlikely to buy newspapers or watch TV newscasts. News ratings and newspaper circulations will decline. Advertisers will forgo expensive newspaper advertising and stop buying spots during TV news. Newsgathering operations will be scaled back. Not only will journalists lose their jobs, but a decline in the quality of news will be unhealthy for our democracy. A democracy depends on its citizens being informed enough about the issues to make wise decisions. Unless the media can interest Americans in the news, voters may not be able to meet these expectations.

Many newspapers editors and TV news producers are experimenting with ways of appealing to readers. However, some ways being suggested to increase the audience for news seem to clash with the basic assumptions of what ethical journalism ought to be.

REDEFINING "NEWS"

When consumers stop buying a product, the owners of the business that produces it worry. They bring in market researchers to find out why customers no longer want their product. Then they instruct their engineers and designers to change the product so it will once again appeal to customers. Finally they hire an advertising agency to find ways of enticing customers to try the "new and improved" version.

The use of these marketing techniques to shape the news product is nothing new at most TV stations. News directors often answer directly to programming directors, and newscasts are often judged by the same standards as other programs — namely, ratings. If the ratings are down, consultants may be brought in to find out why viewers aren't watching. Depending on their findings, the station may build new sets, add new features to the newscast, order new hairdos for its on-air people, or fire its anchors and hire some new ones. CBS anchor Dan Rather was once advised to wear sweaters to make viewers react more warmly to him.

Some print journalists point to the news content of local TV news to show what's wrong with using marketing surveys to make news decisions. For instance, surveys in many markets say that viewers have little interest in politics and don't care about candidates and their policies. Viewers want stories about the weather, the environment, the economy and especially crime. TV devotes so much time to crime that some researchers have reported that people who frequently watch TV are convinced their communities are much more violent than they really are.

"Crime at 11 p.m. sells," a TV news executive once noted. "There is little evidence at this point that [news about] public affairs sells."[60] This probably explains the plight of one candidate for Congress in Central Florida. He complained that his campaign received less coverage on local TV news than in *The New York Times,* published more than 1,000 miles away, and in *Fortune,* a national business magazine.[61]

But stations that buck the marketing experts can get burned. The news director at WSOC in Charlotte, N.C., decided not to follow the advice of the consultants. Instead, the station concentrated its political coverage on issues rather than the candidates' exchange of charges. But when viewers switched to other channels and the ratings went down, the station returned to more conventional coverage.[62]

MARKETING VERSUS JOURNALISM

USA Today is the first major American daily to be conceived with the help of marketing experts. While journalists generally praised the paper's design and use of graphics, many criticized its news coverage. When *USA Today* first appeared, they mocked its short, "quick read" stories that often emphasize "soft news" about lifestyles, entertainers and happy events. They said it avoided "hard news" about government and tough social issues and tried to simplify complicated problems so they could be told in a few paragraphs. Ben Bagdikian charged that the paper selected stories "not because of their inherent importance but on the basis of their potential for jazzy graphics."[63] However, these criticisms became less frequent in the 1990s when the paper began to carry longer, more thoughtful stories.

Until recently, *USA Today*'s reliance on marketing made it a rarity among American dailies; most editors didn't want any help deciding what would be printed. While readership surveys might be useful in picking comic strips and columnists, editors thought they should decide what was news. But in the 1980s many newspaper companies saw that their circulation figures and profits were not growing. They hired marketing firms to do surveys to find out what readers liked and disliked in their paper. They brought in "focus groups," small groups of people selected at random from the community. These focus groups told the editors what they thought ought to be in the paper.

The problem was that sometimes what people said they wanted in the paper clashed with journalists' perceptions of their role. According to nationwide surveys by Weaver and Wilhoit, most print journalists saw their roles as investigating government claims (66.7 percent said this was very important) and informing the public quickly (68.6 percent). Considerably fewer journalists saw their role as appealing to the widest audience (20.2 percent) or entertaining readers (14 percent).[64] Yet many journalists fear that changes in the news content suggested by marketing studies will shift the emphasis of their profession. They fear that they will be expected to find ways of entertaining a wider audience at the expense of covering the serious news of the day.

The clash between traditional news values and marketing approaches is already being felt in many newsrooms. A survey of West Coast journalists found that morale was low among journalists "in newsrooms of chain newspapers where the push toward market-oriented

Giving readers what they want may not be what they need.

journalism is strongest." Although "journalistic principles seemed to be holding their ground," few of the journalists thought the changes were making the papers any better, except for improvements in design and some managerial practices. The general perception was that the changes were making the papers worse.[65]

As newspapers begin to redefine their news content in keeping with marketing surveys, some of the criticisms that had been heaped on TV news are being aimed at newspapers. Some newspapers have been accused of carrying too much "soft news" and easy-to-get crime news and not enough hard news. The *Wausau Daily Herald* in Wisconsin adopted a reader-driven format that devoted news space to grade-school awards and bowling scores. The paper's editor told a *Washington Journalism Review* writer, "We do less government, to the point where the mayor calls and complains."[66]

An extreme example of a newspaper opting for soft news occurred in Winnipeg, Canada. Editors at that city's *Free Press,* a Thomson chain newspaper, put the outbreak of the 1992 Los Angeles riots on Page 56 in the fourth section of the paper. They reserved the front page for stories about edible golf tees and local residents' good deeds. The paper's ombudsman wrote a column calling the editors' decision an example of the paper's "not so subtle" shift away from hard news to softer features.[67]

Probably the most discussed redefinition of news content was the one performed by the Knight-Ridder chain on *The News* in Boca Raton, Fla., an upscale community near Fort Lauderdale and home of a large IBM facility. The paper had been a fairly well-regarded small-city daily with a circulation of about 22,000. Then Knight-Ridder, one of America's most prestigious chains, decided to use *The News* as a testing ground for some of the ideas developed during the corporation's $3 million research project on how to make newspaper readers out of young-adult "baby boomers." The chain, which publishes several Pulitzer Prize–winning papers, including *The Miami Herald, The Philadelphia Inquirer, Detroit Free Press* and *Lexington (Ky.) Herald-Leader,* indicated that it expected some of the changes to spread to other papers it owns.

Among the changes in the redesigned paper were lots of charts, news-in-brief columns and graphics. Every day it ran large locator maps on each of the pages designated for news briefs from the world, the nation, the state and the local area. The maps had numbers that corresponded with numbers on stories about events that happened at those locations.

Preparing all these graphics and briefs required more desk work by the journalists at *The News.* Some reporters had to be taken off news beats and shifted to desk jobs. The paper's editor, Wayne L. Ezell, acknowledged that the pressure to produce more features, graphics and business stories left his staff little time to do real investigative reporting.[68] The news focus of the paper changed too. It ran more "soft news" like stories about Pets of the Day, Heroes of the Day and other lighter topics. When space was tight, government stories were the first to be dropped, according to Lou Heldman, who headed the Knight-Ridder project team.[69]

The way the news was written also changed. Since research repeatedly showed that readers didn't like stories to start on one page and then jump to another page, *The News* did away with jumps. Instead, stories on the front page were rarely more than a few paragraphs long. If the story was important enough, the paper ran a second story on the topic inside. These inside stories were usually short too. The approach was so novel that on the day the Gulf War started, journalists from around the nation called the paper's newsroom and asked if the paper wouldn't run a long story about the war and jump it inside. *The News* didn't. It covered the start of the war in a few paragraphs on Page 1 and ran other stories about the war inside. Lots of other changes were cosmetic: brighter colors, a pink flamingo adorning the nameplate, and more graphics on the weather page.

Not every Knight-Ridder editor was satisfied that the experiment in Boca Raton was the best way to attract lost readers. Davis Merritt, editor of *The Wichita Eagle,* said he was not convinced that *The News* maintains what he calls the "core of a newspaper." His paper experimented with "community connectedness" as a way of appealing to readers. For instance, the paper surveyed readers well before the election to discover the issues that concerned them, then shaped its coverage around these issues rather than "getting [candidate] A's statements and [candidate] B's response," explained Steve Smith, the paper's managing editor.[70]

Other newspapers have also studied the desires of their readers, and their results were much different from those in Boca Raton. In Maine the editors of the *Portland Press Herald* found that their readers did not want a Yankee clone of *USA Today*. Instead, they preferred "a traditional newspaper that emphasized traditional definitions of news. They wanted a newspaper that was easy to read but also had depth, and they were especially interested in local enterprise reporting."[71] After making some of these changes, the paper won regional and national awards, and its executive editor reported, "Feedback from the community and our research also indicate that our readers see us as a much better newspaper."[72]

WHAT DO READERS REALLY WANT?

Why is there so much variation in what readers want? Why would one group of editors think readers want shorter stories, photos of Pets of the Day and lots of color, while another group of editors believes readers want newspapers that emphasize more traditional journalistic values?

None of the research is exhaustive enough to provide a definitive answer. The most obvious response is that each newspaper serves a different part of the country and must respond to the specific needs and interests of its region. But regional differences alone may not explain these wide variations in what readers appear to want in a newspaper. Some current research casts doubt on the assumptions that all non-newspaper readers are alike and that they all lack an interest in news.

A large-scale project for the American Society of Newspaper Editors found that people's attitudes toward newspapers fell into four distinct groups. One group consists of die-hard readers who depend on their newspapers each day. Another is people who would never read a newspaper, no matter what was in it. Between these extremes are two groups who might be enticed to become regular newspaper readers. One group prefers a paper that is easier and quicker to read. These people "would rather have the news presented to them than read it themselves." The other group wants a paper that gives them greater depth and insight into the news.[73]

If this research is right, the challenge to newspapers may be to find ways to appeal to readers who want the "quick reads" that *USA Today* promises and readers who want more. Some newspapers are trying to find that mix. The *St. Paul Pioneer Press* has experimented with a "Read-It-Fast, Read-It-Slow" format. For time-conscious readers, the paper has summaries on many of its stories and lots of news outlines. Yet the stories themselves are thorough accounts of the news and appeal to readers looking for depth.[74] Other papers, like the *Portland Press Herald,* have made efforts to appeal to readers looking for a quick read and readers wanting more substance.

When *USA Today* and other papers emphasizing soft news first appeared, many observers predicted that these papers would be the wave of the future.[75] It is too early to know if they are correct. Academic research suggests that the papers most likely to adopt a *USA Today*-style format of short stories and soft news are small, group-owned ones.[76]

"Hold the presses! I've got a paragraph here that's bound to win a Pulitzer Prize."

Clearly, not all newspapers have shifted their emphasis from hard news to fluff and abandoned traditional journalistic principles. Each year reporters and editors receive Pulitzer Prizes, Society of Professional Journalists awards, and other honors for hard-nosed reporting, an indication that many newspaper owners are willing to foster a climate that expects high-quality, ethical journalism.

Yet for too many papers, the fears Robert Greene expressed more than a decade ago seem to be becoming reality. Greene, a former investigative reporter and editor at the Long Island daily *Newsday* and a former president of the Investigative Reporters and Editors organization, told a meeting of journalists:

> I would submit that we have had our moments of greatness and we will have them again. But at this moment in time, most of our industry is no more deserving of special constitutional preference than General Motors, Lockheed Aviation or the Ideal Toy Company. Our ability to present the news in form if not substance is unparalleled. But our inability to comprehend our public service responsibilities would lead a current-day Otto von Bismarck to repeat his observation that "A newspaper writer is someone who has failed in his calling."[77]

The Power of Advertisers

When advertisers buy an advertisement, do they also buy a say in the nature of the news? In an ideal world, the answer to the question would be easy. If journalists are to live up to their ethical obligation of truth-telling, the search for truth should not be influenced by advertisers. News media owners would be aware of this ethical imperative and refuse to bend to advertisers.

Some have even argued that it is against advertisers' best interests if they try to use their advertising dollars to muscle the media. Businesses buy advertisements so they can increase their sales and make more money. If they get upset about a story and cancel their advertisements, they hurt themselves by losing business. Since they need to advertise and there's usually only one paper in town, their threats of withholding advertising are hollow.[78]

But that's not the way it has worked out.

The news media have become so dependent on advertising dollars that today as much as 80 percent of a newspaper's revenue and nearly all a TV station's come from advertisers.[79] Paying this much of the tab, advertisers often have a lot of clout, and some are willing to use it. If a news organization carries a story they don't like, they threaten to move their advertising accounts to other TV stations and newspapers that haven't offended them or to media that carry no news and therefore cannot offend them—media like direct-mail, all-music radio, or free "shopper" publications.

Advertiser boycotts are taken seriously by many media owners. Editors and TV news directors say this kind of pressure is increasing; a few even consider it their top ethical concern.[80]

All too often, advertisers and other influential members of the business community demand and receive special treatment. Sometimes this special treatment is rather indirect. Reporters may be expected to select sources from businesses that advertise with the paper and avoid sources from businesses that don't. For instance, the editor of a Pennsylvania newspaper complained when a travel story named three travel agents but not one who advertised with the paper. If a story needs to be illustrated with local examples, the editor contended, "our policy is to use the ones who advertise. I don't think that's compromising anything. . . . If you're going to pick only a few people to talk to, pick the ones who spend money with us."[81] A small-city editor in Indiana directed a reporter preparing a story about merchants' Christmas preparations to exclude references to stores that did not advertise with the paper, and some small-budget papers review only restaurants that buy ads. Many journalists are troubled by these mergings of their papers' news and advertising missions.

Of more concern are those cases in which advertisers exert direct pressure on editors. Sometimes they demand that their press releases be used verbatim or that only favorable stories about their products and services be run, even when there is important but negative news about them. On occasion, editors and commentators are pushed to write editorials in support of political positions that advertisers favor.

Otis Chandler, chairman of the executive committee of the Times Mirror Company, which publishes the *Los Angeles Times* and other newspapers, said that "successful newspapers do not have to let the business side into the editorial arena. They have the luxury of letting the editorial department be completely independent to cover the news as it sees it." However, Chandler recalled working for a paper that was not successful financially, the old *Los Angeles Mirror-News,* which his corporation eventually folded. "Every line of advertising was so important, we really killed some news stories because we were trying to get the major department stores to advertise and we did not want to rock any boats."[82]

SOME BATTLE AD PRESSURE

Some newspapers have battled publicly with advertisers who wanted to control news content. When *The Salina (Kan.) Journal* endorsed a city sales tax, the city's car dealers who opposed the measure pulled their ads from the paper. Instead of bending to the boycotters' demands, the paper reported the dealers' actions and published a series of editorials criticizing them. "I think we should let the public know what organizations are trying to impose their will on us, trying to drive us out of business because we don't agree with their point of view," said the editor of the paper.[83]

Many other newspapers have also fought costly advertiser boycotts. *The Washington Post* once ran a story about a Harvard University study predicting a decline in the prices of houses in the Washington area. To provide balance, the reporter included comments from experts who disputed the prediction, but the story did not set well with the real estate community. Major builders withdrew an estimated $750,000 of advertising from the paper.[84]

When *The Seattle Times* and *Seattle Post-Intelligencer* ran stories about labor problems at Nordstrom, a large department store chain, James Nordstrom, co-chairman of the company, called the coverage "the worst in the nation." The chain stopped advertising in the papers and started using other media.[85] But the papers did not soften their coverage. "You can't sell your soul in little bits and pieces and expect readers will understand," the executive editor of the *Times* said. "A lot of newspapers don't understand that."[86]

Editors at *The Virginian-Pilot* and *The Ledger-Star,* sister newspapers in Norfolk, Va., and the *St. Louis Post-Dispatch* showed their independence from their advertising departments, which rejected ads because they were too controversial. The ad rejected by the Norfolk papers was for a winter festival sponsored by a gay and lesbian group. The *Post-Dispatch* advertising department refused an ad by an anti-abortion group that featured a graphic photo of a mutilated doll. Editors at the papers considered the rejections news and printed stories quoting the ad managers and the groups involved. The *Post-Dispatch* even ran in its news columns the photo that the business office had found offensive. The paper's ombudsman wrote a column explaining the seeming inconsistency of a paper first rejecting an advertisement, then printing it free as news. "That apparent anomaly," he said, "was the best demonstration of the separateness of a paper's news department and its business offices I've ever seen."[87]

BUT ADVERTISERS OFTEN GET THEIR WAY

Examples of editors and TV news directors bravely battling advertisers may become less frequent as management scrambles to meet the profit expectations of their corporate owners. Reports in *Columbia Journalism Review, Washington Journalism Review,* various regional journalism reviews, and *The Wall Street Journal* have exposed apparent special treatment given to advertisers and other influential groups. Auto dealers, real estate interests and department stores are frequently cited as recipients of favored status. These groups are among the heaviest advertisers in newspapers.

The Oregonian in Portland destroyed tens of thousands of copies of its Sunday paper after advertising people pointed out a story that was sure to upset real estate firms that buy lots of advertising. The story suggested that homeowners could save money by selling their homes themselves and avoiding the commissions of real estate agents. The paper's managing editor explained that the timing of the story "could not have been worse in view of the assurances we had made" to real estate groups at a meeting shortly before the incident.[88]

The Oregonian is not alone in its efforts to appease real estate people. Wendy Swallow Williams, a journalism professor at American University in Washington, D.C., found that 44 percent of the real estate editors she surveyed said publishers or senior editors would not allow them to present balanced coverage. "More than 80 percent said advertisers had threatened to pull their advertising because of negative coverage; a third said they knew of advertisers who had done so." The attack on their journalistic ethics was painful for many of them. "Several editors said they had been ordered by senior editors or publishers to delay or kill a story that might offend advertisers. For each, the experience was devastating." Many editors filled the survey forms they had been given with long diatribes attacking publishers and advertisers.[89]

"It's not that we want you to kowtow to our biggest advertisers. Just remember to do what our mothers taught us: 'If you can't think of anything nice to say about somebody, don't say anything at all.'"

Some newspapers have advertiser-driven real estate sections with headlines that gush, "Sound Judgment the Basis for Buying at Boca Quay." Some allow advertisers to write newslike stories that are printed as if they were news stories. This blending of ads and editorial copy is often called "advertorials."

A few newspapers have tried to overcome the problems of advertiser influence in real estate sections by labeling these sections as advertising and using special typefaces for the headlines to differentiate them from the news. Fort Lauderdale's *Sun-Sentinel,* owned by the Tribune Co. of Chicago, has been doing this for 10 years. How successful these tactics are at alerting readers to the nature of these sections is open to debate.

Some newspapers successfully print tough-minded real estate sections. When *The Miami Herald* added a real estate section with the same ethical standards of the rest of the paper, an assistant managing editor said, "I argued that the readers were being ill-served by something that cloaked itself as news when it was simply ad messages."[90] Not only were the editors satisfied with the new section, but the advertising department reported a 79 percent increase in paid ad linage. Ad sales in the *Chicago Tribune*'s real estate section also increased when that paper started a consumer-oriented section to replace a classified ad section that ran advertorial copy.[91]

AUTO DEALERS' BOYCOTT

Automotive or transportation sections have also been targets of arm-twisting by advertisers. *The Birmingham (Ala.) News* introduced an advertiser-friendly automotive section after car dealers withdrew ads worth between $300,000 and $500,000 a year. The dealers were upset because the paper ran a story critical of tactics used to sell cars.[92]

Other newspapers have also shown great sensitivity to the image of car sales staffs. The Carbondale, Ill., *Southern Illinoisan* printed an apology and suspended a sportswriter and his editor after the writer compared the St. Louis Cardinal pitching staff to a bunch of used-car lemons polished up for sale by a shady dealer. The publisher said it was an "obsolete stereotype" of used-car dealers.[93]

In Trenton, N.J., *The Times* was hit by a series of advertising boycotts by car dealers who objected to stories about discount dealers who sold cars at wholesale prices. The dealers also attempted to use their advertising accounts to influence the paper's editorial pages. When the paper opposed the federal government's plan to lend the financially ailing Chrysler Corporation millions of dollars to keep the company from closing, the car dealers again pulled their ads. It is estimated that boycotts cost the paper $1 million before Joseph Allbritton bought the paper and decided to make peace with the advertisers. Soon after taking over the paper, he fired 24 people from the staff of 80. Soon 14 other news staffers left, complaining that the business office was taking over the newsroom and catering to advertisers. Some journalists said they were told to run as news flattering stories written by the advertisers.[94]

Car dealers' sensitivities are not limited to stories attacking their sales practices or pricing policies. In 1992, auto dealers in Ogden, Utah, pulled their ads from the *Standard-Examiner* because the paper ran a story about GM's Saturn cars and gave the name of the nearest dealership, which was in another city and competed with the Ogden dealers.[95] And a syndicated cartoon cost many newspapers several thousand dollars in advertising. The cartoon—which showed a proud new-car owner with an "I Buy American" sticker on his bumper watch his bumper fall off—led to a boycott against the Marion, Ind., *Chronicle-Tribune* and to declines in car advertising at the Akron *Beacon Journal* and several of Gannett's suburban newspapers in New York.[96]

Auto dealers have also pressured local TV news. After WCCO-TV, the CBS affiliate in Minneapolis–St. Paul, ran an investigative piece alleging that a string of fires in Ford vans was caused by design flaws, many dealers, including some who did not sell Fords, cut back their advertisements on the station. Many switched to the station's competitor KARE-TV. WCCO management set up talks between the dealers and its news staff, but the talks fell through when the station reported that some Chevy Lumina seat belts were unsafe in crashes. WCCO management did not renew the contract of the reporter who did that story, although she was reinstated after a newsroom protest.[97]

Department stores too have tried to use boycotts as a weapon against unfavorable coverage. When the *Boston Herald* reported on the financial problems of Robert Campeau, the Jordon Marsh chain, owned by Campeau, pulled its advertisements for a week.[98]

HOW OFTEN DO EDITORS CAVE IN?

The frequency of advertiser attempts to influence the press alarms many journalists. Philip Meyer, a former reporter and Knight-Ridder executive who conducted a survey of ethics for the American Society of Newspaper Editors, found that "advertising pressure is a concern at least some of the time on papers read by 79 percent of the American public. . . . And for 9 percent, it happens every week. That's a lot of advertiser pressure."[99]

More recent research paints an even bleaker picture. A survey by professors at Marquette University found that more than 90 percent of the newspapers had been pressured by advertisers to change or kill a story and that about a third of the editors admitted they had caved in and complied with advertisers' wishes.[100] The ethics committee of the ASNE reported that in the past five years, about 90 percent of the nation's largest 100 newspapers had advertisers cancel ads because they were upset by news stories. Only about 10 percent of the time did the newspapers inform readers what was going on.[101]

These figures, as awesome as they are, may underestimate the influence of advertisers. Stephen Rynkiewicz, a copy editor at the *Chicago Sun-Times,* has pointed out that editors rarely kill stories outright, "but any practical reporter or editor uses extra caution when they see a conflict coming. In that respect, business has bought influence in the news media as surely as it has with PAC money in Congress."[102] For instance, in a publication of the Investigative Reporters and Editors organization, consumer reporter Herb Weisbaum of KIRO-TV in Seattle wrote: "We don't even bother with most auto-related stories anymore. These days, even a simple consumer education story on how to buy a new car can draw the wrath of local car dealers. Trying to share such basic advice with your viewers can result in the loss of many thousands of dollars."[103]

In some cases, the "extra caution" Rynkiewicz described is reinforced when reporters learn that their stories about certain advertisers may be scrutinized by high-level editors. At *The Miami Herald,* the executive editor reads all stories relating to major advertisers. He told *The Wall Street Journal* that he does not believe any of his reporters are intimidated by this extra step in the editing process by one of the paper's highest editors. When *The Indianapolis Star*'s largest advertiser (the L.S. Ayres & Co. department store chain) complained about negative coverage, the paper didn't back off, but the managing editor then reviewed all stories about the advertiser.[104]

Steve Singer of Harvard University's John F. Kennedy School of Business believes the problem of advertiser interference is growing. He wrote:

> There is mounting evidence that advertisers nationwide are increasingly taking advantage of weak newspaper ad revenues to pressure papers into more positive coverage of their activities. It's a development that is raising questions about the lengths to which recession-battered publishers will go to court advertisers. . . . The trend also raises questions about the slow erosion of the walls around the newsroom and, ultimately, about what readers should expect from newspapers.[105]

The situation may be even worse for broadcast news. When TV

news directors were asked about their major ethical concerns, many cited the growing pressures to give special treatment to advertisers. One news director wrote: "Our station policy dictates no interference with editorial and content decisions, but sales people still try to manipulate news managers. We are still immune from outside influence, but I worry about what may happen as the recession squeezes us and sales fall." Another news director said he is worried about the "intrusion of sales decisions into newsrooms where there is not a strong history of journalistic independence (especially true with a softening economy and erosion of the audience base)."[106]

What's an Ethical Journalist to Do?

The alternatives for journalists who find that the demands of management clash with their consciences are not very inviting. Traditionally, ethical journalists have quit working for unsavory employers and found jobs at other stations or newspapers. That option is less achievable because of the shortage of jobs in journalism. Some journalists have decided to leave the profession altogether rather than lower their ethical standards.

A code of ethics for newspaper publishers and station owners would be one small step in improving the quality of American journalism. But there has been little discussion of extending codes to publishers, and it is difficult to imagine that the worst offenders, whose publications need codes the most, would agree to one.

It is ironic that many of the owners whose newsrooms have strict codes of ethics for journalists are not covered by codes of ethics. These owners are willing to tell small-town reporters who barely make living wages that they cannot accept free admission to an amusement park for fear that they will compromise the integrity of the news. Yet they are not bound by industry codes of ethics that deal with understaffing newsrooms, reducing the news hole, or yielding to advertiser pressure.

Former CBS newsman Jon Katz and *Columbia Journalism Review*'s Karen Rothmyer urge journalists to make media managers understand the need to commit financial resources to strong news coverage. Rothmyer believes that reporters and editors are going to have to take a more active role in the management of their papers. She wrote:

"Don't tell me my newspaper isn't ethical. We haven't offended anybody in this town for years."

For journalists, the challenge will be to learn to live with the financial realities while, at the same time, fighting against the corporate values that so often accompany them. That will require two forms of activity not now common in American newsrooms: serious financial analysis, by news employees, of their organizations; and collective action—not individual gestures or expressions of concern—aimed at giving journalists a voice as one of the stakeholders in media corporations.[107]

Katz urged broadcast journalists to take an even more aggressive approach. He believes that pressure from outside the broadcast industry is the only way to get station owners to invest in better newscasts.

Katz suggested that TV news directors have lunch with local newspaper editors and encourage them to print stories about the "perilous position of local news" and write editorials that "lean on the television industry to provide air time that's protected . . . from some of the profit pressure."[108] Katz said that it may take the fear of renewed government regulation to improve local stations' commitment to news. Speaking to station managers, he said:

Remember that this deregulatory era can't last forever. Sooner or later some congressman or -woman is going to notice that you're making obscene profits, that you're broadcasting little public affairs programming, that your children's programs exist only to sell sugared cereals, and that you've grown contemptuous of the notion of public airwaves as a public trust. When it hits the fan, you'll have little in the way of public support. Then you'll be forced to get serious. . . . Remember that in other fields executives have learned to view market research as a guide, not a bible.[109]

The answer to the problems of business interference in the newsroom will have to come from media owners themselves. Owners have made a lot of money from TV stations and newspapers. One stock analyst expects newspaper profit ratios to continue to be nearly twice those of other American industries in years to come.[110]

The problem is that these profit ratios may be lower than those that media owners grew accustomed to during the high-flying 1980s. Too many owners want to maintain their high profit ratios by slashing at the heart of the news operation and undermining its commitment to telling the truth. Until these publishers and station owners learn to accept new realistic profit standards, too many journalists will not be allowed to practice their profession in keeping with its highest ethical principles.

Conflicts of
Interest

More than 300,000 people crowded the streets of Washington, D.C., carrying pro-choice banners and singing protest songs.

They were hoping to send a message to the U.S. Supreme Court that they disagreed with its ruling in *Webster v. Reproductive Health Services,* which many believed was a signal that the court was going to overturn its decision in *Roe v. Wade* legalizing abortion.

A protest of this size was a major media event. Hundreds of journalists were on the scene. Among them was Linda Greenhouse, a *New York Times* reporter who covers the Supreme Court. But she wasn't there to report on the demonstration prompted by the court's decision. She was there with the marchers who were protesting the decision. And she wasn't the only reporter who participated in the march. Dozens of journalists from papers all over the country were among the protesters.

When these journalists returned to their newsrooms, many received a jolt. They got messages from their editors telling them that they had violated their newspapers' codes of ethics. The codes specified that they were not allowed to participate in activities that may create or appear to create conflicts of interest.

Many of these journalists and some of their editors said they did not know that participating in the march would be considered unethical.

When Greenhouse told the Washington bureau chief for the *Times* about her participation, his first reaction was that she had done nothing wrong. "People's private expressions are their own business," he told her.[1] Then he checked the *Times'* guidelines on ethics and found a clause that seemed to ban such activities:

> The integrity of *The Times* requires that its staff members avoid employment or any other undertakings, obligations, relationships or investments that create or appear to create a conflict of interest with their professional work for *The Times* or otherwise compromises *The Times'* independence and reputation.

But he still wasn't sure the rule would apply to Greenhouse's participation in the march, so he checked with *Times* editors in New York and learned that Max Frankel, then executive editor, was committed to the policy. He was told, "Max's view is that, as an example, you cannot cover the White House and wear a campaign button."[2]

Greenhouse and other *Times* staffers were not punished by the paper for their participation in the march. She stayed on the Supreme Court beat because, her bureau chief said, "We have full faith and confidence in her professionalism. It's part of our profession that we try to discipline opinions, not that we're opinion-free."

But she was criticized by other journalists. "Most of my colleagues thought I was a jerk to be there," she said, "and they let me know that, either politely or impolitely."[3] Some thought the *Times* let her off too easy. Eileen McNamara, who covered the abortion issue for *The Boston Globe* at the time of the march, said that Greenhouse had made "a terrible mistake" in marching and that the *Times* had "made a bad mistake in allowing her to continue to cover the issue."[4] Greenhouse said she would follow the newspaper's policy and not participate in pro-choice rallies. "I don't intend to make a martyr of myself. I wouldn't want to do anything to undermine the credibility and objectivity of the profession," she told *Time* magazine.[5]

The journalists who joined the protest have encountered one of the thornier concerns facing journalists. Many want to be involved in their communities, but are aware that these involvements can lead to conflicts of interest — or the appearance of conflicts of interest. Conflicts of interest are part of our everyday lives. But when such conflicts occur for journalists, the public is apt to wonder whether these journalists have given up their independence and ability to report truthfully. Such doubts threaten the credibility of journalists in a profession in which being believed is everything.

Journalists and Free Speech

When Greenhouse's editor heard of her participation in the march, his first response was that she had done nothing wrong since she was making a private expression of her opinions on her own time. Bosses in most businesses would probably say the same thing: "At work, you live by our rules; after work, you are free to do pretty much what you want." But often that's not the way it works in journalism.

On the job, reporters are sometimes encouraged to express their opinions in op-ed columns and news-analysis pieces and to appear on TV and radio talk programs. Some small-town papers even pay bonuses to reporters who write editorials. But off the job, journalists are supposed to keep their opinions to themselves. Most newspapers and TV stations have policies limiting what reporters and editors can say and do when they are not at work.

Editors at many papers, including the *Chicago Tribune* and *The Orlando Sentinel,* issued reminders of their conflict-of-interest rules when they learned that some of their staff members had participated in the abortion-rights march. Some papers had newsroom meetings to discuss the matter. A few newspapers, like *The Washington Post,* went a step further. Editors prohibited all staffers who participated in the march from reporting or editing stories about the abortion question. Leonard Downie Jr., who was managing editor at the *Post* during the pro-choice march, told *Time* that some of his staff members "found it kind of shocking that they are called on not to exercise some of their personal rights so that the paper can vigorously defend its own First Amendment rights."[6]

To head off potential problems, many newspapers and TV news departments reminded their staffs of their policies before the march on Washington by gays and lesbians in 1993. ABC News, the Associated Press and the *Post* were among the news organizations that specifically banned their journalists from participating in that demonstration. Other news organizations limited participation to staff members who did not cover issues involving gays.[7]

Marches are not the only way journalists have run afoul of conflict-of-interest codes. Reporters at many papers have been cautioned not to wear campaign buttons or put political bumper stickers on their cars. A pro-choice reporter at a newspaper in South Florida was fired after she mailed miniature coat hangers, symbols of illegal abortions, to every member of the Florida Legislature. A reporter at the Santa Rosa, Calif.,

Cover, but don't participate, most journalists are told.

Press Democrat was taken off coverage of the timber industry after a weekly paper quoted him as praising organizers of an anti-logging protest.[8] And some papers have asked reporters not to join groups like the National Organization for Women because these organizations become entangled in political issues.

The Washington Post not only wants its staff members to "avoid active involvement in any partisan causes" but includes a statement about their families: "Relatives cannot fairly be made subject to *Post* rules, but it should be recognized that their employment or their involvement in causes can at least appear to compromise our integrity."[9]

TOO MANY RESTRICTIONS?

Many journalists think the restrictions now in place at many newspapers intrude far too much into their private lives. They contend that they can express their opinions publicly and still do their jobs.

Some believe that once the public sees that their stories are fair, there will be no loss of credibility. A. Kent MacDougall, now a journalism professor at the University of California, argued that he did nothing wrong when he participated in an anti–Vietnam War protest while he was a reporter at *The Wall Street Journal*. In an op-ed piece for the *Journal,* he wrote, "A well-trained reporter with pride in his craft won't allow his beliefs to distort his stories, any more than a Republican surgeon will botch an appendectomy on a Democrat."[10] Helen Thomas,

UPI's veteran White House reporter, told talk-show host Phil Donahue that she had a 40-year history of expressing her views and still reporting the news fairly.[11]

Many journalists agree. They contend that placing limits on journalists' free speech is only a cosmetic effort to mask the fact that journalists have opinions. They argue that reporters' stories will be the same whether they keep quiet about their opinions or express them openly. "There's a certain hypocrisy in trying to have the public think that just because a reporter doesn't march, he or she is somehow more objective than somebody who does march," *New York Newsday* columnist Gabriel Rotello told *American Journalism Review.*[12]

Other journalists argue that some issues are too important for them to bury their heads in the sand. A *Chicago Tribune* reporter told *Time,* "To me, the struggle for abortion rights is as important to women as the struggle against slavery. This isn't about whether they're going to build some bridge downtown. This is about my body."[13]

And a few contend that when off-duty, journalists should have the same rights as other Americans. Sandy Nelson of the *Tacoma (Wash.) Morning News Tribune* argued that newspapers treat journalists "like serfs." She said, "We have become the company's property 24 hours a day." She sued her paper after editors moved her from a reporting position to the copy desk after she played a key role in a political battle to keep that city's ban on discrimination because of sexual orientation.[14]

WHY JOURNALISTS' RIGHTS ARE LIMITED

Many journalists believe that journalists should not take part in public issues. They argue that as people engage in marches and organizations that promote causes, they become more deeply involved in these issues. These strong involvements may lead to bias unintentionally slipping into their reporting. The concern is not that reporters might deliberately slant their stories — editors are supposed to keep that from happening — but that while gathering information, they might treat sources they agree with more favorably and unconsciously rely on them more heavily.

Many people, both in the newsroom and among the public, have questioned whether this kind of unintentional bias may have affected the news media's coverage of the abortion debate. "If you are a woman reporter under the age of about 50 . . . you are writing about something that could happen to you," said Cynthia Gorney, who covers abortion for *The Washington Post*. She told *Los Angeles Times* media writer David Shaw, "You're going to have a view on it. . . . There's no way you can set that aside. The issue is whether you can, while holding that view, listen seriously to people of all stripes on this issue . . . and really do what reporters are supposed to do . . . shed light and make clear why people hold the positions that they do."[15]

A few journalists have admitted that on the question of abortion, they cannot set aside their beliefs. Reporters at newspapers ranging from the *Vero Beach (Fla.) Press-Journal* to the *Los Angeles Times* have asked to be taken off coverage of abortion issues because they doubted they could be fair. The *Times* reporter did not want to cover planned blockades of clinics by Operation Rescue: "There were moments, probably in the wake of the demonstrations, when I was angry enough that I could not have written dispassionately about the matter."[16]

Many other reporters who cover abortion believe they can separate their personal feelings from their reporting. However, there are questions about how successful they have been at doing this. Some have charged that many reporters unconsciously ask tougher questions of anti-abortion leaders and seem less willing to take their opinions seriously.

Shaw, who has been covering media for the *Los Angeles Times* since 1974, spent 18 months studying the media's coverage of the abortion issue and wrote a four-part series in which he concluded:

> [W]hile responsible journalists do try hard to be fair, the culture in most big-city newsrooms automatically embraces the abortion rights side of the argument, and this results—however unwittingly—in scores of examples, large and small, that can only be characterized as unfair to the opponents of abortion, either in content, tone, choice or language or prominence of play.[17]

Shaw cited a study of *The New York Times, The Washington Post* and the evening news on ABC, NBC and CBS finding that women reporters quoted twice as many supporters of abortion rights as opponents of abortion. Among women newspaper reporters, the tilt was 3–1. During the same period, men reporters were evenly split on the use of supporters and opponents of abortion rights.[18]

Abortion is not the only issue that may prompt concerns about unconscious bias in coverage. Objections have been raised about Jewish reporters who cover the Middle East and African-American reporters assigned to the civil rights beat.[19] Others have wondered if gay and lesbian journalists can cover gay rights issues fairly and write dispassionately about political issues involving AIDS or if reporters with strong feelings about nature conservation should be on the environmental beat.[20]

Leonard Downie Jr., when he was managing editor of *The Washington Post,* was so concerned that journalists might allow their personal opinions to slant their coverage of political issues that he asked his reporters not to vote. Going through the process of judging a candidate's fitness for office may subtly influence what reporters write, in Downie's view. That's why he has refrained from voting in any election in which he played a role in the paper's coverage.[21]

The *Post,* along with papers like *The Philadelphia Inquirer,* does not allow its staff to take part in any activity that might compromise the paper's credibility, regardless of whether they are covering the issue.

OPINIONS CAN AFFECT CREDIBILITY

Many of the reporters who marched in the Washington abortion-rights rally were not only embarrassed by the criticism from their editors but were further chagrined when they learned that pro-life groups were using their participation in the march to "prove" their argument that the media were biased against them.

The possibility that people will presume bias is another reason many news organizations require their journalists to keep their opinions to themselves. Too many people are willing to discount the message if they believe the messenger has an ax to grind. Nancy Monaghan, editor of *Public Opinion,* the daily newspaper in Chambersburg, Pa., was so concerned about public perception of the fairness of her newspaper that she ordered her staff to avoid being involved in any activities that suggested they favored any group or political position. "Public perception becomes the litmus test, determining whether journalists can, as private citizens, participate in extracurricular activities," she wrote. There's danger in alienating the public in nearly every activity. "Someone, somewhere, is going to believe it affects fair and impartial coverage. When you assume the role of journalist, you give up your personal right to public opinion."[22]

"In all my years as a journalist, I have never registered or voted, and I never have an opinion about anything."

Many journalists criticized their colleagues who appeared on a talk show and cast their votes about whether the United States should engage in the Gulf War while the Senate was debating the issue. Judy Woodruff, then a reporter on PBS's *MacNeil/Lehrer NewsHour,* refused to divulge her personal views. "I think it's wrong, and I don't do it," she said. "I think you hurt your credibility."[23]

Other journalists worry that when reporters voice their opinions publicly, they might create problems for themselves by alienating sources on their beats. Kerry Sipe, the ombudsman at *The Virginian-Pilot* and *The Ledger-Star* in Norfolk, Va., has criticized his papers for allowing reporters to write opinion columns sometimes making caustic comments about the people they cover. In one column, the reporter who covered local schools wrote that discipline in the schools was so bad that it was dangerous to enter a classroom. He further charged that administrators didn't care about these unsafe conditions. In another column, the city hall reporter told readers that there was no good reason to vote against a controversial $17.6 million bond issue a city utility was considering.

Sipe wondered whether school officials would trust the reporter to give them a fair shake in future news stories after the reporter had accused them of not caring about safety in the schools. Sipe asked whether citizens opposed to the bond issue would feel good about being interviewed by a reporter who had gone on record as dismissing their objections as unfounded.[24]

Richard Cunningham, former ombudsman at the *Minneapolis Tribune,* has another objection to reporters spending their time writing opinion pieces and appearing on talk shows. He believes they can be of more service to the readers if they stick to reporting:

> [I]n a newspaper world in which readers already have difficulty differentiating among editorials, columns, and news stories, it seems self-destructive for newspapers to let reporters indulge themselves in opinion columns to start with. Every minute spent sucking their thumbs over an opinion column is time taken away from a sacred task: getting the news and writing it.[25]

SOME QUESTION TOTAL BANS

Many editors take a less extreme position than those of Monaghan, Cunningham and Downie. *Time,* for example, does not impose a ban on staff members engaging in political activity as long as it is unrelated to their regular beats. NBC News, the *Los Angeles Times* and *The New York Times* take essentially the same position.

Many editors understand the rationale for letting reporters express opinions about topics they do not cover. But, they say, such a policy would be hard to implement. Defending AP's ban on reporters participating in the gay and lesbian march in Washington, William Ahearn, executive editor of AP, said that because AP reporters cover all kinds of stories, they can't know in advance whether they might have to report stories involving issues like abortion or homosexuality.

And some news organizations run into problems when they try to decide what issues are far enough removed from a reporter's beat that the reporter should be allowed to express opinions about them. Elizabeth Kolbert, a *New York Times* reporter, noted that education writers in New York had spent several months writing about a proposed gay-rights curriculum for New York schools. "Would such a reporter's work be compromised if he or she had marched in a gay-rights rally?" she asked.[26]

Some believe a blanket statement in a code of ethics banning any participation in public issues puts too much limitation on journalists' rights. But they would also acknowledge that when journalists feel very strongly about issues, they should not play a role in covering them. These writers, such as Deni Elliott of the University of Montana, believe all reporters have at least one issue they feel so strongly about that they should not be allowed to write about it.[27]

Journalists and Community Service

Randy Hammer, the editor of the Marion, Ind., *Chronicle-Tribune,* was asked to serve on the board of a workshop for disabled people. It seemed it would be a good opportunity for him. His employer, the Gannett chain, which often moves people from newspaper to newspaper, was making a push to get its people in touch with their communities. And Hammer thought that a workshop for the disabled was one way to be involved with the community, yet avoid any potential for conflicts of interest. After all, helping the disabled is hardly a controversial cause. Yet Hammer soon found himself in the middle of a heated controversy. The board voted to build a group home for the people with disabilities in the middle of a residential neighborhood, but the neighbors didn't want the home.

When the paper editorialized that the home's opponents were narrow-minded, the neighborhood was upset that the local newspaper would be involved in making a decision and then criticizing those who disagreed. "The residents said our news coverage of the issue was slanted and that our editorial was unfair," said Hammer. "They said the newspaper and I were part of a plot to destroy their neighborhood." Hammer's problems increased when the board worked out its strategy to respond to the neighborhood's challenge. As so often happens when journalists serve on such community panels, the board asked Hammer to keep the plans secret. He decided he had to resign from the board.[28]

Hammer's dilemma is one that journalists are increasingly facing. More and more, journalists are seeing a need to get in touch with their communities. But often they are drawn into awkward positions of being newsmakers themselves. Some editors argue that the risk of involvement is worth taking. Steve Crosby, executive editor of the *Journal & Courier* in Lafayette, Ind., joined the Board of Visitors at Purdue University and the foundation board of the Greater Lafayette Museum of Art. He argued that being on these boards has made him a better editor. "You are so much better in touch," he said. "You know the people, the events, the background. Having that knowledge helps editors mold coverage that meshes better with the community."[29] *Rockford (Ill.) Register Star* executive editor Linda Grist Cunningham believes the "we're-observers-only" tradition of journalism hurt newspapers "because we got real out of touch with the people for whom we were writing and about whom we were writing. We had a real superficial knowledge of things."[30]

But many newspapers frown on such involvements. More typical are newspaper policies that have stopped a feature writer whose stories are often about psychological issues from serving on the board of a self-awareness group and a political reporter from serving on the public relations committee of her church.

Editors at *The Hartford (Conn.) Courant* were so suspicious of any appearance of conflict of interest that they refused to run an Ann Landers column suggesting that readers give money to the Hereditary Disease Foundation. Landers was a longtime member of the group's board of directors. *Courant* editors noted that the paper had a policy against reporters writing about groups they were associated with, and they thought the rule ought to apply to Landers too.[31]

On first glance, such conduct may seem hard to justify. No one suggested that the Hereditary Disease Foundation was not a fine charity. Yet there are hundreds of fine charities. The question becomes: Is it right for a newspaper to endorse a charity because a columnist is on the board of directors and not give similar support to the fund-raising efforts of all the others?

RUNNING FOR POLITICAL OFFICE

Some journalists want to play an even more pivotal role in their communities than just serving on the boards of museums, the United Way or workshops for the disabled. They want to be in policy-making positions. *Knoxville News-Sentinel* reporter Jacqueline B. McClary, the mother of three, believed that although her local schools had a good reputation, they had some serious problems. So McClary decided to run for a seat on the Alcoa, Tenn., school board. "I thought that because I am a journalist that I could make a positive contribution," she said. "I've covered city council, county commissioners and those kinds of public governing bodies, and I know how to ask questions and get information." But the *News-Sentinel*'s policy prohibited "participation of an employee in any political activity that could raise questions as to the newspaper's objectivity." Her editor gave her a choice: Keep the $25-a-month school board job or keep her job at the newspaper — but not both.

She chose to fight, arguing that allowing her to serve on the school board would create no problems for the paper. Alcoa is 15 miles from Knoxville, she explained, and the paper hired a stringer (a part-time reporter) to cover the school board. She conceded that reporters should not run for mayor or city council while on the payroll of the local newspaper, but she thought a nonpartisan school board was a different kind of body.[32]

But people both in and out of journalism might argue that even nonpartisan school boards are just as political as city councils because they collect and spend big tax dollars. Others might wonder if news coverage of the school board might not be compromised, especially at a smaller newspaper like the *News-Sentinel*. Suppose she did or said something during a meeting that made her seem shallow or foolish. Would the stringer — who might hope to get a full-time job with the paper — feel some subtle social pressure not to make a colleague look bad? Might her editors be concerned that a story that reflected poorly on McClary would cause her problems on her own beat?

McClary, with support from The Newspaper Guild, won her case before a labor arbitrator, who acknowledged that the *News-Sentinel*'s policy was reasonable but noted that the paper had not been consistent in enforcing it. (The editor who wanted to fire McClary had been appointed by the mayor to a city parking authority, and another staffer had served as a county commissioner while on the newspaper's payroll.)[33]

The Knoxville paper's reactions to McClary's candidacy illustrate the general newsroom taboo against reporters getting involved in politics. Reporters from news organizations ranging from *The Miami Her-*

ald to the Duluth, Minn., newspapers to WESH-TV in Orlando, Fla., have quit or been fired when they decided to become political candidates. Many newspaper codes, like the *Standard-Examiner*'s in Ogden, Utah, ban newsroom employees from running or holding any elective office.[34]

But some reporters have been able to keep their jobs while they sought and held public office. The *New York Times* code of ethics allows public service commitments that are far removed from the journalists' professional responsibilities. "A foreign desk copy editor might properly serve on the Great Neck [Long Island] school board," the *Times* code says, "but a Long Island correspondent should not."[35]

In Connecticut, journalists don't have to worry about losing their jobs if they run for the state legislature. State law protects them. When Steve Powell, managing editor of the *Journal Inquirer* in Manchester, Conn., decided to run for the General Assembly, his publisher, Elizabeth Ellis, was not pleased. Ellis told *Presstime* magazine that having Powell in the race made covering it inconvenient and awkward but noted that Powell's opponent had not criticized the paper's election coverage. Ellis and the paper's news editor shared the managing editor's duties while Powell handled administrative and other non-news tasks.[36]

However, some reporters have covered themselves while they served on governmental bodies. In the 1980s, Dan Meckes covered a city council for *The Daily Herald* in Tyrone, Pa., while he served on it. A second member of that city council was a reporter for another paper; however,

"Remember—Councilman Jones is also our news director, so try not to make him look any dumber than he is."

her paper assigned a different reporter to the meetings.[37] Two journalists for the Washington (Pa.) *Observer-Reporter* covered themselves; one was a member of the city council, and the other was on the county planning commission. Both resigned their political positions when another paper pointed out the obvious conflicts of interest.[38]

NEWS ORGANIZATIONS AND COMMUNITY INVOLVEMENT

Fewer than half the top newspaper editors who took part in a survey thought they could "trust lower-ranking editorial employees to become involved in their communities" without causing conflicts of interest. But nearly two-thirds of the editors thought it was all right for themselves to be involved in community activities.[39] And many want their newspapers to take leadership roles in their communities.

One paper that has played an active role in its community is *The Day* in New London, Conn. Its reporters and editors observed that governments in their area did not work together. Instead of just writing about the problem, they arranged a day-long retreat, invited government leaders and other people from area communities, and started them talking to one another. Reid MacCluggage, editor and publisher of the paper, reported in the *Kettering Review* that the retreat resulted in "a citizens' coalition that is now looking at the region as a whole."[40]

It was not the first time *The Day* took an activist role in the community. After the city's Garde Arts Center had been abandoned, the paper did more than report the city's loss. According to MacCluggage, the paper was instrumental in bringing together people who formed a nonprofit arts center and kept the building alive.

In the past, newspaper publishers often used their role to push their communities in the direction they wanted. They shaped their news coverage and their editorial pages to bring about the changes they wanted and ignored or criticized people who opposed them. Today most journalists are leery of newspapers and their publishers acting more like political activists than fair-minded observers of the community. David Jones, assistant managing editor of *The New York Times,* thought even the activities of *The Day* were going too far. "I guess it's the old-fashioned, traditional view," he said. "Once you get involved in these things, how do you write about them objectively?"[41]

That's the problem that some journalists said they faced at *The Flint (Mich.) Journal.* The publisher and the editor of the *Journal* once sat on a total of 17 community and business booster organizations. The publisher, Robert D. Swartz, had chaired the Flint Chamber of Commerce and was publicity chairman of the fund-raising campaign for Auto-World, a tourist attraction that backers hoped would draw vacationers to Flint but went broke after a few years. The *Journal*'s editor, Alfred Peloquin, founded the Alliance for a Greater Flint and was marketing chairman of the Flint Convention and Visitors Bureau. In addition, the metro editor, Allan Wilhelm, was a member of the Mayor's Committee to Improve Flint's Image.

Some argue that having so many key editors so deeply involved in trying to improve Flint's image affected the *Journal*'s news coverage. They contend that although Flint was in deep economic trouble (its 26 percent unemployment rate was the highest in the nation at the time), the paper's executives downplayed such bad news as the closing of a General Motors plant and pursued a policy of cheerleading. "The *Journal* is in bed with the very institutions it should be covering," said Al MacLeese, then a feature writer on that paper for 17 years. "The paper has begun to resemble a community newsletter."[42]

The answer to the problem of community involvement by news organizations may lie somewhere between the activism of the Flint editors and the complete withdrawal from the community seen at many papers.

Katherine Fanning, former editor of the *Christian Science Monitor,* noted that in the past, publishers such as Col. Robert McCormick of the *Chicago Tribune* and Robert Atwood of the Anchorage, Alaska, newspapers "pretty much called the shots" in their communities. "There was only one viewpoint." That kind of overbearing community activism was replaced by what Fanning called "the objective, hands-off, concerned-about-conflict-of-interest style." She believes that now the pendulum may be swinging back to more newspaper involvement in the community, but not like the heavy-handed kind of the McCormicks and Atwoods. "We are turning to a more bottom-up, grassroots, diverse kind of approach to community leadership for the newspaper, one that involves the community and involves diverse voices within the community; one where the newspaper can help to spark a kind of involvement."[43]

Entanglements, Financial and Otherwise

Philadelphia was once home to the Pen and Pencil Club, a drinking and social organization popular with local journalists. One of the club's irreverent acts was the creation of the Harry J. Karafin Award to memorialize the city's worst journalist. Karafin was a reporter who was fired by *The Philadelphia Inquirer* in 1967 after *Philadelphia Magazine* exposed how he used sources and his access to the news columns of the *Inquirer* to build up his public relations sideline. Karafin would prey on shady businesses under investigation by some legal agency and get them to buy his public relations services. Then he would turn the publicity faucets on or off in the *Inquirer* to suit his clients. He died while serving time in prison for blackmail after his exploits were exposed by a local magazine, not by the *Inquirer,* then owned by Walter Annenberg.[44]

If the Harry Karafin Award had been in existence in the 1980s, R. Foster Winans, a *Wall Street Journal* reporter, would no doubt have won it. At his trial on charges of securities fraud, Winans admitted that he had leaked information to a couple of hungry stockbrokers about what was to be published in the *Journal*'s "Heard on the Street" column, which Winans wrote. The stockbrokers then bought or sold the stocks they thought would be affected by what the column said, transactions that earned them a profit of about $700,000, of which only $30,000 went to Winans and his accomplice, David Carpenter.

The *Journal,* which has for years had one of the strongest conflict-of-interest policies in the news business, fired Winans when it first heard he was under investigation. The paper printed an editorial that explained that leaking market-sensitive information was specifically prohibited by its policies. The credibility of the newspaper "could not be long sustained if readers come to believe that our articles are tainted by some hidden agenda other than informing the public."[45]

One effect of the Winans episode was that many newspapers began to adopt very tough standards, especially for business writers. The *St. Petersburg Times* fired a business writer who covered banking when it was discovered that he was short-selling bank stocks. (Short-selling is a financial move in which the investor is betting the price of the stock will go down.) Then, two days later, the editor who fired the business writer was fired when he acknowledged that some of the money in his retirement account was invested in a mutual fund that had bought stock in bank-holding companies.

Many in journalism circles were surprised at the severity of punishment handed down in St. Petersburg. There was no indication that the reporter who covered Florida banking was planning to write anything that might affect the price of his stock in a West Coast bank. And the editor's mutual fund bought and sold stocks without advance notice to its shareholders. Karen Rothmeyer, then a business journalism professor at Columbia University, said the firing of the editor "begins to get into the realm of the absurd."[46]

OUTSIDE JOBS

Moonlighting, or holding down a second full- or part-time job, has become common in modern society. Other than possible damage to health, moonlighting seems to present few problems to most of its participants. But if you are a reporter, you must be careful when selecting that second job. Writing a book is probably acceptable and may even be encouraged by your editors. It might make you some money and bring credit to you and your news organization. Doing an article for a national magazine will require getting permission of your editor but will probably be OK. But writing a promotional booklet for a local developer can get you fired. Many news organizations have taken a dim view of outside jobs and activities that might cause the public to smell a conflict of interest.

The Boston Globe asked for the resignation of a political columnist when the paper learned that he was working part-time for two companies—doing public relations for a food brokerage firm and writing news for a TV station. The *Globe*'s editor said that if the writer had asked permission in advance, as *Globe* policy requires, it would have been denied. The *Globe,* like many newspapers, usually grants permission only for certain kinds of outside work such as teaching journalism courses or writing books.[47]

The *Globe* and the Rochester, N.Y., *Times-Union* and *Democrat & Chronicle* have made efforts to stop photographers from moonlighting. The Rochester papers objected when one of its photographers worked for the Lake Placid Olympic Organizing Committee, and the *Globe* refused permission to a photographer who wanted to be the backup to the Boston Red Sox official photographer. His role would have been to shoot pictures for the Red Sox yearbook, scorecards and promotional materials. Robert Giles, executive editor of the Rochester papers at the time, wrote in a memo to his staff, "We must avoid activities that can cause suspicion among readers about our ability to report the news in a fair and balanced way. Our relationships with news sources, promoters, advertisers and public relations people must be kept at arm's length."[48]

TV journalists have also run into problems with conflicts of interest. When Bill Williams was news anchor for WBIR-TV in Knoxville, he received $5,741.68 in talent fees and expenses for work on a documentary for the Tennessee Valley Authority. He used pieces of the documentary in a series on water quality for his station. Neither Williams nor his news director saw anything wrong with Williams' working for the TVA. However, a member of the SPJ ethics committee said he was appalled by the "obvious conflict of interest" in Williams accepting money from a news source.[49]

Newspaper Guild officials have questioned the motivation of news organizations that prohibit outside work. When David J. Eisen was director of research and information for the Guild, he claimed that these bans were "not ethical provisions: the public doesn't give a damn about them. They're publishers' interest provisions" that serve the economic interests of employers.[50] Eisen and other officials of the union have argued that newspaper managers use conflict of interest as a justification for extending their authority over their employees and restricting journalists from obtaining the maximum economic benefits of their skills and talents.

In addition to being careful about outside employment, most newspaper and newsmagazine journalists avoid anything relating to their organizations' advertising departments, in deference to long-standing rules about keeping news and advertising separate. But radio and television newspeople, particularly at the local level, feel less constrained. Making commercials, even testimonial commercials, seems to be part of the job in some news departments. This may add to the income of newscasters who do commercials, but it certainly detracts from their credibility as reporters. A news director whose testimonial for a local tire dealer ("These tires get me where I need to go in my job as news director at WJAC.") is inserted in the station's evening newscast is begging the public to lose its trust.

Some TV newspeople get around this problem by having split personalities. During the 1980s, Glenn Rinker was recognizable throughout most of the nation as the happy shopper in TV ads for a furniture store chain. But not in Orlando, Fla., where he was the serious-minded news anchor for the CBS affiliate. Rinker had a clause in his contract with the advertising agency that prohibited it from showing his ads in Central Florida.

Of course, many broadcast journalists will not do advertisements. Early in his career, long before he became anchor of *NBC Nightly News,* Tom Brokaw was a finalist in the search for a new host for NBC's *Today* program. But when he learned he would be expected to do ads, he said he would not accept the job. ABC, CBS, NBC and CNN now have rules against full-time journalists doing ads.[51]

CONTESTS AND NEWS JUDGMENT

Contests can be a good idea. An organization promotes a contest for reporting or editorial writing and lines up some respected editors and journalism professors as judges. Often the winners' work is reprinted and can serve as a model for other journalists, thus improving the craft. Many contests—the Pulitzers, SPJ Awards of Merit, the Society of

Newspaper Design awards, and many regional contests sponsored by journalism groups—have achieved that goal.

But some contests do not serve an altruistic purpose. The sponsors of these contests are trying to get their message, free, in as many newspapers as possible. They hope that by announcing a contest for the best story that promotes whatever they want promoted and by promising a big cash prize, they can lure journalists into writing stories favorable to their causes.

For example, the National Association of Realtors offered a cash prize for "articles dealing with real estate development, property tax relief, etc."[52] Other contests define themselves even more directly. South Carolina sponsored a contest "for articles promoting travel in South Carolina," and the Mexican National Tourist Council wanted articles "that promote travel to Mexico." But whether or not a contest is this blatant, it often isn't difficult to guess the kinds of articles that are likely to win. Paul Poorman, former editor of the Akron, Ohio, *Beacon Journal,* said he doubted that an exposé on the use of faulty concrete in interstate highway construction was likely to win a contest sponsored by the National Highway Contractors' Association and the Cement Institute.[53]

The Milwaukee Journal did not have awards in mind when it assigned reporter Don Bluhm to check out major Mexican resorts after the 1985 Mexico City earthquake. But two months after Bluhm's articles were published, a flyer came to his desk announcing a contest to reward "outstanding press reports abroad which aided in clarifying the image of Mexico" after the quake. Bluhm saw nothing in the newspaper's 10-year-old policy about contests to keep him from entering, so he did, and he won a $12,500 second prize. The size of the award concerned Bluhm and his editors (at that time Pulitzer Prize winners got $1,000). His editors discovered that the contest was sponsored by Mexico's department of tourism, two travel organizations, and a chain of Mexican hotels. The editors concluded that accepting the prize "in a contest intended to promote tourism in Mexico gives the appearance of a conflict of interest that compromises the newspaper's credibility." Bluhm agreed with the editors and returned the money.[54]

Many large newspapers now have written rules that limit the kinds of contests staff members can enter. And the Society of Professional Journalists has adopted guidelines for determining which contests fall within the society's code of ethics. Basically, SPJ rejects contests that "state or imply favorable treatment of a cause or subject," insist that judging panels be "dominated by respected journalists or journalism educators," and tolerate cash awards only in contests wholly sponsored by professional journalism organizations, journalism foundations or universities.[55]

SPOUSES AND KIN

Sometimes conflicts of interest in journalism, real or apparent, are caused by the activities or jobs of the wives, husbands or children of journalists. In Seattle, Elaine Bowers, the new bride of *Seattle Times* managing editor Mike Fancher, quit her job as press secretary to the mayor after only a day. Her job qualifications were not in doubt. She had been a reporter for *The Kansas City Star* and the *Houston Chronicle* and had worked as press secretary to Missouri Gov. Kit Bond for two years. But if she stayed on in her new job in the mayor's office, her husband was going to lose his. *Seattle Times* management informed him that because his wife's new job put him in violation of the paper's code provision that staffers are not to make news judgments about individuals they are related to by blood or marriage, he would be transferred out of the newsroom. Bowers ended up taking a public relations job with the Seattle Public Health Hospital. Fancher still had to remove himself from any news involving the hospital, but he was allowed to continue as managing editor and was later promoted to executive editor.[56]

"You know I'd marry you if I could, Suzie, but my editor says it would create a terrible conflict of interest."

When Charles W. Bailey was editor of the *Minneapolis Tribune,* his paper reported that his wife had made a large contribution to the campaign of a U.S. senatorial candidate. This prompted Bailey to send a memo to his staff:

> The contribution may be a matter of some embarrassment to me. I hope it will not be a source of embarrassment for the *Tribune.* It didn't seem

to me that I had any business trying to tell my wife what she could do with her money as long as what she proposed to do was legal and would be a matter of public record.[57]

Most news executives agree they have no legal right to influence the activities of spouses. When a conflict of interest does arise because of a spouse, all the news organization can do is reassign the journalist if the conflict is serious enough or ensure that the journalist does not handle any news involving the spouse. "Journalists have to be mindful of the problems their spouses can cause," said Phil Currie, vice president/news staff development for Gannett, but he also acknowledged that spouses and other family members must be allowed to live their own lives.[58]

The children of journalists can also raise conflict-of-interest problems. Bill Endicott resigned as Sacramento bureau chief for the *Los Angeles Times* after his editors told him that he would be transferred unless his 23-year-old daughter quit her entry-level secretarial job with Willie Brown, speaker of the California Assembly. Endicott, who was hired almost immediately by the *Sacramento Bee* to be its chief correspondent at the capital, said he could see no moral or legal basis for the request that he ask his daughter to quit her job. "My daughter is an independent adult," he added. "I can't tell her where to work."[59]

When Stuart Bykofsky was doing the television column for the *Philadelphia Daily News,* some of the people he wrote about reportedly arranged job interviews for his daughter, a recent broadcasting-school graduate. Their efforts did not land his daughter a job, but they did get him into trouble. His editor heard rumors that one of his sources was bragging to colleagues that his station didn't have to worry about any harsh criticism from Bykofsky's column because he had arranged for the daughter's interviews. "The impression was that Bykofsky had compromised himself," his editor said.[60] Bykofsky was taken off the TV column and put back on general assignment–features.

Many newspapers at one time had nepotism policies that prevented spouses from working in the same newsroom. Young journalists sometimes postponed their marriages and simply lived together to get around such rules. Many papers still have rules against hiring spouses, but it is becoming more common to find husbands and wives both doing journalism, sometimes for the same employer but often for different news organizations. Sometimes they're on the same beat, as was the case with Charles Bierbauer and his wife, Susanne Schafer. Both covered the Reagan White House, she for the Associated Press and he for CNN. A cursory survey Susan Page did for an article on journalist couples in *Washington Journalism Review* turned up more than three dozen such couples in Washington, not counting the metropolitan staffs of the city's newspapers and local TV stations. Page herself was half of a journalist couple. She worked in the Washington bureau of *Newsday,* and her husband, Carl Leubsdorf, was bureau chief for *The Dallas Morning News.*

Most of these couples have such different assignments that they never run into conflicts of interest, but even those who cover the same stories seem to keep their conflicts under control. Al Hunt, chief of the Washington bureau of *The Wall Street Journal,* said that neither he nor his wife, Judy Woodruff, then chief correspondent for the *MacNeil/ Lehrer NewsHour,* found that their marriage caused problems in their professional lives. He contended that "good reporters can compete against their spouses during the day and sleep with them at night."[61] And couples working together may produce good stories. In 1989 a husband-and-wife team, Nicholas Kristof and Sheryl Wu Dunn of *The New York Times,* shared a Pulitzer Prize for their reporting on China.[62]

SPECIAL PROBLEMS IN SPORTS

An enduring joke in American newsrooms is the reference to the sports department as the "toy department." Things are not supposed to be as serious in sports as in the main newsroom. But that's not the only thing that separates sports from the allegedly more serious news department. Sports journalists have grave conflict-of-interest problems peculiar to their branch of journalism.

The sports establishment — athletes, teams, coaches, owners, fans — expects sports journalists to support and promote sports at every level. Unfortunately, in the past, sportswriters and editors often acted as if they were part of that sports establishment. Sports pages and sportscasts frequently seemed more interested in promoting than in covering sports, being cheerleaders for the coaches and players, often to the detriment of the facts.

Reporters had such cozy relationships with the teams that they could be "trusted" not to write anything that might make the hometown heroes look bad, no matter what the sportswriters saw or heard. If the reporter knew that the team's leading hitter went 0 for 4 in the opening game of the playoffs because he was nursing a bad hangover after spending a night carousing in a trendy night spot, he would forget to mention that detail in his report.

But that's slowly changing. Bill Lyon, a sports columnist for *The Philadelphia Inquirer,* noted that until the 1960s every sports department "was a 'homer' — an arm of the local team's public relations staff." But he believes that "if Babe Ruth played today, you'd know he was a heavy drinker and a womanizer."[63]

There are indications that newspapers are taking sports coverage more seriously. They now spend an estimated $500 million a year covering sports, and that money is spent on more than just pre-game stories and profiles of athletes. Many papers have hired sportswriters who cover the business aspects of sports or concentrate on investigative reporting. *The Philadelphia Inquirer* gave a reporter three months to do a piece on sports doctors; *The Atlanta Constitution* did a thorough investigation of the relationships between sports agents and college athletes; and the *Chicago Tribune* assigned an investigative team to dig into such matters as the academic machinations that otherwise respectable universities go through to make or keep athletes eligible to play.

But this switch from the boosterism of the "homers" to hard-nosed journalism was not welcomed by everyone. Newspapers that have exposed the negative side of sports have met with ugly protests. After the *Montgomery (Ala.) Advertiser* printed stories alleging that Auburn University coaches had made payments to players, some fans spat on adult and youth carriers selling papers at an Auburn football game, and others hired a plane to pull a banner over Auburn's stadium reading "Boycott Montgomery Advertiser."[64]

Things were even more heated when the *Lexington (Ky.) Herald-Leader* reported that basketball players were given cash by University of Kentucky boosters. The paper was besieged with hate mail and bomb threats, one of which forced the building to be evacuated. An anti–*Herald-Leader* rally was held, and 400 readers canceled their subscriptions. "It seemed as if the entire state decided we had violated a sacred law and needed to be punished," wrote Michael York, one of the two reporters who did the articles that so offended Kentucky basketball fans.[65] The articles won a Pulitzer Prize for investigative reporting, but four years after the series ran, the *Herald-Leader* was still getting complaints from Wildcat fans.

Although many editors are demanding more hard-hitting sports pages, some editors and publishers no doubt wonder if exposing the conduct of grown people who make their living playing games is worth all the fuss and bad feelings that these stories often generate.

The shift to harder-hitting sports coverage is often missing from TV and radio reports. A so-called sports reporter interviewing a college or professional coach is apt to sound more like a job applicant than a journalist. Most professional teams and many college teams have veto power over the choice of play-by-play and color announcers for games broadcast on radio and TV. In some cities, the announcers are employees of the team, not the station broadcasting the game. Jack Brickhouse, popular broadcaster of Chicago Cubs games during the 1970s, was a member of the Cubs board of directors.

At one time it was also common for newspaper sportswriters to have financial ties to the home team. Baseball teams in particular hired them as official scorekeepers. In addition to being on the payroll of the organization they were covering, this relationship presented another potential conflict of interest: The sports writer was in a position to make some key decisions that over the course of a season could affect players' careers and could even set the tone for the day's coverage. For example, suppose a hard line drive is hit toward the third baseman. He dives for the ball, but it bounces off his glove. The sportswriter, as official scorekeeper, decides whether the hitter gets credit for a hit or the fielder is blamed for an error. If this happened in the last inning of the game and the pitcher had given up no hits until this play, the sportswriter's ruling might determine whether the story would be about the pitcher's glorious no-hitter — a feat that happens only a few times a season — or the feisty hitter who ended the pitcher's dream of a no-hitter in the ninth inning. The idea of journalists having that much say in the events they were covering left a bad taste in many mouths. Sportswriters rarely serve as official scorekeepers today.

But members of the Associated Press Sports Editors group have debated a related ethical question. Even the most casual sports fan knows that New Year's Day is the finale of the college football season. All three networks feature hour after hour of bowl games with payoffs in the millions of dollars to the teams involved. These teams are sometimes selected by rankings determined by a poll of the nation's sportswriters. And that bothers many of them. "We're creating the news and then covering it," said Steve Doyle, a member of the APSE executive board and *Orlando Sentinel* deputy managing editor overseeing its sports department. "A lot of newspapers just don't like the situation."

But sports journalists are split on the issue. Even at Doyle's paper, sports editor Larry Guest wrote a column during the APSE's debate calling the APSE the "joy police . . . that contemporary breed of pointy-headed extremists determined to take the fun out of everything."[66]

The trend in sports journalism, though, is clearly toward applying the same expectations to sportswriters that are applied to other journalists. Sportswriters are slowly giving up many of the freebies they were accustomed to and shedding some of the relationships with teams, owners and players that have created conflicts of interests in the past.

Corporate Owners Cause Conflicts

When media companies become conglomerates by investing in firms outside the information business or when non-media companies buy and own news organizations, serious conflicts of interest can arise when those news staffs have to write about the other financial interests of their owners. News stories that might reflect poorly on the conglomerate's other holdings may be downplayed or not printed at all. For example, shortly after GE bought NBC, the chairman of GE complained to then NBC News President Lawrence Grossman about the way NBC reporters were covering a big drop in the stock market. The GE executive feared investors might shy away from the market, causing the value of GE's stock to go down even more. Grossman said he never told reporters about the call, but he wrote later that he was troubled that a corporate official "felt no qualms about letting his news division know that he thought NBC's reporters should refrain from using depressing terms like 'Black Monday.'"[67]

On some occasions, NBC's corporate ties with GE have shown through. The news staff on NBC's *Today* decided to leave out of its report on dangerously substandard bolts in airplane jet engines the fact that the engines were built by GE, the network's owner.[68]

Until fairly recently, these kinds of worries were rare because news media companies tended to limit their holdings to media properties. Public awareness of these concerns grew after the Tribune Company's purchase of the Chicago Cubs baseball team. The Tribune Company owns the *Chicago Tribune,* WGN-TV and WGN-AM, all of which cover the Cubs. The company also owns other daily newspapers and several other broadcast stations around the country. James D. Squires, who became editor of the *Tribune* the same day the parent company bought the Cubs, immediately saw the problem the paper would have convincing the public that the Cubs would not be favored over the Chicago White Sox in *Tribune* coverage. The first thing Squires did was to hire Jerome Holtzman from the rival *Sun-Times,* "a baseball writer who had the history of being the most independent, uncompromising, ethical reporter in sports. His word and his background were just impeccable," Squires maintained.[69]

But in Chicago editors soon learned that covering the team was only one of their problems. The paper also had to cover the controversy that arose when the Tribune Company sought a city permit to put lights in Wrigley Field, where the Cubs play. Some people who live around the stadium fought the move, but the major problem for the newspaper was the opposition that came from city and state politicians who apparently saw an opportunity to buy some editorial goodwill from the *Tribune.*

"When the corporation's lawyers go to Springfield to try to get lights in their ballpark," Squires said, "all the politicians down there say, 'Well, can I get the *Tribune*'s endorsement'" in exchange for supporting the Tribune Company's request for lights. The editor claimed that his publisher, Stanton R. Cook, did "not monkey around with the editorial end of the newspaper. And my deal is that if you guys are going to play with baseball teams, television stations, and movie stars, you can't have a damned thing to do with the editorial page. And they observed that." But Squires feared that a lot of people outside the company did not believe that the *Tribune*'s journalists could be that independent from the company's other interests.[70]

In 1993, editors at Denver's *Rocky Mountain News* faced similar criticisms. Readers charged that the paper's coverage of the Colorado Rockies baseball team might be slanted because the *News* was part owner of the team. Officials of the paper dismissed the criticisms. They said they had hired veteran baseball writers and told them to "do a professional job."[71]

Many Floridians became suspicious they might have received tainted news accounts after learning that many of Florida's largest media companies had kicked in $180,000 to persuade voters to reject a measure that would have allowed casino gambling in the state. Nearly all the major media outlets, including WTVJ-TV in Miami, *The Orlando Sentinel, The Miami Herald, St. Petersburg Times,* and *Tampa Tribune,* contributed to the governor's campaign against gambling establishments. Many of them were solicited directly by the governor. (Two notable groups that did not contribute were Gannett, which owned four dailies in the state at the time, and The New York Times Company, which owned eight Florida dailies. Their officials said later they did not give money to the campaign because they feared that financial involvement would compromise reader confidence.)

After Florida voters rejected casino gambling 72 percent to 28 percent, pro-casino forces asked the now defunct National News Council to investigate *The Miami Herald*'s involvement and coverage of the casino fight. They were concerned that by using both their editorial pages and their money against a referendum, the media had "an unprecedented influence" in the campaign. They also questioned the objectivity of the *Herald*'s coverage since its corporate owners had put so much money into the fight against casinos.[72] The council found no evidence of unfairness in the way the *Herald* reported the referendum battle. In fact, the council concluded that "the *Herald* acquitted itself with distinction." It was not asked to examine other newspapers or broadcast stations that had contributed.

But the council was less satisfied with the appropriateness of the media companies' contributions. It cautioned media owners that such financial contributions can lead to three serious risks:

1. "First, they run the risk of undermining public confidence in the fairness of their news columns." The council noted that a *Herald* poll during the campaign showed that a majority of those favoring casinos and those opposed believed that newspapers contributing financially to the referendum could not be fair in their news columns.

2. A second danger lies in the possible "blurring [of] the line of separation that should properly exist between the state and the media." The council was troubled by the *Herald*'s corporate president serving as "chief fund-raiser for the governor" and soliciting funds from bankers and other business leaders outside the media.

3. Another risk is created when news media owners argue that such contributions are needed for the financial health of the media corporation. The council said the argument reinforces the concern that "newspapers and other media corporations are just another form of big business, indistinguishable from other large corporations in their right to claim special protection under the Constitution."

In one of two opinions dissenting from the council majority, William A. Rusher, publisher of the politically conservative *National Review,* disagreed that journalists face risks "if they participate, as citizens or civic-minded corporations, in forms of political activity that would be regarded as downright praiseworthy if engaged in by a nonjournalist." Rusher said, "The American people fortunately do not share the perception of journalists as priests." He argued that journalists should be allowed to be a "fully rounded" people—faithful to their God if they have one and loyal to whatever political creed attracts them. He said people will think more, not less, of journalists who contribute financially to causes they believe in.

In 1986, casino gambling was again on the ballot in Florida and again defeated. Although most of the state's newspapers editorialized against it again, none contributed money. However, 14 executives of the Knight-Ridder chain, which owns *The Miami Herald,* gave a total of $53,000.

What's an Ethical Journalist to Do?

Avoiding all conflicts of interest in modern life seems impossible. For most of us, when our role as family members or obligations as citizens conflict with our jobs, we either solve the conflict as best we can or decide to live with it and get on with our lives. But things aren't that simple for journalists. Their jobs as truth seekers and reporters require that they pay careful attention to certain kinds of conflicts to avoid projecting the impression that they can no longer be trusted.

One answer might be to avoid all non-journalistic activities: Don't vote, don't run for president of the PTA, don't go to church, don't contribute to the fund for the new library, don't party with anybody. Some purists in the news business see complete withdrawal from the world as the only safe course for journalists. But if journalists are going to understand the world about them — the world they are responsible for interpreting and explaining to the rest of us — how can they achieve that by deliberately removing themselves from public life? Being aloof seems a poor way for thoughtful journalists to understand their communities and the world at large.

Walking the conflict-of-interest tightrope.

So journalists end up walking a tightrope — somewhere between living their own lives as citizens of the world and staying away as much as possible from non-journalistic involvements that would reflect on their trustworthiness as journalists. Journalists should avoid entangling involvements with groups and causes that are controversial and/or political. But registering and voting do not create a serious conflict of interest, and affiliating with a political party in order to vote should be acceptable for all journalists. But working for a politician or holding office in a political party or organization, even as an unpaid volunteer, should be avoided. Belonging to a church, social group or neighborhood improvement group should present no problems. Belonging to a group that lobbies Congress, the state legislature, or city hall is not acceptable.

Often the sting of a conflict of interest can be mitigated by simple disclosure. "It may be less important to forbid outside activity than to be sure it is fully publicized if it does occur," Charles Bailey concluded after a study of conflicts for the National News Council. "Journalists prescribe full disclosure as a cure for many problems they see in political, governmental and business worlds; there is no good reason why it shouldn't be applied with equal enthusiasm to the news business."[73]

Finally, ethical journalists are well advised to study themselves and decide where they stand on major questions. All of us have biases, some overall view of the world, what the Germans call *Weltanschauung*. All of us are guided by our upbringing and experience. If journalists are going to be able to separate truth from falsehood and understand humanity and the world, they must first understand themselves and adjust their thinking by knowing their own biases.

The Seducers

What if you are the editor of a metropolitan newspaper in mid-America and you get an anonymous

letter, apparently from a Jeep dealer in town, charging that your popular outdoor editor has free use of an International Harvester Scout? The letter, which seems authentic, also charges that your editor mentions Scouts but never other brands of four-wheel-drive vehicles in his writings. You confront your outdoor editor, and he admits that for almost a year he has been using a Scout free of charge. Although accepting such a "gift" is prohibited in your paper's code of ethics, the outdoor editor, who to your knowledge has no blemish on his 16-year record with the paper, argues that he has done nothing wrong and that use of the free vehicle has not influenced what he has written. What would you do? Do you take him at his word and give him another chance? Do you throw him out?

In Kansas City, Mo., where this happened, Michael J. Davies, then editor of the city's sister papers, the *Star* and the *Times,* gave the outdoor editor another chance but then fired him about a week later when he learned that the writer had failed to come clean about "a couple of other goodies."[1] Davies also assigned two reporters to look into the shenanigans of outdoor writers across America. The stories they wrote painted an ethically ugly picture.

Although some large newspapers bought their outdoor writers four-wheel-drive vehicles and other equipment, reporters Rick Alm and Bill Norton found that it was common at many newspapers for outdoor writers to accept manufacturers' discounts of up to 50 percent on many hunting and fishing supplies and that some were given free merchandise each year worth as much as $35,000. They also learned that their outdoor writer was not alone in accepting long-term loans of boats and recreational vehicles from manufacturers. Many were doing it. Some outdoor writers were being paid to do publicity for the hunting lodges and fishing clubs they covered in their news columns.[2]

"I don't know how I'll be able to thank the Bass Fishing Club for giving me this boat. But I'll think of something."

Surprisingly, none of this violated the ethics code of the Outdoor Writers Association of America, which has manufacturers as "supporting members." The code seemed more aimed at protecting the freebie givers from freeloaders than improving the honesty of outdoor journalism. The OWAA code said loans, gifts and discounts were "commonly accepted practices" in the trade but cautioned writers not to accept favors for other than journalistic pursuits and not to accept free room and board unless a salable story could be produced.

But these activities violated the ethics code at the Kansas City papers: "Gifts of merchandise which might be construed as a reward for past coverage or an inducement to future coverage . . . are to be rejected." Nearly all news codes have similar or even more strongly worded provisions designed to combat the attempts by outside interests to buy favorable publicity through favors to journalists. These favors come in all sorts of packages, including free lunches, free trips and free bottles of liquor. Regardless of the value of the gifts, it is the motives of the givers — and the reactions of the public — that bother thoughtful journalists.

Freebies, Junkets, Perks

The freebie—something given without charge or cost—was once common in the newsrooms of America. Many journalists accepted Christmas presents from the people they covered. Getting free tickets to theaters, circuses or baseball games was common. Traveling free on the train or plane with the political candidate or sports team you were covering was encouraged. Many reporters assumed their news sources would pick up the tab for their drinks or meals. Freebies went with the job; they were perquisites of a trade notorious for underpaying its apprentices. There was "a tradition in journalism of take what you could get," Richard B. Tuttle said when he was publisher and editor of the Elmira, N.Y., *Star-Gazette.*[3]

In other countries, that tradition is still alive. Before the Gulf War of 1991, it was widely reported that Kuwait routinely offered reporters Mercedes automobiles, which many British and Continental journalists were quite willing to accept. German reporters often are given personal computers, large discounts on automobiles, and tax breaks.[4]

Freebies, although not on the Mercedes scale, are still being accepted by American journalists because outside interests are still working hard to buy their way into news columns with favors. But the practice is widely condemned by American media and may disappear here entirely. Many journalists are concerned that some of their colleagues might be seduced into writing "puff," or at least that many in the public will believe that reporters are on the take. Also, the growth of professionalism among journalists has caused many to shun freebies. They note that in our society when one person consistently pays for the meals and entertainment of another, the person paying often does so to feel superior. Many journalists who see themselves as professionals do not like being treated as inferiors.

GOODBYE, FREE LUNCH

Some news sources, including public officials, politicians and public relations people, often insist on picking up the tab whenever they have lunch or drinks with reporters, and some like to wine and dine journalists at parties. They may not expect anything in return for such favors, but they may. Most journalists these days insist on paying for their own meals and drinks, and many news organizations reimburse reporters who pick up the check when they dine with news sources.

Jack Nelson, chief of the *Los Angeles Times* Washington bureau, said it is common for his reporters to take their news sources to lunch. His bureau regularly invited government officials and other news makers in for on-the-record taped breakfast discussions that resulted in news stories.[5]

But newspaper journalists have not always behaved this gallantly, and the rules at some TV stations and most magazines were even less restrained. A *New York* magazine editor, Rhoda Koenig, wrote a piece in 1982, "Diary of a Freeloader," in which she described a round of press lunches, cocktail parties and suppers in Manhattan paid for by such would-be press seducers as American Express, Merrill Lynch, the Gucci Galleria, Columbia Pictures, the French Embassy, the German Information Center, Milton Bradley (games), Ketchum Communications (advertising and public relations), Little, Brown (publishers) and *People* magazine. "Few journalists will admit to being influenced in what they write by the existence or quality of refreshments, yet the public relations people continue to provide so much food that a busy (or shameless) journalist never has to pay for meals," Koenig reported.[6]

It would more difficult for a newspaper reporter to replicate Koenig's freeloading today, even in New York City. Most newspapers now prohibit their journalists from accepting free meals from news sources. However, other news media, particularly business and trade publications and some magazines, seem less fussy about where their journalists get their nourishment.

Some journalists in smaller cities believe the rules ought to be different for them. James Lowman, who spent four years as a one-person news bureau in two small communities for the Elmira, N.Y., *Star-Gazette,* believes it is permissible to accept "lunches, Cokes, beers and so on from sources" in rural settings where "a different set of ethics" is at work. "You have to remember that the person offering the treat has a set of ethics, too," Lowman said. "The moment you turn him down, you are questioning his own ethics. It hurts people for the reporter to turn the treat down. People are grossly offended by that in a small community."[7]

George Osgood Jr., who covered another small town for the Elmira paper, noted that people in small communities "know and trust each other, for the most part, and neighborliness gets more than just lip service." He said that turning down the gift of homemade bread by a public official's family may present the reporter as "too 'big-headed' to accept simple friendship and too set in his city ways to understand rural hospitality."[8]

Lowman and Osgood make sense when they argue that what might be seen as a freebie in an urban journalism setting is often a friendly gesture in a small town. Many big-city papers are also redefining their codes to include accepting a drink in a social setting. But all reporters — both rural and urban — share the risk of being pulled across that thin line between a friendly neighborly gesture and an attempt to influence news policy. And even when that line has not been crossed, there is the additional risk that the public will perceive that it has been.

MERRY CHRISTMAS?

Christmas used to provide a major problem for journalists. The season brought out the effusiveness of the freebie givers. In the mid-1900s, newsrooms often looked like the gift-wrapping desk of a department store as loot from all manner of givers would roll in. Some, like baskets of apples from a well-known senator, would be for everybody; others would be for specific writers or editors. Many older journalists can tell stories of newsrooms awash in bottles of liquor and journalists cheerfully trying to abide by early ethics rules that allowed them to keep what they could eat or drink — on the premises, in one sitting.

But the Christmas presents have decreased in number and lavishness over the past two or three decades. Most public relations people and politicians are now aware of media policies that require the presents to be returned or given to homeless shelters and other appropriate charities.

Different Areas, Different Rules?

Newsroom codes of ethics frequently spell out in detail what reporters can and cannot accept from sources. But in many newsrooms, the application of these codes may vary from section to section. A political reporter is often held to a different standard from a sportswriter or travel writer.

POLITICS AND GOVERNMENT

Political reporters frequently have to travel around the country to cover national political campaigns, conventions and public hearings. In the old days it was common for such reporters to ride free on the candidates' trains and planes. But free rides have virtually disappeared in political journalism.

Nearly all media sending reporters to cover the president and national campaigns for the presidency pay the full cost of transportation.

When the transportation is a chartered airplane, as it usually is, the media pay a proportionate share of the full cost, which often amounts to more than the price of a first-class ticket. Curt Matthews, former Washington correspondent for the Baltimore *Sun* who sometimes traveled with the White House press corps, said he was always "kind of shocked" when the president and the reporters landed somewhere and he heard people standing at the fence grumbling, "It's outrageous that those reporters get to travel around with the president on my tax dollars."[9]

It is difficult to pay for the plane ride when the aircraft is military, as sometimes happens when reporters cover military projects or need to get someplace where only the U.S. military is present. News executives say it's "a pain in the neck" to get a bill from the military, but most are finding ways to pay for such travel these days. Sending reporters, technicians and equipment to cover the Gulf War cost the media millions of dollars in 1991.

One perk that journalists used to accept without question was the use of pressrooms in the White House, statehouses, courthouses and city halls around the country. These pressrooms had one thing in common: The media paid no rent for their use. That began to change in the 1970s as the Watergate revelations sharpened sensitivities of journalists and public officials about their relationships. Some larger news organizations are now paying for the space they use in government buildings. And in some state capitals, such as Sacramento, Calif., and Tallahassee, Fla., the media have moved out of the statehouse and set up their own pressrooms.

The movement to vacate or start paying rent for government pressrooms is still small, and it is more visible in the larger cities and state capitals than in Washington, D.C. But some news media have begun to make financial contributions to the U.S. Treasury for the facilities they use in the White House, Capitol and other government buildings.

COVERING SPORTS

In many newsrooms, sports coverage has traditionally been governed by different ideas of what's acceptable. The argument goes like this: Reporters covering the government, environmental issues, and business are writing about serious matters that have great impact on readers' lives; therefore, these reporters are expected to follow the highest ethical standards. But sportswriters—well, they really don't write about anything too serious, so how they behave isn't such a big deal.

In the past, professional sports organizations and sportswriters often had a cozy relationship. The writers flew free on the team plane, stayed free in the team hotel, and received other nice perks. When teams won titles, it was not unusual for them to give the reporters gifts. For example, when the Pittsburgh Steelers won the 1979 and 1980 Super Bowls, the players got rings cast especially for the occasion. The team also offered to give rings to the sportswriters. Many sportswriters refused the rings because they were so expensive but then accepted cuff links and watches engraved to commemorate the Steelers' victories.[10]

Although such practices have become much less common, every year there are stories about the largess sportswriters receive at major sports events like the Super Bowl. Much of the tab is picked up by corporations, sponsors and tourist industries, who want to ensure that their city looks good in the sportswriters' stories.

At the 1984 Super Bowl in Tampa, the press was "wined, dined and entertained, in the open and almost brazenly," wrote Tom Goldstein, who observed the week of press festivities before the game for his *The News at Any Cost*. About 2,500 working and nonworking journalists and some of their spouses, children and friends got press credentials for that event, Goldstein reported, but "it would be difficult to determine how many of these actually covered the game." In addition to the parties sponsored by the National Football League, Budweiser and others, "there were free passes to Tampa Bay Downs, St. Petersburg Derby Lane and Tampa Jai Alai."[11]

"So this is what they mean by a free press."

The Los Angeles Summer Olympics of 1984 "may be remembered by the press as one of the biggest freebie opportunities in sports history," M.L. Stein wrote in *Editor & Publisher* magazine. Among the freebies given to all accredited journalists covering that event: an official duffel bag, pocket calculator, sun visor, Sanyo pocket radio, film processing from Fuji, camera repairs and loans from Canon, accessory vests from Fuji and Canon, Olympic books and medallion and a commemorative Coca-Cola bottle. The reporters were also invited to numerous parties, including one given by the Olympic organizing committee that featured free liquor, food and a live orchestra.[12]

Perhaps the most obvious perk that sportswriters routinely accept is free admission to the events they cover. Unlike theater and music critics, who usually pay their way into events they plan to write about, sportswriters routinely use press passes to games. However, the practice of sportswriters being given a handful of general admission tickets to pass around to their buddies is no longer allowed except at the most loosely run news organizations.

Disappearing too is the practice of sportswriters traveling free on team flights or staying free in hotels with the teams. Nearly all major dailies have rejected this practice, and the ethical guidelines of the Associated Press Sports Editors forbids it. At smaller papers, sportswriters contend, there is no way they could afford to pay expenses for reporters to staff away games, but many managing editors are beginning to reject that argument. They believe the public may distrust articles written by reporters whose ability to get those stories depend on the largess of the teams they cover. Besides, there are usually plenty of stories closer to home that need to be covered.

Also becoming less common is the custom of sportswriters wolfing down free meals in the press boxes at professional and major college games. Many newspapers now repay the teams for the meals. Sportswriters for *The Dallas Morning News* are allowed to eat the free meals at Rangers, Mavericks and college games, and the paper reimburses the teams at the end of the seasons. "We felt that there shouldn't be any possibility of any perception whatsoever that we may be beholden to a team," said Dave Smith, *News* deputy managing editor. In other stadiums, sportswriters aren't given the choice of eating free. In the early 1990s, the Montreal Expos, Atlanta Braves, Oakland A's and other teams began to charge for the meals up front.[13]

TRAVEL WRITERS

As Americans have been able to travel and vacation more, the news media, particularly newspapers and magazines, have tried to provide travel information. They have hit a rich lode of advertising in doing so — hundreds of millions of dollars each year. Some parts of the travel industry, which includes private and government tourist agencies, airlines, cruise ships and resorts, are willing to pay the expenses of travel writers to get publicity.

For years and years, many travel journalists considered free trips, free meals and even free vacations just a nice perk that came with the job. They visited amusement parks, took Caribbean cruises, and stayed in posh resorts—all free of charge. No one thought much about it. Even a rock-ribbed paper like *The New York Times* had no rule against free travel by travel writers until 1978.

The movement to limit such practices became widespread in the late 1970s and the 1980s. *The Boston Globe, Chicago Tribune* and *The Seattle Times* were among the first papers to adopt or expand no-free-travel policies. Some papers have been slower dealing with the problem. The *Chicago Sun-Times* had no policy until 1990, and a few large papers like the *San Francisco Examiner* and many smaller papers were still allowing their staffs to accept travel junkets in the early 1990s.[14] However, most newspapers with ethics codes now have rules against free travel, and news services like Gannett News Service, New York Times News Service, AP and UPI will not distribute subsidized stories.

Radio and TV stations are less likely to object to the free tickets, although many TV stations and the network news departments do pay their own way. The travel reporter for KABC-TV in Los Angeles said, "At times we find it frustrating. We're out paying these expensive plane fares and hotel rooms, then there'll be another camera crew living it up" on a freebie.[15]

A good many journalists look with disgust on journalists who accept freebies. Robert W. Greene told of an experience he had with junketeers when he was assistant managing editor of *Newsday.* Because of a personal emergency, he was called back to New York from Rome. All he could get was a first-class ticket. "I found myself surrounded by freelance travel writers," Greene recounts. "All of them were either riding for nothing or were on a discount. They were going to these places for nothing or almost nothing and then after a couple of weeks of wining and dining and having a good time, they'd come back and write puff stories."[16]

Greene put his finger on a problem in travel journalism: Most large newspapers forbid their staff members from accepting free travel, but many buy materials for their travel sections from free-lance writers who may not abide by the newspapers' ethics codes. Travel editors at seven of the 15 largest papers in the country admitted that they used stories written by free-lancers on subsidized trips. For instance, the *Los Angeles Times* has paid the travel expenses of its writers for years. But *Times* travel editor Leslie Ward told a writer for *Quill* that when she tried to stop buying stories from free-lancers who accepted free trips, she discovered she had trouble filling her 40-page section. She hoped that eventually the *Times* would be able to use only stories by writers who had paid their own way.[17]

Other papers have found that the ban on subsidized stories by free-lancers is hard to enforce. Travel editors at *The Washington Post* and *The Seattle Times* rely on their gut feelings to weed out subsidized stories. *Post* travel editor Linda Halsey said that if she is suspicious of a free-lance piece, she calls the writer and asks who paid for the trip. "I've waylaid a number of pieces that way," she said. *Newsday*'s travel editors ask free-lance writers for receipts for their travel expenses. But even that rule is not foolproof; some travel companies give free-lancers regular tickets with no indication that the free-lancer did not pay the indicated price.[18]

Most journalists support the ban against travel junkets. They don't believe writers can produce honest stories from the free trips even though travel concerns rarely put overt pressure on writers to produce favorable stories.

But sometimes the pressure is apparent. Some travel concerns ask to see tear sheets of stories after the junkets, and occasionally they let it be known that they are selective about who will be invited on the next junket. Free-lance travel writers understand that if their stories do not satisfy the people arranging the free trips, they won't be invited again. And they know that if they aren't offered the free trips, they will have to find another line of work, probably one that does not involve free trips to the world's top tourist destinations.

A few organizations are more up front about what they expect when they give the media a freebie. Disneyland provides transportation for radio and TV shows to do live remotes from the park in California. John McClintock, supervisor of publicity, said that Disney expects a puff piece. "That will be a deal. No one is expecting objective reporting from that. That is a promotional relationship."[19]

But even if the junket giver does not pressure the travel writer for a favorable article, there is another reason that junkets may produce less than accurate accounts. The resorts know the travel writers are coming and can put on their best faces for them. The publicists take care of all the headaches that most vacationers would experience and make sure that the writers are warmly received wherever they go. Baggage, ground transportation and side trips are arranged for them, and every effort is made to make sure their rooms are spotless and their meals flawlessly served. "Travel writers are never constipated," *Chicago Sun-Times* travel writer Jack Schnedler told *Quill* magazine, "because people are always sending fruit baskets to the hotel rooms."[20]

Not all travel writers believe their stories are compromised by the free travel, food and rooms or all the attention they receive. Alfred Borcover, who covered travel for the *Chicago Tribune* before and after it stopped accepting freebies, said that "even back in the days when we were taking freebies, Kermit Holt [another *Tribune* writer] and I reported things as we saw them. Our responsibility was still to our readers." He argued, "If somebody's going to be influenced by a Bloody Mary, heaven help us! Some newspapers have taken the whole ethics thing and driven it to ridiculous ends."[21]

Yet all too often travel writers select the areas they will write about not because they believe an area might be popular with readers but because they have been offered a free trip. Las Vegas, but not Reno, might be the topic of a travel story because a tourist organization in Las Vegas paid for the trip. Writers might praise the side trip given them by one tour company but mention in passing other side trips offered by companies that did not give them a free trip. In these cases, news judgments are being made by whoever is willing to pay the journalists' expenses.

Some travel editors have found ways to put out successful sections without resorting to freebies or buying from free-lancers who accept free travel. They write stories giving general travel tips and pay newsroom staffers for travel stories about their vacations. If they want a story about a particular tourist destination, they buy pieces from writers who live there. For instance, when *USA Today* wanted a story about Mardi Gras in New Orleans, the paper hired a writer who worked for a magazine in New Orleans.[22]

COVERING THE ARTS AND ENTERTAINMENT

Once, the spoils of covering the arts and entertainment beats included lots of freebies. Some were on a grand scale—expense-free trips to Hollywood and luscious meals with the stars. Arts and entertainment writers wouldn't think of paying their own way to plays, concerts, movies and amusement parks. Even book reviewers found a way to cash in. Book editors receive scores of books every week from publishers. Some editors sold the books they did not review, a practice that over the course of a year could net the book editor a tidy tax-free income. Most papers now donate unreviewed books to public libraries or return them to the publishers.

All of these practices—free trips, free meals, free books—were good deals for promoters. A good review can make or break a play, a book or a restaurant. If free trips and free meals might lead to favorable reviews, they were a good business expense for the promoter.

At most newspapers, those days have long passed. Today legitimate restaurant critics often try to dine anonymously for fear that restaurant owners will give them specially prepared foods and better service; they pay for their meals and put it on their expense accounts. Some TV restaurant critics even appear on air with their faces shadowed so they cannot be recognized. Only on the weakest publications do restaurant critics demand free meals — or worse, require the restaurant to buy ads — in return for the privilege of being reviewed.

Most theater critics buy tickets like the rest of us. Movie critics usually do the same, or they attend special screenings before the movie opens to the general public, so that their reviews can appear on opening day. Some critics avoid these special screenings because they prefer to attend regular showings with real audiences. On a few occasions, critics have boycotted these screenings after theater owners have denied admission to critics who have given bad reviews to similar movies.

The film industry sometimes spends nearly as much to promote a movie as to make it. Newsrooms are often bombarded with gimmicky contrivances that the studios hope will get a reviewer's attention. Jay Boyar, movie critic at *The Orlando Sentinel,* said he receives promotional gambits ranging from flashing red police lights (to promote the movie *Lethal Weapon 3*) to a diaper imprinted with an excerpt from a review of *National Lampoon's Loaded Weapon 1*: "It Made Me Pee."[23]

But these items are mere trinkets. The real gifts come if a writer accepts one of the motion-picture-television industry's junkets. The three major TV networks and the top film studios, seeking advance publicity on new movies and TV shows, arrange special media screenings, complete with interviews with stars, directors, producers and others. To attract reporters, the networks and studios offer to pick up the transportation and on-site expenses of the journalists who attend the screenings, often in Hollywood. Often the writers are entertained at lavish parties that are catered by California's top chefs. Many writers, particularly free-lancers, staff members of trade magazines, and smaller-city broadcast journalists, still accept such junkets, but the number of newspapers and magazines that reject them increases each year.

"The trend in the major newspaper markets is toward paying rather than accepting the studio's free junkets," according to Al Newman, vice president of publicity and advertising for Metro-Goldwyn-Mayer studios in Los Angeles. Newman told the ASNE Ethics Committee that he cheered the "younger generation of hard-hitting journalists who are more honest in their reporting. . . . Naturally, the older practices of courting the press left a stigma, but the trend away from junkets — and a new breed of writer with a more honest approach — will better serve all concerned."[24]

The trend away from junkets seemed to hit a snag when Disney World became Junket World for about 5,000 media people and their guests one weekend in 1986. The occasion was the 15th birthday party of Walt Disney World near Orlando to which Disney brass invited about 14,000 media representatives from small-town radio disc jockeys to big-time publishers. About 10,000 showed up, half at Disney's expense. Well, it wasn't all on Disney's tab. Of the $8 million that Disney figured the party cost, Disney put up only $1.5 million. The rest came from airlines and Central Florida hotels in the form of free transportation and rooms, and from tax-supported state and local tourist bureaus.

Most of the freebie riders were on the fringes of journalism—radio personalities, free-lance travel writers, editors of special-interest magazines, radio and television station employees with little or no connection with news, and the like. But there were plenty of legitimate journalists on the take, small-towners mostly. "It's only the big metropolitan papers that get hung up" about such junkets, said Jerry Wise, publisher of small papers in Louisiana. "We take a more relaxed view in the weekly field." Lee Elby, an editor of the Connellsville, Pa., *Daily Courier,* who brought three other *Courier* employees with him, said that he saw no ethical problem in taking Disney's junket because he does not work in Florida. Radio station WBSB in Baltimore was represented by a dozen freebie riders.

This kind of press representation may help to explain a news-conference question posed to Warren E. Burger, then recently retired chief justice of the United States, who was at the media party to promote the

"Yes, that's just what my publisher husband said: 'Why not take advantage of their offer? We don't live in Florida.'"

200th birthday of the U.S. Constitution. "Could you tell us your favorite recipe?" Burger was asked.

The three-day party was also covered by legitimate journalists whose organizations paid their way. Most of their reports were not about the Disney anniversary so much as the media junketeers. "The biggest story from Florida was the way the press debased itself," *The New York Times* editorialized, "and those who accepted Disney's gifts were the most likely to miss it."[25]

Disney repeated its freebie bash for the 20th anniversary of the park. Fewer journalists attended the scaled-back affair. Disney officials would not tell *Editor & Publisher* magazine exactly how many came. The event also drew less criticism from the nation's papers. Bill Dunn, managing editor of *The Orlando Sentinel* at the time, explained that his paper didn't report on the ethical issue the second time around because he did not believe the public cared much about it.[26] (*Sentinel* employees are forbidden from accepting freebies.)

What's an Ethical Journalist to Do?

The freebie problem is a comparatively new one in American journalism; at least it was hardly mentioned in the early literature on journalism ethics in the 1920s. Today it is almost a fixture in the codes of the news media and journalistic organizations. This is not to say that would-be seducers of the press did not exist in the early years of the century. But their efforts were apparently not perceived by press leaders as a serious threat to journalistic integrity. One theory of why journalists in earlier years showed little concern about freebies is that there were considerably fewer freebies for them to worry about.

Freebies grew out of the U.S. public relations movement, which began to develop in this century, particularly during the 1920s. As government, business and other segments of American society came to depend on the advice of professional propagandists and publicists, currying favor with the press soon came to be seen as a necessary or helpful step in communicating with the public at large. Currying favor has often translated into gifts, free tickets and trips, discounts, free drinks and dinners.

If the history of freebies for journalists could be graphed, the line representing the periods of greatest abundance would rise slowly through the 1930s and 1940s, reaching its highest point in the late 1950s and early 1960s, then drop slowly through the 1970s and 1980s and into the 1990s.

One reason that freebies are decreasing as a problem in journalism is that news organizations, particularly the larger ones, are paying full expenses to send their reporters where the news is. Reporters do not need free tickets, meals and rides to do their job. But some smaller newspapers and TV and radio stations still count on some favors to get the news, particularly if it involves travel for their reporters.

Most American journalists can't be bought with a Gucci bag, a bottle of booze, or even a free plane ride. So the problem for most journalists is not that they can be seduced by freebies but what accepting them says about journalism. Freebie grabbing says: Here are a bunch of people on the take. A business for whom credibility and public trust are indispensable can ill afford that kind of image.

"We pay our own way" is a clear statement that all journalists and news organizations ought to follow. But that should be a standard, not an unbending rule, because reporters should not be prevented from accepting occasional work-related meals or drinks if that helps them do their primary job of getting the news. White House reporters who accept an invitation in order to get close to a shielded president come to mind. So does a city hall reporter having coffee with a brainy member of the mayor's staff or a sports reporter having lunch with a top college coach. Reporters in these and similar circumstances should try to pay their share, of course, but that's not always possible. And when it isn't, it's silly to make a fuss about it. The test has to be whether the freebie was in the line of duty and helped the journalist do a better job of reporting.

The "pay our own way" standard should also apply to smaller news organizations that justify freebies by contending they are necessary to do their job. The problem with that argument is defining what that job is. Most of the small newspapers and radio stations that permit reporters to take free rides and junkets to cover sports events or do travel pieces would be serving the public better by keeping those reporters at home and doing more to cover their own backyards. Why should we expect our smaller news organizations to be inadequate reflections of *The New York Times* or ABC News?

What the small newspaper or radio station can do that the big media cannot is to tell its readers and viewers what's important to them in their town. If a small newspaper wants to give its readers a report on a distant sports event involving an area team, let it get that story from a news service or pay a reporter in the other city to write stories tailored for the paper's readers. Instead of taking junkets to faraway places, hometown journalists could do more for their readers and viewers by digging into local problems, and they wouldn't be tainted by their feelings of obligations to the sponsors of their free rides.

Reporters
and Their
Sources

As editor of a metropolitan newspaper, you learn that a promising new reporter in your Washington bureau had an affair with a politician while covering politics for her previous newspaper two years ago.

The man was one of the reporter's sources, and she helped cover some of his campaigns and other political events. She received a fur coat, a sports car and other expensive gifts from this man, and they shared an apartment. When her supervising editors heard rumors about the relationship and questioned her, she feigned innocence, saying she was the victim of idle gossip by reporters envious of the stories she was breaking.

Do you ignore her past, even though her old newspaper is printing detailed accounts of the relationship and pointing out that she now works for you? Do you reprimand her? Do you have a right to tell her whom she can sleep with and what gifts she can accept? And is she accountable to you for things she did before she came to work at your paper?

Those were the decisions faced by news executives of *The New York Times* when they learned that Laura Foreman, a 34-year-old reporter in their Washington bureau, had had an affair with Henry "Buddy" Cianfrani, a 54-year-old state senator and South Philadelphia political leader, while she worked as a political reporter for *The Philadelphia Inquirer.* Her editors at the *Times* apparently had not heard about the relationship until FBI agents questioned her as part of their investigation of Cianfrani on income-tax evasion charges. At about the same time, the *Inquirer* broke the story of the Cianfrani investigation, including details about his relationship with Foreman and the expensive gifts he gave her while she was covering politics.[1]

Times editors took a hard line when they learned what Foreman had done. They forced her to resign. What bothered them was her having an affair with a man who was both a news source and the subject of many of her articles. Abraham M. Rosenthal, then executive editor of the *Times,* acknowledged that "the penalty was severe but there was nothing else I could do." Foreman "violated a cardinal rule," he said. "She could not continue covering things in Washington, everybody in the Washington bureau agreed. And nobody wanted her here in the main office; her name was an embarrassment." It made no difference to him that Foreman's violations occurred at another paper. "We don't tell our readers that our reporters start being ethical when they come to the *Times,*" he explained.[2]

Also involved in the decision to dismiss Foreman was David R. Jones, then national editor of the *Times,* who had no reservations about the action. "If we had known about it when she was hired, we would not have hired her," he maintained. He dismissed complaints that Foreman was being treated differently than a man would have been. "If I were aware of any similar conflict of interest with any reporter on my staff, male or female, the result would be the same," he said. "A deep personal (particularly sexual) relationship with an important news source is a conflict of interest that merits dismissal."[3]

But many were not convinced that a man would be treated the same. In the past, male reporters used to brag of their sexual conquests. Jay McMullen once boasted that to get information while he was covering city hall for the old *Chicago Daily News,* he had slept with women who worked at city hall. He said, "All those goddamn bluenoses who think you get stories from press conferences—hell, there was a day when I could roll over in the bed in the morning and scoop the *Tribune.* Anybody who wouldn't screw a dame for a story is disloyal to the paper."[4]

He later married Jane Byrne and quit the newspaper business when she became mayor of Chicago in the 1970s.

Some think journalism's randy past may have colored the way editors looked at the Foreman-Cianfrani relationship. Richard Cohen, a *Washington Post* columnist, wrote that if a man was sleeping with a source, editors would consider that he was using her to get information. He wrote that it did not appear that anyone raised the question whether Foreman might have been using the relationship to get information from Cianfrani.[5] But Eleanor Randolph, then a reporter with the *Chicago Tribune* and later a *Washington Post* columnist, said that a man who had committed similar actions would have some explaining to do to his editors, but perhaps for different reasons.

> If a man took gifts valued up to $20,000 from a person he wrote about — love or no love — he would be in trouble. He would have a hard time convincing an editor that it was not a bribe, and in this area a man might have found himself in deeper difficulty than a woman.
>
> As for sleeping with the subject of stories, however, there is little doubt that until very recently a male reporter who took a female source or subject to bed had simply scored with more than a good story.[6]

Foreman and Cianfrani eventually married — after he served a prison sentence for mail fraud, racketeering and conspiracy. The ethical problems raised by their relationship are not the kind that happen every day in newsrooms, but they underscore the ethical pitfalls in the delicate relationships between reporters and their sources.

Friendlies and Unfriendlies

A friendship between a reporter and a news source does not have to go as far as the Foreman-Cianfrani relationship before it becomes troublesome, particularly for the reporter. Clearly, reporters need sources they can depend on. Those minutes spent schmoozing with a source can pay off later in solid information and leads to stories. But reporters who develop friendships with their news sources, seeing them socially as well as professionally, can easily fall into the trap of favoritism.

Sometimes without being aware of it, reporters start taking care of their friends, looking out for them: When you need a good quote or a new angle on your story, call old pal Joe. When your old pal gets into the news, make him look good if you can. When you catch old Joe with his hand in the till . . . ? Sources can also take care of their reporter friends, feeding them news or tips exclusively or at least ahead of their competitors or filling them in on the sort of background information that makes their stories sound more authentic. A kind of a mutual back-scratching pact can easily develop.

"Just a bit lower, Senator!"

It is understandable how such friendships occur. Reporters and their sources often have a lot in common and share an interest in some of the same things. It is no wonder that politicians and political reporters, police and police reporters, coaches and sports reporters sometimes become friends. And in smaller towns, reporters and their sources are more apt to see one another after work because the social network offers fewer opportunities to avoid one another. Friendships can easily spring from church dinners, the evening softball game, the Independence Day parade, and the daily contacts that make up the social life in small towns. Nevertheless, many reporters in both rural and metropolitan environments try hard to avoid deep friendships with their sources for fear these relationships might interfere with perspective and the ability to treat news subjects fairly.

"My rule is I try not to become friends with my sources," said veteran Washington reporter Mike Feinsilber of the AP. "It's asking too much of human nature to separate the reporting function from your social function. This is hard because many of my sources are about my age and are fine people I'd like to have as friends."[7]

Often, though, reporters develop friendships with sources and their families, and sometimes these relationships cause problems. According to Jack W. Germond and Jules Witcover in their book on the 1980 presidential campaign, Roger Mudd, then a reporter for CBS News, and his wife were good friends of Ethel Kennedy, Robert's widow, but not particularly close to Sen. Edward Kennedy. Although the Mudds often went to parties and casual evenings at Ethel Kennedy's home, where the senator was sometimes present, they had been in the senator's home "perhaps three times on social occasions." Mudd had the kind of social relationship with Edward Kennedy that "many Washington reporters have with many members of Congress they have covered for years," Germond and Witcover wrote.

These friendships with members of the Kennedy family caused Mudd to hesitate when he was asked to prepare an hour-long documentary for CBS News on Sen. Kennedy, who had announced his candidacy for president. Mudd eventually agreed to do the documentary, and it became a major political event. Mudd's tough questioning, spurred perhaps by his not wanting to be seen as a "Kennedy insider," and the senator's often incoherent replies created a furor that some saw as contributing to the senator's failure to obtain the Democratic nomination. The program also killed the Mudds' friendship with Ethel Kennedy and caused a "great freeze" to descend on Mudd from Edward Kennedy and his immediate family and staff.[8]

Dinner parties like the ones the Mudds attended, involving the families of journalists and their sources, happen "all the time" in Washington, according to Lyle Denniston, longtime Supreme Court reporter for the Baltimore *Sun,* but he doesn't approve of them. "How can you have sources to your house and have intimate personal relationships and be their adversary the next day if you have to be?" The same thing happens in state capitals, according to Denniston. "There's too much intimacy between reporters and sources," he charged. "The press is a captive of government almost everywhere it has a relationship with it."[9]

Ellen R. Findley worked in one of those state capitals as a reporter for the Baton Rouge, La., *Advocate.* She told about calling up an attorney who was a "very good friend" to ask him about the mayor's race. She was interviewing him for a story, but he thought they were talking as friends. When her story appeared, she said, "We both got a lot of flak — me from him, him from the politicians he offended."[10]

It's not just friendships between reporters and sources that worry some observers. Several of the nation's top reporters and editors were criticized for attending a victory party after Bill Clinton won the presidency. Columnist James J. Kilpatrick wrote that journalists from *The Washington Post, The New York Times, The Wall Street Journal,* CBS, NBC, ABC, PBS and other news organizations had no business at the Democrats' bash. Kilpatrick said he doubted that the reporters "are going to toss cream-puff questions at Clinton just because they ate puff pastry" at the party, but he worried about "the danger of crossing the invisible line that socially separates newsmen from their sources."[11]

Attending parties with sources can cause other problems. Occasionally some VIP, cocktail in hand, will start talking openly about some newsworthy topic—a merger deal under consideration or a secret decision to force out the police chief. Some reporters say that anything they hear at social gatherings is fair game, but most think it is fairer to call the VIP the next day and to try to get the "party talk" on the record. Occasionally they learn that the great story they heard was the result of too much wine combined with dinner-party bravado and not based on solid information.

Broadcast journalists may have a special source-relationship problem, according to ABC newsman Brit Hume. He explained that in television reporting, because you often don't have as much time as you do in print, you "develop a handful of people who can help you . . . and you come to depend on them. Then it becomes tough to take a shot at them." Also, he explained, broadcast journalists need access. The picture of the president walking toward the helicopter is important in a visual medium like television, even if what the president is saying is "pure word salad." TV reporters "have to be able to get to people, to be in the main scheme of things, to be known by the VIPs." Hume acknowledged that there were risks in such a dependence on certain top sources. "You have to make sure you are not compromised by this need for access."[12]

Reporters who have covered the same beat for many years can encounter special problems. Although the public may benefit from reporters who have a deep understanding of the area they cover and have close friendships with many of the people they write about, sometimes beat reporters develop too many cozy relationships with their sources, and their reporting suffers. That's why some editors rotate reporters on beats. Other times, editors feel it is important not to reassign reporters who have established themselves with the people on their beats, so they send another reporter when a special or negative story has to be done that the beat reporter could not do without losing prize sources.

SOURCES AS ADVERSARIES?

A concept that has appeal for many journalists is that reporters are, or ought to be, adversaries of their sources, particularly political sources. They argue that an adversarial relationship between reporters and sources is necessary if the press is to be a true watchdog of government and other important institutions of American life. There are times when journalists must ask the hard questions and be firm when sources begin to avoid questions or talk around the issues. To get at the truth, reporters sometimes must play tough.

But treating all sources as adversaries can be just as unfair to them and the public as treating them all as buddies. Reporters who act as if most public officials were crooks or potential crooks are not only wrong in that assessment but are apt to let their prejudices dictate their questions and their news sources.

That doesn't mean reporters should let their guard down. Many sources must be approached with caution not because they may be covering up some vital information but because they have their own agendas and want to see their ideas presented positively. They may be willing to flatter and manipulate the reporter. J. Anthony Lukas, who won two Pulitzers during his career, recalled a time when he believed he was manipulated by a source. He was interviewing Elliott Richardson, a Republican political figure best known for refusing Nixon's order to fire the Watergate prosecutor. About halfway through the interview, Lukas thought to himself, "He likes me. Elliott Richardson likes me. And he trusts me and he is speaking to me not as a subordinate, not as a mere reporter, but as a literate and perspective man who can understand." Later, when he was on his way home, Lukas was hit by the thought "Schmuck, you've been had. You've just been treated to the treatment that this guy is exceptionally good at, and you fell for it — and may have taken a little sting off some of your questions in return." Lukas described long-term relationships between sources and reporters as "being filled with collaboration and manipulation, with affection and distrust, with a yearning for communion and a yearning to flee."[13]

When their sources are ordinary people, journalists must adjust their questioning style. There is no need to browbeat them with questions in a manner more appropriate to Hollywood fiction. Pulitzer Prize–winner David Halberstam said he tries to treat ordinary people who are not used to being interviewed as if they were members of his family.[14]

Checkbook Journalism

While not a common practice among American newspapers, paying sources for information, photos or interviews — exclusive or otherwise — is an accepted practice in other countries. "The British tabloids are notorious for buying their 'scoops,' and the juicier the scandal, the higher the price," Tamara Jones, a *Los Angeles Times* foreign correspondent, discovered. Throughout Europe, government officials often demand "honorariums" before they grant interviews. And sports stars like Boris Becker, Steffi Graf, and soccer players often receive large sums before they will talk with European reporters.[15] In Moscow, interviews with law enforcement officials can cost as much as $400, an interview with death-row inmates can be arranged for $1,000, and getting guards to allow picture taking inside the Lenin Mausoleum can cost $5,000.[16]

Checkbook journalism on that level has not come to the United States, although there have been notable exceptions. CBS once paid $100,000 for an interview with H.R. Haldeman, Richard Nixon's top White House aide, then several years later gave Nixon $500,000 for a 90-minute interview.[17] The editor of the *Los Angeles Times* admitted that his paper paid a court official "quite a bit" of money for sealed court documents during the investigation of the Manson murders in 1969.[18] Both CBS and the *Times* were heavily criticized for their activities. The *Times* has since adopted a formal practice against paying for information.

In the early 1990s, the debate over paying for interviews was rekindled by talk shows like *Donahue* and *The Jenny Jones Show* and tabloid TV news programs like *Hard Copy* and *Inside Edition*. These programs were often willing to buy interviews in hopes of scoring bigger ratings. When a religious cult in Waco, Texas, had a shoot-out with federal officers and touched off a siege of the cult's compound, one of the tabloid TV programs paid the mother of the cult's leader, David Koresh, for interviews. The rush for ratings was so great that several programs got into a bidding war to interview a group of high school boys whose claim to fame was that they had formed a club that awarded points for sexual conquests of girls at their school.[19]

The mainstream media often smirk, but they are not entirely virtuous. During the 1992 presidential campaign, *Star,* a grocery store tabloid, paid Gennifer Flowers (reportedly $150,000) for her account of an affair she said she had with Bill Clinton. Although most American dailies would not stoop to pay Flowers for her story, nearly all repeated her unsubstantiated allegations once the *Star* announced its coup. (This episode is discussed further in Chapter 10.) The *Star*'s stories touched off a media hunt to find more women willing to tell stories about Clinton. *The Washington Times* reported that a British tabloid was offering $500,000 to anyone who could confirm Flowers' story. Michael Hedges, a *Times* reporter, said he was told that several women were willing to invent stories of affairs with Clinton if the price was right.[20]

WHY NOT PAY FOR INTERVIEWS?

That these women might be willing to lie or exaggerate to sell their stories to news organizations is one argument against checkbook journalism. *Newsweek* magazine learned that lesson in 1990. For a story on the spread of AIDS, *Newsweek* reporters found a prostitute who said she had AIDS but continued to work the streets. The magazine paid her $60 for her story. After the article appeared, the woman told authorities and other reporters that she had lied to *Newsweek* to get money to feed her heroin habit. The public defender who handled her case told the *San Francisco Chronicle,* "When organizations like *Newsweek* pay people for stories, what happens is that people like Linda get victimized by it. The money was an invitation to someone using drugs and who wanted more drugs to say things that were not necessarily true."[21] Police were unable to determine if she had AIDS and did not press charges.

Legal and media scholars are bothered by the growing number of cases in which news organizations offer payments to jurors *before* highly publicized trials. When Bernard Goetz was on trial for shooting would-be muggers in a New York subway, *The New York Post* arranged before the trial to buy the comments of one juror for nearly $5,000, and the *Daily News* gave another $2,500.[22] What troubles people in the legal community about these payoffs is the fear that jurors may try to make verdicts more sensational in hopes of getting more money.[23]

A second argument against checkbook journalism is that many will withhold information unless they are paid for it. Some of the police officers on trial in the King beating stopped talking to reporters in the middle of their second trial. They had decided to peddle interviews to the highest bidders. The *Donahue* show paid two of them $25,000 each; *A Current Affair* paid one, Stacey Koon, $10,000.[24]

Moments before a former member of the Waco cult was to be interviewed live by Ted Koppel on ABC's *Nightline,* he canceled his appearance because he had made a deal with a tabloid TV show for exclusive rights to his story.[25] Koppel is not alone in having trouble getting people to appear without being paid. A producer for ABC's *PrimeTime Live,* which does not buy interviews, said it now takes "a lot more persuasion" to get people to appear on that program.[26]

When gang violence in Los Angeles became a national story in the early 1990s, a county government official with ties to the gangs often helped arrange interviews but told reporters that the gang members would want money. "The money is not buying a story," he argued. "It is showing respect" to gang members.[27] Other reporters have been hounded for payoffs by eyewitnesses at crime scenes and disasters and during interviews for other stories. Some have even been threatened. A reporter and a photographer with the *Detroit Free Press* said they feared a drug addict they were interviewing "might become violent if he wasn't given any money." The reporters at first refused to pay but then agreed to buy a portable radio and a sausage from the man. When editors found out what they had done, they were suspended without pay for a few days.[28]

A third argument against checkbook journalism is that it may lower the quality of the reporting. If a TV program or tabloid newspaper has paid big bucks for an interview and promoted it to get higher ratings or street sales, the people doing the interview may be less likely to push the source with tough questions and to expose inaccuracies in the information. A *PrimeTime Live* producer noted that since the programs pay for the interviews, "they also script them, so it's not really real."[29]

A fourth argument is financial. News organizations are fearful that if they begin to pay for interviews, they will be required to shell out a constant stream of cash.

IS INFORMATION A COMMODITY?

Some reporters see contradictions in outright bans on checkbook journalism. John Tierney, a reporter for *The New York Times* who wrote a series of stories about street people in New York, said many of them asked for payment in exchange for being interviewed. "Sometimes I explained that I couldn't pay them, but that I could buy them a meal during the interview," he said. "Things would go well until we sat down in a restaurant and the person announced: 'I'm not hungry now. Just give me the money and I'll eat later.'" Tierney said it is difficult to explain why it is "ethically superior to buy a homeless man a $30 dinner than it was to give him $10 in cash."

To learn about the drug culture, Tierney once paid a drug user to give him "a tour of shooting galleries and crack houses." He said he considered the fee much like paying an interpreter or guide in a foreign country. But Tierney balked when his "tour guide" offered to take him to a crack-driven sex party the next day. When Tierney asked what time the party would begin, the guide told him to name a time. Tierney said it was obvious that his money was going to be used to arrange the event.

Tierney contends that some interviews would go more smoothly if there was a cash transaction between source and reporter because it would have "clarified the relationship." The sources would understand that the reporter was neither a friend nor an advocate but a reporter who had paid them for information to use in news stories. But Tierney cau-

*"Lady, can you spare a couple of bucks for
food? Or would you like to buy my life story
for a hundred bucks?"*

tioned that not all sources should be paid and that the reader should be
told when paid sources were used.[30]

Some media people argue that some stories are worth paying for.
Appearing on ABC's *Nightline,* Phil Donahue, a pioneer of the TV talk-
show format, said, "I think checkbook journalism is here. We operate in
the marketplace." Donahue said that if Adolf Hitler were discovered
alive today, he doubted that many news organizations would refuse to
interview him because he demanded $100 in advance.[31]

Others contend that in our society information is commonly bought
and sold. Jack Landau, a journalist and lawyer who directed the Reporters Committee for Freedom of the Press, said he can't understand
why newspapers buy photographs of news events if their own photographers were not there and pay columnists for their ideas but balk at
paying eyewitnesses and experts for their help in covering news.[32] Others
note that news organizations make their profits selling information.
Why shouldn't the people who are interviewed for those stories—the
original sources of the information—share in the profits?

But journalists remain overwhelmingly opposed to checkbook journalism. In one poll only 17 percent said they thought paying for an
interview would ever be justified.[33] Polls have found that the public also
opposes the practice. Fewer than a third believe checkbook journalism is
ethically acceptable.[34]

Secret Sources

Reporters at *The Seattle Times* presented executive editor Michael R. Fancher with a difficult news decision. They reported that eight women had told them they had been sexually abused by one of the state's U.S. senators. One of the women claimed the senator raped her. The reporters said they had confirmed as many of the details given by the women as possible, but they couldn't confirm the key charges since they happened in private.

The problem was that the women did not want to be identified. They were all Democrats who earned their living as lobbyists and full-time employees of the Democratic Party. They believed their careers with the party would be over if it was known they caused the downfall of one of the party's elected officials.

The reporters explained to Fancher that they had tried for years to get the women to let their names be used, or at least identified to the senator, but they had staunchly refused. The reporters asked Fancher to make an exception to the paper's policy against using accusations made by anonymous sources or sources who would not confront the people they were accusing. The decision was made harder because the senator was involved in a re-election campaign. If the paper printed the story, some would charge the decision was politically motivated. But not using the story would cause others to say the paper covered up important information.

Fancher decided to use the story about Sen. Brock Adams and to print a front-page message explaining the reasons for violating the paper's policy against printing anonymous charges.

Fancher told readers that the paper had been working on the story for more than three years and that it involved "abuses of power and women" over a long period. He said he decided to print the story while the campaign was under way because he believed the voters had a right to hear the allegations and the story's development had reached "critical mass"—the paper had enough information from enough people to believe the story was true. "The bottom line is that we thought the basic choice we had was to withhold an important story we believed to be true or to tell the story without named sources, and it was a reluctant choice," Fancher said.[35] Once the story appeared, the paper's ombudsman said she received more than 200 phone calls, most against the paper's conduct.

Journalists are worried about the use of anonymous sources. Some would not have used the Adams story, even with the precautions the *Times* took. "We'd need papal dispensation to use one anonymous source in any story," said Madelyn Ross, managing editor of the late *Pittsburgh Press.* "In all cases, we demand on-record information to maintain our credibility with readers."[36] Other papers have similar bans on anonymous sources. *San Diego Union-Tribune* editors said they didn't want to second-guess Fancher's decision but noted that the Adams story would run afoul of their policies, which discourage reporters from repeating criminal charges made by anonymous sources if they have not taken them to proper authorities.[37]

But many editors agreed with Fancher's decision. *St. Petersburg Times* editor Andrew Barnes said his editors argued about whether they would use the story if it had happened in Florida. "I came away thinking I would twitch a lot and then do it," he said.[38]

A NEEDED TOOL?

Many journalists in the United States believe that certain kinds of information cannot be obtained unless the identities of some sources are kept secret. They point out that many major exposés by American journalists were possible only because reporters extended confidentiality. "I don't think we can function without it," said Robert M. Steele, director of the ethics program at the Poynter Institute for Media Studies in St. Petersburg, Fla. "It's an essential tool to use at the right time and in the right place."[39]

But deciding the right time and right place—and the right degree of secrecy—is no simple matter. Claude Sitton, former editor of the Raleigh *News & Observer,* said that at his paper these decisions weren't made until he, the reporters involved, and other editors had "prayer meetings" that sometimes included the paper's libel lawyer.[40]

Several factors go into making these decisions. The importance of the story is one consideration. Probably the most famous secret source in journalistic history was "Deep Throat," the name that Robert Woodward and Carl Bernstein gave to the anonymous insider who helped them break the Watergate cover-up for *The Washington Post.* Deep Throat was only one of many secret sources used to develop the stories that contributed to the eventual resignation of President Richard Nixon and the jailing of several White House aides. The importance of that information would probably convince most editors that using unnamed sources for the Watergate story was justified.

The background and motives of the sources are another consideration. Some sources, knowing they will not be named, may invent information or exaggerate problems. Because of this, journalists must make sure the sources know what they are talking about and are unlikely to be using the newspaper to plant an untrue story. They must also weigh the hazards for sources if their names are used. Some sources might lose their jobs or the trust of those from whom they are getting the information. In a few cases, sources might be physically harmed or even killed if they are identified.

Editors are also more likely to bend the rules if regular sources are being unreasonably closemouthed. During the 1991 Gulf War, the U.S. military tried to limit press coverage, and the number of stories using anonymous sources increased in many newspapers.[41]

Fierce competition among reporters on some stories can cause a softening of rules. Editors at the *St. Petersburg Times* said that competition combined with tight-lipped officials led them to break their written guidelines about unnamed sources during their coverage of the mutilation murders of five female students at the University of Florida. *The Florida Times-Union* in Jacksonville maintained its policy of requiring reporters to confirm with other sources all information that came from unnamed sources, and editors acknowledged that their coverage wasn't as good as that of papers with fewer restrictions.[42]

EDITORS GROW WARY

Many editors are trying to limit the use of unnamed sources in their papers. They fear that (1) too many reporters are using unnamed sources because they are too lazy to find on-the-record sources, (2) there is too great a risk of reporters making up things and passing them off as comments by unnamed sources, and (3) too many unnamed sources are passing along information that is either inaccurate or self-serving.

Some editors have had firsthand experience with lazy reporters who do not press to get information on the record. Norman Isaacs, retired newspaper editor and former chairman of the National News Council, said he was startled by "reporters calling up people and saying right away, 'If you don't want to be quoted, that's all right.' "[43] William J. Small, former president of UPI and NBC News, said he wished he had a dollar for every time a reporter called him and said, " 'Look, why don't we do this off the record?' They're always shocked when I said I never talk off the record."[44] Nancy Woodhull recalled that when she was managing editor of the Rochester, N.Y., *Democrat & Chronicle,* one of her reporters turned in a story with no specific identification of his sources. Asked about this, the reporter said, "Well, gee, I didn't think they'd want their names used."[45]

But other editors have a more serious concern. They fear that some of the material attributed to anonymous sources may have been the product of reporters' creativity. The most notorious case of phony unnamed sources involved Janet Cooke, a *Washington Post* reporter who wrote a gripping tale of a child drug addict. After the story won a Pulitzer Prize, she admitted that she had made the whole thing up. (Her case is discussed more fully in chapters 9 and 12.)

Although deception on that level is rare, editors suspect other reporters have spiced up their sources with fictitious sources. Robert Greene, who was a top investigative reporter and editor at *Newsday,* said he has known reporters who tried to pass off their own ideas by attributing them to anonymous sources. "I'm enormously suspicious of it," he said.[46] Mark Washburn, an editor at *The Miami Herald,* reacts to anonymous sources even more strongly: "Anytime I see 'sources said,' the hairs go up on the back of my neck and I want to say 'Oh, bullshit, you made it up.' "[47]

"I'll quote you as an unimpeachable source, and you can quote me as highly reliable."

Many editors argue that readers will be less likely to believe stories with unnamed sources. But several studies have found that readers are no more likely to distrust a story with anonymous sources than one with named sources.[48] However, when pollsters asked the readers directly if they approved of the use of anonymous sources, more than half said no.[49]

If editors are more skeptical of unnamed sources than the public appears to be, it may be because editors have seen too many stories based on unnamed sources turn out to be wrong. *The New York Times* apologized to its readers in 1991 after one of its reporters used information from an "unnamed corporate official speaking on condition of anonymity" in stories about negotiations involving the *New York Daily News.* When everybody involved told *Times* editors one of its stories was wrong, the editors asked the reporter who this "corporate official" was. The reporter admitted that he didn't know. He said he had based the stories on an anonymous phone caller who seemed to have inside information about the talks.[50]

In the fierce competition among Florida papers to get the best stories about the slayings of five women students at the University of Florida, papers used unnamed sources and occasionally got burned. Patrick May, who covered the story for *The Miami Herald,* said that there was a lot of exaggeration by anonymous sources. "If you go back and look at the coverage, you see that there were 'sources' saying things that turned out to be total bullshit. Lots of it." He thought reporters "seemed really out of control."[51] Similarly, Rob Hooker, an editor at the *St. Petersburg Times,* explained later: "We had a case here where the competition was so intense among Florida newspapers that a lot of newspapers made some mistakes." For example, many papers identified a young man who lived in the Central Florida area as the chief suspect and all but pronounced him guilty. They printed lengthy stories about his past and his mental problems and used information from unnamed informants to link him to the crimes. But later a drifter from Louisiana was tried and convicted of the murders.

The New York tabloids and some of the Florida media got into a no-holds-barred hunt for news when a woman accused members of the New York Mets baseball team of gang-raping her during spring training in Port St. Lucie, Fla. The papers used stories based on unnamed sources who supposedly had ties to the prosecutor's office or the sheriff's office. Many of those stories were dead wrong, according to a follow-up story in the *St. Petersburg Times.* Papers reported erroneously that the woman had been to the hospital after the alleged rapes, that she had submitted a lengthy statement to police in Florida, and that the players had been interrogated at the stadium by police.

But the biggest scoop was scored by the *New York Post* when it named three Mets and said they would be charged with the crime "within the next few days." When several days passed with no charges, the *Post* reported that the investigation had hit a snag. No charges were ever filed in the case, and officials told the *St. Petersburg Times* that there was never a time when they thought they were even close to bringing charges.

The *Post*'s editor was not overly troubled by his paper's mistakes. "Inaccuracies happen on all kinds of stories, in plane crashes and rapes," editor Lou Colasuonno told the St. Petersburg reporter. "But this was a very hot story, a very sexy story, and very fast moving. I'd rather be a little aggressive on something like this than a little timid."[52]

But other editors argue that the likelihood of inaccurate information causes them to be very cautious when allowing the use of unnamed sources. "When people's names aren't attached to a story, it becomes much easier for them to say things that aren't necessarily true," said *USA Today* editor Peter Pritchard. "They're protected. A lot of savvy people will use that protection to float stories that aren't true or that embarrass someone else."[53]

THE DARK SIDE OF SECRET SOURCES

When most of us think of anonymous sources, we think of disgruntled employees who want to tell about the shenanigans of their bosses. Or we picture public-minded individuals who are fed up with waste and wrongdoing. And most reporters have run into bureaucrats who leak information, as a Justice Department official once observed, "simply for the thrill of seeing their quotes in the paper."[54]

But not all anonymous sources are even that pure of heart. "The motives of leakers have always been an issue with journalists," Eleanor Randolph wrote in *The Washington Post*. "If a private individual or low-level official calls with a leak, most journalists understand the motives — perhaps anger at a boss or anger about a policy. But a leak from a high-level official is more often a strategic move to help formulate or further a policy, and many journalists fear that they are being used as part of the process rather than as disinterested reporters relaying facts to the public."[55]

Perhaps the classic perversion of the use of secret sources is the "trial balloon" — bogus stories floated by political leaders to test which way the wind of public opinion is blowing. For example, a city official might tell a reporter, on a not-for-attribution basis, about one of the mayor's plans. Once the story appears in the paper or is broadcast, the officials listen for reactions from the public. If there are no complaints, they may go ahead with the plan. But if the plan is attacked, they announce that there was no truth to the news report whatsoever. The mayor assures voters that such an awful idea would never be considered.

Prosecutors sometimes use similar tactics. They may leak details of an investigation when they do not have enough evidence to bring charges. They hope that the news accounts will put pressure on the people under investigation or encourage more witnesses to come forward.[56] A prosecutor in California acknowledged that people in his office "vastly overstated" things when they told reporters about a case they were investigating that involved alleged child abuse at a day-care center.

For instance, the media reported that the children had been used in thousands of child-pornography pictures and films. When the case came to trial, it became clear that police had found no pictures or films.[57]

Trial balloons like these are an all-too-common ploy, but reporters say there is little they can do to avoid them. When President Clinton was formulating his economic package, the administration used trial balloons to test reactions to many of its provisions. "We probably have been used as much as anybody in this," Albert Hunt, the *Wall Street Journal*'s Washington bureau chief, told *Washington Post* reporter Howard Kurtz. "There are days when I pick up the paper and cringe. But if you say we're not going to participate in this, they float it to someone else and you wind up chasing it the next day."[58]

Others leak information so that if things go wrong, they won't be blamed. Kurtz said that when James Baker took over President Bush's re-election campaign, he started leaking stories to key reporters that the campaign was "in shambles." As Baker had hoped, the stories reported the mess and suggested that if Bush lost, it wouldn't be Baker's fault.

And some people leak stories to avoid risking confrontation with their colleagues. Several Democratic congressmen were unhappy with their leader, Speaker Jim Wright, but they did not want to ask him face-to-face to resign. Instead, they leaked anonymous stories to the news media, according to David Rosenbaum of *The New York Times*. Wright got the message, and the congressmen didn't have to risk alienating him.[59]

For similar reasons, several insiders in the Reagan White House leaked their concerns about a controversial budget proposal because they did not think their objections were getting a fair hearing by Reagan's top advisers. After a barrage of leaks reporting information contrary to the Reagan economic assessments, the budget proposal was modified, according to political scientist Doris Graber.[60] The Reagan administration used leaks to send other kinds of messages. When his administration wanted to scare Libyan dictator Col. Muammar el-Qaddafi, aides planted exaggerated stories that the United States was about to make additional military moves against Libya. The stories, of course, cited unnamed sources. Reporters stopped writing them after *The Washington Post* uncovered and published a memorandum in which Reagan's national security adviser outlined the scheme. He referred to it as a "disinformation program."[61] Similarly, President Bush reportedly ordered a leak to *The New York Times* that was to serve as a warning to Lebanon. The day after the *Times* printed its story, the White House correspondent for Knight-Ridder uncovered the ruse.[62]

The Kennedy administration ran into other kinds of problems when it tried to use leaks to advance its policies. When some Cuban exiles attempted to launch a military attack on Cuban dictator Fidel Castro, stories were leaked to the Miami media that 5,000 U.S. troops would join the fighting. The administration apparently hoped that information would cause more Cubans to join the uprising. But when it became clear the exiles were being defeated by Cuban soldiers, administration officials wanted to distance themselves from the invasion, so they told other reporters that the Miami reporters got the story wrong. The real story, the leakers said, was that the United States had deployed only a few hundred American soldiers to help with supplies but not to do any fighting. Later it turned out that both leaks were wrong. About 1,000 American soldiers were involved. Political scientist Graber wrote, "When reporters discovered that they had been used to spread false stories, they were furious."[63]

Stephen Hess, who studies press-government relations, adds another variety of leakers to this list. He said that some people will leak stories to get on the good side of a reporter they think can be helpful to them.[64]

Occasionally, even seasoned Washington observers can't figure out the motives of people in what Kurtz calls the "shadowy world of unnamed sources." He cited a *New York Times* story that said Gen. Colin Powell was so upset with President Clinton that he might step down as chairman of the Joint Chiefs of Staff. The story, which appeared shortly after Clinton became president, attributed the information to "several close associates" of Powell. The morning the story appeared, Powell appeared on all four network news shows to deny the account. Kurtz wonders if the *Times* had been duped by people who wanted to embarrass Clinton during the early days of his presidency—or if Powell had leaked the story to give himself a forum to show support for his new boss.

If reporters know that using unnamed sources can lead to these kinds of games, why don't they refuse to play along? One reason is the competitive urge of reporters to score good stories. R.W. Apple Jr., Washington bureau chief of *The New York Times,* told Kurtz: "Ours is a competitive business, and if someone with an authoritative voice says to us a decision has been made to do X, and we check it a couple of other places, we run it. So does *The Washington Post.* So does the *Los Angeles Times.* You're going to be used on occasion. You do your best to get around being used by figuring out motivation and checking the story out from a number of angles."[65]

Sometimes reporters play along because they think a secret source is better than no source at all. NBC's Timothy Russert noted that reporters covering some criminal investigations may have no other way to get news.[66] Similarly, reporters covering the fighting in Central America interviewed U.S. Embassy people but attributed the information to "Western diplomats" because that title would "inspire confidence in readers" and because they did not want to risk losing access to embassy sources, according to Frank Smyth, who covered El Salvador for several years.[67] Other times, reporters say, they simply don't have time to find sources who will talk on the record. "You're operating on deadline and you need the information," so the sources are able to demand that their names not be used, said Nina Totenberg of National Public Radio.[68]

Occasionally, reporters and news organizations have tried to reduce their use of secret sources. James McCartney, longtime Washington correspondent for Knight-Ridder newspapers, argued that the best thing "that could happen in the journalistic community would be if every reporter were required to take an oath that he would walk out of the office of any official who insisted on talking to him off the record."[69] *The Washington Post* wanted the Washington press corps to boycott backgrounders in the early 1970s, but the effort failed when many newspapers, especially *The New York Times,* refused to go along. Abe Rosenthal, *Times* executive editor at the time, said he recognized the problems with backgrounders but he said that sometimes reporters can get solid information at them. "I profited from many of them when I was a reporter, but I'm sure I was used many times."[70]

RITUALS OF CONFIDENTIALITY

Journalists and their sources have invented a variety of labels for various degrees of confidentiality, such as "off the record," "without attribution," "on background," and "on deep background." One problem is that not all reporters mean the same things when they use these terms, and many sources are understandably confused. Sometimes reporters and sources use "off the record" to mean what others would call "without attribution."

"Off the record" usually means that reporters will listen to the information but never use it. Since off-the-record information is supposed to be kept secret, many reporters never go off the record. Other reporters, however, have found that some off-the-record information has kept them from writing stories that are mistaken or incomplete. More frequently, reporters accept off-the-record information in hopes of finding another source who will go on the record. But this tactic has one major drawback: The reporter may burn the source without meaning to. If the reporter seems to know too much about what's going on, other officials may recognize that someone has leaked information, and they may be able to guess who it was. Many reporters will not take off-the-record information unless the source understands that they will try to verify it elsewhere. Without that provision, reporters are afraid that they will hear a lot of great stories they will never get to write.

"But, General, you can't go off the record in front of twelve hundred people!"

When sources ask to go off the record, most reporters try to talk them into staying on the record. Reporters have found that many people who approach them with information want to get things off their chests and will decide to talk on the record. But if they refuse to go on the record, some reporters will ask the sources to let them use the information without attaching their names to it. "Without attribution" is the normal label for this agreement.

The phrase "on background" is used by journalists in two ways. Sometimes it is used much as the name suggests: Sources offer reporters background information that will give them a better understanding of complicated news events. Business writer Gary Ruderman considers backgrounders essential when he is working on stories about complicated topics. He said if he was assigned a story on the "intricacies of floor and ceiling guarantees on the London Interbank Offering Rate," he would call a banking source for a "fast course" on "how it works and what are the pitfalls." He could then begin reporting the story with more expertise.[71] Since much of the information would be common knowledge to the industry, he probably would not attribute it to his source.

Other times, background sessions are meetings between reporters and government leaders, sometimes at breakfast, for free-form discussions of the issues. The participants agree in advance whether the information will be on or off the record. In Washington, however, the backgrounder has evolved into an art form. Often backgrounders are briefings by officials with several reporters, almost like a full-blown press conference. Usually the understanding is that the information and opinions expressed at these briefings can be used but must be attributed to "a senior White House official," a "State Department adviser," "key congressional aide," or some other such designation. When Henry Kissinger was Richard Nixon's secretary of state, he often gave backgrounders in which he was to be identified as "a high State Department official traveling on the secretary of state's plane." Most readers soon figured out who the source was.[72]

Alex Jones of *The New York Times* divides confidential sources into two broad categories: visible and invisible. Visible sources are people who are identified as "a source in the sheriff's department," "a previous client of the lawyer," or "a senior State Department official." Invisible sources do not appear in the stories but are instrumental in their publication. These people may tip the reporter about the story and even provide names of sources and documents the reporter may need, documents that will be described only as "obtained by" the newspaper.[73]

When reporters agree never to name or even quote invisible sources but to use them only to confirm information, some reporters call them "deep background sources," a term invented by Woodward and Bernstein during their Watergate investigation for *The Washington Post*. Deep Throat was a deep background source.[74]

Occasionally, at the end of an interview, reporters are hit with a tricky request. The source will ask, "You're not going to quote me, are you?" Before reporters answer that question, many take into consideration how media-smart the person is. If the person deals with the media regularly and the reporters make it clear they were talking with the person to get information for a story, most reporters believe the interview is on the record and feel justified in using the information and the person's name. But many reporters temper that rule if their source is not used to dealing with reporters. Ruderman said that if he is convinced the source is not "playing dumb," he may consider using the quotes but not the person's name.[75] (Dealing with unsophisticated sources is also discussed in Chapter 12.)

BREAKING PROMISES

On rare occasions, reporters and their editors get so bothered by their dealings in this shady business of leaks and clandestine sources that they decide to expose their secret sources.

One such incident involved Oliver North, a Marine lieutenant colonel who played a key role in several secret international dealings during the Reagan administration, including supplying weapons to guerrilla forces in Central America. When he was charged with lying to Congress, he admitted that he had not told Congress the truth about his activities. But he testified at hearings that he lied because he could not trust Congress to keep the information secret. North then cited some specific cases where he believed his work had been hindered by leaks from Congress. Many journalists were stunned by North's allegations. They knew it was North himself, not members of Congress, who had leaked the information in those cases. *Newsweek* editors believed this violation of trust was so great that they broke their pledge of confidentiality and identified North. "Given these unusual circumstances, we felt an obligation to point out to our readers that North himself was a frequent source of administration leaks," *Newsweek*'s editor said.[76]

Sometimes reporters decide to break confidences because they believe that informing the public what the source said is more important than keeping their word. That was the decision Milton Coleman made when he was covering politics for *The Washington Post*. When Jesse Jackson was running for the Democratic nomination for president, he said to Coleman, "Let's talk black talk." Coleman, who is black, had heard Jackson use the phrase before and understood it to mean that the conversation was off the record. "Jackson then talked about the preoccupation of some with Israel," Coleman wrote. "He said something to the effect of the following: That's all Hymie wants to talk about is Israel; every time you go to Hymietown, that's all they want to talk about." Coleman said he had never heard Jackson use those words before, and he made a mental note of the conversation.[77]

Although Coleman did not write a story about the remarks because he felt there was no context for them in his stories, he passed Jackson's comments on to another *Post* reporter who was doing a story about Jackson's difficulties with Jewish voters. The 37th paragraph of his 52-inch story read: "In private conversations with reporters, Jackson has referred to Jews as 'Hymie' and to New York as 'Hymietown.' " The comments seemed to go unnoticed at first until the *Post* published an editorial calling on Jackson to explain his use of those "degrading and disgusting" words. After first insisting he could not recall using them, Jackson finally conceded that his remarks were "insensitive" and denied that what he said "in any way reflects my basic attitude toward Jews or Israel."[78]

Coleman said he thought he was right to repeat Jackson's racist remarks because Jackson "was presenting himself for the highest elective office in this land" and "had said something that appeared to at least stereotype if not . . . denigrate a group of American electors. That statement ought to be brought to the public's attention." He argued that "the convention of background and nonattribution has never been intended to hide remarks that would denigrate a particular group of people."[79]

Many journalists supported Coleman's and *Newsweek*'s decisions to violate their pledges to sources. But other journalists vehemently criticized them, and many *Newsweek* staffers let it be known that they opposed their editors' decision in the North case. These journalists worry that incidents like these may persuade other sources to believe that they can't trust reporters' promises and to refuse to provide information. Sources for information might dry up. Besides, many journalists find the whole idea of not keeping their word distasteful.

Sources drying up.

A Supreme Court ruling in 1991 gave journalists another reason to abide by pledges of confidentiality. The court ruled that such a pledge is a binding contract between the reporter and the source. The case grew out of stories in the Minneapolis *Star Tribune* and the *St. Paul Pioneer Press.*

A Republican politician gave reporters copies of documents revealing that the Democratic candidate for lieutenant governor had been convicted of shoplifting 12 years before. The man passed out his copies a week before the election with the understanding that he would not be identified as the source. All the newspaper and broadcast reporters agreed, and none of the reporters used the man's name in their stories.

But editors at the two newspapers weren't so sure that keeping the source's name secret was a good idea. At the *Star Tribune,* about 15 editors debated the story. Many thought the 12-year-old conviction was not news. The real story, they thought, was the use of dirty tricks by Republicans. After having another reporter confirm that the only person who had checked out the court file on the case in several years had ties to the Republican politician, the *Star Tribune* decided to print his name despite the pledge the reporter had made. Editors at the *Pioneer Press* came to a similar conclusion. John R. Finnegan, vice president and editor of the St. Paul paper, accused the politician of "trying, in the most blatant way, to manipulate the Twin Cities media for maximum exposure with no risk to himself or his party."

When the story broke, both reporters were angry. So was the source. The bad publicity cost him his job with a public relations firm. He sued the papers for breach of contract, misrepresentation and fraud and won.[80]

EDITORS REVISE RULES

The Supreme Court decision in the Minnesota case and editors' doubts about using unnamed sources have prompted some papers to review their guidelines on promising confidentiality. Many papers now require reporters to tell senior editors the names of sources who ask for anonymity and their reasons. At papers like *The Tennessean* in Nashville, the senior editors then decide if the request is merited. If they decide it isn't, reporters can't use information from those sources in their stories.[81]

While a system of checks like *The Tennessean*'s would seem to lessen the chances of abusing the promise of anonymity, reporters say these rules may not work well in practice. "When you're sitting over a meal with a source, nobody is going to say, 'Excuse me, I'm going to go call my editor,' " said Fredric N. Tulsky, chairman of the Investigative Reporters and Editors organization and a reporter for *The Philadelphia Inquirer.* He noted that the *Inquirer* received a Pulitzer Prize in 1991 for a story that used secret sources to reveal mishandling of funds at Cumberland Farms Inc.[82]

The rules for secret sources vary. Some newspapers require reporters to have two sources for information that will be used anonymously. The rules at *USA Today* require the reporter to be "absolutely positive" about the accuracy of the information, according to editor Peter Pritchard.[83] And a few papers ban anonymous sources altogether.

Claude Sitton, former editor of the Raleigh *News & Observer,* preferred that his reporters use secret sources only as leads to on-the-record sources, not as a basis for news stories. Sitton, who distinguished himself covering civil rights for *The New York Times,* observed that "once you go beyond using confidential sources for leads, you're on dangerous ground."[84]

Although indications are that editors are tightening the rules about granting anonymity, some believe the use of anonymous sources is becoming more common, not less. One researcher found that nearly a quarter of the stories in the main news sections of *The New York Times, The Washington Post* and the *Los Angeles Times* included anonymous sources.[85] However, earlier research found that major papers like these tend to use considerably more anonymous sources than other American dailies.[86]

SECRET SOURCES, REPORTERS AND JAIL

Virtually all journalists who grant sources anonymity keep their names secret when they write their stories. The touchier decision sometimes comes after the stories are printed. Prosecutors, defense lawyers or lawyers in civil cases may read the stories and demand that the reporters reveal their sources. These attorneys contend that unless these sources testify in court, innocent people may go to jail, guilty people may go free, or injured parties will be denied just settlements. They ask judges to order reporters to name their sources or be held in contempt of court.

Many reporters have had to make that decision. Tim Roche, a 24-year-old reporter, was sentenced to 30 days in jail in 1993 for refusing to reveal his sources in stories about a child-custody battle he covered for *The Stuart (Fla.) News.* The child's foster mother said his initial stories may have helped save the life of the child who was going to be returned to an abusive home.[87] Timothy Phelps of *Newsday* and Nina Totenberg of National Public Radio were threatened with contempt of Congress when they refused to identify sources they used in revealing the sexual-harassment charges against Supreme Court nominee Clarence Thomas.[88]

Once in a while, reporters are saved from jail when their blind sources identify themselves. Susan Wornick, a reporter for WCVB-TV in Boston, had been sentenced to three months in jail after she defied a judge's order to name the sole eyewitness to a drugstore burglary. Wornick told the judge that she had promised confidentiality to the eyewitness because he feared retaliation by police. The burglary was allegedly committed by members of the Revere, Mass., police force. After the man came forward and testified before a grand jury, the judge withdrew his contempt ruling against the reporter.[89]

Not all stories that can land reporters in jail are the kind that save children from abuse, protect people from corrupt police officers, or question the integrity of a Supreme Court nominee. The first reporter in modern times to go to jail to protect a source was Marie Torre, radio-TV critic of the old *New York Herald Tribune.* In 1958, she refused to identify the CBS executive she had quoted in her column to the effect that Judy Garland, the actress who played Dorothy in *The Wizard of Oz,* was being dropped from a program because she was too fat.

Many news organizations believe anonymous sources are so basic to journalism that they have sought laws to shield reporters from having to identify their sources. About half the states have "shield laws," which vary greatly in effectiveness. In states without shield laws, judges have applied either common law or provisions in state constitutions to give some protection to journalists.[90]

But still, the sight of a subpoena being served in a newsroom is not a rarity. More than 3,000 subpoenas were issued in 1992 ordering news organizations to turn over news articles, photographs, videotapes and reporters' notes. Most were complied with because the material had been printed or broadcast. But about a third were contested by the media, and 97 were quashed by shield laws.[91]

Using secret sources can create other legal problems. News organizations may have trouble winning libel suits if the sources will not testify in court. At some newspapers, editors consult with libel attorneys before using sensitive stories based on anonymous sources. An APME committee has suggested that if reporters can't get sources to go on the record, they should ask them to agree that the paper will keep their identities secret unless there is a libel suit.[92] *The Seattle Times* took this step when it decided to mask the identity of the women who accused Sen. Adams of sexual harassment.

When People Use Offensive Language

Although movies, recordings and even daytime TV shows are becoming very graphic in their use of four-letter words, newspapers remain almost prudish protectors of their readers' modesty. Stories of editors' efforts to avoid being offensive are common in every newsroom. David Shaw, media writer for the *Los Angeles Times,* said a headline in his paper in the 1970s once called a 69-car crash on a freeway a "70-car pileup" to avoid "titillating or offending readers." At about the same time, the paper removed the genitals from a picture of a male lion at the zoo because editors were afraid children might see them.[93]

Although those cases are extreme, reporters must occasionally decide how to handle quotes by sources who sprinkle their conversations with off-color words. They and their editors consider many things when deciding how much will be quoted verbatim. The prominence of the person is one major consideration. "If the president of the United States says 'fuck,' I'm going to quote him," observed Benjamin Bradlee when he was executive editor of *The Washington Post*. At *The New York Times,* Abe Rosenthal put it this way: "We'll take 'shit' from the president of the United States, but from nobody else."[94] That was probably the reasoning when newspapers editors and network news producers once quoted President Reagan as calling reporters "sons of bitches." (A spokesman the next day said Reagan didn't recall using that phrase but thought he might have said, "It's sunny, and you're rich.")[95] Athletes, however, usually aren't treated this candidly. "You can't quote most pro athletes verbatim because of obscenity," said Bill Lyon, a sports columnist for *The Philadelphia Inquirer*. "You have to launder their words."[96]

"That's a great quote, Lefty, but now try cleaning it up so I can use it."

Editors also consider the nature of the story and may allow the use of graphic language if it is needed to make a point. In a story about racist and sexist attitudes among Los Angeles police officers, reporters and editors at the *Los Angeles Times* disagreed about how much of the crude language used by cops should appear in print. The top editors decided to use the word "tits" but substituted the phrase "a four-letter vulgarism for vagina" in place of a word the officers used to refer to women. The woman who wrote the story and many editors at the *Times* argued that the vulgarism should have been used because otherwise the story would "fail to accurately portray the severity of the officers' demeaning attitudes toward women."[97]

However, *The New York Times* asked its reporter to be more graphic in her descriptions of a homoerotic art exhibit that had been picketed in some cities and led to the arrest of a museum official in Cincinnati. "It seems to me you have to come as close to describing it as you can to show why, to some people, it's offensive," deputy national editor Jeffrey Schmalz told *Newsday*. "Otherwise you're not telling the story." But the *Times* (like nearly every major paper) chose not to print any of the more controversial photographs that appeared in the exhibit. The *Times'* handling of this case involving the photography of Robert Mapplethorp was an exception for the paper, which tends to encourage its reporters to write around the cruder facts of life.[98]

Editors at other publications are equally uneven in their decisions about vulgar language. *Newsweek* found that its editors had allowed the use of the word "fuck" three times in 16 years but during the same time period had also substituted "f—k," "bleep," "f'ing" and "motherf—."[99] When editors at the *Los Angeles Times* assigned David Shaw to write an article about newspapers' use of vulgarisms, he was told he could use the words in his examples. But when Shaw submitted his story, the editor changed his mind and deleted most of them, including words that had appeared in the *Times* more than 17 years earlier.[100]

Many editors are concerned that their efforts to find euphemisms for vulgarities may give readers a false idea about what was really said. For example, when Jimmy Carter was running for president, he agreed to be interviewed by Robert Scheer for a feature in *Playboy*. Carter, whose image was that of a straight-and-narrow Baptist from rural Georgia, used the words "screw" and "shack up" and admitted that he had "lusted" after women in his heart. *The New York Times* considered those words too raw for a family newspaper, so when the *Times* first reported Carter's comments, it substituted the phrase "a vulgarism for sexual relations" for the word "screw." But the next day, editors recognized that readers might have assumed he had used the "f-word" instead of "screw," so they reported that he had used "a common but mild vulgarism for sexual relations." As Shaw pointed out, it took the *Times* "eight words to clear up the confusion originally caused by having used five words to replace one word."[101]

Other papers, including *The Milwaukee Journal,* have left readers befuddled about what people really said. The *Journal* quoted baseball player Barry Bonds as telling manager Jim Leyland to "get the . . . out of here," leaving readers to guess the censored word. According to half a dozen newspapers that carried the full quote, he said "hell."[102] Readers of the *Journal* may also have guessed wrong when the *Journal* used five dashes instead of the word "bitch" when New England Patriots owner Victor Kiam called sports reporter Lisa Olsen "a classic bitch" after Olsen claimed she had been sexually harassed by the Patroits. Linguist Reinhold Aman noted that *Journal* readers might have assumed he called her "a whore, broad, hussy or whatever other five-letter word fits."[103]

THE EARL BUTZ TEST

In a classic offensive-language case, newspaper editors and broadcasters dug into their dictionaries for euphemisms they could use to report a racist "joke" that caused President Ford to fire Earl Butz, who had been secretary of agriculture for five years. The media first learned of Butz's comments in a report on the 1976 Republican National Convention in *Rolling Stone* written by John Dean, former White House counsel to President Nixon. Dean said that on the plane coming home from the convention he got into a discussion with entertainers Pat Boone and Sonny Bono. They were joined shortly by a man Dean did not name in his article but identified as "a distinguished member of Ford's cabinet." Dean asked the unnamed secretary why convention delegates had given such a cool reception to a speech by their vice-presidential nominee, Sen. Robert Dole:

> "Oh hell, John, everybody was worn out by then. You know," he said with a mischievous smile, leaning over the seat in front of Pat and me, "it's like the dog who screwed a skunk for a while, until it finally shouted, 'I've had enough!' "
>
> Pat gulped, then grinned and I laughed. To change the subject Pat posed a question: "John and I were just discussing the appeal of the Republican party. It seems to me that the party of Abraham Lincoln could and should attract more black people. Why can't that be done?" That was a fair question for the secretary, who is also a very capable politician.
>
> "I'll tell you why you can't attract coloreds," the secretary proclaimed as his mischievous smile returned. "Because coloreds only want three things. You know what they want?" he asked Pat.
>
> Pat shook his head no; so did I.
>
> "I'll tell you what coloreds want. It's three things: first a tight pussy; second loose shoes; and third, a warm place to shit. That's all."
>
> Pat gulped twice.[104]

A writer for another magazine tracked down which cabinet official was on the plane. He got Boone to confirm that it was Butz who made the comment. "I took it as a joke," Boone said. He said he did not think it was funny and was surprised that Butz would use such language when talking to a reporter. "I cringed for him," said Boone.[105]

Clearly, such inappropriate comments by a high-ranking government official were news. But editors weren't sure how to deal with the language. The AP decided to send two versions, one with the words Butz used and one that said Butz had referred to blacks as "coloreds" and "discussed in derogatory terms what he said were their sexual, dress and bathroom preferences." The UPI was a little more forthcoming. It paraphrased him as saying "good sex, easy shoes and a warm place to go to the bathroom."[106]

The New York Times reported that Butz had referred to blacks as "coloreds" and said they wanted only three things, which he "listed, in order, in obscene, derogatory and scatological terms." After Butz resigned, the *Times* loosened up a bit and used the euphemisms "satisfying sex, loose shoes and a warm place for bodily functions—wishes that were listed by Mr. Butz in obscene and scatological terms." The *San Francisco Examiner* employed the old crossword-puzzle trick: "first, a tight p— —, second, loose shoes, and third a warm place to s— —."[107]

Some newspapers told their readers that Butz's comments were unprintable but that adult readers could see them at the office or write for copies. More than 100 people visited the Erie, Pa., *Morning News* to read the "joke" for themselves. About 350 showed up at the Lubbock, Texas, newspaper, including a farmer and his wife who drove 70 miles to copy it for their neighbors.[108]

What's an Ethical Journalist to Do?

Reporters must develop regular sources they can depend on for quick, reliable insights into the news. Often the nature of these relationships is shaped by the nature of the people involved. Reporters will take a personal liking to some sources: Their personalities and humor may jibe to form a pleasant working relationship. Everyone can benefit from such relationships. The sources have a channel for making their views known, the reporters get good stories, and the public gets a better understanding of the news.

How friendly these relationships ought to be is not an easy call. Sometimes the news organization and the public are served by chummy relationships. Most journalists have known police reporters who knew nearly every officer and firefighter in town, their spouses' names, and the

Little League teams their children played on. Although these reporters may not write tough investigative stories, they are called upon when their news organizations need a quick and accurate account of some breaking story involving the police or firefighters. Some veteran police reporters argue that because so many departments now have so-called public information officers who see their jobs as keeping the public from getting information, it is even more important to develop friendly relationships with some officers.[109]

But it is essential for journalists to be independent in their search for facts and truth. For reporters, that means among other things not allowing their relationships with sources to get so friendly that their journalism serves sources better than the public. Reporters can't afford to let themselves be compromised, even unconsciously, by a need to keep their sources happy at all costs. This does not mean that sources have to be turned into enemies. Sometimes adversarial treatment becomes necessary — say, in a Watergate-type relationship in which sources try to lie to the public through the news media — but reporters have to be cautious about loosing their aggression on sources undeserving of such incivility.

In deciding how to handle profane and obscene words expressed by people in the news, journalists have found no easy answer. They want to be truthful in their reports, but sometimes precise accuracy can be so shocking that the truth gets lost in the telling. Journalists have to put the use of offensive language by sources in the larger context of what the public needs to know: High-ranking government officials and politicians with foul mouths need to be quoted accurately if they are insensitive about what they say in public. Citizens need to know when their political leaders exhibit such poor judgment. But when ordinary folks use offensive language, journalists should consider "cleansing" their remarks unless the dirty words are important to understanding the story.

Athletes in the limelight create a special problem. The argument that the media should protect the hero image of star athletes seems weak alongside the larger obligation to truthful reporting. Athletes who want to be treated like heroes need to act and speak like heroes. Journalists must walk a fine line between creating a false impression of sports heroes and offending readers with the language athletes sometimes use.

Secret sources present other problems. Some reporters and news organizations grant anonymity without hesitation. They may beat the competition to a lot of stories by doing this, but they also put out news that is sometimes inaccurate, incomplete or at least misleading. And they leave themselves open to being used by sources who care more about shaping the news to fit their own needs than informing the public.

Most news organizations are more hesitant about building stories on unnamed sources. They grant anonymity only for important stories and only when there is no other way to get the information. They are even willing to lose a story occasionally to maintain their faith in the news they offer the public. They believe that avoiding anonymously sourced information also helps build public faith in journalism and the news media.

The Government Watch

As manager and former news director of the only TV station in this southern city

of about 46,000 residents, you get an urgent call to come to a cabin owned by the U.S. attorney for your area. When you get to the cabin, you are met by the U.S. attorney, the district attorney for your city, and the director of police, all men you know from your days as a reporter for your station. Also present are some police detectives, and you are soon joined by the managing editor and the police reporter for the city's only daily newspaper.

The law enforcement authorities tell you that they believe a contract has been put out to murder a local businessman. An undercover police officer posing as the "hit man" has been unable to meet or learn the identities of the person or persons willing to pay $35,000 to have the local businessman killed, but the officer has been told by the "money man" on the telephone that the $35,000 will be paid 24 hours after he reads in the news that the hit has occurred.

The authorities say the intended murder victim is in their custody and is willing to help them stage a hoax. What they intend to do that afternoon is plant the victim's truck somewhere in the area with blood on it. When the abandoned truck is "discovered" by police, they want you and the local newspaper to give the event full coverage as if it actually happened. Authorities will not tell you the name of the intended victim unless you promise them you'll cooperate.

Would you cooperate with law enforcement officials in this case? Even if it means airing what you know to be a false report? How does putting out a fake news story stack up against the life of the local businessman?

That's the dilemma faced by Cliff Brown, manager of WDAM-TV in Hattiesburg, Miss. He decided to cooperate. That evening his TV station showed videotapes of the abandoned pickup truck of local cattleman Oscar Black III. The report suggested that a struggle had taken place on the country road where the truck was found with Black's pistol and other possessions in it. It also implied that Black had disappeared and was probably murdered.[1]

The next afternoon the newspaper, the *Hattiesburg American,* published a one-sentence item in its daily roundup of police news. The sentence read: "Police are seeking information concerning suspected foul play directed toward Oscar Black III."[2]

That sentence was written by the newspaper's publisher, Duane K. McCallister, in an apparent attempt to walk the tightrope between not exposing the police hoax and not lying to the public. McCallister saw that one-sentence report as a refusal by his newspaper to participate in the hoax staged by the police. "An important principle was at stake — you just don't lie to your readers," wrote McCallister.[3]

Brown went along with the authorities in this case because, he said, he believed there was a real threat to Oscar Black's life. The U.S. attorney, George Phillips, and most of the other officials who asked him to cooperate were people he had worked with while he was in news. "They had never misled me or used me in any way," Brown recalled. "I had no reason to think that they would mislead me after all the years I had worked with them."

He saw this case as being a clash between the "life ethic" and the journalistic ethic. He said he has always subscribed to the journalistic ethic "of presenting the news so that it is truthful, factual and balanced, . . . but when the value of a person's life hit me square between the eyes, I realized there are few absolutes in this world." Brown also felt he was influenced by his fairly strong religious beliefs.

After he told Phillips he'd cooperate, but only for a week, Brown returned to his station with the intention of *not* informing his news staff, letting them cover the staged murder as if it were for real. However, after that first false report was broadcast on the 6 P.M. news, Brown had to reveal the hoax to the assistant news director because the latter had gotten so involved in the story he began to smell something. But the rest of Brown's news staff, including the news director, didn't know they were reporting a false story for three days until police called a news conference to announce that the hoax had failed.

At the news conference, District Attorney Glenn White claimed that police came close to finding out who tried to murder Black, an owner of Custom Cattle Co. in Lamar County, Miss. But the operation fell apart when the money man sensed somehow that police were involved and called off a rendezvous with the undercover hit man at which the latter was to get his $35,000 for the hit. White commended *Hattiesburg American* reporter Janet Braswell, WDAM-TV, "and the law enforcement officers involved for putting their credibility on the line when it came to a human life and perhaps putting their ethics aside in order to save a human life." He did not commend the newspaper itself.[4] Later Phillips and the Hattiesburg public safety commissioner condemned the *American* for being more concerned about the reaction of the rest of journalism than human life.[5]

Reporter Braswell put police onto the investigation that spawned the unsuccessful hoax. A longtime police reporter, Braswell got a call one day from a man who said he was "Pete," a private investigator, and he knew there was going to be a hit in Hattiesburg. He said no more. Braswell reported the strange conversation to her managing editor, Frank Sutherland. They decided that the caller must be some kind of nut, but when he called again eight days later, she and Sutherland decided she should inform the police.

"My guiding rule is to let law enforcement enforce the law and let us cover them," Sutherland explained. But "sometimes if a reporter witnesses a murder, you cannot hide behind a journalistic shield and say I'm going to write about it but I'm not going to tell police what I saw." He felt Janet Braswell "was thrust into that same kind of problem. She answered the phone and she was forced to cooperate with police. Somebody calling up and saying I'm going to kill somebody—you don't keep that within the walls of the newsroom, you have to tell authorities. I think she did the responsible thing."[6]

Braswell subsequently persuaded her "private investigator" to deal directly with police. It was on his information that police provided an undercover officer to pose as hit man in an attempt to learn the identities of those who were trying to buy Oscar Black's death. Although the undercover hit man failed to flush out the alleged death buyers and dealers in this initial operation—hoax and all—the same money man tried again to hire a killer a few months later. This time police used an undercover hit man as before but they did not involve the local news media. They ended up arresting and charging two men. One of them was convicted and sentenced to 17 years for attempted murder.[7]

Some editors around the country have suggested that the TV station and the newspaper should have at least threatened to blow the whistle on the police hoax at the outset. They reasoned that the law enforcement people were way out of line when they presented the local news executives with a fait accompli—a staged, phony murder that they were supposed to treat as real. Such an unreasonable request should have been rejected because it would compromise the local news media in their responsibility for factual reporting. Although that rejection would seem to have put a life in jeopardy, it probably would have forced police to come up with a different scheme, as they did successfully in their second opportunity to trap the contract killers.

Sutherland, who at the time was president of SPJ, said he did consider publishing a story that police had staged a hoax, but rejected it because "it would blow the case." His paper was not sure of what was happening at that point—"and we didn't know what we were endangering. . . . If we exposed the hoax, we didn't know what that would do." Sutherland was not happy with what his paper did in the initial reporting of the Black incident. He recalled that he opposed running the one-sentence report the day after police staged the murder. "I was reluctant to run it the first time and I'd be reluctant to run it again," Sutherland said.

Although Sutherland represented his paper at that first conference when authorities sought media cooperation in publicizing their hoax, he immediately consulted his publisher, McCallister, who ended up making the final decision about how the paper would handle the situation. The newspaper and television station executives arrived at their differing decisions without conferring with each other.

This complicated case illustrates how difficult it is for journalists in the American system to decide how far they should go in cooperating with and helping the government they feel they are bound to watch. How can journalists work with government and government officials and still do their jobs as critical observers and reporters of governmental activities?

JOURNALISTS AS WATCHDOGS

American journalists have developed what Peter Braestrup calls a "public theology" in which the press serves as a watchdog of government, representing and providing information to citizens so that they can intelligently participate in democratic government.[8] Government news is a staple of American journalism. Government beats, from the White House to the county courthouse, are among the most important on any editor's assignment sheet.

This ennobling image of journalists as watchdogs protecting the public from abuses of government is rooted in the First Amendment, many journalists believe. They argue that a free press is an essential of democratic government. Without journalists observing and reporting on government actions and inactions, the voters would be ignorant and unable to make intelligent decisions in elections.

The press as a watchdog of government.

"If you look at the history of this country . . . the thing that makes this experiment in government unique among democracies has been the continued independence of the daily newspaper serving as a critic and watchdog of government," said James D. Squires, when he was editor of the *Chicago Tribune*. "It goes hand in hand with us being the forum in which the political debate is played out." Squires also believes that freedom of the press is "most sacred when it is covering government."[9]

The watchdog role, of course, gets interpreted differently from journalist to journalist, from newsroom to newsroom, and from time to time. Some journalists see themselves as representatives, almost champions, of the people, particularly the powerless ones, and they tend to be aggressive watchdogs, sniffing out government wrongdoing at every opportunity. Other journalists are more like lapdogs — "too cozy, too intimidated, and too respectful of people in power," as Les Payne of *Newsday* put it.[10] Journalistic watchdoggery also seems to wax and wane with the times, showing its more aggressive fangs during the Watergate era and wagging its tail during the Reagan presidency, for example.

Journalists also keep watch on other orders in American life, such as business, sports and entertainment, but government has traditionally gotten the most intense and vigorous surveillance. "Government can take away your freedom and legislate you into prison, into debt," Squires explained. "Government always operates on tax dollars, on public money. . . . I don't think we have nearly as strong an obligation and an inherent right to look into the personal business of a movie star as we do the mayor of our city, or our city councilmen."

Government officials show less enthusiasm for the idea that journalists are obligated to be their critical observers. Authorities frequently feel the need to do business behind closed doors or to seek the cooperation of individual journalists or their organizations in certain projects or operations. Both of these compulsions of government — to be secret and to involve journalists as partners — threaten the watchdog concept. They also present journalists with difficult ethical decisions about their responsibilities as citizens as well as their functions as reporters and evaluators of their own government.

Government Cooperation and Secrecy

American journalists are no longer "on the team." That expression came from a remark that Admiral Harry D. Felt reportedly made when he met Malcolm Browne, one of the early AP correspondents covering the Vietnam War: "So you're Browne," Felt said. "Why don't you get on the team?"[11] The admiral was expressing his anger at Browne and other correspondents who were beginning to defy the official line in their reporting of that war in the early 1960s. American war correspondents had not acted that way in World Wars I and II and Korea. Their patriotism came out in the positive, morale-boosting stories most filed.

The spirit of cooperation between the press and government that prevailed during America's wars in the first half of this century seemed to carry on for a while after World War II. During that war and for the period after it known as the "Cold War," some U.S. journalists worked or cooperated with the young and still small Central Intelligence Agency. It was only natural that our spy agency would turn to journalists, many of whom had contacts in and special knowledge of other countries. But the love affair between the CIA and some journalists did not last long because of something that was happening between the press and government in this country.

As the U.S. government grew in size and complexity during and after World War II, it became obvious to government leaders that effective communication with the citizens was required. American business had already discovered this essentiality some years earlier and had turned for help to a new breed of specialist—the public relations expert. Government soon followed suit, adding scores, then hundreds, and finally thousands of such specialists to the public payroll. Today, in both government and the private sector, no major enterprise is without public relations counsel.

With the help of its public relations specialists, government began to find better ways to assemble and package information so it was more apt to be used by the press. It also found other ways of communicating with the public, so that it did not have to depend entirely on independent, nongovernmental channels of communication. And somewhere along the line, government discovered that certain kinds of information were better than other kinds, that you did not have to tell the people everything. Image making and manipulating information to certain ends became instruments of government strategy. Even the lie was not out of the question, as the press and the country learned in 1960 when the government said it was not using the U-2 plane to spy on the Soviet Union, and then the Soviets produced the captured pilot of a downed U-2 who said that was just what he was doing. And in 1962 Arthur Sylvester, spokesman for the Pentagon under Presidents Kennedy and Johnson, admitted that the lie had been added to the government's public relations arsenal when he told a meeting of journalists: "I think the inherent right of the government to lie—to lie to save itself when faced with nuclear disaster—is basic, basic."[12]

Well, this was something new. It was one thing for the press to cooperate with government, as it did in World War II, to keep news from the public. But having the government manage the news, even to the extent of lying, to keep information from the press was more than most journalists were willing to take. So in Vietnam reporters began to ask tougher questions and to go out on their own without military escort to find out what was happening. One reporter, Harrison Salisbury of *The New York Times,* even went to Hanoi, the enemy's capital, to file reports that cast doubts on Pentagon claims that we were not bombing civilian targets in North Vietnam, only military targets. Salisbury's stories in 1966 and the increasingly critical coverage by all reporters and photographers covering Vietnam undoubtedly contributed to the snowballing public disenchantment with that war, which eventually forced the government to disengage from the conflict without victory.

The more aggressive and less cooperative attitude of the press toward government also was expressed in the publication by *The New York Times* and other periodicals of the secret Pentagon Papers and the coverage of the Nixon administration, which brought about the resignation first of Vice President Spiro Agnew and then Nixon himself in 1974. Some leaders of journalism believe the press may have overdone its aggression in the period right after Watergate, and the watchdog's growl has tempered a bit of late, but the press is certainly not back on the government's team.

COOPERATION PAYS

Although the relationship between press and government has become more adversarial, journalists and government officials still find that cooperation pays. Governments at all levels in the United States have traditionally provided the news media with press rooms, press tables and facilities they need to report on government. Press cards issued by government, particularly police and security agencies, help reporters pass through police lines and other barriers to the general public. Government public information people may not always be truthful in their dealings with the press, but they provide reporters with tons of legitimate information and help them get to the officials who make and carry out government policies. Everywhere government is covered by the news media in this country, there exists a degree of cooperation that serves both interests.

Although he feels strongly that the press should be independent from and not work for government, Andrew Barnes, editor of the *St. Petersburg Times,* sees the need for cooperation. For example, he says, "one of the functions of civil defense in this coastal Florida city is to let people know where to go if a storm is coming. . . . We provide that information to the citizens for government." Another way the press cooperates with government is in "informing citizens when there are open houses at schools." And although he suspects many public officials would not agree with him, Barnes says "we cooperate when we let people know what our elected and appointed officials are doing."[13]

A kind of cooperation that sometimes leads to trouble occurs when public officials, candidates or other news sources turn to journalists for advice. If the source is of some importance, such a request can be very flattering and difficult to turn down. Then if friendships develop between the advice seeker and giver, serious conflicts of interest can result for the journalist. That's what happened to George F. Will. He's one of the new breed of newspaper columnists who did not come out of the ranks of reporters but straight from political employment. Will had been a legislative assistant to a U.S. senator. Similarly, columnist William Safire of *The New York Times* had been a speech writer for President Nixon, columnist Jody Powell was President Carter's press secretary, and Bill Moyers of PBS was President Johnson's press secretary.

As a participant in conservative politics, Will had many friends among conservative politicians, one of them being President Reagan. When Reagan asked Will to help him prepare for his 1980 debates with President Carter, Will agreed. Later, in his column and as a part-time ABC News commentator, Will praised Reagan's performance in the debates without disclosing his role as one of Reagan's coaches. His involvement came out in 1983 when a House subcommittee investigated Reagan's use of some Carter briefing papers in preparing for the debates. Will defended his aid for Reagan by contending that the relationship columnists have with politicians can be different from that of straight news reporters. But columnist Mary McGrory of *The Washington Post* spoke for many in journalism when she wrote that what Will was saying when "he stoutly maintains he is not a journalist" was that "he is not subject to our rules and conventions, and I find that a bit arrogant." The *New York Daily News* dropped Will's column for what it called his "violation of journalistic ethics." Although none of the 400 other papers subscribing to his column followed the example of the *News,* Will wrote later that he would "not again come as close to a political campaign" as he did in 1980.[14]

Will may have a point when he separates opinion writers from fact reporters in how much distance should be maintained between them and politicians. But what should journalism then do about the increasing number of fact reporters who go into the government and then come back to the fact side of journalism? Aren't they even more of a threat to journalism's credibility than somebody like George Will?

"Turnstile journalists" is what critics have labeled people like Leslie Gelb of *The New York Times,* who has gone through that government-press turnstile more than once. A former head of the Defense Department's policy planning staff during the Vietnam War, Gelb was working for U.S. Senator Jacob Javits when the *Times* hired him. He left the *Times* a few years later to direct the State Department's Bureau of Politico-Military Affairs from 1977 to 1979, returning to the paper in 1981 as national security correspondent and columnist.

Gelb is just one of scores of turnstile journalists in the news business today. Diane Sawyer of ABC News was Nixon's assistant press secretary. Pete Williams, Pentagon spokesperson during the Gulf War, has since joined the Washington staff of NBC News. John Hughes, former editor of the *Christian Science Monitor,* went into government in 1981, serving in the U.S. Information Agency and as State Department spokesman until 1984 when he returned to running his weekly newspapers on Cape Cod and writing a column. NBC commentator John Chancellor served for a period as director of the Voice of America. Roger Comstock, executive editor of the Hackensack, N.J., *Record,* took a two-year leave to be state director of public information. Even an old government watchdog like Clark Mollenhoff left the Washington bureau of *The Des Moines Register* for a year to work in Nixon's White House. The list could go on and on. Almost every one of the big newsrooms in the country has at least one former government official wearing a journalist's hat.

WORKING WITH POLICE

As we saw in the opening of this chapter, police can sometimes lean hard on journalists to cooperate to help them fight crime. The ethical question is how much cooperation between the news media and law enforcement can be tolerated without threatening the independence and credibility of the press.

Most journalists seem to believe that at the working level a little cooperation between reporters and police is usually not harmful, but they draw the line at becoming just another arm of law enforcement. There seems to be considerable disagreement, however, about how much cooperation is acceptable.

William F. Thomas, when he was editor of the *Los Angeles Times,* warned that "you never cooperate with law enforcement in a way that jeopardizes your independence." For example, his paper refused to cooperate with police who wanted staff testimony and photographs of college riots back in the 1960s and early 1970s. "Helping police that way would have hurt our effectiveness as journalists." But Thomas argued that if a journalist is walking down a street and sees a crime, there is no reason why he or she should not testify. As a city editor for many years, Thomas conceded that he often cooperated with law enforcement by trading information. "You do this very quietly and it helps you both."[15]

The way Robert W. Greene, retired assistant managing editor of *Newsday,* sees it:

> All the cops are required to give a police reporter are the basic skeleton details on the blotter report. But they give him more, plenty of background. They volunteer that information. Now there comes a time when the reporter and the police are each working on the same thing, both convinced that the other is working toward the same good end, and so you prime the pump by exchanging information.[16]

Greene, a longtime officer of IRE, said that "a vast majority of reporters I know cooperate with government agencies—senate committees, local police, district attorneys—given certain circumstances." Greene believes journalists do not have a right to withdraw from society. "To say that we will not cooperate when we have seen a crime committed, that because we're reporters we don't have to testify, is to say that we're not citizens, that we're privileged people," he added.

A considerable degree of press-government cooperation was evident when the *Chicago Sun-Times* bought and operated the Mirage Tavern to expose shakedowns by city inspectors (detailed in Chapter 8). Then editor Ralph Otwell, who believes that journalists witnessing a crime in progress have a duty to report it, noted that the reporters who posed as operators of the tavern made daily reports to the Illinois Department of Law Enforcement. Their memos "summarized their encounters with various inspectors in cases where the inspectors were soliciting bribes."[17] The principal reporter on that undercover project, Pamela Zekman, who later moved to WBBM-TV, Chicago, said the agency "understood that they were not to make arrests while our investigation was still going on, because if you arrest the first inspector in a chain of inspectors, that's the end of the project."[18] The department started making arrests when the investigation was finished but before the *Sun-Times* published its report. Otwell emphasized that the paper would not have collaborated with law enforcement "if there had not been an actual crime being or about to be committed" because "we don't want to be perceived of as an arm of law enforcement."

Many newspapers and television stations oppose giving police prints or videotapes of any pictures unless they have been published or broadcast. But Michael J. O'Neill, former editor of the *New York Daily News,* believes that "if we have a photo that will help the cops solve a murder case and we accidentally didn't run it, there's no crime in giving it to them. We are citizens, too."[19] And when he was president of NBC News, William J. Small said, "The FBI asked for our outtakes to see if John W. Hinckley Jr., [charged at that time with trying to assassinate President Reagan] had been at any Carter or Reagan rallies. We culled through our tape files and put the pertinent ones on the air."[20]

COVERING COURTS

The press and the bar have long disagreed about whether media coverage of crime and the legal process does or does not get in the way of justice. At the extremes of the argument are the journalists who want absolute freedom to cover crime the way they see it even if that stirs up the populace, and the lawyers who seek a pure justice through a process that is conducted in a vacuum immune from the stones and shouts from the street. Numerous press-bar discussions have not settled the disagreement but seem at least to have given both journalists and lawyers a better understanding of their differing approaches to news versus evidence, charges versus convictions, justice versus advocacy, and a free press versus a fair trial.

Ethical issues are raised by the way the news media cover crime and courts: Should reporters play cop and investigate crimes on their own? Should the media report confessions or prior police records of accused persons when those matters may not always be used as evidence in a trial? Should reporters interview and report statements of people who are apt to be witnesses in the trial? Should the media so emphasize certain very interesting cases that community opinion is aroused against a defendant, making it more difficult to draft an impartial jury? Should reporters interview jurors? Should the news media allow trial lawyers to try their cases in the news columns and newscasts, to use publicity to affect the outcome in their favor?

There is a community and public interest in reporting crime, of course. Journalists have an obligation to watch the criminal justice system — from arrests to sentencing — in the same way they are supposed to watch the other branches of government. The public is well served when diligent news reporting assures against secret arrests and trials, both contrary to an open and civilized society.

But what bothers many people is the way some segments of the news business publish or broadcast material that seems to jeopardize the Sixth Amendment rights of the accused to a fair trial. Lawyers for news organizations argue that the courts have remedies when they think publicity may get in the way of a fair trial: Trials can be delayed until the impact of publicity has diminished; juries can be sequestered; trials can be moved to other jurisdictions; or juries can be brought in from other places. News media representatives also question whether pretrial publicity has the power to prejudice a jury.

A case that raised the issue of whether publicity affects trials was the John DeLorean trial in Los Angeles. Just as the jury was about to be selected to hear drug conspiracy charges against the auto maker, CBS

News and its Los Angeles affiliate, KNXT-TV, aired videotapes taken by the FBI during a sting operation. Among other things, the tapes showed DeLorean beside a suitcase supposedly loaded with cocaine as he toasted a $24 million drug deal with champagne. With him were the other men allegedly in the deal with him who were actually undercover agents. The tapes were slipped to CBS and KNXT by Larry Flynt, publisher of *Hustler* magazine, who claimed he had bought them from an unnamed government official. Hearing that the broadcasters had the tapes, the trial judge, Federal District Court Judge Robert M. Takasugi, asked CBS and KNXT to hold the tapes for a week "in view of an individual's right to a fair trial." When the broadcasters replied that the tapes were too newsworthy to keep off the air, Judge Takasugi ordered them not to use the tapes. A day later, the Ninth Circuit Court of Appeals overturned his decision, calling it an unacceptable prior restraint of the press. The tapes went on the air that evening. Judge Takasugi put off the trial until the next term of court and the next round of jury selection.[21]

Despite the outrageous airing of evidence before it was introduced in court, DeLorean was acquitted in September 1984 by a jury that had been sequestered during his four-month trial. Eight of the twelve jurors answered reporters' questions as a group after the lengthy trial and explained that they felt DeLorean had been entrapped by the FBI.

BEHIND CLOSED DOORS

"Every government has an interest in concealment; every public, in greater access to information," Sissela Bok wrote. "In this perennial conflict, the risks of secrecy affect even those administrators least disposed at the outset to exploit it. How many leaders have not come into office determined to work for more open government, only to end by fretting over leaks, seeking new, safer ways to classify documents, questioning the loyalty of outspoken subordinates."[22]

The drive for secrecy leads government officials who are otherwise honest and open people to resort to deceptions, half-truths and lies. Often they justify their concealments in the name of national security. The revelation of some government secrets obviously would jeopardize the nation's security, but recent history has taught us that our leaders also invoke national security improperly to cover up embarrassing mistakes, administrative incompetence, and plans they don't want the public to know about for strategic reasons.

This systematic lack of candor in government at all levels tests American journalists every day. When they occasionally pierce the shield of government concealment — as Bob Woodward and Carl Bernstein did in uncovering Watergate — the test then becomes one of deciding whether the secrets uncovered would harm the nation if published. Journalists lean toward revealing government secrets when they can find them — they see that as their duty extending from the First Amendment — but they have often restrained themselves when the possible harm has been obvious. That was the case after the Iranian militants seized the American embassy in Tehran and captured several hostages in 1979. American reporters and news media were aware for weeks that six members of the embassy staff escaped being taken hostage and were hidden in the Canadian embassy. The story was suppressed until the Canadians succeeded in smuggling the six Americans out of Iran.

One way that journalists learn things government officials try to keep quiet is through "leaks" of information from other government officials. (News leaks are discussed more fully in Chapter 6.) Howard Simons, former managing editor of *The Washington Post,* said it's impossible for journalists in Washington to do their daily jobs "without bumping into a secret." He noted that about four million bureaucrats have access to classified information and estimated that 20 million government documents are classified as secret each year. "It is a constant wonder how any of" those dealing with secret information "can remember what is secret and what is not secret," Simons said. He recalls the meeting that *Post* lawyers had with a National Security Agency deputy in judge's chambers when the U.S. government was trying to get the courts to stop that newspaper from publishing the Pentagon Papers. The deputy brought along a top-secret document sealed in several envelopes in a double-locked briefcase, claiming that the document was also contained in the Pentagon Papers, which if published would jeopardize American lives in Vietnam. Ordered to open up the secret, the deputy revealed an intercept from a North Vietnamese radio transmitter, a verbatim quote from a message to their armed forces. Publishing that quote would tell the enemy that we had tapped this valuable source of information, which they could then seal, the deputy contended. Fortunately for the *Post,* the lawyers had brought along George Wilson, respected Pentagon reporter for the paper, who remembered that the quote had been read before an open hearing of the Senate Foreign Relations Committee. And Wilson had the committee transcript with him so that he could point to the quote in the public record. As Simons added in telling this story, "That clinched that for the *Post.*"[23]

The government, of course, failed in its attempt to keep the *Post, The New York Times,* and other papers from publishing the Pentagon Papers, which contained a detailed record of the origins and conduct of the Vietnam War. The papers "should never have been kept secret in the first place," Bok argued. "This information was owed to the people, at home and abroad, who were bearing the costs and the suffering of the war; keeping them in the dark about the reasons for fighting the war was an abuse of secrecy."[24]

SECRECY IN WAR

One of the important lessons the American military thought it learned from the Vietnam War was that the news media had to be controlled. The mostly friendly relationship that the press and the military experienced in World War II and Korea began to fade as the American military was drawn into the quagmire of a war in Indochina and reporters sent back truthful but often negative reports. According to Malcolm W. Browne of *The New York Times,* who spent eight years as a war correspondent in Vietnam, government officials and reporters in that war "settled into a more or less permanent state of confrontation" because of the increasingly "gloomy tone of reporting from Vietnam, which told of corruption, bungling and defeat."[25]

Since Vietnam, the military has tried to control and censor American war correspondents in their coverage of the Grenada, Panama and Persian Gulf expeditions. Many Americans appear to agree with imposing restrictions on reporting wartime military operations. At least the news media do not seem to get much public support when they complain publicly about losing their freedom to cover wars just as they cover everything else.

The new attitude of the military became obvious when American journalists were blocked from covering the U.S. invasion of the Caribbean island of Grenada in October 1983. It was the first time since the Civil War that the government had denied front-line access to journalists in military engagements. The secrecy of the Grenada operation began to fall apart when Caribbean radio stations and newspapers issued stories saying the United States was about to invade Grenada. When reporters asked about these stories on Oct. 24, White House press secretary Larry Speakes, after checking with a member of President Reagan's national security staff, labeled the stories "preposterous." The invasion took place the next day.

Within hours after President Reagan announced at a press conference that the landing had occurred, more than 400 American journalists had flown to Barbados, about 160 miles northeast of Grenada. With no help from the military and no arrangement for a pool of journalists to be taken to the invaded island to report to the other journalists in Barbados, some reporters and photographers rented boats or planes and tried to reach Grenada on their own. At least two boats and a plane were turned back by American ships and aircraft.

Two days after the invasion, the military agreed to fly a pool of 15 journalists to Grenada, but the pool was delayed in returning to Barbados. The reports based on what the pool had seen missed the big network newscasts that night. Somehow, though, the films taken by military camera crews made it back in time. This prompted *The Washington Post* to describe the invasion in an editorial as "the first official war in the history of the United States, produced, filmed, and reported by the Pentagon, under the sanctions of the President."

Another press pool was permitted on the island the third day after the landing, and on the fifth day the press was given unlimited access. By then, the president and the Pentagon had issued a lot of misinformation. The most serious misstatements related to the number of Cubans on Grenada and whether they were soldiers or construction workers. President Reagan at first said there was "a military force" of 400 to 600 Cubans on the island. Adm. Wesley L. McDonald made the situation even more alarming when he stated the next day that captured documents showed there were at least 1,100 Cubans there, all "well-trained professional soldiers." The Reagan administration claim that the Cubans were about to take over Grenada seemed valid. But it turned out that the number of Cubans on the island had been 784, according to the State

Department, and that only about 100 of them were soldiers. That figure seems to swing the validity pendulum back to Cuba's claim that the men were there to build an airport and help an ally.

Why did the Pentagon and the White House defy more than a century of military precedent and prevent nonmilitary observers from seeing the Grenada invasion? At first the Pentagon told reporters that secrecy was necessary to ensure military success and avoid the need for military leaders to be concerned with the safety of journalists. But the real reason seems to lie in a later statement by Secretary of State George Shultz: "These days, in the advocacy journalism that's been adopted, it seems as though the reporters are always against us and so they're always trying to screw things up," said Shultz. "And when you're trying to conduct a military operation, you don't need that."[26]

Protests from virtually all major news organizations and journalistic associations apparently pushed the Pentagon to agree to a press-pool arrangement for future Grenada-type military operations. When military aircraft bombed Libya in retaliation for terrorism in 1986, a pool of eight journalists was allowed aboard the USS *America,* an aircraft carrier from which some of the attacking planes were flown.[27]

In press-pool coverage, the pool journalists cover the story for the entire press corps by sharing their reports and photos. Very few journalists like press or media pools, but they thought that having at least some reporters and photographers present when military operations began was better than no coverage at all, as happened in Grenada for the first two days.

POOLS BECOME TOOLS

Unfortunately for journalism and the public, the media pools after that short-lived Libyan operation did not work well. When U.S. troops invaded Panama in late 1989, a pool of reporters and photographers was flown to Panama by the Pentagon but was then prevented from getting anywhere near the military action. The military said it had to protect the journalists. Instead of seeing the invasion by American troops, the journalists were led by their military handlers on tours of deposed dictator Manuel Noriega's various hideaways. The military handlers apparently hoped that pool reports of the cocaine, firearms, skin magazines and a Hitler portrait found in Noriega's lairs would help justify the purpose of the invasion, which was to oust the dictator, arrest him, and take him to the United States for indictment and trial on drug charges. The journalists rightly thought they were being used as propagandists.[28] The pool never got near the major story that came out about six months later—

that more than a dozen U.S. soldiers were killed or wounded by friendly fire.[29]

Pool reporting was similarly abused by the military in the 1991 Gulf War, the "worst-covered major U.S. conflict in this century," in the judgment of Stanley W. Cloud, Washington bureau chief of *Time* magazine and former Vietnam War correspondent. Not only did the Pentagon restrict coverage to rigidly controlled pools, but the pool reporters had to agree to submit their reports to military censors for "security review," Cloud noted. Looking back on the 1985 agreement between national news organizations and the Pentagon to create the national media pool, Cloud said its purpose was to "insure that a rotating group of reporters would be available to cover the initial stage of any U.S. military action." But because "journalists naively failed to insist on binding rules about how and when it would operate, the national media pool quickly became a tool for government control of the press."[30]

A few Gulf War correspondents like Chris Hedges of *The New York Times* broke out of sole reliance on pool reports and official military briefings. Hedges, who speaks Arabic, wrote about how he did it:

> For two months several colleagues and I bluffed our way through road-blocks, slept in Arab homes, and cajoled ourselves into (military) units. Eventually, following armored battalions in our jeeps through breached minefields to the outskirts of Kuwait City, we raced across the last stretch of open desert and into the capital before it was liberated. Our success was due in part to an understanding of many soldiers and officers of what the role of a free press is in a democracy. These men and women violated orders to allow us to do our job.[31]

And then there was Peter Arnett, who had won a Pulitzer Prize in Vietnam and was in Baghdad for CNN when the Gulf War broke out. He and his CNN crew showed us Baghdad under bombing by U.S. and allied warplanes, just as Harrison Salisbury of *The New York Times* had when he reported on the impact of U.S. bombing of Hanoi in the Vietnam War. The difference was that Salisbury's reports were uncensored, while Arnett and other correspondents later allowed to join him in Baghdad had to do their reporting under heavy Iraqi censorship.

Should American journalists have gone to the enemy's land and submitted their reporting to enemy censorship? Didn't they then become tools of the enemy? Those kinds of questions continue to be discussed. One justification journalists gave for being in Iraq during the fighting was that the Pentagon was so tightly controlling information that the truth was being abused by both sides. "The notion of American correspondents reciting reports approved by the enemy is uncomfortable, but noncoverage is not an attractive alternative," wrote Walter Goodman, television critic for *The New York Times*.[32] Others noted that the journalists were not required to transmit any Iraqi-written reports but had to submit their reports to censors.

If the Pentagon continues its control of the coverage of post–Gulf War military actions, it had better be prepared for more reporters like Chris Hedges and Peter Arnett. But there must be a better way of ensuring that the public is well-informed about U.S. military operations without risking lives. To give democratic judgment and decision making a chance to work, the public has to get more and better information than it did during the Grenada, Panama and Persian Gulf episodes. That's a responsibility of both the Pentagon and the press.

PACK JOURNALISM

Media pools have been suggested from time to time as a solution to the problems that arise when journalists gang up on big stories. So many reporters and photographers try to cover certain events that they get in one another's way and often become part of the story. As many as 15,000 cover the Democratic and Republican national conventions, for example. And it seems that every sports reporter in the land manages to get assigned to the Super Bowl every winter.

Pool coverage is sometimes dictated by government for non-military events — presidential trips, for example. But by and large, except in serious military operations, American journalists successfully resist efforts by government and others to restrict them to pool coverage. Journalists want their own front-row seats and want to be able to do their own stories based on the facts they have collected, even if that means having to stumble over one another in the process.

A pack of journalists seeking consensus.

If that's the case, then why do so many stories have the same spin, preach the same line? "Consensus journalism" is the reason, concluded David Shaw of the *Los Angeles Times* after analyzing why there is so little diversity and so much uniformity in news reports, particularly those originating from Washington, D.C.[33] That uniformity is the most serious consequence of consensus journalism, also known as "pack" or "herd" journalism.

After interviewing more than 60 journalists and public opinion specialists, Shaw uncovered at least the following explanations for journalists quickly arriving at a consensus interpretation of virtually all events they cover:

1. Journalists, particularly the 4,000 covering the national government in Washington, tend to use the same sources, the same experts. As we've noted in previous chapters, journalists come to depend on sources who sound authoritative and speak their spins in the kind of clear, short sound-bites TV producers love. The same sources get used over and over, often because they are available and cooperative.

2. TV news is playing a larger role in setting the agenda for what journalists regard as important news. The major print media such as *The New York Times, The Washington Post, The Wall Street Journal, Time, Newsweek* and the AP still influence the journalistic pack, but increasingly the quick judgments and interpretations of major TV news shows become the conventional wisdom for all of journalism on most events. But because TV is so fast getting the news out, even the brightest anchors and producers seldom have enough time to come up with the most accurate and truthful interpretations of major events. Yet their shoot-from-the-hip explanations quickly spread through the news-absorbing population. Very rarely do other journalists vary from those quickly formed interpretations, which then become the consensus view. All this might be acceptable if the consensus were always right, but it has not been, as historians frequently discover.

3. Journalists may like to think of themselves as iconoclasts and risk takers, but they aren't. They may have been in an earlier day, but most contemporary journalists are "more serious, more formal — both more corporate and more conformist," Shaw wrote. "Journalism is now a Profession, with codes of ethics, pension plans and newsrooms that look more like insurance offices than the cluttered city rooms of generations past. . . . [T]hose in the press are now more inclined toward responsibility than sensationalism, and with responsibility often come respectability and caution."[34] This decline in individuality causes most

journalists to play it safe and go with the consensus. "Conformity journalism," it might be called. These conforming journalists also share a similar education, background, economic status and views about the system, according to *Wall Street Journal* editor Norman Pearlstine.[35]

What's sad about pack journalism is that it works against diverse and varying explanations of what's going on in our communities and our society, which should be one of the great benefits of a free media system. So many of the best and highest-paid journalists are glued together on the same interpretation for everything they cover, and they cover mostly the same things. More nonconforming reporters, editors and producers are needed to break from the pack and take on that hastily formed journalistic consensus.

Are Journalists Biased?

One of the major problems in assessing how well American journalists are monitoring politics and government is the incessant criticism that journalists are biased. In the 1992 presidential campaign, for example, all three major candidates in one way or other complained that the media had treated them unfairly.

The public also sees bias in the news media. Opinion polls indicate that more than half the public believes that journalists favor one side or the other when reporting political and social issues.[36] People with college educations are more likely to see bias and less likely to believe that the news media have been doing a good job than the less well-educated.[37] Although occasionally people have attacked the press as a tool for big business, most who see bias believe the media are liberal and favor the Democrats. In that unusual 1992 presidential election, for example, more than half thought the media wanted Clinton to win the 1992 presidential election; only 17 percent thought journalists favored Bush.[38]

When asked whether the media in general were liberal or conservative, 41 percent of Americans said liberal, and only 19 percent said conservative. The rest were equally divided between "neither" and "don't know."[39] Even when given the choice "middle of the road," 31 percent said liberal, 28 percent middle of the road, and only 13 percent conservative.[40]

POLITICAL LEANINGS OF JOURNALISTS

Surveys have shown that those who complain that journalists aren't like the rest of Americans are right. By and large, journalists are not representative of the population. They're more likely to be white, male and college-educated. According to surveys, the religious background of journalists is about the same as the rest of the nation: about 60 percent Protestant, 27 percent Catholic and 2 percent Jewish.[41] But they are less likely to say they were strongly religious. About 42 percent of the journalists — but only 18 percent of the public — said they were "non-practicing."[42]

Journalists tend to be more liberal, or at least less conservative, than the general population on most political and social issues. A *Los Angeles Times* poll found that newspaper journalists were

- More likely to call themselves liberal (55 percent to 23 percent).
- Less likely to call themselves conservative (17 percent to 29 percent).
- More likely to favor abortion than the general public (82 percent to 51 percent).
- More likely to favor government help for people who are unable to support themselves (95 percent to 83 percent).
- More likely to support employee rights for homosexuals (89 percent to 57 percent).
- More likely to support affirmative action for blacks and other minorities (81 percent to 57 percent).
- More likely to support stricter handgun controls (78 percent to 50 percent).
- More likely to support government regulation of business (49 percent to 22 percent).
- Less likely to support prayer in public schools (25 percent to 74 percent).
- Less likely to favor the death penalty (47 percent to 75 percent).

The 1992 presidential campaign seemed to provide more ammunition for those who contend the press favors Democrats. A Times Mirror survey of 3,000 journalists during the campaign found that Bill Clinton got a "significantly higher favorability rating from the press" than President George Bush. The poll also found that Vice President Dan Quayle had an "unusually high unfavorability rating."[43] Another poll during the 1992 campaign found that 44 percent of the nation's journalists called themselves Democrats and only 16 percent said they were Republicans.[44]

Journalists working in the "media elite" — the network news departments and a handful of major newspapers — were even more liberal than the rest of the press. One study found that more than 80 percent of these big-time journalists regularly voted for Democrats, 90 percent of them were pro-choice on the abortion issue, and most of them had a definite anti-business bias. Other surveys found journalists at prestigious publications to be more liberal, but not to this degree.[45]

It seems clear that journalists are probably more liberal than the public they serve. But these findings alone do not prove that the news itself is slanted by reporters to suit their political leanings. A University of California sociologist suggests that "many reporters, inclined to be Democrats themselves, bend over backwards to avoid the appearance of being unfair to Republicans" and end up being more critical of Democrats.[46]

EDITORIAL PAGES TELL ANOTHER STORY

Since so many journalists seem politically liberal, one might expect newspaper editorial pages, traditionally the pages where opinion is supposed to be expressed, to advocate liberal positions, endorse liberal Democrats, and attack conservative Republicans. That is not the case.

On their editorial pages, newspapers have been strong supporters of conservative presidential candidates. The majority of newspaper endorsements preferred conservative Republican Ronald Reagan to middle-of-the-road Democrat Jimmy Carter in 1980, Reagan to liberal Democrat Mondale in 1984, and conservative Republican Bush to liberal Democrat Michael Dukakis in 1988. Conservative Republican Richard Nixon got more endorsements than any of his three liberal Democratic opponents, including John F. Kennedy.

The conservative leanings are so strong that since 1936, when records of such things were started, newspapers have endorsed 13 of the 15 Republican presidential candidates by overwhelming margins. For instance, in 1940 Republican Wendell Willkie won the endorsement race, 59 percent to Democrat Franklin Roosevelt's 19 percent, and in 1948 Republican Thomas Dewey was preferred to Democrat Harry Truman 79 percent to 10 percent.[47]

The only exceptions to this Republican landslide in newspaper endorsements were in 1964 when Democrat Lyndon Johnson edged Republican Barry Goldwater 440 endorsements to 359 and in 1992 when Democrat Bill Clinton got 183 endorsements to George Bush's 138. An overwhelming majority chose not to make an endorsement in that race, and a handful endorsed Ross Perot.[48]

If journalists are so liberal, why do newspapers endorse so many conservatives? The explanation for this seeming paradox is that most working journalists, liberal or otherwise, have little say in editorial policy of the newspapers they work for. These decisions are usually made by the top editor and an editorial board, and these editors tend to be more conservative than their reporters. In the *Times* poll, 35 percent of the editors said they were conservative, compared to 17 percent of the rest of the news staff. On many political and social issues, top editors were more like the general public than their news staffs.

Moreover, most of the top editors answer to general managers and publishers, who are often employed by large corporations to run the paper. At about 60 percent of the papers these executives play a direct role in the direction of the editorial pages, and often they are even more conservative than the editors. One survey found that 72 percent of the top editors at chain-owned papers and 68 percent at non-chain papers believed they were more liberal than their publishers or general managers.

That means that sometimes the top editors may not agree with the positions taken on their editorial pages. These editors said that nearly a fourth of the time they do not vote for the candidates their papers endorse. Sometimes the number of editors who disagree with their papers' endorsements is striking. For instance, 65 percent said their papers endorsed Reagan over Mondale, but only 35 percent of the editors said they voted for Reagan.[49]

Because editorials and particularly editorial endorsements of candidates are so rare as to be nonexistent in TV and radio news, comparisons of the editorial positions of print versus broadcast media would be meaningless.

DOES THE NEWS HAVE A LIBERAL SLANT?

One of the cornerstones of objectivity as it has developed in this century is the notion that opinions should be expressed only on the editorial pages. American readers tend to think that news and opinion should be separated and that reporters should keep their opinions out of their stories. But many do not believe journalists succeed in doing that. They don't seem to agree with journalists who contend that they can cover issues fairly without injecting their own views.

Trying to find a conclusive answer to the question of political bias in the media is difficult because journalists' decisions are often individual ones. There is no easy way to know what is going on in journalists' minds when they select information for the lead paragraph or decide which paragraph to trim from a story. Prejudices may be at work that even the journalists themselves are not aware of.

"I can't seem to write a good story with my jacket on."

Critics might say that all you have to do to determine if there is bias in the media is to read newspapers and watch some TV news. It's not that easy.

Sometimes people see bias where there is none. Longtime CBS newsman and commentator Eric Sevareid observed that there was plenty of "biased reading and hearing." By that he meant that many people see bias when the facts in a story do not jibe with the way they would like the world to be, especially if they are true believers in a cause or a candidate.

Los Angeles Times media reporter David Shaw saw this phenomenon when he reviewed two books critical of the media — one written from a liberal perspective and one conservative. He said that reading the books back-to-back "is a bit like listening to two people's accounts of a football game in which each rooted for the opposite side." One book saw liberal bias in the same news accounts where the other book saw conservative bias.[50]

Even people with similar political leanings can interpret the same information much differently. As researcher Michael Robinson has pointed out, some people said that Ronald Reagan won a landslide victory in 1984 despite hostile coverage by network TV. Others said that his campaign received a major boost from the TV networks because their "superficial, picture-oriented coverage fit perfectly with his masterful media management."[51]

Researchers have tried to develop methods of looking for bias that are as scientific as possible. So far, much of this scholarly research has failed to find consistent political bias in media coverage of presidential candidates. After intently studying three presidential campaigns, Robinson and his colleagues at George Washington University concluded:

> Ideological bias is one of those mistakes that the network news doesn't make. In the 1980 primaries CBS treated "liberal" Ted Kennedy worse than it treated "middle-of-the-roader" Jimmy Carter, and in the general-election campaign CBS treated Carter worse than Reagan.[52]

In the coverage of the Reagan-Mondale race they found that there were 10 times as many negative things about Reagan as positive and seven times as many negative things about him as negative things about Mondale. They pointed out, however, that the bulk of the news about the candidates was neither positive nor negative. They concluded that "overall the biased pieces were so few and the bias so weak in implication that real issue bias hardly existed at all."[53]

Robinson's study concentrated primarily on story content. Other researchers, like Doris Graber, have made efforts to include the impact TV's pictures and graphics might have on voters in the same election. She found that the words reporters spoke were more favorable to Mondale, but that a disproportionate share of Reagan's coverage dealt with traits favorable to him, like his personableness and good looks.[54]

Not everyone will agree with Graber's and Robinson's findings.[55] Robinson observed, "Can anyone other than a Democrat conclude that political reporting is unbiased against Republicans and conservatives? Perhaps not." But both researchers made one observation that many will agree with. They were surprised by the news media's emphasis on bad news about the candidates. Robinson concluded that "over the long haul the national press is biased against everybody, but in near equal proportions."[56]

THE TILT TOWARD BAD NEWS

Robinson's contention that the media are "biased against everybody" is a frequent criticism. Robinson saw so much negativity in newscasts that he described the news as a "cacophony of carping and criticism." His research found that bad-news messages outnumbered good ones 20 to one, although most of the news was neutral. In 100 days of watching all three network news broadcasts, his researchers found only 47 positive statements by correspondents.[57]

Some people believe that the larger problem with the news media is not political bias but a bias in favor of bad news. James Squires, the former *Chicago Tribune* editor who became Perot's press spokesman in the 1992 presidential campaign, said he believed the media attacked Perot not because reporters disagreed with his politics but because it was the best way to advance their careers. Squires argued that reporters are so intent on getting front-page stories that they stoop to "hit-and-run journalism." They know that reporting negative news about a candidate will get more play than reporting positive news. So journalists will report rumors and break promises to sources because "simply taking the story to a new level and creating controversy does more for a reporter's career today than the more mundane truth ever could."

Squires is no Johnny-come-lately critic of journalists' preference for bad news. When he was editor of the *Chicago Tribune,* he criticized young reporters at Chicago's city magazines: "They go out of their way to bash the big institutions. . . . They're not going to attract any attention if they have a very positive kind of story." He explained:

> If you go to *Chicago* magazine and say, "Boy, the *Tribune* sure has changed in the last seven years; it's a great newspaper now," there's not any interest. If you go to them and you say, "You know, I hear there's great conflict of interest in the editor's office at the *Tribune* and he had a temper tantrum the other day and wet on his desk," then they say, "Jesus Christ, that's a great story; let's get that."[58]

Other journalists have come to the same conclusion. Reluctantly, they have agreed with Spiro Agnew, Richard Nixon's vice president until he had to resign amid a bribery scandal, who once described reporters as "nattering nabobs of negativism."

Many people mistake this negativism for bias because they just do not understand the "dynamics of the journalistic process," according to the *Los Angeles Times'* Shaw: "They don't understand that good news isn't news, for example, or that the bias most reporters have is not political but journalistic: They are biased in favor of a good story, a juicy, controversial story that will land them on Page 1 or on the network evening news." Shaw acknowledged that reporters may get more pleasure from writing negative stories about candidates they don't like. "But almost every reporter I've ever known would rather break a really juicy story exposing the wrongdoing of a politician he agrees with than do a routine story making that same politician look good. Does that make us ghouls? Nattering nabobs of negativism? Yes. Is that good? Probably not. But it sure as hell doesn't make us ideologues or cheerleaders for the left."[59]

Syndicated columnist Richard Cohen said it more pointedly: "Liberal or conservative, a reporter is a primitive being who would go after his own mother if he thought that was a good story."[60]

These "primitive" instincts may explain the coverage of George Bush's re-election campaign in 1992. Many people, including several journalists, believe Bush was treated more negatively than Bill Clinton. Even *The New York Times* headlined a post-election article "Maybe the Media DID Treat Bush a Bit Harshly." But Everette Dennis, director of a foundation that studies the media, wonders if Bush's treatment may have been the result of reporters' willingness "to go for the jugular when any candidate is trailing." He noted that the press savaged liberal Democrat Mike Dukakis' inept campaign in 1988 when he ran against Bush."[61]

Time magazine made a similar observation:

> Some of the toughest stories about Clinton have emerged from the liberal *New York Times* and *Los Angeles Times.* Bush's two most ferocious critics, syndicated columnists William Safire of *The New York Times* and George Will of *The Washington Post,* are staunch members of his own party. That summarizes the deepest objection most politicians have to journalists—not that they are liberal, nor that they are conservative, but that they are stubbornly individualistic and persistent.[62]

While the *Time* writer presents journalists' leanings toward negativity in almost heroic terms, polls show that the public doesn't like the media's emphasis on bad news. Two-thirds in one survey complained that the media were too negative.[63]

THE NEW DEMANDS ON REPORTERS

When reporters followed the theory of strict objectivity, the opportunities to inject bias in their stories were relatively few. They saw their role in almost mechanical terms. They were to pass along the information just as it was given to them.

But for reasons that were outlined in Chapter 1, many reporters began to believe that journalists should not be just "fancy stenographers," as Geneva Overholser, editor of *The Des Moines Register,* put it. They began to believe that their job was to provide background, to present a wide range of opinions, and to explain the significance of the news. Journalism professors taught their students to provide "point of view" in their stories and "voice" in their writing styles. Editors said they wanted reporters to "write with authority." Readers, too, have indicated that they want journalists to write more about the issues and to give them more analysis.

In doing this, journalists are walking a tightrope. They want to use their knowledge and experience as reporters to make their stories more complete and more truthful. But they run the risk of appearing biased. They want to provide analysis based on the insights they have gained by spending weeks or months covering a story, but they want to avoid the appearance of giving their work a purely partisan slant. Readers "tell us they want analysis, background, interpretation, and when we do that and it's not entirely keeping with their view of the world, they say we're biased," *St. Petersburg Times* political editor Ellen Debenport told *Washington Journalism Review.*[64]

What's an Ethical Journalist to Do?

The relationship between journalism and government in the American system was probably never meant to be peaceful. A degree of tension is inevitable when journalists and government officials try to outfox one another to do their important but often conflicting jobs.

Journalists need to keep their perspective and prevent this built-in tension from coloring their attitudes toward people in government, most of whom are honest and reasonably competent. Americans who view government officials only as bumbling bureaucrats skilled solely in corruption and graft have undoubtedly been influenced by what they have read, seen and heard in the media. There have been bumblers and grafters in government service, just as in law, entertainment and journalism. But journalists who see corruption under every government desk are apt to report government news from that point of view. Their reporting risks becoming a journalism of cynicism that does little to protect the people from the real and potential abuses of government, which is what the press-as-watchdog ideology is all about.

Journalists must scrutinize government with a skeptical eye, but they must be careful not to become so cynical, hard-nosed and narrowly focused that they turn every bonfire into a four-alarmer. That "Big Exposé" of trouble in the Clinton White House travel agency was a good example of much ado about very little. Washington reporters, particularly those covering the White House, got all stirred up about it, but the public seemed to see it as a very small matter that got too much attention in the media.

Richard Harwood, former ombudsman and editor of *The Washington Post,* used the word "travelgate" to describe the exaggerated coverage of the sacking, then the reinstating of the people who staff the travel office:

> [I]t revealed rather clearly how the personal interests of reporters can color their assessment of the news. The travel office was their personal fiefdom. It exists to provide the first-class comforts and VIP treatment they demand on travels with the President at home and abroad. Messing with the travel staff was equivalent to messing with their rice bowls. Enraged, they created a firestorm of negative publicity. After *The Washington Post* published 11 stories, three editorials and several columns on the affair in 19 days, Travelgate was described in a news story by *Post* White House correspondents as "relatively trivial."[65]

White House reporters, as well as those covering the smallest police department, must also be careful when government officials, as they too often do, ask them to hold or suppress certain information. If lives are at stake, as they were when officials asked news organizations to delay reporting the six Americans hidden in the Canadian embassy in Tehran, journalists can justifiably cooperate with authorities. But delaying a story to save lives was an easy call, unlike the Hattiesburg case that opened this chapter. The reasons the authorities in Hattiesburg gave for seeking the cooperation of local news executives may also have seemed valid, but they asked too much. What they sought was not a mere delay in getting some legitimate story to the public; they wanted the local newspaper and TV station to help them pull off a questionable hoax, to join them in a lie. It may be OK for cops to lie and set deceptive traps to catch criminals (although many disapprove of such techniques), but journalists should report police sting operations, not join them. Knowingly lying to the public destroys the basic trust that people must have in journalism if it is to do its essential job in a democratic society.

What journalists should do when government officials deliberately lie to them is difficult to say. Out-and-out lying, of course, is rare. What we see more often are half-truths, false leaks, and attempts by government public relations specialists to control what events journalists will pay attention to each day and what kind of "spin" their reports will get. It's a kind of game. Journalists understandably work hard to expose these manipulative efforts by government officials, but that often means shunting their larger responsibility to inform the public about how and what their government is doing. As Dean Kathleen Hall Jamieson of the University of Pennsylvania School of Communication sees it, "When everything the president does is covered as 'how is he doing?' rather than 'what does it mean?' you lose your ability to evaluate governance."[66]

Government officials deserve to be condemned for using disinformation techniques, trying to fool the people by fooling the press. The government has a right to get its story told, but by legitimate and truthful means, not by lies, half-truths and manipulative leaks.

Government secrecy in wartime is commonly accepted and supported in this country, despite the Pentagon Papers and other post-war revelations of how the government and the military have abused secrecy in the name of national defense. In general, journalists have a good record of cooperation with the military in war situations when lives are at stake. The exceptional cases where some reporter or news organization has put lives of soldiers and civilians at risk by irresponsible reporting have been as severely criticized by the profession as by the public. But since the Vietnam War, for reasons discussed earlier in this chapter, trust between journalists and the military has broken down. Both sides need to work on this problem.

Journalists who claim that they are without bias are kidding themselves. No one is without bias, if we mean by "bias" the way each of us looks at the world and not merely prejudice, prejudging individuals or groups, usually without knowledge. We may be able to eliminate prejudice in ourselves — many people do — but bias is with us to stay. Journalists who want to be respected must understand themselves, understand their own biases, and adjust their reporting and editing accordingly.

Frankly, bias among journalists is not the great problem that some critics would have us believe. Even though most journalists tend toward liberal positions on social and political issues, they usually keep their biases under control. For example, most critics thought the press would go soft on the Clinton presidency since most reporters are Democrats and Clinton was the first Democratic president in 12 years. But the Clinton honeymoon with the press after he took office was so short as to be unnoticeable. Advocacy, good stories, proof that watchdogging is still our main game — all turned out to be more important to the Washington press corps than their personal politics. They may have voted for Clinton, but they showed him no mercy (less, most observers thought, than the two preceding Republican presidents). What that says is that bias in government coverage is a minor problem in the context of the exaggeration and alarmism by reporters playing the advocacy game — and God help any president or White House flak who gets in the way.

Some scholars scoff at the notion that the press is a watchdog of government and other orders in American life. They see the press as part of the system, not an independent critic of it. Its dependence on advertising for financial survival, it is argued, makes the press an extension of the industrial order. Likewise, many Americans outside academe often seem unappreciative of journalism's role in a democratic society, particularly when the press goes after one of their political favorites. But some great things have been accomplished in American journalism in the name of that watchdog. Despite its financial moorings, journalism has not only uncovered large and small abuses of governmental power but has been about the only check we have in modern times on the increasingly efficient secrecy of government at all levels.

Although journalists can justifiably pat themselves on the back for being a check on government secrecy, they still need to work harder at explaining the substance of government to the public and restoring mutual trust between themselves and our public servants. That might help to bring about a greater and much needed trust in both journalism and government by the public.

Deception

Imagine that you are executive editor of a metropolitan daily newspaper.

A veteran reporter on your staff has been doing an exhaustive study of the prison system in the United States. He has spent months investigating American prisons and jails, inspecting dozens of them and interviewing scores of prisoners and experts. But he does not believe he could truly describe the psychological effect of being inside just from talking to prisoners. He wants to pass himself off as a criminal and spend a few days in a big state penitentiary to find out what it's like inside. This means that he will have to deceive some people because if the warden knows who he is, he will get special treatment, and if the other inmates know who he is, his life may not be worth a plugged nickel. But the reporter believes he can arrange to get himself incarcerated without the people at the prison knowing he is really a journalist.

Do you approve of your reporter posing as a criminal for a few days, assuming that his security can be ensured? Are you concerned that he will not be able to identify himself as a reporter? Does it bother you that the people he will talk with will assume they are having private conversations with a fellow inmate when they are really being interviewed for a newspaper story? Is all the deception needed to pull off his scheme going to add that much to his story?

Those are the kinds of problems that confronted the editors of *The*

Washington Post in 1971 when Ben H. Bagdikian wanted to get inside the Huntingdon State Correctional Institution in Pennsylvania as an inmate. His editor decided to allow him to do it. Bagdikian made arrangements through the state attorney general's office and assumed a false identification, a false name and a false history. The warden and Bagdikian's fellow inmates did not learn his true identity until five weeks after his release when he described his experiences inside Huntingdon in the second of an eight-part series called "The Shame of the Prisons."[1]

When Bagdikian ran into the warden at a conference on prisons some months after his article was published, the warden accused him "of unethical behavior, of coming into his prison under false pretenses." Bagdikian tried to explain, but the warden was too angry. "No warden or administrator likes to think he was spied upon for public use," Bagdikian said.[2]

Ironically, the editor who approved Bagdikian's posing as a convict began to reconsider his paper's use of deception and came to a conclusion much like the warden's. He no longer thought he could justify using "false pretenses" to get a story. Bagdikian's editor was Benjamin C. Bradlee, who played a key role in the *Post*'s Watergate probe that uncovered the deceptions of high-ranking officials during the administration of President Richard Nixon. Bradlee began to believe that if the news media were going to criticize other people for lying and using dirty tricks, reporters should not lie and trick people either.[3] Bradlee's change of heart coincided with the growing belief among newspaper journalists that honest reporting rarely needed to begin with dishonesty.

But as newspapers began a full-scale retreat from the use of deception in the 1980s, TV news began to adopt it with gusto. The ethics of deception can still stir heated debate among serious-minded journalists.

The Three Faces of Deception

What Bagdikian did in passing himself off as an inmate to report on prison life from inside is often called "undercover" reporting. That term creates an exciting picture in most people's minds of reporters disguising themselves as police sometimes do. In fact, most of the undercover techniques journalists have used came from police investigations.

Undercover reporting always involves some degree of misrepresentation by journalists to their sources. Even when journalists merely pose as members of the public, their motive is still to get a story, which sets them apart from other members of the public and results in their misrepresenting who they really are.

Nevertheless, students of journalistic deception, and that includes many journalists, talk about three types of activities:

1. So-called active deception, in which reporters stage events so they can expose wrongdoing.
2. Misrepresentation or masquerading, in which reporters pass themselves off as persons other than reporters.
3. So-called passive deception, in which reporters allow themselves to be taken as members of the public so they can observe people without their knowing a reporter is present.

ACTIVE DECEPTION

Interviewing people who have been victimized is not enough documentation for some journalists, nor are they willing to wait patiently in the shadows hoping to observe wrongdoing. They believe they must take an active role in arranging events so they can uncover wrongdoers and get the most accurate and complete story.

For example, producers from CBS's *60 Minutes* had heard that owners of clinics were receiving illegal kickbacks from the laboratories that processed their medical tests. The practice was costing Medicare and Medicaid programs millions of dollars a year and was growing. After a citizens-action group, called the Better Government Association, told *60 Minutes* that the scheme was widespread in Chicago, *60 Minutes* rented office space there and announced that a new clinic would open soon. Members of the citizens group posed as staff while a camera crew hid behind one-way mirrors. Soon a salesman from a laboratory came in and offered to pay kickbacks. After hearing the offer, *60 Minutes* reporters popped out of a back room and confronted the salesman. He told them kickbacks "were a way of life in inner-city Chicago."[4]

An even more dramatic example of active deception was carried off by the *Wilmington (N.C.) Morning Star.* In 1983 America was mourning the loss of 241 Marines who were killed when terrorists drove a truck loaded with explosives up to a U.S. Marine barracks in Beirut and set off the bombs. Reporters at the *Morning Star* wondered if terrorists could do the same thing at nearby Camp Lejeune. They decided to find out by staging their own terrorist assault. One team of reporters drove trucks filled with boxes that could have contained explosives into the base; another team entered the base by boat. Once inside, they roamed the base taking pictures of their trucks outside buildings they thought terrorists would probably target, like barracks and communication offices. A couple of reporters were even able to get inside base headquarters and the base commander's house simply by asking to use the rest room. They left notes pointing out that if they had been terrorists, they could have planted bombs in those buildings.

The Marines later said that they knew in advance that the reporters were coming and used their assault to practice counter-terrorist drills. But after the raid, security was tightened, and the base's two top officers were soon reassigned, according to the paper.[5]

PASSIVE DECEPTION

No staging of sting operations is required for passive deception. Reporters simply do not identify themselves as reporters. They let others assume they are members of the public, part of the crowd. Perhaps the most benign use of this kind of deception is restaurant critics failing to inform their waiters that they are dealing with a journalist or reporters doing consumer stories posing as customers to check the honesty of repair shops and other businesses.

A more elaborate example of passive deception was provided by Neil Henry, a reporter from *The Washington Post* who was working on a story in 1983 about the exploitation of jobless and often homeless men in Washington. He learned they were recruited for jobs picking vegetables in the South with promises of good pay and good living conditions. But what they encountered after they were hauled to the fields was back-breaking work, filthy bunkhouses and overpriced meals of pig ears. Sometimes after a day's work they had earned only enough to pay for their meals and a night in the bunkhouse.

Wanting to get a firsthand taste of this treatment, Henry decided to hang around soup kitchens in Washington. As he had expected, one day a recruiter asked him if he wanted a job. The reporter answered all the recruiter's questions honestly—he used his real name and Social Security number—and said he was willing to work. He did not volunteer that he was a reporter, although he carried his press card. After working in the fields but before writing his story, he returned to the farm as a *Post* reporter and interviewed the operator of the camp, the man who had recruited him, and others who knew about the legal and illegal harvesting of crops in that part of the world.[6] Henry contended that to understand "this particular subculture," he had "to become, as nearly as possible, one of these people, to suffer as they do, to yearn as they do. The only way to really get the story was to become part of the story."[7]

Many journalists do not condone the active deception used by reporters in the invasion of Camp Lejeune but are more likely to approve of Henry's conduct. When he was editor of the *Chicago Tribune,* James Squires acknowledged that passive deception can be as "deceptive as lying." But "I'm more comfortable if I can be deceptive by silence and not deliberately lie and mispresent myself."[8] Rules at *The Washington Post* no longer allow a reporter to pose as a prison inmate, but they are less clear on the passive deception Henry used.

MISREPRESENTATION

Tales are often told about Harry Romanoff of the old *Chicago American* who would pose as a police officer, a coroner or even a governor to get a story.[9] He once got the mother of mass murderer Richard Speck to talk to him by telling her he was her son's attorney.[10] Romanoff died in 1970, but his techniques have lived on.

Many older journalists have known reporters who made calls from the press room in police headquarters and introduced themselves this way: "Hi, I'm Mike Jones. I'm calling from police headquarters." The ploy often worked; people assumed they were talking to a police official.

This kind of misrepresentation was taken a step further by Bob Greene, who had an illustrious career as an investigative journalist for *Newsday* and helped form Investigative Reporters and Editors. According to a *Quill* article, Greene was having no luck getting information about a man in France for a story about heroin trafficking in 1974, so Greene called the man's wife and told her he was an attorney and that her husband had been left $8,000 in a will. But before the woman could collect, Greene would need some information so he would feel sure he had found the right family. To complete the masquerade, Greene had phony business cards printed, wrote a seven-page will, and had another reporter play the role of his secretary. Greene's ploy was so convincing that the man's wife not only provided Greene the information he wanted but gave him a picture of her husband.[11]

Other journalists have used equally successful disguises. When Lester Piggott, the great English jockey, was riding in a race in Florida in 1992, his horse fell, throwing him to the ground and shattering several bones. Although hospital employees had been told to keep visitors away from the jockey because he needed rest, they allowed a priest, a mortician and a laboratory technician to enter his room. But they weren't the people they appeared to be. They were reporters for British tabloids wanting to get pictures of the jockey and maybe even a quote or two.[12]

A few American journalists have posed as hospital employees to eavesdrop on conversations they were not supposed to hear. When

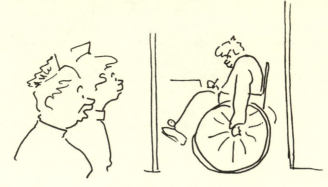

*"Pretend you don't notice him — but make
sure he knows how to spell your name right."*

Eugene Roberts, former editor of *The Philadelphia Inquirer,* was covering a murder case as a reporter for the Raleigh *News & Observer,* he
picked up a stethoscope in a hospital and walked nonchalantly into the
emergency room where police were questioning a suspect. No one
stopped him as he went into the interrogation room and heard the suspect confess to police. Years after the trick, Roberts still believed he was
justified. "I didn't lie to anyone," Roberts said. "We're not obligated to
wear a neon sign."[13]

But some reporters believe that it is important to tell people who
you are, even to the point of wearing signs. David Halberstam, who won
a Pulitzer Prize for his reporting from Vietnam for *The New York
Times,* said that when he was in Vietnam, he and Horst Faas of the AP
"got these little tags that we sewed on our fatigue jackets that said
'Halberstam, New York Times' and 'Faas, AP.' Most of the reporters
began to do this. We didn't want anyone to speak to us with any misim-
pression of who we were."[14]

Surveys indicate that most journalists today would agree with
Halberstam. Seventy percent of those polled said claiming to be someone else could never be justified. Almost the same percentage of the
public has told pollsters they feel the same way.[15] However, the majority
of journalists were more willing to accept reporters taking jobs with
organizations to see what happens from the inside,[16] although only
about 30 percent of the public believe that reporters should pose as
people they aren't.[17]

INSIDER REPORTING BOOMERANGS

Editors at *The Wall Street Journal* at one time allowed their reporters to engage in misrepresentations, but they found that often the

undercover reports created unwanted problems. The *Journal* once allowed reporter Beth Nissen to get a job in a Texas Instruments plant to see how that company tried to keep its workers from forming a labor union. The reporter deliberately talked about the union to her fellow employees, which caused many to shun her. After three weeks, TI fired her when it discovered she had lied on her application. The article she wrote reported that security was tight and heavy anti-union pitches were part of the orientation program for new employees, that working conditions were pleasant, but that pay and benefits were only average.

Before the story appeared, corporate officials learned what she was up to. They complained to top management at the *Journal* and threatened to sue the paper for trespassing. The paper reported in the fourth paragraph of the story that the company "strenuously objected to the way in which the story was obtained." The paper was more heavily criticized after the story was printed and received lots of letters "expressing a deep sense of outrage that we had given ourselves the right to do something nobody else could do," said Lawrence O'Donnell, then the paper's associate editor. *Journal* editors were also concerned about the TI employees who had talked to Nissen thinking she was just another new employee. The paper was stung by criticism that when Nissen openly talked to fellow employees about unions, she may have jeopardized their jobs. "People don't know who you really are when they bare their souls to you, and then you smear them by invading their privacy," O'Donnell said.[18]

Much as the *Journal* tried to use undercover reporters to find out what was going on in non-union factories, many papers have sent young reporters into the public high schools as "undercover students." But some of these investigations have raised more questions about the reporters' ethics than about the quality of the public schools. Many editors now place stringent controls on such projects if they choose to do them.

The Albuquerque Tribune in 1983 allowed one of its young-looking reporters to enroll in an Albuquerque high school, claiming her family had just moved to town. Not only did she lie to school officials and students about who she was, but to avoid getting caught, she had to impersonate a school official. She realized that the Albuquerque high school would request a transcript from her old school, which they did, so she called her old school and, posing as a school official, told them to disregard Albuquerque's request for a transcript because it was a bureaucratic mistake. After spending 11 days as a student, she wrote a series of articles that criticized the competence of the school's teachers, reported illegal drug and alcohol abuse by students, and claimed that there was a general lack of interest in education at the school.

"Students, teachers, parents and school administrators reacted with shock and anger, not to the meat of the articles but to the ethics of the method," the reporter later confessed. "They felt violated, intruded upon and tricked into trusting an individual who lied for no good purpose." The reporter believed her conduct was justified because it was the only way she could get the trust of high school students. Her editors, however, decided against using the method again "because of the obvious questions about their credibility and fairness."[19] Many wondered if someone fresh out of journalism school knew enough about teaching high school to make valid criticisms about the teachers.

Four years later, *Milwaukee Journal* editors decided to do their version of that story. But they required their reporter first to get the permission of school officials, who then told high school administrators and teachers a reporter was going to pose as a student. The reporter limited her story to the attitudes of students, but she said she did not ask students leading questions. "I never tried to steer the conversation to drugs, for example, or liquor or sex," the reporter explained. "When those subjects came up, they came up naturally. I played a passive role and observed whatever I could." Ruth Wilson, the paper's ombudsman, defended the *Journal*'s actions. She said the stories let readers get an inside look at what high school life was like. "I suspect that look reassured many readers that high school today isn't very different from what it was in their day," she wrote.[20]

San Francisco Chronicle editors decided to put even more controls in place before they allowed a reporter to pose as a student in 1992. Not only was she required to get permission from school officials, but she had to check with every student and teacher mentioned in her stories and delete anyone who did not want to be included.[21]

From Nellie Bly to Diane Sawyer

For nearly 100 years journalists used variations of the three kinds of deception and rarely gave the ethics of them a second thought. When Bagdikian asked Bradlee if he could pose as a prisoner, Bradlee's "chief concern was security not the ethics of it," Bagdikian said.[22]

Undercover reporting goes back at least to the 1890s when Nellie Bly (her real name was Elizabeth Cochrane) pretended to be insane to find out how patients were treated in the Blackwell's Island Insane Asylum. Her three articles for the old *New York World* were headlined "Ten Days in a Madhouse."[23]

The heyday for undercover newspaper reporting was in the 1930s, perhaps because most cities had two or more papers battling for dwindling depression dollars. Nellie Bly's inside report on a mental institution was repeated by the old *Chicago Times* in 1933 when one of its reporters posed as mentally ill so that he could be voluntarily committed to the state mental hospital at Kankakee, Ill., by another reporter posing as his brother. When the reporter was released to his "brother" a week later, he wrote about the dreadful conditions he had seen inside. His article was headlined "Seven Days in a Madhouse." Silas Bent, writing about his undercover report, said it caused the *Times'* circulation to go up considerably "but that was of minor importance in comparison with a drastic cleanup of the institution."[24]

When journalism historian Frank Luther Mott started publishing collections of the best news stories each year, undercover reports were a mainstay. The best news stories of 1934, for example, contained an exposé of the Drake estate swindlers by a *Milwaukee Journal* reporter who pretended to be a prospective investor and a story by an *Omaha World-Herald* reporter who posed as a transient and spent a night in a shelter for homeless men.[25]

Undercover reporting by newspapers continued into the 1960s and 1970s. Even Nellie Bly's madhouse story had a copier in 1975. Annapolis *Capital* reporter Doug Struck conned his way into the Crownsville (Md.) Hospital Center, a mental institution, and wrote about the jail-like conditions he found during his six days as a patient there.[26] Pulitzer Prizes were given to Edgar May of *The Buffalo News* for stories he wrote after he posed as a social worker in 1961 and to William Jones of the *Chicago Tribune,* who took a job as an ambulance driver for a story about collusion between police and ambulance companies in 1971. The *Tribune* also won Pulitzers for stories by reporters who posed as election judges to uncover vote fraud in 1973 and worked in hospitals to document patient abuses in 1976. The *New York Daily News* got a Pulitzer in 1974 after a reporter and photographer posed as Medicaid patients with the knowledge of New York Medicaid officials and exposed doctors who were cheating the system.

MIRAGE CAUSES TURNAROUND

To find out about reported shakedowns of small businesses by government inspectors in Chicago, the *Chicago Sun-Times* went into the tavern business. Reporters Pamela Zekman and Zay N. Smith posed as a couple from out of town and bought a tavern they called the Mirage. With help from Chicago's private muckraking Better Government Association, Zekman and Smith rigged the tavern with obvious plumbing and electrical problems. They also built little hideaways where photographers could snap pictures as dozens of electrical and building inspectors solicited bribes to overlook the deficiencies. Zekman and Smith allowed state officials to set up a special auditing team to uncover tax fraud by accountants who offered to do the tavern's books.

"Let's make sure I understand: All I have to do to get you to stop ticketing my customers is slip you a hundred dollars a month and all the beer you can drink."

The *Sun-Times* exposé rocked Chicago with four weeks of exciting, dramatic stories and pictures. Scores of electrical and building inspectors were indicted on charges of soliciting bribes. Ralph Otwell, then editor of the *Sun-Times,* called the series the most successful undercover investigation the paper had done for 40 years. "It reached the most people in a way that they related to what we learned," Otwell said, "and it documented something that had always been a truism in Chicago but yet had never been documented by anybody to the extent that we did it."[27] Journalism schools sought Zekman and Smith as guest speakers.

Although the series attracted a lot of attention around the nation, it did not attract another Pulitzer Prize to the *Sun-Times'* display case.

Why no Pulitzer for such an enterprising piece of reporting? Like *The Washington Post's* Bradlee, many editors were growing concerned about the ethics of deception. Eugene C. Patterson, a member of the

Pulitzer advisory board in 1979 and 1982, said the Mirage series caused a debate on the board. Many believed that by honoring undercover reporting, they were endorsing it. Patterson, then chief executive officer of the *St. Petersburg Times,* said he was among those opposed to giving the Mirage series a Pulitzer. He called undercover reporting "a fashionable trend I don't like to see encouraged." He believed that "the press as a whole pays a price in credibility when a newspaper that editorially calls for government in the sunshine and candor in business shows itself disposed to shade the truth or mask its motives." Undercover reporting should be limited to "extraordinary circumstance that would require a policy decision by the editor."[28]

When the Pulitzer board did not give the *Sun-Times* the prize for the Mirage in 1979 because it questioned the reporters' methods and rejected another undercover story in 1982 for the same reason, most newspaper journalists began to reconsider the ethics of undercover reporting, and many newspaper editors decided to put limits on the use of deception by their reporters. The *Sun-Times* has since stopped the practice. "I don't think we should pretend to be things we're not," *Sun-Times* editor Dennis Britton explained.[29]

UNDERCOVER REPORTING REBOUNDS IN TV

While newspaper editors were showing disdain for the use of deception and misrepresentation in gathering stories, hidden cameras and phony identities became standard tactics of many TV news programs in the early 1990s. Tabloid TV shows like *A Current Affair, Hard Copy* and *Inside Edition* were getting large ratings with their mixture of hidden-camera exposés, re-enacted news events and frequent stories on topless dancers and sexy murders, and network news magazine programs like ABC's *20/20* and *PrimeTime Live,* CBS's *60 Minutes,* and similar programs on NBC were using hidden cameras to uncover insurance fraud, auto repair rip-offs, and poor treatment of children in day-care centers.

That's not to say that TV had not done undercover reporting before. *60 Minutes* has a long history of using hidden cameras. Before he became a talk-show host, Geraldo Rivera did serious undercover reporting for ABC. Even some local stations like WBBM in Chicago developed reputations for their investigative work, which occasionally made use of undercover techniques. But in those days the use of undercover reporting on TV was relatively rare. Now hardly a day goes by that a viewer can't see hidden cameras at work on one of the tabloid TV shows, a network newsmagazine, or even the local news.

Perhaps the biggest flap over a TV undercover story was created by

Diane Sawyer's report on ABC's *PrimeTime Live* about unsanitary conditions in a supermarket chain. A labor union that was trying to organize workers for Food Lion, a fast-growing supermarket chain, tipped the show's producers about unsanitary practices in some stores and gave them a list of employees to interview. Satisfied there might be a story, *PrimeTime* decided to have one of its researchers get a job at a Food Lion store and take along a hidden camera to record what happened. At first the researcher couldn't get hired. So producers had to step up the level of deception. Union members gave her a crash course in how to wrap meat, created a phony work history for her, and supplied her with a glowing recommendation from her "previous boss" at an out-of-state grocery. She wrote on her application, "I really miss working in a grocery story, and I love meat wrapping." She said she hoped to have a career with Food Lion.

Once on the payroll, she began videotaping her fellow employees as they gave her advice on how to do her job, including ways to sell old meat and deli products as if they were fresh. The most striking claims were that meat-counter employees would soak outdated meat in bleach and repackage it and that they sometimes would douse old meat in barbecue sauce and sell it at a premium price since it was ready to grill. Company officials rejected an offer to appear on camera and answer the charges.

Public response to the segment was dramatic. Sales at Food Lion dropped immediately, the value of its stock fell, and the company delayed plans for expansion. The company fought back with TV ads emphasizing the cleanliness of its stores and pointing out that the chain had an "above average" rating from state health inspectors. The chain also filed suit against ABC claiming among other things that the network violated federal racketeering laws and that the researcher had committed fraud by lying on her application. The suit sought more than $30 million in damages.[30]

A Controversial Method

For at least 20 years people in and out of journalism have been debating whether the media's use of undercover reporting is justified. An informal survey for an earlier edition of this book found journalists evenly split on the question, and hardly anybody was willing to endorse or condemn the method without qualification. Those who favored it did not believe that it should be done casually on virtually every story that comes along. Those who disapproved believed there might be some special and rare circumstance in which the method might ethically be used.

ENDS VERSUS MEANS

That division of opinion among journalists was evident in the Tampa Bay area. Reporters for WFLA-TV heard that two Salvation Army workers were selling items that had been donated to help victims of Hurricane Andrew and pocketing the money. The reporters tracked down the pair and posing as people in need of help, bought supplies that were supposed to be given to hurricane victims from a Salvation Army truck. Once the tape was aired on the station's 6 o'clock news, the Salvation Army labeled it an isolated incident and fired the two workers.

Many journalists criticized the conduct of the reporters. A columnist in the *St. Petersburg Times* wrote that she worried about reporters engaging in such practices when the media's "credibility is increasingly questioned." She described the ploy as fraud committed by "journalists playing a role to get the news, pretending to be guys wanting diapers and dog food when they were pros wanting a story." A libel lawyer who works for the *Times* said the reporters should have called police when they learned workers were stealing items from the Salvation Army and selling them. The journalists could then have reported the arrests. She said reporters should observe a story, not participate in it.

The station's news director later said he didn't understand why people were focusing so much attention on the method used to get the story. He said people "should focus on a charitable institution which solicited and collected goods, then mismanaged them." In his view, the story was warranted because it had exposed a wrong.[31]

In many ways, this discussion of the Tampa station's conduct exemplifies what happens when journalists discuss the ethics of deception. They often get embroiled in a controversy that's been around since Plato: Do the ends justify the means? As Valerie Hyman, a former TV journalist and ethics teacher at the Poynter Institute, phrased it, "If truth-telling is one of the values we hold dear as journalists, then we have to think awfully hard before we decide to be deceptive in our pursuit of telling the truth."[32]

Some journalists who have thought hard about the use of deception have concluded that it is readily justifiable. They believe the ends often justify the means. "It's the small crime versus the greater good," Don Hewitt, *60 Minutes* producer, argued. "If you catch someone violating 'thou shall not steal' by your 'thou shall not lie,' that's a pretty good trade-off."[33] And Pam Zekman, one of the *Sun-Times* reporters in the Mirage bar, said journalists working undercover were simply allowing themselves to experience things that happen to people every day: "Just because we're reporters should not stop us from being able to see how the public is being abused."[34]

Others believe that you have to weigh the merit of the story against the dishonesty of the method. "I don't think the American public loves the idea of surreptitious taping unless it is in a really good cause," said Richard Kaplan, executive producer of *PrimeTime Live*. "You have to make sure, when you use a hidden camera, the story is important, or you end up looking like some KGB chief." Kaplan said he would like to have an undercover segment each week on his program, but explained, "If you use it for trivial cases, you demean it."[35] Mike Wallace, *60 Minutes* reporter, said he believes that deception can be justified if it is needed to get the truth. "You don't like to baldly lie, but I have," he said. "It really depends on your motive. Are you doing it for drama or are you doing it for illumination?"[36]

But many journalists have come to the conclusion that deception can never be justified. Former *Washington Post* executive editor Ben Bradlee said: "In a day in which we are spending thousands of man hours uncovering deception, we simply cannot deceive. How can newspapers fight for honesty and integrity when they themselves are less than honest in getting a story. When cops pose as newspapermen, we get goddamn sore. Quite properly so. So how can we pose as something we're not."[37] Many papers have outlawed deception and misrepresentation. "At our paper you can't do that," said Mark Middlebrook, an assistant managing editor of *The Florida Times Union* in Jacksonville and former president of Investigative Reporters and Editors. "You can't pretend to be somebody you are not. Period."[38]

Syndicated columnist Colman McCarthy has listened to the argument that some stories merit undercover reporting, and he isn't impressed. "In Hewitt's and other news executives' justifications for their 'small crimes,' a tone of self-importance — *60 Minutes* and *PrimeTime Live* as the Truth Squad — came through," he wrote. He noted that many of the stories on these programs use undercover reporting to expose petty crimes, which they treat as if they were "damned important stuff."[39]

Other concerns are raised about undercover reporting as a means to a story. Often reporters working undercover may intrude on people's privacy. The argument is not that undercover reporters are necessarily breaking privacy laws. Most news organizations have attorneys who guide them through the maze of state privacy laws and court rulings. For

"And now for our undercover feature of the week: an inside look at a Barbie Doll factory!"

example, when CBS reporters used hidden cameras to photograph fathers who weren't paying child support, they went to their places of employment. If the reporters had taken the same pictures in their homes, CBS might have been open to lawsuits.[40]

Although nearly all the undercover reporting now being practiced may satisfy the letter of the law, many think it invades privacy in an ethical sense. They note that people think they are engaged in private conversations with fellow employees or new acquaintances when what they are saying may be broadcast to millions of people watching network TV.

"I just think it's wrong," Tom Goldstein, dean of the journalism school at the University of California at Berkeley, told *The Washington Post*. "Journalists should announce who they are. I'm uncomfortable living in a world where you don't know who you're talking to. . . . I don't think journalists are cops."[41] Columnist McCarthy wondered how ABC or CBS would react if a reporter from *Hard Copy* "secured employment through fakery and then, equipped with a hidden camera and mike, caught *PrimeTime* executives or Don Hewitt in their less than noble moments."[42]

BEST WAY TO THE TRUTH?

Another question usually raised during debates about deception is whether it is the best way to get the story. Zekman, one of the Mirage bar reporters, thinks it always is. She said undercover reporting is "a much more valid way to get at the truth of things than any other technique there is."[43] But the majority of undercover reporting's most ardent practitioners recognize it is not suited to every investigation. An NBC executive said, "We don't like to do it, and we try not to do it." His counterpart at CBS agreed: "We would much rather have someone consent to an interview or consent to appear on camera."[44]

Some believe that deception should be a last resort. Undercover reporting can be "a terrific way to get stories when no other way is possible," said Hyman, a former TV journalist who now teaches ethics. "When the more straightforward, more conventional alternatives have been considered and dismissed for legitimate reasons, and when the story itself is of such import that it must be told, deception is warranted. Our job — as journalists — is to inform, not to conceal."[45]

The problem, of course, is trying to decide when conventional techniques won't work. Zekman contended that the *Sun-Times* buying the Mirage bar was the only way to uncover corruption in Chicago. She rejected using traditional methods or working undercover in someone else's bar. "You had to own the bar to find out whether businessmen were being extorted by building inspectors." But Eugene Patterson of the *St. Petersburg Times* argued that the *Sun-Times* could have exposed corruption in Chicago without the theatrics of buying the bar: "Hard work and shoe leather could have unearthed the sources necessary to do the Mirage story."[46]

Columnist McCarthy makes the same argument about the Food Lion story. "Other ways — truthful, ethical — exist besides hidden camera footage to nab wrongdoers," he wrote. "Classic investigative reporting relies on public documents, skilled interviewing, exhaustive research and cross-checking." He called undercover work "lazy journalism, not aggressive reporting."[47]

Nearly everyone who advocates undercover reporting, though, agrees that there must be safeguards built into the technique and that it should be only one part of an investigation. Without adequate research before the undercover project begins, reporters cannot provide enough background so that the public can understand whether the story has uncovered a few bad apples trying to spoil an otherwise legitimate endeavor or whether it exposed a widespread and ongoing problem.

That's why Bagdikian, the reporter who wanted to go inside a prison, had already spent a long time researching the problem before he asked if he could go undercover. He had talked to experts, visited prisons, and studied available public records. Armed with this information, he knew what he was likely to encounter and that he would be able to judge whether his experiences in prison were typical of most prisoners'. His undercover work was only one story in an eight-part series. Similarly, the *60 Minutes* producer knew the scope of illegal kickbacks to clinics treating Medicare patients, that it was a growing problem, and that it was common in Chicago before opening the store-front clinic.

Some worry that not all stories are this carefully researched before the undercover work begins. People in and out of TV journalism expressed concerns about ABC's *PrimeTime* Food Lion report. "I cannot believe that such a story would be done that way on any CBS program," Joe Peyronnin, CBS's senior vice president for newsmagazines, told the *Chicago Tribune.*[48]

The pictures *PrimeTime* had of Food Lion workers were clearly powerful. Viewers watched as workers appeared to be doctoring meat and listened to them as they rather smugly discussed other equally unpleasant tricks of the grocery business. It was good television and exposed a serious consumer problem. But some contend that the reliance on undercover reporting at a few Food Lion stores may have lessened the story's impact.

Russ W. Baker, in a *Columbia Journalism Review* article, put his finger on the problem many people had with the Food Lion episode. *PrimeTime* may have fallen "into a typical trap — focusing in on a villain when the problem is systemic." The episode showed a few workers at a handful of stores in one chain. Baker noted that at the same time *PrimeTime* was preparing its Food Lion story, a local station in Atlanta, WAGA-TV, was doing a larger-scale investigation of food safety. The Atlanta report found that every one of the 20 supermarkets it tested were repackaging old meat. The markets included both national and local chains.[49]

Although most journalists would agree that stories should ideally explain the significance and scope of a problem, they contend that it is unrealistic to expect them to produce detailed examinations of every problem they write about. They argue that much as traffic cops can stop only a few speeders, journalists can expose only some wrongdoers. Kaplan, who produced the *PrimeTime* segment, said that to his way of thinking, the Food Lion story accomplished the goal he wanted to achieve. "The story was about one thing," he said. "You're a consumer. You go in and see a date on a piece of meat. You expect that freshness date is honest."[50]

NEWS AS PROFIT

Many charged that this sudden growth in undercover TV reporting was prompted less by a desire for good journalism than by financial motivations and improvements in technology. It wouldn't be the first time money and gadgets have changed the face of journalism. The rowdy reporting by newspapers in the 1930s was partially prompted by the depression and circulation wars. And as soon as small cameras became available in 1928, a photographer for the *New York Daily News,* which then billed itself as "New York's Picture Newspaper," strapped one on his leg and tried to photograph an execution.[51]

By the early 1990s, TV news shows were facing tremendous competition. The tabloid TV shows were pitted against one another in the early-evening schedules, and the network newsmagazines battled TV's more traditional prime-time fare of sitcoms and police dramas. "Nothing matters anymore, except the competition for audience," Reuven Frank, former president of NBC News, told a *Chicago Tribune* reporter. He said the competition from the tabloid TV shows and the decision by networks to consider news departments profit centers have eroded journalistic ethics and made hidden cameras possible. "Everybody in the spectrum is fighting everybody else for audience, so you're getting a mushing up of standards. Standards are fine, if they don't lose audience."[52]

If news programs can score well in their time slots, they can make big money for their producers. In 1993 CBS expected to generate more than $300 million from *48 Hours* and *60 Minutes,* the latter the most profitable series on TV. ABC was expected to bring in more than $200 million from *PrimeTime Live* and *20/20.* Wanting to get in on this bonanza, NBC tried 17 times to create a successful newsmagazine before it finally hit pay dirt with *Dateline NBC.* The three major networks and Fox were planning to add more newsmagazine programs to their prime-time lineups in the mid-1990s. They recognized that these shows could generate profits even if they did not win the ratings battle in their time slots. News shows can be produced for half the cost of an entertainment program, and the networks don't have to pay residuals for the reruns.[53]

Producers recognized that the most successful of the new programs had found "dramatic visual ways to express themselves," as some writers noted. "You cannot produce a prime-time TV [news] program the way you do a Sunday morning program," said Sid Feders, an executive producer of one of NBC's prime-time news shows. "People want to be entertained more, they want their attention held more."[54]

This push to entertain is growing. "Once they became profit centers for the networks, they became susceptible to all of the same pressures that the entertainment divisions always had in terms of keeping the audience and keeping the ratings up," Everette Dennis, director of a center that studies media, told *American Journalism Review.* "There's enormous pressure on these TV magazines for pictures, pictures and hype."[55]

Technological advances have made these pictures possible. At one time, TV cameras were large machines that were shoulder-mounted. Undercover reports were shot from camouflaged vans or with hidden cameras that produced grainy and often poorly focused images. Today, cameras as small as pencils and microphones hidden in earrings and tie tacks can produce high-quality work. *Chicago Tribune* reporter Kenneth Clark said that many network newspeople were divided on the ethics of hidden cameras, "but all agree on one thing: As cameras become smaller and easier to conceal, their hidden use is bound to increase."[56] And that bothers Stephen Klaidman, an ethics scholar at Georgetown University. "If they're doing it simply to hype ratings, that's not an acceptable justification."[57]

TWO NEWSPAPERS, TWO ANSWERS

Reporters at *The Miami Herald* and *Newsday,* a Long Island, N.Y., daily, heard reports of racial discrimination in housing. They knew this was a story that had been done by many newspapers during the past 30 years, including college newspapers, small dailies, large dailies and network TV news, but they were convinced it was still a major problem in their communities. So they began work on how they would go about documenting the story. Both papers have long histories of first-rate investigative reporting.

The technique adopted by the *Herald* in 1986 is probably typical of most of these investigations. Reporters Paul Shannon, white, and Larry Bivins, black, created almost identical backgrounds for themselves so they would be "ideal tenants — well-dressed, professional, relatively affluent, and no kids or pets." Then they went from apartment office to apartment office using classified ads. The black reporter went in first, the white reporter 10 to 30 minutes later, so that they were apt to deal with the same rental agent. They used their own names but fudged their occupations: Bivins said he worked as a minority recruiter for the *Herald,* which was part of his job, and Shannon said he worked in an office for the Knight-Ridder Corporation, owner of the *Herald.* "No one caught on," Shannon said.

They found both overt and subtle discrimination. One rental agent would tell Bivins that an apartment complex was filled up and 20 minutes later tell Shannon that he could have an apartment there immediately. Sometimes when they compared notes after their visits, they would find that the white reporter had been shown such amenities as a swimming pool, sauna and Jacuzzi, while the black reporter was never told about them.

Heath Meriwether, *Herald* executive editor at the time, defended the misrepresentation used to get this important story even though he is very cautious about approving any kind of deception. "There are times when undercover reporting with very stringent . . . safeguards, preceded by full discussion, is OK."[58]

Newsday reporters had heard complaints about real estate agents steering whites to white areas of town and blacks to black areas. They wanted to expose this illegal practice. Their methods were described by Marcel Dufresne in a *Columbia Journalism Review* article.[59] *Newsday* editors had read several stories about the problem in other papers, and they were troubled by the inconclusive nature of many stories. They noted that reporters in many of the earlier investigations had tested only a dozen or so salespeople even though there were hundreds of offices with countless agents in each city. After the stories based on these probes appeared, the companies often claimed that the violations had been done by individual agents and that the company itself promoted equal opportunity. At best, a few agents were reprimanded or fired, but the practice of housing discrimination continued.

Newsday wanted more than that. Originally, project editors planned to use 20 teams of reporters and trained actors who would visit 200 real estate offices on Long Island. As the project team began to overcome many of the tactical problems inherent in an investigation of this size, some of the reporters wanted to begin some limited testing to see how well the plan worked and to get some anecdotes that might add color to the final story. But project editor Joye Brown was hesitant to approve the trial run because she knew *Newsday* editors generally did not approve of undercover operations and she did not want "to propose undercover testing just to make stories lively," according to Dufresne.

When Brown was convinced the overall project would work, she took the idea to managing editor Howard Schneider, no fan of undercover reporting. He indicated that he was not enthusiastic about the project. However, Brown and her group still wanted to do the story. They brought in a Chicago expert on documenting racial discrimination who assured them that by using trained testers it would be possible "to show the extent of steering on Long Island with 95 percent accuracy." The expert's presentation was strong enough that Schneider decided to go ahead with the undercover work.

The project team starting looking for ways to guarantee that each of the 20 teams would present themselves to the real estate agents the same way, so that differences in body language and nuances of speech would not affect how they reacted. Almost 10 months after the idea was first proposed, the *Newsday* team thought the time had come to go undercover and begin testing for discrimination. But then Anthony Marro, the paper's editor, vetoed the idea.

A year later, *Newsday* published a 10-part series, "A World Apart: Segregation on Long Island." The articles were based not on undercover revelations but interviews with African-Americans (who had been shown homes only in black neighborhoods), brokers, agents, housing advocates and state prosecutors. Dufresne said the series used "moving personal accounts and startling statistics to bring readers face to face with racial segregation." The series, which was nominated for a Pulitzer, described Long Island as a place where many black residents were "trapped in neighborhoods beset by drugs and crime, where the police are unresponsive, and where the schools are inferior." After the project ended, Brown was asked whether she believed the story would have been better if they had gone undercover. "Did we need the test? The truth of the matter is no, we didn't."

Both newspapers discovered a serious problem in the community. The *Herald*'s story showed that racial discrimination was occurring in the city's rental offices. The story could be done rather quickly. *Newsday*'s story was a thorough documentation of the extent of the racism in housing and its impact on communities. But the series required a team of reporters at a newspaper known for its willingness to invest in investigative reporting.

What's an Ethical Journalist to Do?

Probably no other ethical issue discussed in this book has sparked such strong but diametrically opposite reactions from thoughtful journalists. There is no easy explanation of what constitutes ethical behavior in the use of deception.

In its handbook *Doing Ethics in Journalism,* the Society of Professional Journalists suggests these guidelines for deciding when deception by a journalist is justified:

> • When the information obtained is of profound importance. It must be of vital public interest, such as revealing great "system failure" at the top levels, or it must prevent profound harm to individuals.
> • When all other alternatives for obtaining the same information have been exhausted.
> • When the journalists involved are willing to disclose the nature of the deception and the reason for it.
> • When the individuals involved and their news organizations apply excellence, through outstanding craftsmanship as well as the commitment of time and funding needed to pursue the story fully.
> • When the harm prevented by the information revealed though deception outweighs any harm caused by the act of deception.
> • When the journalists involved have conducted a meaningful, collaborative, and deliberate decision-making process in which they weigh:
>   a. the consequences (short- and long-term) of the deception on those being deceived.
>   b. the impact on journalistic credibility.
>   c. the motivations for their actions.
>   d. the deceptive act in relation to their editorial mission.
>   e. the legal implications of the action.
>   f. the consistency of their reasoning and their action.

The SPJ handbook also suggested some criteria that *cannot* be used to justify deception:

> • Winning a prize.
> • Getting the story with less expense of time and resources.
> • Doing it because "the others already did it."
> • The subjects of the story are themselves unethical.[60]

On the surface, it is difficult to condone lying or deceiving to get information. We do not want to think of ourselves as liars. But who among us has never told a lie? As with most things, there are degrees of lying. There are also degrees of deception that journalists have practiced in pursuit of their stories. Hardly anyone finds fault with the lesser deceptions of restaurant reviewers or travel writers who do not identify themselves while checking out eateries or cruises. But some of the big guns of journalism have been challenging the use of more serious and active deception, which is the main reason that undercover reporting has declined in American journalism, particularly in newspapers. The method has been kept alive mostly by TV journalists whose motives may have as much to do with profits as good reporting.

The argument from defenders of undercover reporting that the ends justify the means (the importance of the story makes it OK to deceive) is seldom persuasive. You can't separate ends and means that easily. If the means (the methods you use to get your story) are tawdry, that's bound to rub off on the story and the way it is received by the public. Yet the best of our undercover reporting — Bagdikian's prison series, *Newsday*'s exposé of world heroin trafficking — has exposed evil, advanced knowledge and improved civilization. That kind of journalism — when it is done by skilled, ethical and careful journalists, because there is no other way to get a vital truth — can still be justified.

Fakery

Let's say you are a wire editor of a daily newspaper in California. A wire service has a news story that begins like this:

LOS ANGELES — The $100,000 Lamborghini Countach shoots up the on-ramp at 65 mph in first gear, 80 mph in second.

Once in the fast lane, the speedometer inches toward 200 mph. Signs along the deserted freeway flip past in a blur and gentle curves become hairpin turns. Make a mistake at that speed and both car and driver would likely disintegrate in flight.

This is a "banzai run" with an outlaw racer, a man pursuing an illegal, dangerous and expensive hobby that goes beyond the speed limit and even beyond the reach of the law. For these racers, speed is a kind of intoxicant.

"Military jets take off at 200 mph," the driver of the Countach says with a terse laugh. "If this car had wings. . . ."

He eyes the Ferrari Boxer and Victor Twinturbo V12 behind him in electronic rear-view mirrors. The exotic cars in this high-speed caravan are barely visible out the Lamborghini's tiny back window. "It's the Italian philosophy of driving," he said of his sports car. "You don't have time to look back."

Indeed, looming suddenly ahead is a dreaded black and white cruiser of the California Highway Patrol. The distance eaten up in a second, the sports cars rocket past in a flash. As seen in the mirrors, the patrol car seems to be hurtling backward as if shot from a cannon. Are its red lights turned on?

"Doesn't matter—might as well try to catch a Russian spy satellite," sneers the driver, who asks not to be identified. Nevertheless, some banzai runners take no chances—they've installed switches in their cars to flip off their tail lights and make their vehicles more difficult to follow.

By the time the patrol radios for help, the banzai runners will be hiding safely in some small town miles up the coast, slinking down back streets maybe parking in a dark alley until things cool down.[1]

"Good Lord!" in Italian slang.

The rest of the story tells of police surprise that this new "sport" is as organized as it is and describes the banzai drivers as former race-car drivers or the "newly rich," such as rock stars, actors and Middle Eastern princes. Would you publish this story? Would you question the story? Does it bother you that the writer of the story, who presumably was on the banzai run described, has protected (by not identifying) the drivers who were obviously breaking the laws?

When the story was sent out by the AP to its member papers in California and Nevada, many published it. Three weeks later, they had to publish what the AP calls a "corrective." The story was partly phony and partly plagiarized. The reporter who wrote it, Gloria Ohland, had not been on the banzai run she described or on any run. What she portrayed as if she had been a witness or participant was fabricated. She had also lifted parts of the piece from an article that appeared nine months earlier in *New West* magazine. In addition, she attributed statements to a California Highway Patrol officer who denied that he had ever talked to her and said that the patrol had not had a problem with banzai runners. When AP President Louis D. Boccardi confronted Ohland, she eventually admitted that her story was a misrepresentation. The 29-year-old reporter, who had worked in the Los Angeles bureau for more than two years, decided she had no future with the AP and resigned.

Boccardi, who wrote the corrective himself, called the episode "a serious lapse in our standards." Ohland did not fabricate the phenomenon of banzai racing, Boccardi conceded. "But she misrepresented the circumstances under which the story was gathered, she took some material from a magazine without credit, and she inaccurately attributed some quotations."[2]

Besides being an embarrassment, the Ohland story is one of several that have caused questions about the reporting and writing methods of some journalists: fabricating news stories, plagiarizing, making up quotations, embellishing the facts so much that a false picture is presented. This kind of fakery is rare, but that it occurs at all is disturbing to those seeking a more ethical journalism.

Fabricating News

In earlier days, newspapers enjoyed manufacturing news for their readers. The most celebrated journalistic hoax was the lengthy account, complete with drawings, of the manlike creatures with wings discovered on the moon. This discovery of "man-bats" and other lunar life was supposedly made by a Sir John Herschel employing a giant new telescope. This 19th-century version of pure baloney, published in the *New York Sun* in 1835, was one of the stunts that helped it achieve the largest circulation of any daily in the world. After the hoax was uncovered, the paper's editors told readers it was a slow time for news and they just wanted to brighten their readers' days. The readers were apparently not angered by the hoax; circulation remained high after the disclosure.[3]

Newspapers today are more concerned about their readers' reactions to fabrications. The *Chicago Sun-Times* fired a sports reporter who apparently made up a story about some "good ole' Texas boys" watching the Chicago Bears thrash the Dallas Cowboys on TV in a bar in Eden, Texas. Some reporters and editors thought there might be something wrong with the story. "Some people felt . . . it was just too pat a story," said the managing editor. The next week, the managing editor and another reporter went to Eden. They found no "Bonner's bar" and no townsfolk with the names in the story.[4]

Broadcast news has also had its fabricators. Jessica Savitch, in her *Anchorwoman,* told of a fellow anchor at KYW, Philadelphia, who "always came up with cuter, funnier, more interesting closing pads than I did." She couldn't figure out how she was missing those good items in the newspapers and magazines she scoured each day. "Finally I begged him to tell me where the hell he was getting his information," Savitch wrote. "I make it up," he said. His tenure at KYW was short.[5]

JANET COOKE AND JIMMY'S WORLD

The Washington Post, a newspaper that has been a leader in setting higher ethical and professional standards, ran the most famous hoax of the modern era, a hoax every bit as shocking as man-bats on the moon. The story that embarrassed the *Post* was a dramatic account of an 8-year-old heroin addict. The writer, Janet Cooke, gave him the name Jimmy, and her Page One article was headlined "Jimmy's World: 8-Year-Old Heroin Addict Lives for a Fix." Illustrated by a moving drawing of what *Post* artist Michael Gnatek Jr. imagined Jimmy would look like while he was getting a fix, Cooke's article began:

> Jimmy is 8 years old and a third-generation heroin addict, a precocious little boy with sandy hair, velvety brown eyes and needle marks freckling the baby-smooth skin of his thin brown arms.

The article went on to paint a dreary and hopeless picture of "Jimmy's world" in Southeast Washington where he lived with his mother, an ex-prostitute, and her lover, Ron, a pusher who got Jimmy hooked on heroin. Jimmy wanted to be a dope dealer like Ron, the article said, and "he doesn't usually go to school, preferring instead to hang with older boys between the ages of 11 and 16 who spend their day getting high on herb or PCP and doing a little dealing to collect spare change." At the end of the article Cooke described Jimmy being "fired up" with an injection of heroin:

> Ron comes back into the living room, syringe in hand, and calls the little boy over to his chair: "Let me see your arm."
> He grabs Jimmy's left arm just above the elbow, his massive hand tightly encircling the child's small limb. The needle slides into the boy's soft skin like a straw pushed into the center of a freshly baked cake. Liquid ebbs out of the syringe, replaced by bright red blood. The blood is then reinjected into the child.
> Jimmy has closed his eyes during the whole procedure, but now opens them, looking quickly around the room. He climbs into a rocking chair and sits, his head dipping and snapping upright again, in what addicts call "the nod."
> "Pretty soon, man," Ron says, "you got to learn how to do this for yourself."[6]

The story of Jimmy saddened, outraged, angered and upset many Washingtonians, including the mayor, who ordered a search for the child. The police chief threatened to have Cooke and the *Post* editors subpoenaed if they did not reveal who Jimmy was. *Post* lawyers replied that the paper had a right under the First Amendment to protect its sources. As Robert Woodward, the famed Watergate reporter who was then an assistant managing editor, put it, "We went into our Watergate mode: Protect the source and back the reporter."[7]

The *Post* withstood the legal challenges, but three weeks later, the managing editor told the city editor to find Jimmy and "take Janet with you." Cooke said she had recently revisited the house and the family had moved. So that was that. Exit Jimmy.

The *Post* entered the story in the Pulitzer Prize competition, and the jurors — with the dissenting vote only of *St. Petersburg Times* editor Eugene Patterson, who called the story "an aberration" that should never have been printed — awarded it the Pulitzer for feature writing. Cooke, who had been on the *Post* staff for a little more than eight months, had won herself a Pulitzer at the age of 26.

But then her house of lies began to crumble. The *Post* had submitted a biographical sketch of her from her applications. It claimed she was a Phi Beta Kappa graduate of Vassar College; had worked for two years at the *Toledo Blade,* where she had won an award; and could speak French and Spanish. But when she filled out her background for the Pulitzer, she wrote that she had earned a master's degree, done advanced study at the Sorbonne in Paris, won six awards while at the Toledo paper, and spoke Portuguese, Italian, French and Spanish fluently. When the *Blade* decided to do a "local woman makes good" story about Cooke, it found that biographical information in the AP story didn't jibe with the paper's records of its former employee. She had attended Vassar for one year but had returned to Toledo and earned her B.A. at the University of Toledo. She studied French in high school and college but was not fluent.

Editors at the *Blade* passed along their findings to *Post* editors. By early the next morning, she confessed to her editors that "Jimmy's World" was a fabrication. She had never encountered or interviewed an 8-year-old drug addict. He was a "composite" of young addicts whom social workers had told her about. She resigned, and the *Post* gave back the Pulitzer.[8]

Why did she do it? When her fakery was discovered, Cooke refused to be interviewed, but about nine months later, she allowed Phil Donahue to interview her on NBC's *Today* show. She told Donahue that after spending about two months looking for the 8-year-old heroin addict her sources told her were out there, her "whole mind-set was in *The Washington Post* mentality: He must be there and it's being covered up; I must find him." She decided to make up an 8-year-old addict because "the last thing I could do was to go to my editor and say, 'I can't do it.'" Cooke said she does not excuse what happened: "It was wrong; I shouldn't have done it. . . . I simply wanted . . . not to fail." Asked why she lied on her job application, Cooke said she believed she would not have been hired otherwise and felt "a need to be perfect."[9]

Other Kinds of Fakery

Not all kinds of fakery are as brazen as Janet Cooke's wholesale creation of an 8-year-old drug addict. Some journalists fudge the facts to make their stories more readable and dramatic. And some pass off someone else's work as if it were their own.

THE NEW JOURNALISM

Unfairly perhaps, what became known as the New Journalism has taken much of the flak for pieces by writers whose stories were not based in truth. New Journalism is the label placed on the technique of writing news stories as if they were short stories or novels, using the devices and modes of fiction writing to make the articles more dramatic and readable. Practiced by skillful writers and reporters like Tom Wolfe and Gay Talese, New Journalism has produced some lively articles and books that have also been fairly truthful.

Younger writers have tried to imitate the style of these writers and have received applause and promotions from their editors. But a few have practiced New Journalism without the careful research and reporting needed for truthful portrayals. Some have even argued that they should be allowed to embellish their stories because the important truths are the impressions they leave in the readers' minds, not the factual documentation.

The New Journalism became suspect when Gail Sheehy did an article for *New York* magazine detailing the lives and fortunes of a prostitute Sheehy called Redpants and her pimp, Sugarman. These names were not just pseudonyms, a device journalists sometimes use to protect a news source or subject. They were names that Sheehy made up for the two composites she created from the prostitutes and pimps she had interviewed. Instead of reporting what each of her sources said and did, she expressed their words and actions through Redpants and Sugarman.[10]

Many journalists criticized this use of composites when it became known. They didn't find out about it from reading the articles. Although she had written a paragraph explaining what she had done, her editor had removed it.[11] Her use of composites came out later when Sheehy was interviewed by other journalists. Sheehy apparently saw the composite technique as a way of protecting the identities of her sources but also as a way of telling of what she had learned in a more dramatic and interesting way.

"You know what you can do with your New Journalism. What I want are straight, factual news stories — and keep 'em short!"

Other journalists have carried the search for the dramatic and interesting beyond composites. They have written books and articles ascribing thoughts to presidents, judges, convicts and others in the news. For instance, Bob Woodward, one of the two *Washington Post* reporters who broke the Watergate story, has written books reporting the thoughts of President Richard Nixon and various Supreme Court justices, the deathbed comments of CIA Director William Casey, and what Gen. Colin Powell said to himself during the Gulf War in 1991.[12] These "new journalists" contend that they have studied their subjects so intensely that they can accurately describe the subjects' thoughts.

Many people find that argument unconvincing. Haynes Johnson, a columnist for *The Washington Post,* is turned off by this technique. "When Tom Wolfe and the people who call themselves the new journalists use composite characters and tell us what people are thinking because they've talked to so many of them, well, they're playing God," Johnson says. "I find that pretentious."[13] Using composites and guessing the personal thoughts of newsmakers are not generally accepted in daily journalism as ways to tell stories.

STAGING THE NEWS

One of the reasons people watch TV news is that they are able to see news events as they happen or at least see where they happened. And newspaper readers have also become accustomed to photographs that capture the mood of an event. Sometimes this demand for pictures pushes the media into some ethical quicksand.

A small-time deception is occasionally used by TV reporters who can't get to the scene of a news event. They do voice-overs as if they were on the scene when they are showing videotape supplied by another source.[14] Other times reporters seem to be reporting directly from the scene when they have hardly left the station. To make the news seem more current, they may stand on the station's parking lot with a highway or a fence or a lake in the background—whatever would be appropriate to the story. The reporters then give their "live" reports and are interviewed through their earpieces by the anchors sitting in studios perhaps a few hundred feet away. This technique is not limited to small-town stations. Careful viewers of network news may notice how similar government buildings appear on the nightly news. Reporters in Washington sometimes use a downtown church with large white pillars as a backdrop for stories about Congress, the White House or the Supreme Court to create the illusion of being at those buildings.[15]

But sometimes the efforts by TV journalists to present the news in a dramatic way move away from these rather innocent tricks. In the early 1990s several lawsuits were filed against General Motors charging that GM pickup trucks had a design defect increasing the likelihood that the gas tank would explode if the truck was hit in the side. The NBC news magazine *Dateline NBC* wanted to illustrate the problem, so they bought one of the trucks, filled it with gasoline, and crashed a car into it. The truck exploded in a sea of flames while cameras recorded the event from outside and inside the vehicle. The pictures appeared to make a vivid point about the safety of the GM trucks.

After the segment ran, GM investigators tracked down the remains of the wrecked truck and bought it from a junkyard. They X-rayed the gas tank and discovered that it had not ruptured as NBC had suggested. The alleged defect in the trucks had nothing to do with the fire NBC had shown. GM further discovered that remote-control incendiary devices had been placed on the truck to make sure that there would be a fire when the car and truck collided.

After GM announced its findings at a press conference, NBC officials took the unusual step of having a four-and-a-half-minute apology to GM read during the program. Anchors Jane Pauley and Stone Phillips, who apparently did not know of the deception, pledged that such "unscientific demonstrations" would never again be used on the program.[16]

Unfortunately for NBC, at about the same time GM was challenging the story about exploding pickup trucks, *NBC Nightly News* ran a story about the environmental damage caused by clear-cutting by the timber industry. The report was illustrated by footage showing fish floating belly-up in a river, fish NBC said had died as a result of clear-cutting in the Clearwater National Forest. A few days later, NBC acknowledged that there were two problems with the report: The fish were not in a stream in Clearwater National Forest, and they were not dead. They had been stunned by forestry officials as part of a fish count in another stream.[17] Shortly after these incidents, Michael Gartner resigned as president of NBC News.

Making reality fit the needs of journalists is nothing new. When Don Black was assistant managing editor at the *Statesman-Journal* in Salem, Oregon, he recalled, a photographer at another paper was sent to a school to get a picture of young people smoking in a school lounge. The lounge was empty when he got there. "So he rustled up a couple of kids, gave them some cigarettes and set up the picture," Black said. "The paper got into a big hassle, because one of the kids did not smoke and came from a family strongly against smoking."[18]

Reporters at two TV stations were arrested after similar exploits in the name of journalism. In Minnesota, a TV reporter for KCCO wanted pictures to illustrate a story about under-age drinking. When he couldn't find any, he bought two cases of beer for six teen-agers, then filmed them happily downing the free beer. When the ruse was uncovered, the reporter and cameraman were not only fired; they were arrested and charged with violating state liquor laws. They pleaded guilty and were fined $500, sentenced to 10 days in jail, and required to do community service.[19]

In Denver, the NBC affiliate wanted to expose the illegal sport of dogfighting. Breeders train bulldogs to fight in pits, and spectators bet on which dog will leave the pit alive. The KCNC series featured videotape of a dogfight the reporter said had been mailed to her by an anonymous source. But after an investigation by police, two cameramen for the station pleaded guilty to videotaping the dogfight themselves. The reporter, who denied any role in the scheme, was later convicted of arranging the dogfight.[20]

Although no one contends that such stories are typical of TV journalism, there is concern that the great demand to get graphic video causes many producers to forget journalism ethics. Syndicated columnist

Richard Reeves has criticized the new generation of TV journalists. They "don't think of themselves as reporters or producers, but as 'filmmakers' with little interest in words, and heavy interest in dramatic effect," he wrote.[21]

More troublesome, incidents like these often lead the public to believe that all news is filled with dishonesty. A few months after NBC News rigged the GM fire story, the *Los Angeles Times* asked people how common fakery was in the news media. Surprisingly, 56 percent said they thought it was a common practice.[22]

PLAGIARISM

When Steve Lovelady first joined *The Philadelphia Inquirer* as an associate editor after reporting for *The Wall Street Journal,* he started searching through *Inquirer* clips to learn who the good and not-so-good writers were. He was very impressed with one article he found, but something about it seemed familiar. Then he figured it out. It was his article, one he had done for the *Journal,* that an *Inquirer* reporter had plagiarized. Such dishonesty is serious enough when a college student does it, but it can be career-smashing for a professional writer. The *Inquirer* reporter got off with a warning that time, but he was dismissed about a year later when *Fortune* magazine informed the *Inquirer* that one of its articles had been picked up verbatim by the writer.[23]

Some newspapers react more quickly to plagiarism. The *St. Petersburg Times* obtained a resignation from a reporter after she passed off as her own about a third of an article on credit cards from *Changing Times* magazine. She put a letter on the newsroom bulletin board the day she resigned:

> Twelve years of dedicated journalism down the drain because of a stupid mistake. I am writing this public explanation for a selfish reason. It will be easier for me to live with myself knowing that the truth is known. But I hope my mistake will serve as a lesson to others. I have let the *Times* down. I have let myself down. But most of all, I have let the profession down. And for that I am truly sorry.[24]

Stephen Isaacs, associate dean of the Columbia School of Journalism, told *The Boston Globe* that plagiarism by journalists is common. "Hundreds of incidents of plagiarism have taken place that I know of." John Seigenthaler, former publisher of the Nashville *Tennessean* and editorial director of *USA Today,* agreed: "I'm confident plagiarism happens with a lot more frequency than any of us knows. Part of it is new technology, but more of it is just plain misunderstanding and absence of sensitivity. And sometimes it's a total lack of ethics."[25]

Technology has made it easier to acquire stories from other newspapers quickly. A reporter with a computer can tie into data bases like Nexis and Dialogue and read the offerings of newspapers and wire services throughout the nation. The *Chicago Sun-Times* dropped a columnist after he admitted using information in his columns he had not reported but had gathered through a computer data-base search, according to *Editor & Publisher* magazine. He had credited the newspaper's librarian who helped him with the search, but not the newspapers that created the material.[26]

Sometimes writers accused of plagiarism say that the real crime they have committed is sloppiness. David Hawley, the drama critic for the *St. Paul Pioneer Press* for nearly 10 years, resigned and wrote an apology to readers after he used part of a *New York Times* review written six years earlier in his review of a play produced in Minnesota. He said that he had not intentionally copied the *Times* review but that his notes got "commingled" with part of the earlier review.[27]

Isaacs, a newspaper editor and producer at CBS News before he joined the faculty at Columbia, said that plagiarism is even more common in television. He told *The Boston Globe* that it "happens all the time. People steal other people's pictures."[28] Some TV and radio stations have been known to read news out of newspapers without crediting them. CNN admitted that it lifted a *Newsweek* article as a basis for one of its reports.[29]

Not all cases of plagiarism are as straightforward as these. Some reporters recycle quotes. They see a good quote in another newspaper or on TV and copy that quote in their stories without acknowledging the work of the original reporter. A 13-year veteran of the *Fort Worth Star-Telegram* resigned after it was discovered that he lifted quotes from the New Orleans *Times-Picayune* and TV news reports without crediting them. About the same time, the paper disciplined an editorial writer for repeating several paragraphs from an opinion piece in *The New York Times*.[30] Both *The New York Times* and *The Washington Post* have had to punish reporters for lifting quotes. A *Times* reporter took quotes from a *Boston Globe* story, ironically about a university dean who was accused of plagiarism. A reporter in the *Post*'s Miami bureau lifted quotes from *The Miami Herald* and the Associated Press.[31]

Tactics used by some reporters to sidestep ethical questions about recycling quotes worry Eleanor Randolph of *The Washington Post*. These reporters call the person who gave the great quote to the other publication and get the same quote directly from the source, usually by merely asking whether it was accurate, then use it without crediting the original reporter. Randolph wrote that she also wonders about ethics when a small paper comes up with a big story and other media send their own people in and report the story under their own bylines without mentioning the paper that originally broke the story. Randolph suggests that if these activities aren't plagiarism, they are close to it. She would prefer that the reporters and news organizations credit their colleagues who originated the stories or got the quotes in the first place. "The easiest way to avoid plagiarism is to give credit. But the average journalist enjoys giving credit about as much as your local 7-Eleven."[32]

QUOTE TAMPERING

Most editors believe that quotation marks are supposed to say to the reader, "What's inside here are the exact words of whoever is being quoted, verbatim." And most of the time what we read in the press inside quotation marks is a fairly accurate facsimile of what the source said. Careful writers do not use direct quotation unless they are sure they are presenting the exact or nearly exact words of the speaker. If they are not sure, they use indirect quotation by paraphrasing what the speaker said as accurately as possible and not enclosing any words in quotation marks.

Although handling quotations may seem pretty straightforward, journalists often encounter some difficult decisions in dealing with them. For instance, most journalists "clean up" quotes when they are ungrammatical or difficult to understand because they believe it is more important to convey the person's thoughts clearly than to confuse the reader. The question becomes: How much cleaning can you legitimately do?

Kevin McManus, for a *Columbia Journalism Review* article, asked two journalists how they deal with quotes. He quoted one verbatim:

> We have an informal policy which is a, uh, policy that's, uh, not uncommon in newsrooms around the country, which is, uh, that if you, uh, uh, uh, uh, put a sentence, uh, between quote marks, uh, that ought to be what the person said.

The other journalist told McManus he edited quotes in "certain inoffensive ways." When asked what they were, the journalist said:

> Well, ways that, uh, you can, for instance, uh, if the language is, um, horribly ungrammatical and, uh, makes the speaker—as spoken language sometimes is—makes the speaker look like a complete idiot, you can, quote, correct his or her grammar slightly, or make the person agree with the verb. The noun agree with the verb, something like that.[33]

McManus wonders how much you can "clean up" quotes like those and still use quotation marks.

A few journalists contended in a *Washington Journalism Review* article that it is not their job to clean up quotes to make sources sound better. Famed Texas reporter Mollie Ivins argued that "people stand up on the floor of the Texas legislature and make jackasses of themselves all the time. It is not my responsibility to make them look good."[34] Similarly, *Chicago Tribune* reporter Timothy McNulty told McManus that changing a quote misrepresents the way the person really is. In his view, changing a quotation to make a person sound better is like altering a photo to change the way the person dresses.[35]

But some sources ask the reporter to "make that proper English," and many journalists are willing to oblige. "Don't quote what I said, quote what I mean," the late Richard J. Daley, longtime mayor of Chicago, used to demand of reporters. Daley was famous for his fractured English. John Drury, who covered him for WLS-TV, recalled that Daley once told reporters: "The policeman isn't there to create disorder, he's there to preserve disorder." Chicago's print journalists reported what he meant; the electronic media replayed the quote the way he said it.[36]

When President Reagan didn't have a script or TelePrompTer in front of him, he could bewilder reporters who tried to quote him verbatim. For example, tape recordings indicated that he predicted he would win the 1980 presidential election because the voters were changing and,

"Don't quote what I said, quote what I mean!"

in his exact words, "uh . . . it's kind of encouraging that more of the people seem to be coming the same way, believing the same things." The AP "cleaned up" the quote: "It's remarkable how people are beginning to see things my way."[37]

Although that carries quote cleansing beyond the comfort limits of many journalists, some, like Reuters' Micheline Maynard, confess that they will sometimes add words to a quotation if they will help make the source's point.[38] But most journalists balk at shaping quotes for stylistic purposes — compressing a quote or taking various statements a person made during an interview and presenting them as if they were one coherent thought.

Sometimes quote tampering gets even more serious. Wayne Thompson, associate editor and veteran reporter for the Portland *Oregonian,* was suspended without pay for eight weeks when he fabricated some quotations from an interview with Washington Gov. Dixy Lee Ray. The nightmare that occurs to all reporters who use tape recorders became reality for Thompson when his recorder malfunctioned without his knowing it during an hour-long interview with the governor. He could make out parts of the tape when he got back to his office, but most of it was an unnerving hum. Because his paper had already promoted the upcoming interview with Ray to its readers and he could make out about 15 quotes clearly, Thompson decided to reconstruct other quotes from his notes and the imperfect sound of his tape. That was a mistake. The governor complained, sending the paper a transcript of the interview from her own taping. The transcript showed that many of his quotes were inaccurate and some were completely his inventions. *The Oregonian* ran a retraction and punished Thompson, who had 28 years of reporting experience.[39]

Probably the most discussed incident involving supposedly fabricated quotes involved a feature profiling psychoanalyst Jeffrey Masson by Janet Malcolm for *The New Yorker* magazine. Masson claimed that Malcolm had libeled him by making up quotes that made him appear unscholarly, irresponsible, vain and dishonest. For instance, Malcolm quoted Masson as describing himself as an "intellectual gigolo," but a tape recording showed him saying nothing like that. During the trial, she acknowledged that she had rearranged words within quotation marks and had compressed lengthy interviews over several months into what she presented as a single conversation over lunch.

The suit put many journalists in a bind. Many were shocked when the evidence suggested that Malcolm had doctored the quotes. Few supported what she had done. But many journalists feared that if Malcolm lost the libel action, reporters all over the country would be sued if their quotes were not letter-perfect. The U.S. Supreme Court decided it was possible for reporters to libel people by deliberately fabricating or doctoring a quote in a way that damages the reputation of the speaker. But the court preserved protection for writers who make honest errors or deliberately change quotes in ways that do not materially change the speaker's message.[40] In June 1993, a jury found that Malcolm had libeled Masson but deadlocked on the issue of damages.[41]

MANIPULATING PHOTOGRAPHS

That idea that writers get quotes wrong is not new to most readers. They've all heard characters in movies and on TV accuse reporters of putting words in their mouths. But newspaper and newsmagazine readers and TV news viewers give great credibility to the pictures they see. "Seeing is believing" is an even older saying than "The jerk misquoted me."

When newspapers first began to print photographs, the combination of poor reproduction and lack of concern about ethics made it possible for many papers to pass off phony pictures as real. Some papers even pasted photographs of the faces of people onto pictures of actors who were posed to make it seem as if the pictures were taken while the news was happening. The expressions on the faces rarely suited the situation, but printing quality was so bad, the reader couldn't tell.

Fortunately, those days have passed, although occasionally a newspaper photographer tries to improve on reality. In 1981, the *St. Petersburg Times* dismissed a veteran photographer who was caught on film by a photographer from the rival *Tampa Tribune* as he staged a picture. Attempting to liven up routine coverage of a baseball game between Eckerd College and Florida Southern, he asked a barefoot student in the stands to print "Yeah, Eckerd" on the soles of his feet. After the picture appeared in the *Times,* editors heard rumors about the picture being posed and eventually saw the pictures taken by the *Tribune.* The photographer was fired, a *Times* editor explained, because "one of the cardinal sins of a journalist is to tell a lie."[42]

But this kind of manipulation pales in comparison to what can be done by computers. They can rearrange images so competently that even experts cannot separate real from faked photographs. In one infamous incident, staff members of *National Geographic* magazine found themselves with a great picture of a camel in the foreground, one of the great pyramids of Egypt in the background. But the picture couldn't be cropped so that both the camel and the pyramid would be on the magazine's cover, so they used a photo-imaging computer to move the pyramid and make the picture fit. Similarly, the *St. Louis Post-Dispatch* used computers to remove a Diet Coke can from a front-page photo because the editors thought it detracted from the image.

The Orange County (Calif.) Register had a more noble purpose in mind when it altered a picture one of its photographers had taken. After the picture was processed, editors noticed that a young man's pants were unzipped. A technician zipped them up for the man, using the paper's photo-imaging computer.

At first, manipulations were limited to still pictures. But technology in use at all four network TV news organizations makes it possible to do all kinds of fancy tricks with moving pictures. Tom Pettit of NBC News said, "With the highly sophisticated editing of videotape, we can reshape reality with great ease." Victor Porges of ABC agreed: "Fifteen years ago, I could not put on my newscast something that I had not heard or seen or recorded, unless it was something that an artist might have sketched. Now I can create pictures and sounds . . . that never happened. And that opens up all kinds of ethical problems for everybody."[43]

Thomas Wolzien, a senior NBC News vice president, said the unwritten policy at his network is not to manipulate news footage, but he worries about the use of computers by governments to manufacture news film. Some government could produce footage of one of its ships being attacked by a destroyer from another nation. Even experts would be unable to detect such manipulations by sophisticated computer-graphics machines. The danger of phony pictures being shown on network TV has increased, Wolzien noted, because American networks can no longer afford to staff as many foreign bureaus as they once did. Often the networks depend on international exchanges for videotapes of news events. "The sources of this 'video river' range from state-run broadcasting organizations to stringers, and it can be very difficult to determine where a video image has come from—let alone whether it has been altered."[44]

Even before computer manipulation of video was possible, the networks learned the danger of buying videotape on the international market. After a nuclear power plant near Chernobyl in Russia had a near meltdown in 1986, ABC showed dramatic footage supposedly taken inside the structure. Later, the network apologized when the pictures turned out to be the work of a con man who had doctored pictures of a cement factory in Italy.[45]

KEEPING PICTURES HONEST

Many news organizations are trying to establish policies to deal with the ethics of photo-imaging technology. Some have outlawed any manipulation of pictures; others require editors to explain any alterations in the cutlines. The *Chicago Tribune*'s policy is succinct: "We do not alter editorial photos, period." *The Dallas Morning News* takes a similar stand. The Associated Press Managing Editors association was even more blunt. In a report on electronic imaging, APME said, "This is supposed to be about electronic photo manipulation, but it's really about lying. The more we mess with pictures, the more we mess with our credibility."[46]

But not everyone thinks the ethics of this new technology can be dismissed that quickly. Deni Elliott, Mansfield Professor of Ethics at the University of Montana, distinguishes between the manipulation of pictures and deliberate deception. "If the manipulation of images creates a false depiction of reality or if the manipulation fails to disclose some relevant piece of reality, the manipulation is deceptive," she argued. She believes *The Orange County Register* did nothing wrong when it made the sky bluer in its pictures of the explosion of the space shuttle *Challenger* because the intent was not to deceive the public but to show the sky more as it had appeared on TV. (The *Register* had been accused of making the sky bluer so the colors of the exploding shuttle would be more vivid.) However, she would not approve editing out people in the background of a picture because that would be changing reality to suit the desires of the picture editor.[47]

Editors at *The Herald* in New Britain, Conn., have manipulated photographs on at least two occasions — when a child's underwear was exposed and when a child's zipper was undone. "Is that tampering?" executive editor Henry Keezing asked. "I don't think so. That's old-fashioned enhancing that did nothing to change the nature of the pictures. It spared the children from embarrassment."[48]

Some scoff at the concern over the new equipment. Lou Hodges, a professor of professional ethics at Washington and Lee University, has contended that the only reason people get upset about technology is that they believe the myth that photographs objectively portray an event. No photograph captures "what really happened." Photographers have already imposed their subjectivity onto the image when they decide to take a picture or not take one. "And once the noteworthy event has been chosen and the photographer is on the scene," Hodges said, "other crucial value judgments follow: What aspect of the scene is most important and how can I capture it? What angle, background, framing, light, distance, moment to shoot?" Hodges also pointed out that even in a traditional darkroom, photographers routinely use techniques like burning and dodging to emphasize parts of the picture, and in the cropping process remove elements that do not contribute to the photograph's major emphasis. In his view, the real challenge of photo-editing computers is to use them to produce better pictures.[49]

The National Press Photographers Association agrees that computers may be used ethically to improve some pictures. The association's code permits some computer manipulation—lightening a football player's face in a contrasty photo, for example. More serious manipulations would need to be discussed with newsroom officials before publication. The code bans manipulation that deceives readers. The group is concerned that as the public learns about the ability of computers to alter photos, many may begin to doubt the honesty of most pictures they see in newspapers or on TV.

Researchers at the University of Wisconsin surveyed news photographers and found that about 29 percent would remove telephone wires from a picture if they detracted from the image, 27 percent would close a zipper, and 19 percent would combine two photos to produce a better image.[50] Other photographers would like to see the American media adopt a system like the Norwegians'. The media there agreed to put a warning logo on all altered photographs, even if the alterations are relatively minor.[51]

PHONY ADVICE COLUMNS

Advice columns have been standard in American newspapers for a long time. Columns by "Ann Landers" or her sister "Dear Abby" have been popular with readers of nearly every daily in the nation. Many papers in recent years have adopted the advice-column format for all kinds of things. Some of them, often called "Action Line," answer consumer complaints. Others give advice on subjects ranging from investing in the stock market to gardening. In most cases, the people writing letters to these columns are given anonymity. That opens the door for various kinds of fabrication, from the silly letters Ann Landers used to get from Yale undergraduates pretending to be "Panting Patty From Paducah" to the more serious manufacturing of letters by staff members of newspapers publishing the advice columns.

When *The Philadelphia Daily News* started a new advice column by psychologist David Stein, "Ask David," the first day's offerings included questions from "Frustrated Mom, East Falls," "Perplexed, S. Phila.," and "Mark, Mt. Airy." As the column warmed to its task, letters appeared from "Irritated Hubby, Ardmore," complaining that his wife's "best friend is a lying creep," and from "Carol, Bala Cynwyd," who was concerned that her husband was too liberal because he told their young daughter details about their lovemaking ("Your husband's no liberal, he's a pervert," David replied). But when David printed a letter from "Worried, Kensington," asking advice because after 22 years of marriage her husband "all of a sudden wants to tie me down to the bed during sex," it was too much for Clark DeLeon, who wrote a column for *The Philadelphia Inquirer.* DeLeon snooped around and reported that all those heavy letters David had received had been written by *Daily News* staff members. *Daily News* editors said the in-house efforts would end as soon as enough legitimate letters started rolling in. "Sign us, 'Cynical, South Philly,'" DeLeon concluded.[52]

"Rats! I have to come up with two more letters for our new advice column!"

Rich Stim, a former editor of the "Hot-Line" column for the Bloomington, Ind., *Herald-Telephone,* told *Columbia Journalism Review* that he created about half the questions he used during his final year at the paper. He said he started slowly, making up two reader queries based on facts he found in the *World Almanac* so he could leave work early to practice with a rock band. Nobody said a word, so soon he was making up one or two questions for each of his columns. Unaware of what Stim was doing, his editor unwittingly encouraged the practice when he selected questions for the "Best of Hot Line" column at the end of the year and chose a majority from those Stim had dreamed up.[53]

The *Wilmington (N.C.) Morning Star* carries a question-and-answer column that received a "dart" from *Columbia Journalism Review* because most of the questions came from employees of the paper, who are asked to submit them. Readers were not told who wrote the questions.[54]

What's an Ethical Journalist to Do?

Journalists pride themselves on exposing the dishonesty of others. They delight in uncovering the deceit of crooked pastors, phony doctors and greedy businesspeople. They see it as their obligation to debunk misleading advertisements and keep track of broken promises by political leaders and unfulfilled promises by bureaucrats. Presidents have been brought down and politicians' careers ruined when reporters caught them circumventing the truth.

But journalists are not always as conscientious about holding themselves to the same standards of honesty. Incidents like Janet Cooke's fictitious heroin addict and NBC's rigged crash tests are sorry tales of reporters trying too hard to score the big story. Deceptions like these damage the credibility of all reporters.

But lesser deviations from honest reporting also make a mockery of journalism's supposed devotion to truth-telling. Reporters who make up quotes so their stories will have more punch or so they can express their opinions are being dishonest. So are reporters who take the rambling words of an interviewee, turn them into polished sentences, then put quote marks around them to make it seem as if that were the way the person spoke. Cleaning up quotes can in some instances be justified. Because informal and not-prepared-in-advance statements from sources are sometimes ungrammatical, journalists usually make some minor changes. But these changes should not mislead the reader. Material in quotation marks ought to be an honest reflection of what people said and how they said it. If interviewees speak so poorly that readers would be confused by verbatim quotes, the reporter should paraphrase. Skilled writers can blend paraphrases and direct quotes in a way that captures the emotions of sources without resorting to fake quotes.

Everyone would agree that copying stories and passing them off as your own is dishonest, but not all examples of plagiarism are that clearcut. "In its worst forms, plagiarism is a sickness," said *Newsweek* media writer Jonathan Alter. "In its lesser forms it's a kind of carelessness that I think every journalist sweats over." He contends that all journalists borrow, "so it's just a question of how much you borrow and what kind of credit you provide."[55]

Some reporters who would never borrow the words of other writers see nothing wrong with lifting quotes and using them. Although newspapers were once more cavalier in their handling of borrowed quotes, most now consider it a dishonest practice. Lifting a quote makes it seem as if the reporter had tracked down the person and asked the right question to prompt the great response. When ethical reporters copy quotes from another reporter today, they acknowledge the paper or TV station that first carried the quote, either in the body of the story or a note at the end.

At one time staging pictures was considered a trick of the news photographers' trade. Old-timers tell of photographers who kept all kinds of stage props in their cars. If they arrived at the scene of an accident involving a child, they could toss a doll or a ball on the road and be sure of a good picture. That kind of fakery is not accepted anymore by photographers or by the public. But photo-imaging computers can make that kind of deception seem like small potatoes. These machines have opened the way for flawless deception. Unscrupulous technicians can create images and modify them to any end. Fortunately, we have not seen many abuses in newspapers or TV. Most news organizations and professional societies have been calling for standards against such practices. But all of journalism needs to be alert to the new ease with which visual images can be distorted.

Whether we're talking about words or pictures, truth still must be journalism's enduring goal. There is no place for fakery in a profession in which truth-telling is its most fundamental principle.

Privacy

As the managing editor of a large metropolitan daily newspaper, you have to decide how far to go in identifying the eight victims of a fire at a gay film club.

All of them are men, and most are married. None is well-known, but one is an aide to a congressman, one an Army major, and one a former pastor. Six other men were injured seriously enough to require hospitalization, but authorities have withheld their names and other identification. Because flames blocked the front door of the club, the only unlocked exit, firefighters had to smash through a locked rear door to reach the dead and injured men, who had been watching all-male X-rated films on the second floor.

Would you identify the dead men fully—their names, ages, addresses and survivors? Would you use the name of the theater? Would you mention the nature of the movies shown? Would you tell your reporters to press authorities to name the injured men?

The editors of *The Washington Post* and the old *Washington Star* had to decide how far they would go in identifying the eight men who perished in just such a fire at the Cinema Follies, a gay-oriented theater.

And the decisions they made differed. The *Star* decided to identify the dead men fully, and the *Post* decided not to name them. Both papers revealed the nature of the theater, but neither published the names of the injured. The ombudsmen for the two competing papers discussed their papers' different approaches to this story in columns about a week after the tragedy. Charles B. Seib of the *Post* said his paper's "main motivation in not using the names was compassion for the wives and children of the men."[1] But George Beveridge of the *Star* wrote that "the identity of the victims in a local tragedy as substantial as this one was so vital an element of the story that the printing of the names never arose" as an issue in the minds of *Star* editors who handled the story.[2]

Beveridge argued that being in a gay-oriented theater didn't prove the men were gay and that whether they were gay didn't matter to the story. He said the overriding obligation of the media in stories like these was to report the information:

> The purpose of those stories, in *The Post* and *The Star* alike, wasn't to disclose or suggest the sexual preferences of anyone. The stories were written solely because eight human beings who happened to be in a certain place at a certain time, tragically died in a fire. That was news. I won't argue that the sexual orientation of the Cinema Follies added no element of additional reader interest to the story. But the point is that eight deaths in a fire at the Kennedy Center, or an uptown X-rated movie, for that matter, would be no less a story. The victims would be no less or no more important to the story in those instances than they were in the Cinema Follies fire. And I can't for the life of me imagine a like tragedy in any other location in which the victims should not be identified as a matter of legitimate reader interest.

Beveridge was concerned about the precedent the *Post*'s approach might create. While "it is hard to imagine that anyone fails to share the *Post*'s compassion for the families of the fire victims," he wrote, the *Post*'s failure to identify the victims of the disaster amounted "to a sort of double standard of press responsibility that is much easier started than stopped."

Seib, the *Post*'s ombudsman, also disagreed with the decision made by *Post* editors. He said he found it "disquieting" because "in effect, *Post* editors said that homosexuality is so shameful that extraordinary steps had to be taken to protect the families of the victims." He questioned whether the *Post* approach did not underscore "the stigma of homosexuality" just when "efforts are being made to bring it out and address it as a social fact."

Seib contended that the *Post* should have fully identified all the fire victims. "By all the measures we normally use, the names were news, and the business of a newspaper is to print the news," he wrote. "Any other course results inevitably in confusion and precedents that cause trouble later." But, in his postmortem on the *Post*'s decision not to fully identify the victims, Seib suspected that if a poll could be taken, "the public would favor the course the *Post* took" because the "public generally feels, I think, that the press is much too insensitive to the harm and pain it can cause innocent people."

Questions like these as to whether a journalist should reveal intimate details about the lives of people are privacy questions. Some people think of privacy as a legal issue involving lawyers and standards set by the courts. And they are partly right. Several famous and not so famous lawsuits against the media have involved invasion of privacy as the law has defined it. But the privacy decisions that journalists usually face are more ethical than legal: Not whether it would be legal to seek and report certain private information but whether it is ethical.

Much of the information published and broadcast in this country is regarded by some of the people involved as private. The political candidate may consider it a private matter that his legal career ended when he was disbarred for mishandling clients' money; a drunken driver may not welcome news accounts about his accident in which a child was killed. The question for journalists is not whether to invade privacy but when and how much. At what point does an invasion of privacy pass from reasonable to unreasonable?

Three Conflicting Obligations

In making these difficult decisions, American journalists have traditionally given different treatment to ordinary citizens and to prominent people, particularly politicians. In effect, the news media afford less privacy to public officials and celebrities. But regardless of the prominence of the people in the news, journalists deciding how far to go in invading privacy seem to be pulled by three sometimes-conflicting obligations: to get the news out, to show compassion, and to educate society.

Although these conflicting obligations are considerations in most privacy decisions, some of the most public discussions of them have come out of the debate about the use of rape victims' names in news stories.

TO GET THE NEWS OUT

Many journalists argue that the obligation to broadcast or print the news is paramount in most privacy decisions, including the question of whether to name rape victims. Charles M. Houser, executive editor of the Providence papers when they named a woman who was gang-raped on a tavern pool table in New Bedford, Mass., said he was bothered by giving rape victims the special treatment of not identifying them. "Any time we are suppressing public information, we are deciding what is good for society, for the public, for an individual."[3]

Although her paper, the Louisville *Courier-Journal,* does not routinely name rape victims, managing editor Irene Nolan thinks maybe it should. "It's basically wrong to treat rape differently from other violent crimes. I know people who've gone through this, and I've seen the horrible agony they go through, but we're not doing anything to help."[4]

Alan Dershowitz, a professor at Harvard Law School, puts a different spin on the get-the-news-out argument. He contends that if the news media name the accused man (who is presumed innocent until proved guilty), they should name his accuser. "In this country there is no such thing as anonymous accusation."[5] That was apparently the thinking behind the decision by editors at the *New York Amsterdam News,* a black-oriented newspaper, to name a jogger who was raped and beaten in Central Park. The editors wanted to protest the fact that the media were withholding the victim's name while using names and pictures of the six African-American youths, ages 14 to 16, accused of attacking her.[6]

THE NEED FOR COMPASSION

Most people who have been in the news business very long know of facts that weren't reported because they would have brought unnecessary harm to people. In the 1980s, for example, news organizations from around the world carried stories about the "bubble boy," a child born in Houston who had an immune deficiency that forced him to live in a germ-free bubble. But none of the stories gave his complete name — he was called only David — or hinted where he lived so that his family could live as normal a life as possible.

That same sentiment now guides many newspapers in their decisions about naming rape victims. Until the 1960s, many newspapers routinely printed names of women who said they had been raped, particularly if their cases were tried in open court. But women's groups argued that publishing rape victims' names made them victims twice — once when the crime was committed and again when the story was reported.[7]

*"I don't know — using the names of these
Sabine women might stigmatize them for life."*

Women's groups wanted rape treated differently from other crimes because of its stigma in our society. As Robin Benedict, a Columbia University journalism professor, wrote in her recent book on the media coverage of sex crimes: "As long as people have any sense of privacy about sexual acts and the human body, rape will, therefore, carry a stigma — not necessarily a stigma that blames the victim for what happened to her, but a stigma that links her name irrevocably with an act of intimate humiliation."[8] By the early 1990s, most news organizations, from compassion for rape victims, had policies against naming them in nearly all circumstances.[9]

TO EDUCATE SOCIETY

Some argue that there are times when newspapers should invade the privacy of some people to overcome stereotypes and undermine stigmas that contribute to public ignorance and bigotry. The news media have raised public awareness of various diseases and social problems, sometimes at the expense of our sense of privacy. Particularly when public people have suffered from them, alcoholism, prescription-drug abuse, various cancers and AIDS have received detailed, sympathetic news coverage that has raised public understanding and lowered the secrecy that once surrounded these conditions.

Some argue that it is the duty of the news media to educate society about these kinds of issues even if it means intruding on some people's privacy. Editors at *The Des Moines Register* believed that not printing the name of a rape victim and writing about the nature of the crime contributed to the stigma attached to rape. They assigned reporter Jane Schorer to write a series of stories about a rape in a rural Iowa town. After finding a volunteer for the story, Schorer used her name and gave explicit details of the crime and the woman's feelings during the police investigation and subsequent trial. Naming the victim was criticized by many and became a hot topic on call-in radio talk shows in Des Moines. But most people who called the paper expressed appreciation that the veil of secrecy had been lifted from the crime. Schorer said she hoped the series would "mark the point where society at large first showed itself as ready and willing to listen" to rape victims and their problems.[10] Her stories won a Pulitzer Prize.

Some feminists have applauded media efforts to cover rape with more candor. Isabelle Katz Pinzler, director of the Women's Rights Project of the American Civil Liberties Union, has said: "There are feminist arguments why it might not be a bad idea to name the victims. It might be a step toward destigmatizing and, by making rape less of a faceless crime, it brings home the horror."[11]

That's the reason Henry Gay, publisher of *The Shelton-Mason County Journal* in Washington, routinely publishes rape victims' names. Concealing the identity of rape victims perpetuates the Dark Ages thinking that such a woman is now "defective," her life ruined, Gay contended. "And at the end of the trial is the Big Daddy newspaper editor with his unctuous promise: 'Don't worry little lady. No one will find out from me that you're ruined forever.' "[12]

One problem with trying to make decisions based on what will be best for society is that it is difficult to predict how people will react to the stories. Although Gay and others argue that printing the names of rape victims might help society by lessening the stigma of the crime, there are those who maintain that society will be hurt if the media use names. They fear that fewer women may be willing to press charges against their assailants. They cite an opinion poll finding that more than two-thirds of the women surveyed said they would be more likely to report sexual assaults if there were laws against disclosure of their names.[13] However, Joe Doster, publisher of the Winston-Salem, N.C., *Journal,* said that does not seem to have happened in his county. The *Journal* prints the names of all women who file rape complaints; papers in neighboring counties do not. He said more rapes are reported in his county than in the more populous surrounding counties.[14]

THE ARTHUR ASHE CASE

Celebrities, of course, get more public attention than ordinary folks. They put themselves in the limelight, and some court the media to keep their names — and thus their careers — fresh in the minds of the public.

Although celebrities will clearly receive more media attention than ordinary people, journalists wrestle with the same issues when trying to decide when to grant them privacy and when to report the details of their lives. Sometimes the decision is not to print. For example, reporters did not write stories about TV journalist Linda Ellerbee's breast cancer and double mastectomy. They kept quiet until she announced it.[15] Other times, the media have not shown such civility. The way reporters treated Arthur Ashe, the revered tennis player, divided the journalism community.

Ashe won nearly every major tennis title but was forced to retire early from the game because of heart problems. However, he stayed in the public eye. He became a tennis commentator for HBO and ABC, wrote columns for several major publications, and coached the 1983 U.S. Davis Cup team. He also remained active in social causes, raising millions of dollars for several groups, giving countless speeches, even being arrested during an anti-apartheid protest at the South African Embassy.[16] One sports writer said Ashe was "a good tennis player, but an even better man."

After receiving a transfusion of blood that had been tainted with the HIV virus, Ashe developed AIDS. Many sportswriters learned of Ashe's illness and decided that the need to show compassion outweighed the pressure to publish this information. Some had known about Ashe's condition for several years but had not reported the story, as one national sports correspondent explained, "out of respect for Arthur Ashe."[17]

Then a reporter at *USA Today* got a tip about Ashe's illness. Gene Policinski, sports managing editor of *USA Today,* called Ashe and told him what his reporter had heard. He said that unless Ashe denied the rumor, the paper would keep investigating but would not publish anything until the story was confirmed by someone with direct information about Ashe's medical condition. Believing the newspaper was about to break the story, Ashe called a press conference so that he could tell his story rather than letting *USA Today* tell it. He said he would have preferred to wait and make the announcement when his 5-year-old daughter was older and could better understand. He also said he feared she might be taunted and shunned by her classmates at school once they knew her father had AIDS.

Ashe's revelations at his news conference were reported in nearly every newspaper and TV newscast. But journalists were divided on the ethics of the way *USA Today* pursued the story. As in many discussions of privacy issues, the debate about the Ashe story centered on trying to balance those three basic pressures: the obligation to get the news out, the need to show compassion, and the desire to educate the public about social issues.

Many journalists argued that the story was news and that it was therefore their obligation to print it when it was confirmed. *USA Today* sports editor Policinski called it "a significant news story." The paper's editor, Peter Pritchard, supported him: "Journalists serve the public by reporting news, not hiding it."[18] Top editors at the *San Jose Mercury News* and *The Kansas City Star* told *Washington Journalism Review* that they agreed. "With the level of interest about AIDS and the level of interest about Ashe, you have a powerful story," said Arthur Brisbane, the *Star*'s editor.[19]

Not everyone applauded the conduct of those journalists who chose not to reveal Ashe's illness. Barry Bingham, who published a media ethics newsletter, wasn't so sure that these journalists were showing compassion as much as taking care of a friend. He said that not reporting the story out of respect was acceptable, "but we cannot expect every newspaper or broadcast station to judge the newsworthiness of a story by personal friendship."[20]

Exposing Ashe's condition was also justified by the argument that printing the story educated the public about AIDS. *USA Today* editor Prichard contended, "By sharing his story, Arthur Ashe and his family are free of a great weight. In the days ahead, they will help us better understand AIDS and how to defeat it."[21] Others defended the story on the grounds that it taught the public a lesson about how AIDS was spread, or in this case, not spread. Many papers printed sidebars explaining that health officials have changed the procedures for handling blood to make transfusions safer than when Ashe received contaminated blood. Some suggested that the Ashe story may have helped break down the stereotype that AIDS is mostly a gay men's disease. The public, it is argued, may become more sympathetic to the need for better AIDS treatment when they read of cases like Ashe's.

Jonathan Yardley, a *Washington Post* writer, disputed the claim that the story served a larger societal need. "No public issues were at stake," he said. "No journalistic 'rights' were threatened. The fight against AIDS will in no way be hastened or strengthened by the exposure to which Ashe has been subjected."[22] Similarly, William Rubenstein, director of an AIDS project for the American Civil Liberties Union, said that if the media wanted to do something about AIDS, they could find much better stories, such as the inadequate health care available to people with AIDS and discrimination against them.[23]

Many other journalists and members of the public argued that the need to show compassion to Ashe and his family outweighed the need to get the news out or the public benefit gained by reading Ashe's story.

Randy Shilts, the late newspaper columnist who wrote two books about AIDS, acknowledged that the Ashe story made people more aware of AIDS. "As a person who cares about AIDS, this is good for the epidemic. But as someone who cares about the human condition, this guy deserves some privacy."[24]

Stephanie Salter of the *San Francisco Examiner* said that most reporters she knew would have experienced a "sickening feeling" if they had been asked to call Ashe and ask him about AIDS. "That sickening feeling, I contend, is our basic human knowledge that what we are about to do is wrong."[25] And Floyd Abrams, a constitutional lawyer and champion of First Amendment rights, said if the rumors had been about a presidential candidate, he would have supported *USA Today*'s actions. But in this case, the potential for harm was so great and the information it provided so little, "I find even the concept of such a story abhorrent."[26]

Ashe himself spelled out the ethical question journalists faced: "Are you going to be cold, hard, crass purveyors of the facts just for the sake of peoples' right to know, under the guise of freedom of the press—or are you going to show a little sensitivity about some things?" Ashe conceded that if the story had been about someone in a position of trust, "from the president down to the conductor of the subway," the public should be informed. But, he said, "I would hope that the so-called newsworthiness of that story will be tempered with sensitivity."[27]

INVASIVE PHOTOS

News cameras obviously have great potential for invading privacy. Responsible photographers and editors who realize that danger try to exercise care in deciding what pictures to take, then how and whether each image should be passed to the public. Poking a camera into personal moments of grief and tragedy can clearly strike many as an invasion of privacy. The arguments over the ethics of invasive photos are similar to those in other privacy decisions.

Photographers and editors at *The Orange County Register* in California and the Pottstown, Pa., *Mercury* maintained that controversial photos in their papers were news and showed the realities of life. The *Mercury*'s Tom Kelly won a Pulitzer Prize for his photos of a blood-stained young man who had gone berserk and killed his wife, stabbed his daughter in the eye, and seriously injured his 71-year-old grandmother. Kelly admitted the photos were "shocking and very emotional" but did not believe the press "should hide what's going on. It's life. It happened."[28]

A photograph on the front page of *The Orange County Register* captured a grief-stricken wife who had been driving to work when she came upon a car crash in which her husband had been killed. A freelance photographer snapped the picture just as a police officer confirmed that her husband had died in the wreckage. Readers called in to protest that running the photo was insensitive and irresponsible, but the paper's ombudsman, Pat Riley, defended it: "It mirrored emotional reality in a powerful way and aroused our empathy. It did not, in my view, hold the woman up to ridicule. It showed her expressing natural understandable suffering, and we could all feel it."[29]

Several editors have justified controversial pictures by arguing that the pictures taught society a valuable lesson. For example, when John Harte, a staff photographer for *The (Bakersfield) Californian,* responded to a call he heard on a police scanner, he arrived in time to see divers bring up the lifeless body of a 5-year-old boy. As the boy's distraught family gathered around the body that had been placed in an open body bag, a sheriff tried to hold back onlookers, including Harte and a local TV crew. The TV crew did not film that moment, but Harte did, ducking under the sheriff's outstretched arms and shooting eight quick frames.[30] Robert Bentley, *The Californian*'s managing editor who decided to use Harte's moving picture, said he thought the photo might remind people to be more careful when their kids are swimming.

A family's anguish: As the weeping father kneels over the body of his young son, a rescue worker (*left*) tries to console the drowning victim's brother and other family members. The editor who ran this picture said he wished he hadn't. (Photo courtesy of *The Californian,* Bakersfield, Calif.)

A similar argument was used by editors of *The New York Post* when they ran a front-page picture of the crushed body, uncovered and face-up, of a 4-year-old boy who fell to his death from a 53rd-floor window in an apartment building. The boy was the son of singer Eric Clapton. The editors claimed that they used the picture not because he was Clapton's son but because they wanted to warn people of the dangers of children playing near open windows in high-rise apartments.[31]

A variation of this reasoning was advanced by the Rochester, N.Y., *Times-Union* after it published an amateur photographer's picture of a 49-year-old woman who had doused herself with gasoline and set fire to herself on a quiet suburban street that morning.[32] The woman, who had left a suicide note, was still alive when *Times-Union* editors decided to use the photo, but she died later that day. In answer to calls and letters of protest, Nancy Woodhull, managing editor at the time, pointed out that the woman had taken her life in a very public place. Besides, the editor added, "the world needs to know this is what happens to a person if pushed to the brink. . . . This is what we're talking about when we talk about mental health facilities and mental health care."[33]

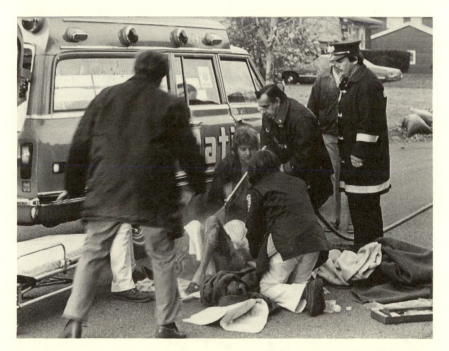

Firefighters and ambulance crew members fight to save the life of a woman who tried to take her life by setting fire to herself. Should this picture have been published?

This "the public needs to be reminded" argument, so often heard in American journalism to justify offensive photos and articles about crime, accidents and other tragedies, doesn't impress journalism professor George Padgett. "Despite the good intentions, the prevention justification simply does not hold up." He contends that if newspapers were truly dedicated to promoting safety, "they could do a lot more than publish an occasional photograph of a victim's grieving survivors."[34] Steve Bauser, editor of *The Salisbury Post* in North Carolina, is more blunt: "That's a bunch of crap," he told *Presstime*. "We print it because it's a dynamite picture."[35]

Many readers don't buy the argument either. After *The Californian* printed the picture of the dead child and his family, it got 500 calls of protest, one bomb threat, some canceled subscriptions, and more than 200 irate letters. "Some claimed *The Californian* showed callous disrespect for the victim," Bentley, the paper's managing editor, wrote in his column the next week. "Others felt the photograph had forced their visual intrusion on what should have been a family's private time of shock and grief. Most combined the dual protests."[36] *The Californian* editor told readers he believed that in the future he would not let the desire to print a sensational picture make him forget the feelings of the families involved. The most important lesson his staff should learn from his error "is the stark validation of what readers — and former readers — are saying not just locally but across the country: That the news media are seriously out of touch with their audiences."[37]

His call to remember the feelings of the people involved was echoed by Minneapolis *Star Tribune* ombudsman Lou Gelfand after that paper in one month printed two pictures that many thought invaded people's privacy. One was of a man falling to his knees and crying after he learned his daughter had died; the other was of a young man weeping after hearing that a friend had been killed in a car crash. Gelfand said he did not think his paper should ban such pictures, but he proposed a moratorium because of local community standards. "I believe those standards in St. Paul-Minneapolis differ from those in bigger cities where life is more impersonal." He contended that "newspapers can show compassion without compromising their mission. Denying the readers this view of someone's grief would not have shortchanged the news report."[38]

Privacy of Ordinary People

When ordinary people get caught up in the news, journalists — for the moment at least — tend to treat them like public figures. It does not seem to matter whether the private persons thrust themselves into the news (marchers, protesters and demonstrators) or fall into the news through no deliberate action of their own (victims of disasters or crime). Many journalists worry, however, about hurting people who with no intent find themselves being interviewed and photographed for display in newspapers and news broadcasts.

IDENTIFYING GAYS AND LESBIANS

Oliver W. Sipple, a 33-year-old ex-Marine, became a national hero when he grabbed the arm of a would-be assassin and stopped her from shooting President Gerald Ford as he left the St. Francis Hotel in San Francisco. Soon after the incident, Harvey Milk, a San Francisco politician, and other gay rights activists said they were proud that "one of us" had saved the president's life and claimed that Ford was slow to honor Sipple because he was gay. The activists asked the Bay area media, which had made no reference to Sipple's personal life during the first two days of coverage, to acknowledge that Sipple was gay in hopes that it would help break the stereotype.

But Sipple would not answer reporters' questions about his lifestyle directly. "My sexual orientation has nothing at all to do with saving the president's life, just as the color of my eyes or my race has nothing to do with what happened in front of the St. Francis Hotel." He explained that he had never told his employer, his mother or his family about his lifestyle and wanted to keep it that way.[39]

Although most news organizations were slow to use the story, Herb Caen, a widely read columnist for the *San Francisco Examiner,* reported the remarks of Milk and the activists. Then a *Los Angeles Times* reporter wrote a story that was picked up by the national wire services. Although the story quoted Sipple as unwilling to discuss his sexual orientation, the reporter used information, given to him by gay activists, that Sipple had participated in well-publicized activities in San Francisco's gay community.

The exposure of Sipple's personal life had one result that the reporters and gay activists had not anticipated. When the *Times* story appeared in Sipple's hometown newspaper *The Detroit News,* it was read by his parents, who were stunned to learn about their son's lifestyle.[40] Sipple and his mother, who died four years later, never spoke to each other again. Sipple sued the newspapers, but the courts ruled that the stories did not meet the legal understanding of invasion of privacy.

Some gay groups continue to pressure the media to engage in "outing," a term for exposing gays and lesbians who have not gone public with their lifestyle.[41] In the early 1990s there were magazines devoted to "outing." But media ethics scholar Deni Elliott wonders if the ploy may backfire. In a column she wrote shortly after Sipple died in 1989, she said stories that make a big deal of the fact that a hero is gay may contribute "to the idea that there was something bizarre about a man who is both heroic and homosexual."[42] And even if these stories might contribute to better understanding of gays and lesbians, Fred Friendly, former president of CBS News and journalism professor emeritus at Columbia University, asked, "Whatever the cause, do we as journalists have the ethical or moral prerogative to strip away anyone's privacy, unless there is an overriding and prevailing justification?"[43]

By and large, the media have answered Friendly's question with a resounding no and have resisted efforts to get them to out gays. In 1991 a free-lance writer reported that at the same time the Pentagon was enforcing a ban on gays and lesbians in the military, a high-ranking Pentagon official was gay. Many news organizations carried stories about the allegations, usually in the context of the larger question of outing. But only a handful, including *The Detroit News, The Patriot* of Harrisburg, Pa., WPIX in New York, and CNBC, a cable news channel, used the man's name.[44] However, many editors who refused to identify the Pentagon official printed stories acknowledging that a conservative columnist who had frequently taken anti-gay positions was gay and had died of AIDS.[45]

Most gay and lesbian journalists believe the real challenge for the news media is to improve their overall coverage of gays and lesbians. A survey found that many do not believe their news organizations do an adequate job of covering events in local gay communities.[46]

DISEASES

Americans have traditionally been squeamish about diseases that cause death. At one time the word "cancer" was spoken only in whispers. News accounts would not say someone died of cancer but a "lingering illness." It took several public-education campaigns to get cancer recognized as a disease and not a moral failing.

As the story of Arthur Ashe showed, the media are now wrestling with the issue of how to report AIDS. Many publications have balked at naming people with AIDS. When *The Boston Globe* ran a story about doctors at a city hospital who denied treatment to a person they suspected had AIDS, it did not name the patient. The paper's ombudsman, Robert J. Kierstead, explained that people with AIDS, "because of the public's inordinate fear of them, may often require the type of voluntary media protection accorded rape victims."[47] A majority of newspaper editors surveyed in 1991 said their papers did not routinely list AIDS as a cause of death.[48]

An equally tough problem for the media was explaining some of the ways the disease was spread. Scientists learned that many gay men had acquired the disease during anal intercourse. But many newspapers saw themselves as family-oriented and would not print those words. As Daniel Lynch, managing editor of *The Times Union* in Albany, N.Y., noted, papers used euphemisms for anal intercourse such as "exchange of bodily fluids" or "intimate sexual contact." Lynch said that this shyness in reporting the way the disease is spread contributed to two misunderstandings. First, many incorrectly guessed what kinds of "intimate sexual contact" spread the disease. Second, since the media were not forthcoming in reporting the way the disease was spread yet gave so much attention to people who had contracted the disease through blood transfusions, many believed they were typical of AIDS patients.[49]

The AIDS discussion also opened the media to the use of the word "condom." Bill Wheatley, former executive producer of *NBC Nightly News,* recalled that in the mid-1980s, staffers at NBC had a lengthy debate about whether America was ready to hear that word on a network newscast.[50]

But many readers believe that some body parts are just too private to be shown in daily newspapers. Many complained when the Minneapolis *Star Tribune* ran a story about ways to detect breast cancer and illustrated it with a photo showing a woman giving herself a breast examination. One woman asked if the paper would illustrate a story about prostate cancer with a similar picture of testicles.[51]

CRIME VICTIMS

The news media's treatment of crime victims has been questioned by many, including some journalists who have become the victims of crime. Thomas Oliphant, a columnist for *The Boston Globe,* wrote: "I got mugged the night before last, a humiliating opportunity to be reminded that the allies of crime victims are the cops, not the press. . . . Any crime, of course, is humiliating. Most cops understand this and treat crime victims as people. Most journalists don't understand this and treat us as subjects."

Oliphant said that after the crime, he was pulled in two directions.

He wanted to call the police in hopes the mugger would be caught. Yet he knew that by dialing 911 he would give up his privacy. He knew that some people would wonder what he was doing walking where he was that late at night. And others would chuckle that a liberal columnist had been the target of street crime. "What infuriates me as a crime victim," he said, "is that the press would insist that it alone can decide when I lose my privacy, and that my recourse to contest that decision is virtually nonexistent."[52]

Other crime victims have complained of being so hounded by reporters that they felt forced to leave their homes to get some peace. A few tell stories of being duped by journalists into giving them pictures of family members. Complaints like these prompted the National Victim Center to create a media code of ethics that calls for reporters to remember that victims are under no obligation to be interviewed and encourages photographers to get permission before taking pictures of victims. Victims' organizations in some areas are trying to get laws passed that would allow police to restrict information about victims. In some South Florida cities, police officers already give victims leaflets explaining that they do not have to talk to reporters.

Few argue that the news media should not cover crimes. Even the National Victim Center acknowledges that news organizations should provide the public with "factual, objective information" about crime. The argument is that reporters should be sensitive to the feelings of crime victims. *Washington Post* ombudsman Joann Byrd insists: "There are ways to report the news without invading people's privacy, without adding to the pain they are experiencing. It often means more reporting, a different approach to the story, a different kind of picture, a different angle. [But] it's quite possible to describe . . . the agony of an experience without being ghoulish about it."[53]

DETAILS OF CRIME

As recently as the 1970s, many newspapers thought the word "rape" was too explicit a description of the crime and banned its use. A reporter could write that a woman had been "criminally assaulted" or "molested," but not "raped." One Houston paper even changed a woman's direct quote. Instead of "Help! I'm being raped!" she was quoted as yelling "Help! I'm being criminally assaulted!"[54]

But fewer news organizations today are that squeamish about details of crime. When some students at the University of Florida were found murdered in their apartments near campus, some papers printed graphic accounts of the mutilation of their bodies. And many readers were given more details of Milwaukee killer Jeffrey Dahmer's cannibalism than they wanted.

Journalists disagree on how graphic these accounts should be. When a jogger was gang-raped in New York's Central Park, the gruesome details of the crime and intimate information about her previous sex life were part of the court record and were available to reporters. Many papers printed much of this information. Some journalists told *Newsday* they had no problems with the explicit coverage. John Corporon, vice president for news at New York's WPIX-TV, said, "It's a tragedy on top of a tragedy she already suffered, but I don't think the media can turn their backs on a story to protect her privacy." And Thomas Mulvoy, managing editor of *The Boston Globe,* argued that the story transcended considerations of privacy. "It's more of a symbolic story than it is about one person's privacy," he said. "It has to do with what's happening in society."

But other journalists were bothered. When *Newsday* managing editor Howard Schneider read his own paper one morning, he found a verbatim account of the rape as contained in a videotaped confession. "I was stunned," he said. "It really troubled me. I thought, 'My God, this is incredibly explicit.' " He learned that day that the story had been approved by the paper's editor. Veteran reporter Gabe Pressman of WNBC-TV in New York said he too believed the media coverage of the rape of the jogger was an "outrageous violation" of her privacy. "I think there's a kind of prurient or scatological tendency in the press and television these days," he said. "Unconsciously, we like to use those little morsels. We know we're titillating people by giving them some of the raw details of the crime."[55]

INTERVIEWING SURVIVORS

Many journalists have drawn the thankless task of interviewing survivors of people who have died in wars, murders and other tragedies. Most journalists and members of the public understand that these interviews, when appropriately done, can help society understand the tragedy better. But it's the kind of assignment few people want, and it's one that many reporters don't handle well. "Some smart people ask dumb questions when they have to intrude on grief," noted Brian Healey of CBS News.[56] Journalists and the public alike cringe when a reporter pushes a microphone in someone's face at the scene of a tragedy and asks, "How does it feel . . . ?"

However, reporters who approach families with courtesy and respect usually find that families are helpful. When reporters experience

"Thank you for the picture of your daughter, ma'am. And for talking to me about her. I can't tell you how much I dreaded having to bother you so soon after your loss. I'll take good care of her picture and get it back to you safely."

hostility, it is often from people who are not involved in the tragedy. For example, when reporters from WISN-TV in Milwaukee tried to interview people at the high school attended by a man killed in the 1991 Gulf War, they were greeted with cries of "Vulture, vulture." Ironically, a block away, reporters from another TV station were interviewing the man's brother, who wanted to talk to reporters.[57]

Other journalists have experienced similar reactions. Reporter Rene Stutzman, then with UPI, was covering the collapse of a walkway in a Kansas City hotel that killed more than 100 people. She approached a victim's family sitting in the lobby of a nearby hotel and asked if she could interview them. "If they had made the slightest indication they did not want to be interviewed, I would have stopped," she said. But family members asked her to sit down and began to talk. "Then people in the lobby came up and started calling me names, and I had to leave."[58]

The editor of the *Chicago Sun-Times* was so concerned about invading the privacy of relatives of people killed during the 1991 Gulf War that he ordered reporters not to contact the families. The paper carried a note saying that it would talk only to families who volunteered to be interviewed. However, a columnist for the competing *Chicago Tribune* pointed out the inconsistency in the *Sun-Times'* decision not to cover funerals of war dead. The paper had given considerable coverage to the funerals of a child who died of AIDS and the mother of a Notre Dame football player.[59]

But most journalists would agree that interviews with the families of war victims are essential to the story. "There is a value in portraying the human condition, including misery, including grief about the loss of a son," said Reese Cleghorn, dean of the University of Maryland College of Journalism, when he was asked about media coverage after 241 Marines were killed in Beirut in 1983. Although he thought the public should be outraged when reporters do not treat families civilly, he saw a value in invading privacy "in some cases to show people what has gone on. It adds a dimension to our understanding of war. . . . People come home dead from war."[60]

ADDRESSES AND AGES

At one time, the rule was clear. Reporters were supposed to get the exact names, including middle initials, of people in the news, their exact ages and their exact addresses. It was argued that full identification saved the reputations of innocent people. If the story said John G. Smith, 62, 1234 Primrose St., was charged with drunken driving, then John L. Smith, 24, 1252 Primrose St., would be off the hook.

However, full identification can also create problems. Many papers have stopped using exact addresses because that may endanger the residents. One small-town editor said that when her paper reported a gun had been stolen from an address, other burglars would target the home because they figured the resident would replace the weapon.[61] And many newspapers have printed stories about burglars who read obituaries to find out when families will be at funerals. Other editors say that not using complete addresses eliminates embarrassing errors caused by sloppy record keeping by officials or criminals who give wrong addresses to police.

The Charlotte Observer found that publishing a name and address, even in a routine feature story, can sometimes spur harassment. The *Observer* ran an interesting but fairly standard photograph on its front page showing a mother taking her 6-year-old daughter to the first day of classes at her elementary school. The caption identified the mother and daughter and gave their address. Four days later the mother called the paper to complain that she had received more than 100 telephone calls — some obscene, some threatening, some from men in jail, some from men who wanted to meet her, some from men who wanted to meet her daughter. "Do you realize that hundreds of sick people know who I am and where I live?" she asked city editor Greg Ring. The calls and letters stopped after about two weeks, but the mother's anger continued long after that. "Newspaper editors need to pay attention to what they're doing to innocent people," she said.[62]

Many editors have got the message. It is becoming more common for newspapers to use block numbers rather than specific addresses. An APME poll in 1988 found that more than 17 percent of the papers it surveyed no longer used exact addresses, up from less than 6 percent just three years earlier.[63]

Using exact ages is another kind of problem. If people's ages appear in the paper, it is unlikely to increase the chances that they will be burglarized or harassed. But for many people, age is a very private matter. Some editors believe ages should be used only when they are relevant to the story. They contend that ages of people who speak at governmental meetings usually add little to a story. But other editors aren't so sure. Although *The Dallas Morning News* has a policy of using ages only when they are relevant, "age seems always to be relevant," John Davenport, assistant to the managing editor of the paper, told *Presstime*.[64]

Age is also a concern at many newspapers in deciding whether to name teens who have committed crimes. At one time nearly all newspapers backed away from naming crime suspects if they were under 18. Usually these teen-agers were tried in juvenile courts where their identities were often protected by law. But in the 1980s the courts and public became troubled by the increase in the number of major crimes committed by young people. Now, if the crimes are serious, judges often decide to try teen-agers as adults in open courts rather than juvenile courts.

Although some news organizations have maintained the policy of not naming suspects under 18, many more now use the names even of middle-school-age children once the names are made public by the legal system. But many believe that the media should consider the effect of identifying children as felons. The label will have little effect on the truly incorrigible teen who commits crimes, but on youthful first offenders, it may be a heavy burden to carry into adulthood.

Privacy and Political Leaders

An outgoing president is unhappy with the way he was treated by the media. In his early drafts of his farewell address, he attacks the news media and calls them "savage." Perhaps he is reacting to rumors reported in some newspapers that he is sexually impotent.

Or maybe he is reacting to the media's treatment of his secretary of the treasury, an accomplished politician who some had hoped might succeed him. Many papers had reported juicy details about a love affair this man had with a married woman. According to the reports, the woman was down on her luck when she had asked the wealthy politician for help, and he obliged her by giving her some money—that night, in her bedroom. The affair continued until the woman's husband found out. He tried to blackmail the politician, who then ended the affair, leaving the woman heartbroken and suicidal, according to newspaper accounts.

But don't think this politician's chief political rival was given a free ride in the media. His moral standards were attacked too. At one point he was so angry, he told the press that he would not dignify with a response newspaper stories that he was having an affair with a woman and that he was the father of some of her children.

When many Americans hear stories like these about the media invading the private lives of political leaders, they wonder if the Founding Fathers wouldn't roll over in their graves if they saw what the press was doing. But the Founding Fathers didn't have graves when those stories were printed. Those stories were *about* the Founding Fathers. It was George Washington who thought press coverage was "savage";[65] Washington's secretary of the treasurer, Alexander Hamilton, who eventually admitted to the affair with the married woman;[66] and Thomas Jefferson who was reported—falsely, some now believe—to have fathered some of the children of one of his slaves.[67]

Newspapers during the early days of our republic were highly partisan. Some received the bulk of their money from political factions, and they were quite willing to print rumors and gossip about opposition candidates' private lives. Often they weren't too concerned about the truth of the rumors. Few political leaders escaped the newspaper rumor mill, according to John Seigenthaler, former publisher of *The Tennessean* in Nashville. Andrew Jackson was accused of convincing Rachel Robards to leave her husband and move in with him. Martin Van Buren was said to wear women's corsets that made it "difficult to say whether he is a man or woman." William Henry Harrison was reported to be senile and mentally failing. Henry Clay was reported to spend his days gambling and his nights in brothels. And Franklin Pierce and John Fremont were alleged to be heavy drinkers.[68]

The partisan press had faded from the scene by the mid-1800s, but papers continued to have a field day exploring the private lives of candidates. For example, in 1884 most observers thought Democratic candidate Grover Cleveland had little chance of winning the presidency. His hopes were further dimmed when the newspapers reported that Cleveland had fathered a child out of wedlock while he was the sheriff of Buffalo, N.Y. The woman reportedly had other lovers, but Cleveland, the only bachelor she was seeing, accepted responsibility and had paid child support faithfully. When these payments were disclosed during the campaign, the *New York Sun* called him "a coarse debauchee who might bring his harlots to Washington . . . a man leprous with immorality."[69]

Most Republicans thought those stories would clinch the election for their man. But then another scandal made the front pages. Papers reported that the first child of Republican candidate James Blaine was born only three months after Blaine and his wife were married. Blaine announced that it was all a misunderstanding, contending that he and his wife were actually married twice — six months apart. His message apparently failed to convince many voters, and Cleveland was the only Democrat elected president between 1861 and 1912.[70]

THE ERA OF THE "LAPDOG"

In the 20th century, the press went from watchdog of candidates' morals to lapdog, as Professor Larry Sabato wrote in his book *Feeding Frenzy*. The press looked the other way as candidates and political leaders engaged in drunkenness and carousing. Even when some were so drunk that they had to be carried off the floor of the House and Senate, the voters back home would never read about it in their papers.[71]

These reporters were adhering to a gentlemen's agreement that political leaders' private lives were off limits. Sabato, a professor of government at the University of Virginia, contends that this informal agreement intensified during Franklin Roosevelt's presidency in the 1930s and 1940s. The press took the position that if Roosevelt's polio did not affect the way he handled his duties, it would not be reported. The news media deliberately avoided doing anything that might show that the president was physically disabled. Of the 35,000 published news photos taken of FDR, only two showed his wheelchair. When Roosevelt was seeking his fourth term in 1944, he was desperately ill, yet many publishers, even some who supported Roosevelt's opponent, chose not to run pictures that hinted how sick he was.[72] Some believe that because the United States was involved in World War II at the time, news executives did not want to suggest that its leader was physically weak.

But the press did not limit its discretion to Roosevelt's health problems. Roosevelt was all but estranged from his wife and had a long-term relationship with his secretary, none of which was ever reported.[73] The lack of interest in such stories was not limited to Roosevelt. His Republican opponent in 1940, Wendell Willkie, openly kept a mistress before and during his bid for the presidency, but it was not a story to the press of that era.[74]

Even if a politician's public image bore little relation to the truth, reporters would not write about it. President Dwight Eisenhower's quick temper and salty language were never mentioned. The media in the 1950s portrayed him as a kindly, soft-spoken grandfather figure. Albert Hunt, a *Wall Street Journal* reporter, told Sabato about a married congressman who left his family in his home district and lived with another woman while he was in Washington. Yet every two years the man would run for re-election, and his campaign would feature pictures of him as an upstanding family man with a wife and four kids. "I never wrote about it, though today . . . I surely would," Hunt said.[75]

The heaviest criticism of the media's willingness to look the other way came when the public learned of President John F. Kennedy's many affairs. Kennedy has been linked romantically with actresses, an airline attendant, one of his secretaries, even the girlfriend of a Mafia chieftain — all while he was serving as president. Even before Kennedy became president, many journalists were aware of his amorous adventures. They were so legendary, according to Sabato, that the press corps covering his presidential bid joked that his campaign slogan ought to be "Let's sack with Jack." But not one newspaper or TV reporter did a story during the campaign or his term in office that hinted at Kennedy's extramarital exploits. "Not only did the media not want to dig for the unpleasant truth, they willingly communicated a lie, becoming part and parcel of the Kennedy public relations team," Sabato wrote. "In the press reports, Jack Kennedy, champion philanderer, became the perfect husband and family man."[76]

Some contend that Kennedy got such special treatment because he was well-liked by the press. But the press also overlooked indiscretions in the personal lives of at least three presidents who preceded him and the president who followed him.[77] Seigenthaler pointed out that it was historians and biographers, not journalists, who revealed the relationships between Warren Harding and Nan Britton, Franklin Roosevelt and Lucy Mercer, Dwight Eisenhower and Kay Summersby, Lyndon Johnson and Alice March.[78]

This see-no-evil agreement was probably one reason people had more respect for politicians and reporters than they do now, according to Ellen Hume, executive director of a center that studies press and politics at Harvard University. "The news was much more upbeat in the 1940s and 1950s when [the] nation's political leaders were treated by the journalists with deference and respect," she told the *Los Angeles Times*.[79]

GROWING CONCERNS

Most writers believe the event that triggered journalists to wonder if their coverage shouldn't include more honest reporting of candidates' personalities was Watergate, the name given to the investigation by newspapers and Congress of President Nixon's role in an attempted break-in at Democratic offices in the Watergate hotel during the 1972 campaign. The problems that ultimately cost Nixon many of his supporters and led to his resignation had more to do with his character (suspicions that he lied and was meanspirited and foulmouthed) than his policies.

But Sabato argues that by the time of Watergate, reporters had already begun to reconsider their responsibilities. In 1969, Sen. Edward Kennedy, who had a considerable reputation for drinking and womanizing, waited until the next day to report an auto accident at Chappaquiddick in which a woman in his car was killed. "Kennedy had been too flagrant, his actions too costly for one young woman, and his excuses too flimsy and insulting to the many perceptive minds in the press corps," Sabato wrote. "Good reporters were ashamed of, and the press as a whole was severely criticized for, the process of concealing Kennedy's manifest vices that had preceded the senator's own cover-up of the facts surrounding the accident."[80]

Other reporters believe it was neither Chappaquiddick nor Watergate that brought more openness to reporting private lives. Seymour Topping, who was assistant managing editor of *The New York Times* during the 1970s, argued that changes in society like the sexual revolution of the 1960s allowed newspapers "to explore things that we wouldn't explore in the past." And Richard Wald, the president of NBC News at the time, noted that politicians themselves were more open in the 1970s, admitting to alcoholism and talking publicly about their divorces.[81]

For whatever reason, the debate over news coverage of the private lives of political leaders intensified in the mid-1970s. Stories of abuses by congressmen began to appear. But none of those stories made a bigger splash than those about the carryings-on of Wilbur Mills, the Democratic congressman from Arkansas who headed the powerful Ways and Means Committee. Reporters who had covered Mills knew he was a heavy drinker and appeared to be drunk at some committee meetings, but they would not pursue the story because they did not think they should invade his private life.

Then one night in 1974 Mills was stopped by police for speeding and driving with his headlights off. A young woman climbed out of Mills' car and jumped into the Tidal Basin, a body of water near the monuments in

"Yeah, that's old Senator Bacchus again. But he's off duty now, so we won't have to do a story."

Washington. The passenger was Fanne Foxe, a striptease dancer who billed herself as the Argentine Bombshell.

Now Mills was named in a police report, and his drinking was no longer a private matter. Stories about Mills' problems began to appear in the media. A few nights later, a drunken Mills climbed on stage while Foxe was performing, and many more reporters began to shed their adherence to the boys-will-be-boys notion of privacy for public officials. "The guy was falling down drunk, but the press in general portrayed him as one of the great legislative leaders in American politics," David R. Jones, then national editor of *The New York Times,* said later. "Now, he himself says that his drinking affected his job."[82] After undergoing treatment for his drinking, Mills admitted that sometimes the day after committee meetings he had to ask aides what had happened and what he had said.

Neither the Watergate controversy nor the Mills affair in 1974 led to an "anything goes" mentality among reporters. The old gentleman's agreement may have been weakened, but it was still the rule of the day, as *Newsweek* reported in 1975:

> There is hardly a journalist in Washington who cannot identify at least one alcoholic or philandering congressman. Such behavior only becomes news when it either interferes with the congressman's duties — say, by preventing him from voting on an important measure — or lands him in trouble with the law, as happened in the Mills case.[83]

But more and more journalists were wondering if they should not write about these "character issues." As Ben Bagdikian, a journalist and media critic who would later become dean of the journalism school at Berkeley, said in 1975, "Since Richard Nixon, there has been a growing feeling that the character of leading politicians is important—and that you've got to know something about their private lives to understand their real character."[84]

THE "PIRANHA PRESS"

Just as the privacy pendulum began to swing from the gentlemen's agreement of earlier years to a more probing kind of reporting, Gary Hart stumbled into the media spotlight. Hart, a Democrat, attempted to run for president in 1984 but lost support when he gave inconsistent explanations why he had changed his last name (from Hartpence), subtracted a year from his age, and changed facts in his official biography.

When Hart decided to try again for the presidency in 1988, rumors about his womanizing were already rampant. Even his campaign workers and big campaign contributors were concerned, and he promised them that he would mind his manners and make sure his sex life was not a campaign issue. In meetings with reporters and political columnists, he assured them he was doing nothing wrong. Hart was so insistent in his denials that he may have invited his own downfall. In an interview with a *New York Times* reporter he said: "Follow me around. I don't care. I'm serious, if anybody wants to put a tail on me, go ahead. They'd be very bored."

Not surprisingly, since it came at a time when many reporters were reassessing their history of not reporting the foibles of elected leaders, Hart's challenge was accepted. Two *Miami Herald* reporters staked out his home in Washington that weekend. Instead of being bored, they watched as a young woman entered the town house and apparently spent the night. Hart at first tried to explain away the story. (The reporters, he said, had missed seeing her leave, and the reporters admitted that they had not kept constant watch on both doors, making it possible that she had left unseen.)

But then came reports that a few weeks earlier Hart and the woman, a model named Donna Rice, had taken an overnight cruise to Bimini on a yacht called, of all things, *Monkey Business*. When one of Rice's friends sold the *National Enquirer* snapshots of Rice sitting on Hart's lap, Hart's efforts to explain away the reports became more difficult. The final straw came when *Washington Post* reporters told him they had evidence of other affairs. Hart decided to drop out of the race.[85]

Although many journalists were uncomfortable with the idea of reporters acting like two-bit private eyes, many justified the story on the grounds that it raised questions about Hart's honesty and his willingness to engage in risky behavior. The *Herald* reporters were honored by the Society of Professional Journalists.

The times had changed. President Kennedy's affairs had at least some impact on his job performance. Sabato notes that occasionally his trysts required him to be out of touch with the military command when the Cold War demanded that the president always be accessible in case of a Russian sneak attack. Kennedy also opened himself to blackmail, and some argue that then FBI director J. Edgar Hoover used his knowledge of Kennedy's affairs to gain more power for himself and autonomy for his department.[86] But by the standards of reporters of that era, Kennedy's affairs were private. Twenty-five years later, Hart was not to receive that courtesy.

The public had trouble making up its mind about how far the press should go. Polls during the Hart-Rice controversy found that about 70 percent of the public thought the reporters had gone too far.[87] Only a few years earlier, news organizations had been criticized for covering up President Kennedy's affairs.

The often-heated debate over whether the media had treated Hart fairly did not cause some reporters to back off the "character issue." Early in the 1992 presidential campaign, Democratic candidate Bill Clinton had refused to answer questions about his personal life. Then the *Star,* a tabloid that usually prints gossip about actors and singers, paid Gennifer Flowers—reportedly $150,000—to tell about a 12-year affair she said she had with Clinton. (Paying for information was discussed in Chapter 6.)

Most news organizations feigned horror about the use of checkbook journalism to get the story, and many were concerned that Flowers' charges were unsubstantiated. Yet most newspapers and TV news departments gave major play to Flowers' press conference sponsored by the tabloid to promote its journalistic coup. Some newspapers relied on an old journalistic ploy to get around their uneasiness at printing unsubstantiated rumors. They asked Clinton about them, and once he responded, the papers felt justified in repeating the rumors in a story saying that Clinton had denied them.[88] Flowers' allegations became part of a detailed scrutiny of Clinton including reports that he had visited Moscow while he was a student, that he used influence to avoid serving in the military during the Vietnam War, and that he had smoked (but not inhaled, he claimed) marijuana.

The public response to all the digging by the media was less than enthusiastic. Interviewed more than a year after Flowers made her splash, almost two-thirds in a national poll said the news media "reveal too much about the private lives of public figures."[89] However, many in the media have noted that there is often a touch of hypocrisy in the public's reactions to these stories. People complain about them, but they often follow them closely and discuss them around water coolers at work and at dinner parties with friends. An NBC News executive called adultery "a tiny issue this year" but noted "it was the No. 1 topic of conversation."[90]

Yet in hindsight many journalists believe they overplayed these stories. Peter Jennings, anchor of ABC's evening news, told the *Los Angeles Times,* "While we were all trying to run Bill Clinton into the ground on the subject of Gennifer Flowers, the voters in New Hampshire wanted to know about the economy. We got in their way."[91] Marvin Kalb, a former CBS reporter who became director of a Harvard center that studies press conduct, said he believed that in most journalists' souls "there has always been the thought, 'Maybe I went too far on this.' "[92]

One of the reporters who participated in the stakeout of Gary Hart didn't think the media coverage of the Flowers affair was justified. Doug Clifton, who had become executive editor of *The Miami Herald* by the time of the Clinton campaign, said: "I don't think the Hart reporting set a precedent that sexual conduct is fair game to report. Hart's conduct spoke to his judgment; if Clinton had an affair in the past, that doesn't."[93]

But some media people contend that reporters backed away from the adultery story too quickly in 1992, given the nature of the campaigns the candidates were running. Phil Donahue, host of a popular talk show, noted that both campaigns were emphasizing "family values" and "character" as key issues. "The same citizens decrying press probing of the candidates' alleged monkey business are also telling pollsters that 'character' is important in this year of 'traditional family values,' " Donahue wrote in *The New York Times.*

Donahue, who was booed by his audience when he asked Clinton about the allegations, does not believe that because the majority may not care about the marital fidelity of the candidates, the media should shy away from "information that might make a difference in some voters' choices of who should occupy the most important office in the world."[94] In many elections, one should note, a shift of only a few percentage points can determine the winner. During the 1992 elections, some polls reported that 14 percent of the public said the revelations about Clinton's affair might sway their vote.

Other writers believe that candidates' past indiscretions can provide a clue to the kind of people they are. Thomas Reeves, author of a biography of John F. Kennedy, contends, "Sexual indiscretions, particularly if they are prolonged and varied, can reveal much about a person's integrity, fidelity, prudence and other qualities that make up character."[95]

A few journalists believe the media are overly concerned about re-spectability. "Look at the Clinton story, that concentration on his sex life. Tut! Tut!" said Geneva Overholser, editor of *The Des Moines Register*. She contended that some editors are so fearful that readers will call their papers "scandal sheets" they have made their papers boring. "Do I approve of all this gossip?" she asked. "It's not up to me to approve or reject it. It's up to me to acknowledge it, and yes, to publish it. This, for heaven's sake, is human nature. I'm willing to bet that part of why newspapers have become less read is because we've become *less* gossipy."[96]

The media's transformation from the lapdog coverage of earlier presidencies to the attack-dog coverage of recent candidates may have one unintended side effect. Harvard's Ellen Hume argues that the coverage "doubtlessly feeds the public's cynicism and distrust of its political leaders — and of the piranha press corps which seems willing to devour anyone, at any time, for frivolous infractions as well as serious ones."[97]

RELATIVES OF PUBLIC PEOPLE

As candidates come under increasing scrutiny from the press, their relatives are often seen as fair game, and many both in and out of journalism are troubled by this. A *New York Times* columnist chided the press for some meanspirited humor about the clumsiness of Chelsea Clinton, the president's then 12-year-old daughter. And Mona Charon wrote in *The Atlanta Constitution:* "Scrutiny of presidential candidates is one thing. Even attention to candidates' spouses is legitimate. But let's have mercy on the kids."[98]

But journalists don't always agree when they try to define the limits of mercy for political leaders' children. In 1991, the 20-year-old son of Oklahoma Gov. David Walters was charged with a misdemeanor, posses-sion of drug paraphernalia, after a pipe and other drug-related items were found in his room. Although the newspaper coverage was low-key, the arrest and subsequent court hearing at which he pleaded no contest were covered more extensively on TV news. Six weeks after the trial, the young man took his life by overdosing on prescription drugs. The governor argued that the media had driven his son to suicide.

Ed Kelley, managing editor of *The Daily Oklahoman* in Oklahoma City, told *Presstime* that his staff weighed the facts that Walter's son was not a public official but had participated in the campaign and was the son of the state's highest elected official. Kelley said the paper ran five or six short stories, none on Page 1, between the arrest and the overdose. "I think we did no more, and no less, than the story required," he said.[99]

Other editors have argued that stories involving the relatives of the mighty are justified because the stories tell us something about public people. One such story involved the arrest of the 41-year-old daughter of U.S. Sen. Hugh Scott of Pennsylvania in a drug raid. She was charged with selling $100 worth of hashish to an undercover agent. Most newspapers in Pennsylvania named the woman but not the others arrested in the raid. *The Philadelphia Inquirer* ran a lengthy story and pictures of her modest home and her with a sweater over her head as she was being led to her arraignment. *Inquirer* editors may have felt information in the last paragraph justified the story: "Her father has been a strong supporter of presidential moves to tighten drug controls" and four years earlier had opposed efforts to legalize marijuana.[100]

The *Inquirer* was criticized when it reported that the daughter of the mayor of Philadelphia was about to marry a convicted bookmaker. Steve Lovelady, then associate executive editor of the paper, argued that it was news and said that if the top editor of the *Inquirer* had become engaged to a bookmaker, the paper would report that too.[101]

Other journalists are not as sure as Lovelady about the ethics of focusing on the families of political leaders. Brit Hume, an ABC News reporter, said he regrets a story he did in the early 1970s when he was working for columnist Jack Anderson about the son of Vice President Spiro Agnew. Hume tracked down young Agnew in Baltimore and confirmed that he had broken up with his wife and moved in with a male hairdresser. He said he is "more ashamed of that story than anything I've done in journalism. I'm sorry about it to this day. We ought not make relatives public persons by extension."[102]

No other name in America seems to draw as much attention as "Kennedy." The press's hounding of the Kennedy family reached a low point in 1984 when David Kennedy died of a drug overdose at the age of 28. He was the son of Robert F. Kennedy, who was assassinated while campaigning for the presidency. The heavy coverage the press gave to the investigation of David's death was questionable, but the attention paid to the family wake and burial seemed ghoulish. It so bothered Eric Schmitt, a young reporter who covered the wake for *The New York Times,* that he later wrote in *Quill* that it made him ashamed to be a journalist. "Instead of what should have been a private moment for the family, the press declared the sad gathering of Kennedys a newsworthy event." He asked, "Why were three dozen journalists at Hickory Hill chasing hearses, interviewing priests and cornering family friends as they left the house?" He rejected the notion that the coverage was justified just because it was about the Kennedys. "Who was David Kennedy other than the son of the late United States senator?"[103]

The name "Kennedy" brought notoriety to two previously private people when William Smith was accused of rape in 1991 while vacationing with his uncle Sen. Edward Kennedy at the Kennedy compound in Palm Beach, Fla. Because a Kennedy relative was involved, this incident mesmerized the nation. (To make sure no one would forget his bloodlines, the media usually referred to him by his full name, William Kennedy Smith.)

Not only was Smith given national exposure, but the woman who accused him was the subject of media attention. At first she was named only by two of the least savory members of the press—an American supermarket tabloid and one of the British scandal sheets. But soon several others, including *The New York Times* and NBC News, used her name. The *Times* even printed a lengthy story about her lifestyle and background, including the number of traffic tickets she had accumulated.

After days of new revelations about Smith and his accuser, particularly on TV shows like *Inside Edition* and *Hard Copy,* parts of the trial were broadcast on television and radio. These broadcasts included graphic details of the incident, which Smith described as consensual sex and the woman called rape. Technicians tried with only moderate success to cover the woman's face with a large blob as she testified. Lawyers, of course, spoke her name, which occasionally made it over the public airways, and eventually the woman gave the media permission to identify her. The jury found Smith not guilty of rape, but many Americans believed the media were guilty of violating Smith's and the woman's privacy.

Invading Privacy to Get the News

To most of us, privacy means that we can go about our lives and work without being monitored secretly by other people, including our bosses, the police and reporters. But some journalists believe that to get the information they need for their stories, they must use clandestine methods. (Deception in journalism was treated in Chapter 8.)

SECRET RECORDING AND PHOTOGRAPHING

Most tape recording in journalism today is done not in sensitive investigations but in more routine ways such as recording interviews, speeches, news conferences and the like. Usually it is obvious to news sources that they are being recorded. But when the telephone is injected between reporters and sources, the sources have no way of knowing whether they are being recorded unless informed by the reporter. Some sources object to having their remarks taped because they believe that a tape recording can more easily be transferred and perhaps misused by persons other than the reporters who interviewed them. They don't see a reporter's handwritten notes as that transferable. Other sources, particularly those in politics, object to being recorded because they want to be able to deny what they said and not have a reporter produce a tape of what they said.

Many reporters, however, say that they see no ethical difference between writing down what people are saying and using tape recorders. Many reporters routinely type their notes while talking to sources on the phone, and some can type nearly as fast as many sources talk.

Ten states require that people be informed when calls are being taped.[104] But even when notification is not required by law, most editors demand it. More than 80 percent of newspaper editors surveyed said they were opposed to secret recording of interviews, even when sources know they are talking to a reporter.[105] A.M. Rosenthal, former editor of *The New York Times,* said that "it doesn't sit well in the stomach to tape someone and not tell them you're doing it. It's not honest. It's not fair. Period."[106]

But some newspapers, even those with rules against secret taping, have allowed their reporters to do it on some stories. The *Lexington (Ky.) Herald-Leader* used surreptitious recordings in an investigation that won a Pulitzer Prize in 1986. The series, written by reporters Michael York and Jeff Marx, revealed that boosters had made cash payments to University of Kentucky basketball players and that those players had also profited illegally by selling their complimentary tickets at inflated prices. The reporters used tape recorders for all their interviews with former players and other sources. Their sources knew they were being taped when they were interviewed in person, but they were not told about it when they were interviewed by telephone. York and Marx were given permission to bypass the paper's general policy against taping interviews without letting the source know because "we thought there was a good chance that some players would develop . . . 'amnesia' after the story appeared," York explained.[107]

Similarly, many photographers justify using cameras with long lenses so that their subjects do not always know their pictures are being taken. *Washington Post* photographer-reporter Linda Wheeler said she doubted the *Post* would allow her to use hidden cameras, but editors permitted her to use long lenses to photograph a police decoy pretending to be asleep on a doorstep while a thief stole his radio and was then arrested by police. And William Sanders, former president of the National Press Photographers Association, said his editors at the Fort Lauderdale *Sun-Sentinel* approved his use of long lenses on investigative stories like one involving a city official who was using city trucks and work crews for personal jobs.[108]

OLD-FASHIONED EAVESDROPPING

Most older journalists tell stories about secretly listening in on conversations they knew they were not supposed to hear. More recently, some television and radio crews have used long-range microphones to eavesdrop on police officers and politicians. Although these kinds of antics were at one time considered acceptable, some journalists are becoming leery of them.

During the early part of the crisis after the Three Mile Island nuclear power plant breakdown in 1979, two *Philadelphia Inquirer* reporters pretended to be a couple of bickering lovers so they could stay in a hotel corridor to eavesdrop on a meeting of public relations executives for the utility. Each time a motel official or some guest came by, the two reporters struck up a lovers' quarrel — which is a great way to get people to look the other way.

"Are you sure we want our Debbie to go into journalism?"

Although reporters often use what they overhear while eavesdropping only as ideas for stories, these *Inquirer* reporters reported what they heard through the door and told readers how they got their information. The reporters said they had tried for days to talk to the officials but were always told that the head of public relations for the utility was too busy discussing the "nuclear question." But when the reporters listened through the door, they heard conversation "about the press question, about how to get us off their tail. They had lied to us."[109]

Although the reporters were obviously angered by the deception, they were not troubled by their own deception and eavesdropping to get the story. Eugene Roberts, *Inquirer* executive editor at the time, said: "We have to have high standards, but we can't get so finicky about ethics that we use them as excuses for not doing our jobs. . . . There's no ethics in being docile and the pawn of whoever wants to prevent you from getting the story."[110]

Getting caught eavesdropping is embarrassing and not in keeping with the image most journalists like to project. Two reporters for the high-minded Louisville newspapers embarrassed their bosses when they got caught eavesdropping on a police meeting in 1974. The reporters were arrested after police found one of them lying on the floor while the other had his ear to the door of a room in which the local Fraternal Order of Police was holding a closed meeting. Charges against both reporters were eventually dropped. What was going on that was important enough for them to take that action? The police wanted to discuss the action of their chief in bugging their squad cars to check on possible police misbehavior.[111]

Michael Davies, managing editor of one of the reporters, said "the resultant publicity was awful." The papers' publisher issued a statement trying to justify the reporters' conduct, but, Davies recalled, the statement "didn't sit well with anyone outside the papers." Davies said he opposes eavesdropping. "We should conduct ourselves the way other people do."[112]

Journalists are divided about how far journalists should go to get information in closed meetings. Philip Meyer, a former journalist and now a journalism professor at the University of North Carolina, asked newspaper editors and reporters to respond to a hypothetical case in which a newly nominated presidential candidate is holding a meeting to discuss his choice for vice president. A reporter asks a person who will attend the meeting to carry a briefcase to the meeting and to leave it there to be picked up by someone else. Unknown to the person, the briefcase contains a tape recorder that tapes the secret meeting. About 45 percent of the editors and staff said they believed the reporter should be admonished and the story killed; 29 percent would admonish the reporter and use the story only as background for other reporting; 7 percent would admonish the reporter but use the story; and 20 percent would reward the reporter.[113]

How often do journalists eavesdrop? There probably is no firm answer. When editors were asked how often their papers engaged in a variety of questionable reporting practices, including false identity, stolen documents, concealed recording, and eavesdropping, 28 percent said their papers never did any of these things. Only about 8 percent said that any of these activities happened as often as once a month.[114]

FORAGING FOR NEWS

In the past it was rather common for journalists to enter private property after a fire, a crime or some other human tragedy, unless the police stopped them. Jerry Thompson, a reporter for *The Tennessean* in Nashville, once beat the police to the scene of a celebrated murder case. He went into the house just before police arrived and heard a police sergeant order the house sealed so that no journalists would be allowed in. Thompson quickly found a picture of the dead woman in an upstairs room and threw it out the window. Fortunately for him, the picture landed safely on some shrubbery, and Thompson was able to retrieve it. He was proud that his paper was the only medium to have a photo of the dead woman for three days.[115]

And there are tales of journalists sneaking into crime scenes. When police charged a man with New York's notorious Son of Sam murders, three journalists were arrested the next day after they broke into his apartment. Sometimes such escapades blow up in the reporters' faces. A newspaper reporter, who went on to become a network anchor, broke into a house to get a photograph only to learn later that he had the wrong address.

The days of journalists doubling as cat burglars and thieves are fading away. A reporter for the Rochester, N.Y., *Times-Union* thought he had scored an exclusive story when he went to the house where police had rounded up a group of suspects. He found two envelopes that apparently had been dropped by the police. He took them back to the newsroom and used the information in his stories. When editors asked him about some of the unattributed details, he told them what he had done. He justified his actions by saying he had seen reporters do that in movies. The editors weren't impressed, and he lost his job.[116]

Although most journalists are now wary of breaking into people's homes to get news, they have fewer problems when dishonest methods are used to get information from governmental files. Some reporters have even rifled trash cans. Reporters in Anchorage, Alaska, searched through a grand jury's trash for information about an investigation of the state's governor.[117] And a good many reporters would probably admit that at one time or another they've glanced at documents on desks in the halls of government.

Les Whitten, a senior investigator for the Jack Anderson column for 12 years, admits he once committed a felony by taking some papers from a U.S. senator's files, copying them and returning them the next day. He had help from a person he would not name, who opened the Senate office door for him and told him the letter of the alphabet he should seek in the files. "It was a hell of a story that helped prevent a multi-million-dollar insurance fraud, and I couldn't resist it," he admitted.[118] Although most journalists would not steal documents, they might be willing to use documents stolen by others. One editor said that if he was given documents showing that Lee Harvey Oswald, the man accused of killing President Kennedy, worked for the CIA, he would use it "no matter how it got in my hands."[119]

A newer way of foraging for information is to use computers. Massive amounts of information are available in computer data bases, including information that many would never tell their best friends. People adept at using computers may be able to find all kinds of personal information about people: their age, height and weight as listed on their drivers licenses; their home addresses and phone numbers; and their neighbors' addresses and phone numbers. They can find out if people are married, if they've been involved in any sticky divorce proceedings, and if they've been sued or have sued someone for any reason. They can also learn how much people paid for their homes, whether they own other real estate, and whether they have ties to major corporations. They can track down driving records and cars owned. They may be able to find out which political party people prefer from voting registration records and if they have contributed money to candidates for federal offices. Even some health records may be accessible.[120]

To test this ability, writers at one magazine used computer data bases to acquire much of this information — along with credit data and biographies — about many movie stars, sports figures, and political and civic leaders. Many of these people want to be so private that they do not list their phone numbers, but with some knowledge and a $100 computer modem, the magazine had no trouble obtaining this information.[121]

Many journalists use data bases routinely to access driver-license and tax data. And some first-rate investigative pieces have used public access to government data bases. *The Atlanta Journal/The Atlanta*

"I was just trying to access real estate transfers when up came this spicy stuff!"

Constitution searched through 5.4 million computer files to track down 43 drivers who had at least 15 drunken-driving convictions. Many had repeatedly renewed their licenses.[122] And the *St. Petersburg Times* used computers to identify substitute teachers who had criminal records, some for sex offenses.

As governments begin to rely on computers, they will create even more data bases with information available to people who can tie into them. In states with strong public-records laws like Florida, courts have ruled that most data on government computers is public, although it's up to the media to get at it.[123] But in other states, legislators are limiting access to much of this information, and some bureaucrats are finding their own ways to make access difficult.

But journalists too are concerned about invasion of privacy by marketing firms that get the same data. Many reporters have done stories about the personal information readily available to telephone solicitors and other salespeople. The irony may be that those stories will lead to laws restricting access to some of those data bases. Those laws in turn would keep journalists from getting valuable information for stories in the public interest.

What's an Ethical Journalist to Do?

It is obvious that most Americans value their privacy highly. It is also obvious that journalists have not given enough thought to dealing with the conflicting pulls of privacy and public curiosity, of informing the public and showing compassion.

News stories can cause harm. As former *Washington Post* ombudsman Richard Harwood wrote, "The 'media' in their long history have
shattered countless reputations and destroyed countless careers. We have
driven people to suicide. We have caused immeasurable emotional pain,
suffering and humiliation not only to individuals but to families and (if
the testimony of many black Americans is credible) to entire communities as well."[124]

This potential for harm is part and parcel of journalism. In covering
the news and exposing the problems of their communities, journalists
will never be able to eliminate entirely intrusions into privacy. But they
can hold themselves to a standard that demands that these intrusions
serve some good other than giving readers a good tale to go with their
morning coffee or providing 15 seconds of sensational viewing on the
evening news. Stomping on the privacy of others is not justified by the
demand for a good front-page story or the chance to add a couple of
rating points.

If no public interest is involved, reporters ought to leave people
alone. For example, the Arthur Ashe story would have been just as good
if the media had waited until he was ready to announce he had AIDS.
No real public need was served by rushing his revelations, and lots of
goodwill among readers was lost. Reporters and photographers who
brazenly intrude on the grief of ordinary people are justifiably criticized.
And even if the grief is an essential part of some very public tragedy,
treating ordinary people in very private moments without compassion
and sensitivity is intolerable. There are some clods who badger people,
poke their cameras through windows, and act, as mothers used to say, as
if they were raised in a barn. Such brutish tactics might be justified by
journalists investigating life- or society-threatening situations but not
when they're covering crimes, real-life dramas and tragedies involving
ordinary people.

The profession is advanced by reporters who sincerely ask people
involved in a tragedy if they would mind answering some questions,
photographers who ask if they can take a picture of children involved in
a sensitive story, and journalists who treat friends and relatives of victims with compassion.

The standards of privacy are different for political leaders. In our
democratic society, the people are given the obligation of electing leaders
and thereby deciding the direction our nation is to take. Their actions
may have great impact on our lives in such everyday matters as the
quality of our schools and the condition of our economy. These leaders
may be called upon to vote on some of the most divisive issues of the
day, like abortion. And on some occasions they will make life-and-death

decisions like sending American soldiers into war-torn areas. These decisions will be shaped by their characters and personalities, and therefore voters are entitled to know the kind of people they are. Responsible media must provide this information. It would be unthinkable for journalists to return to the days when they covered up the fact that drinking and womanizing by some leaders interfered with their ability to do their jobs.

We should also be able to expect public leaders to be honest about who they are. A politician who wants us to elect her mayor because she was successful at running her small business ought to have been in fact a successful businesswoman, just as a politician who tries to win votes by portraying himself as a God-fearing family man ought to be a God-fearing family man. The media should check the claims politicians are making in their speeches and TV advertisements.

But journalists should show some sensitivity, compassion and judgment even with politicians and political leaders. As *Washington Post* ombudsman Joann Byrd has suggested, there should be some "privacy zone where what happens is absolutely nobody's business."[125] Journalists must decide if the information is important in helping people understand the politician or necessary to expose violations of public trust. Dredging up long-forgotten and long-forgiven mistakes would not meet this test.

Journalists need to reconsider reporting the activities of relatives of political leaders. Should politicians be held accountable for the conduct of their adult children? Should these adult children's misdemeanors be covered simply because their parents are in public life?

None of this is to advocate a toothless press backing away from all stories that intrude on privacy or might upset some readers and viewers. But all members of the press suffer when journalists seek stories for shock value instead of news value. And all members of the press suffer when the insensitivity of some journalists causes the public to regard them as vultures. As Joann Byrd has suggested, trying to treat people with compassion may require reporters to work harder and take different approaches in gathering information and writing the news. Photographers may need to search for different kinds of photographs taken from different angles and sometimes not take them at all. But a responsible, respected journalism is worth the effort.

Errors and
Accountability

Suppose you are a sexual-harassment officer at a large university.

To do your job, you must win the trust of the college community. Students must feel free to talk to you about very personal problems. They must believe you will take their problems seriously and do your best to solve them. Faculty and administrators must be able to rely on your judgment, sensitivity and diligence in dealing with these delicate issues. Since part of your job is educating people about the problem, you give speeches to campus and community groups and frequently grant interviews to reporters.

One day, reading your local paper, you are shocked. You see a story about efforts to reduce sexual harassment on your campus. The story cites a case you know about, an incident involving a note-taking pool in the medical school. Two male students took notes at a lecture on the female reproductive process and passed them to other students in the pool. The notes included many sexist comments, and one of the students in the pool filed an official complaint with the university. Then you see your name in the article and begin to read what you supposedly said. In the article, you sound as if you don't take harassment complaints very seriously. You are quoted as saying you believe the note-taking incident "is a situation for an apology and a night at the bar rather than a formal investigation."

The article goes on to quote you attacking professors in the university's professional schools. It says you expected a lot of sexual-harassment problems in those schools because "the whole construct of their reality is male and power-oriented." And, although you know that the university has no double standard in the way it treats students or faculty accused of sexual harassment, you are quoted as charging that it is a lot trickier to get your university's administrators to deal with complaints against faculty than those against students.

You know these are not your opinions. And you know you did not say these things to a reporter because you were never interviewed for the story! What can you do?

This was the circumstance that Donna Ferrara-Kerr, a sexual-harassment officer at the University of Calgary, found herself in after she was quoted in the *Calgary Herald*. When the story appeared, she said, the reaction was "immediate, fierce and detrimental" to her ability to do her job. The misquotations undermined her ability to win the trust of harassed people and damaged her relationships with many people on campus. She said she received several calls from outraged people, many of whom doubted her when she said those were not her opinions. After she complained to the newspaper, the reporter sent Ferrara-Kerr a note admitting she had mistakenly attributed to Ferrara-Kerr statements made by someone else. The paper printed a correction.[1]

Unfortunately, Ferrara-Kerr's experience is not unique. Journalists make mistakes. When pollster George Gallup Jr. asked people who had dealt with newspaper and TV reporters what their experiences had been, about a third said the reporters had gotten some of the facts wrong.[2]

That statistic would not come as a surprise to journalists who have been the victims of other reporters' sloppiness. Several top editors, including Norman Pearlstine, managing editor of *The Wall Street Journal,* and Louis Boccardi, president of the Associated Press, said they have been misquoted so often by reporters that they now tape-record all interviews they give. Some newspaper editors now demand that they be allowed to read stories about them before they appear in print, a luxury few newspapers would give to ordinary citizens.[3]

Why So Many Errors?

Newspeople make mistakes. ("Doctors bury their mistakes," some editor once said. "We print ours.") All too often, errors are caused by incompetence, irresponsibility or both. Whether journalism has more incompetent and irresponsible people than other professions in America is impossible to determine, but it certainly has its share.

Sometimes journalists are blamed for errors that are not solely their fault. Sources sometimes give incorrect information, and reporters and editors fail to challenge or check it. Occasionally, sources deliberately bend the truth to serve their own purposes, and there's no way the reporter can tell. But many errors are caused by carelessness, often aggravated by deadline pressures or a desire to "scoop" the competition. Other mistakes come from ignorance. Journalists lack the knowledge needed to recognize errors. And even when they know something about the subject, some stories are so complex that journalists can err while simplifying them for mass audiences.

"Why would you expect me to know how to spell Wilson Boulevard? I'm not from around here."

A growing number of errors in news stories are caused by reporters' isolation from their communities. Ironically, some of this isolation is the result of tougher ethical guidelines that require journalists to be wary of all conflicts of interest. Most journalists today are supposed to be very careful about the people they hobnob with outside their newsrooms. This may prevent conflicts of interest, but it does little to increase journalists' sensitivity, understanding and knowledge about the people and events they cover.

The problem is worsened by the tendency of journalists to socialize primarily with other journalists. Although it is understandable for people to develop friendships with co-workers, many journalists work unusual hours, which makes it more convenient to socialize with other journalists. Also, journalists often share a view of the world that differs from most people's.

The mobility of newspeople also keeps them from becoming part of their communities. Many journalists at smaller dailies and small-market TV stations expect to live in the community only until their big break comes along and they land a job with a major paper or larger station, so they don't bother to develop ties and friendships or learn much about their communities. Some may even be openly contemptuous of the communities where fate has brought them. All of this further contributes to the distance between them and the people they serve.

Journalists tend to be isolated from their communities in other ways too. Walking into the offices of the larger newspapers and stations today is like visiting your cousin in prison. Because of bomb threats, problems with "crazies," and the expensive equipment lying around modern newsrooms, nearly all news organizations have uniformed guards and security systems.

CARELESSNESS

Sometimes carelessness can lead to silly errors that make the paper look foolish, as did this paragraph in *The Seattle Times:*

> It isn't as though the use of nitrous oxide by dentists has just appeared on the scene. It was first used as an anesthetic gas Dec. 11, 1844. That's not a typo. Eighteen Eighty-Four.[4]

Other times sloppy note taking can result in stories that hurt reputations. Recall what happened when the Calgary paper put someone else's words in the mouth of the sexual-harassment officer.

But carelessness in reporting can result in more subtle errors. Hasty efforts at trying to report what someone said or thought about difficult societal issues can result in serious misinterpretations. That's what Colorado Gov. Richard D. Lamm thought happened to him when *The Denver Post* broke the widely used story that quoted him as saying that elderly people with terminal illnesses had a "duty to die." The remark was the interpretation of a *Post* reporter who taped Lamm at an informal session with lawyers in Denver. The story said in its opening:

> Elderly people who are terminally ill have a "duty to die and get out of the way" instead of trying to prolong their lives through artificial means, Gov. Dick Lamm said Tuesday.
>
> People who die without having their lives artificially prolonged, Lamm said, are similar to "leaves falling off a tree and forming humus for other plants to grow up."

"You got a duty to die and to get out of the way. Let the other society, our kids, build a reasonable life," the governor told a meeting of the Colorado Health Lawyers Association at St. Joseph's Hospital.

Senior citizens groups and others throughout the country were outraged when they read this story, distributed by the Associated Press. So was the governor, who claimed he was quoting a philosopher and that he did not urge terminally ill oldsters to get out of the way but urged society to take a harder look at life-extending machines. The *Post,* standing by its news story but wanting to be fair to Lamm, gave him the reporter's tape of the session. The transcription of the pertinent section of the tape, which the governor's office sent to major news organizations, read:

> The real question gets into, then, high-technology medicine. We have a million and a half heart attacks a year. Every year in the United States we have a million and a half heart attacks. Six hundred thousand of them die. How many Barney Clarks can we afford? You know we at least ought to be talking about that. . . .
> A terrific article that I've read, one of the philosophers of our time, I think, is a guy named Leon Kass. Has anybody seen his stuff? He's just terrific. In *The American Scholar* last year he wrote an article called "The Case for Mortality," where essentially he said we have a duty to die. It's like if leaves fall off a tree, forming the humus for the other plants to grow out. We've got a duty to die and get out of the way with all of our machines and artificial hearts and everything else like that and let the other society, our kids, build a reasonable life.

The *Post* published a correction of its use of "you" instead of the "we" the governor used, but it did not correct the reference to "elderly people" because its reporter said the governor had made several allusions to the aged in his remarks. Over at the rival *Rocky Mountain News,* however, ombudsman Mal Deans wrote that the governor had been treated badly. Deans said the original stories, first in the *Post* and then in his own paper and others throughout the country, erred in reporting that Lamm was talking about the elderly. "Had these remarks received careful attention and paraphrased accurately, the furor never would have developed," Deans wrote. "The focus on the elderly was strictly a media creation that has continued unabated."[5]

The Washington Post got egg on its face when it dug into the background of John W. Hinckley Jr., the young man who attempted to assassinate President Reagan in 1981. In its 10,000-word report put together by eight reporters was this 31-word passage right after a description of Hinckley's purchase of handguns during the 18 months he was a student at Texas Tech University in Lubbock: "A penchant for guns hardly strikes anyone as ominous in free-wheeling Lubbock, where some university students carry guns to class and the pistol-packing frontier tradition runs deep and long."[6] The good people of Lubbock took exception to that picture. Their complaints spurred *Washington Post* ombudsman William L. Green Jr. to discover that one of the reporters on the *Post* article, Chip Brown, had based the offensive passage on material he had lifted, without independent verification or source credit, from a similar article about Hinckley in *The Philadelphia Inquirer* three days earlier.

Donald C. Drake, who wrote the *Inquirer* story, said that although his story did say that guns were common in Lubbock, "it didn't give the sense that Lubbock was a wild town, but quite the opposite." Drake called attention to this section in the *Inquirer* story:

> An official in the Lubbock office of the Federal Bureau of Alcohol, Tobacco and Firearms confirmed yesterday that records showed that Hinckley had purchased at least six handguns over 18 months from various Lubbock pawnshops.
>
> "Should that have raised a warning signal somewhere?"
>
> "Naw," the official said. "We have people that buy a hundred or two hundred a year around here."
>
> Rolf Gordhamer, who directs psychological testing and counseling at Texas Tech, said it was quite common for students to carry weapons at the college.[7]

Drake saw not only a difference in tone between this segment and that in the *Post* but "a small but important difference in the actual information reported." Carrying "weapons at the college," as the *Inquirer* said, is substantially different from the *Post* statement that "students carry guns to class." Drake added, "The thought of a student carrying a pistol in a classroom is much more disturbing to me, as a reader in a northeastern city, than the image of them carrying a gun outside on campus for target shooting or some other sporting activity." The *Inquirer* further quoted Gordhamer as observing:

> "Seriously, this is frontierland. People do have guns. Their grandparents were pioneers. There are a lot of small towns and isolation, and change comes very slowly. People shoot rattlesnakes and coyotes and," he paused to laugh, "trespassers."
>
> "Still," Gordhamer said, "the campus is placid, the calmest, quietest place I've ever seen. Basically, the kids obey authority. They don't protest or march up and down the streets here. They take life pretty easy. They just kind of enjoy it. People out here believe in mother, apple pie and The American Flag."

"As you can see," Drake explained, "the *Inquirer*'s picture of Lubbock is much more complex than the one suggested in the segment of the *Post*'s story. . . . I think this is a particularly interesting example of how the basic facts in two stories might be the same—Lubbock is a town where guns are common and pioneer independence predominates—but one story, the *Post*'s, leaves the impression that Lubbock is the set for a John Wayne movie and the other, the *Inquirer*'s, suggests something more like Thornton Wilder's 'Our Town.'"

The *Post* corrected the passage about Lubbock 25 days after it ran. The correction said that the article "presented an inaccurate depiction of Texas Tech University and the city in which the university is located, Lubbock. Texas Tech students do not carry guns to class, as the article stated, and the city itself is a quiet town with orderly and law-abiding citizens. There is no 'pistol-packing' tradition in Lubbock, as the article incorrectly implied." The *Post* also carried four letters from Lubbock, all disagreeing with the implications in the *Post*'s reference to the city and the university.

IGNORANCE AND INADEQUATE EDUCATION

Journalists are no longer the uneducated louts the legendary editor and writer H.L. Mencken saw in the American newsrooms of the 1920s. Mencken wrote, "It is this vast and militant ignorance, this widespread and fathomless prejudice against intelligence, that makes American journalism so pathetically feeble and vulgar, and so generally disreputable."[8]

But unfortunately ignorance is sometimes still a problem. Errors in news reports, some serious, occur every day because some journalist didn't have the knowledge or intelligence to get the facts straight. Perhaps it is asking too much that journalists have at least above-average knowledge of the many subjects they deal with every working day, but citizens depend on the information they get from the news media to guide them in the decisions they make in the polling place, the marketplace, and their lives in general. Bum information leads to bum decisions.

One important area that has been unevenly reported because of reporter ignorance is the legal process. David Shaw of the *Los Angeles Times* looked into that problem a few years ago and concluded that such reporting is improving but that "media coverage of the nation's legal system is still largely inadequate."[9] At least some of the blame for inadequate coverage of this important institution has to be placed on lack of knowledge by reporters. Although an impressive number of top legal reporters have legal training and even law degrees, the average reporter has none. Shaw, who interviewed almost 100 attorneys, judges, legal scholars, journalists and journalism professors, found that most favored some legal training for reporters assigned to this area. Such training "enables a reporter to speak the same, often arcane language as the people he covers, and it also enables him to invite confidences not easily given to non-lawyers—and to provide historical perspective to his daily reportage," Shaw concluded. Several lawyers told Shaw they were "astounded by the number of reporters who accepted what they said—or did not say—without either question or challenge, either out of laziness, ignorance, or a fear of being perceived as ignorant."

Another area in which sources often complain about journalists' lack of knowledge is business and economics. Although the larger newspapers and network news departments have beefed up their coverage of business and economics in recent years, "media coverage is often simplistic, careless and cursory," A. Kent MacDougall wrote in the *Los Angeles Times*.[10] A recent survey of business executives found that only 27 percent thought business reporting was fair and accurate.[11]

One explanation for errors in business reporting can be surmised from the experiences of the late Cortland Anderson, who worked as a newspaper journalist and in corporate public relations before becoming director of Ohio University's School of Journalism. Anderson commented that when he was public relations chief at the New York Telephone Company, "we had to educate reporters seemingly thrown in at the last minute to cover specific complicated rate stories." He recalled how John de Butts, then chairman of American Telephone and Telegraph, ended an interview with a reporter from a "highly respected publication specializing in business news" when de Butts "discovered the reporter did not know the difference between stocks and bonds." Anderson also told of a reporter gathering information from him (as vice president of the Washington Post Company) to prepare for an interview with Katharine Graham, then chair of the Washington Post Company, for a story on the company's state of business. "In a discussion preceding that interview, my concern rose and my confidence fell when I learned that this reporter did not understand the implications of a company repurchasing its own stock. That was a process in which the company was deeply involved at the time—a vital part of the story."[12]

Some of the ignorance in processing news could be avoided by more preparation—journalists doing their homework before asking questions. Robert Scheer of the *Los Angeles Times* sees library research as the first line of ethical reporting. He believes reporters have to make themselves authorities on the subjects they write about. The ethical question, he said, is "whether you're really going to put out, or whether you're going to surrender to . . . cynicism . . . and just shove it into the paper." Scheer's primary standard is "I want to be able to pick up the piece two or three years later and say 'God, this holds up!'"[13]

Journalists might make fewer errors if they broadened and deepened their education. Although more than 80 percent of newspaper and television journalists have at least one college degree,[14] few have taken advanced education in the specialized areas that journalists have to interpret. There are several explanations for the dearth of specialists who have done work beyond the bachelor's degree in legal matters, political science, business and economics, the sciences, engineering and other fields. The news business is perceived as a business for generalists: reporters and editors who can handle any type of story on any given day. When editors and news directors hire, they are usually not interested in specialists; they want people who can do everything, at least well enough to get by. A second explanation relates to the abysmally low beginning salaries in news work. Although salaries for experienced journalists are satisfactory, the low pay at the entrance level discourages apprentices from carrying their formal education beyond the minimum—now a bachelor's degree. There is a third reason: The streak of anti-intellectualism that has been part of American journalism from its beginning has not dissipated.

As newspapers begin to expect reporters to engage in "expert journalism" in which they are expected to do more explanatory reporting and analysis, many believe journalism education will need to be overhauled. Gene Patterson, editor emeritus of the *St. Petersburg Times,* has called for more specialized and graduate education. And the American Society of Newspaper Editors continues to push for requirements that journalism majors spend most of their undergraduate days taking classes in the liberal arts and sciences.[15]

CORRECTING THE RECORD

You may recall the case of the Louisville doctor discussed in Chapter 2. The *Courier-Journal* printed a chart that mistakenly listed the fees he charged his patients as nearly twice what he charged. The paper not only printed a correction but reported on its front page the National News Council's criticisms of the report. And the paper's executive editor apologized to the doctor in his column.

While few newspapers print front-page corrections and apologies, nearly all make an effort to correct most or some of their errors, and many print their corrections in a set place every day to make them easier to find. Some even print clarifications of stories that were not so much incorrect as misleading. Exactly which errors will be corrected and which overlooked varies from paper to paper. *The Hartford Courant* runs corrections for even minor errors like an incorrect middle initial and averages 100 corrections a month. Other papers show more restraint. "We won't correct the most arcane mistake," says John Bull of *The Philadelphia Inquirer*. "It has to be an error of reasonable substance."[16]

"Don't you think we're carrying our new corrections policy a little far?"

Some newspapers have been known to drag their feet when it comes to printing corrections. The *New York Post,* rarely considered a leader in media ethics, gave banner-headline treatment to the rape of a 3-year-old. The story said motorists on a major highway in Manhattan stopped their cars to watch. "Shame of the City — Shocking Story of New York at Its Worst," the headline charged. The paper never corrected the record with the real story. A rape did take place, but three motorists saw the incident and pursued the rapist. Traffic was stopped not because people were watching the rape but because the rescuers of the little girl had left their cars on the highway in their haste to help the child.[17]

Broadcast journalism has an equally unimpressive history of correcting errors. Although the ethics codes at all the networks require prompt corrections, representatives of CBS News and CNN told Steve Brill, editor of *The American Lawyer,* that they could not recall the last time their networks ran a correction. ABC said it ran three in 1992.[18] As for NBC, even after another reporter and a state senator told the network about misrepresentations in its report on the impact of loggers in

Idaho, the network "stood by" its story for two months, then admitted its error after the report was criticized on the floor of the U.S. Senate.[19] Similarly, NBC did not confess to putting incendiary devices on a GM truck to make sure it would explode in a crash test until GM found the truck in a junkyard, had the gas tank X-rayed for fractures, and arranged a satellite feed of its side of the story to the nation's TV stations.[20]

Many local stations are also not very forthcoming in admitting their mistakes. Some studies have suggested that as many as one-third of the stories on local TV news have inaccuracies, but only a sixth of stations responding to a survey said they ran corrections as often as once a month. Many news directors said they feared that airing corrections might cause viewers to lose confidence in their news.[21]

It is not journalistic integrity but fear of libel that causes some newspapers and TV stations to run corrections. In some states a correction can be a mitigating factor in libel suits. But more important, legal studies have found that if news organizations are willing to admit mistakes, they can often head off lawsuits. Many libel suits are filed only after the people who are already angry because of the news report call the news organization and are snubbed by the journalists who did the story.[22]

Occasionally, people do not want corrections printed. They believe the correction simply calls attention to the original report for those who missed it. Although it rarely happens, there is also the risk that you will get the kind of apology that George Papadakis did when he took offense at the *Signal Hill (Calif.) Tribune* for calling him a "Greek orator" in an editorial. Papadakis, who was a council member in that city, said the reference to him was a "racial slur." This was too much for editor Ken Mills. "The Tribune apologizes, George," Mills wrote. "What we meant to call you is a loquacious asshole, a bore without peer. . . . We've reported your councilmanic doings accurately and without malice. So stuff it." Mills explained to the AP that he used "Greek orator" to mean that Papadakis was articulate.[23]

ARE CORRECTIONS ENOUGH?

Not all people mistreated by the media are satisfied that running a correction rights the wrong. Sexual-harassment officer Ferrara-Kerr is one. The paper printed a nine-line correction, but as she told the paper's ombudsman, many more people read the story than saw the correction. Months after the correction appeared, she was still getting phone calls from people angry at her for what she was quoted as saying. "How do you repair the damage?" she asked.[24]

Jim Stott, ombudsman at the *Calgary Herald* at the time, understood her plight. He said papers ought to do more than print paragraph-long corrections when they make mistakes like the one involving Ferrara-Kerr. He suggested in his column that papers might adopt a "more flexible" policy on corrections. The regular correction box was adequate for most errors, but in the case of Ferrara-Kerr the paper should have run a "prominent article on the same page where the original error occurred."[25]

Other ombudsmen have faced similar questions about repairing the damage of journalists' mistakes. When he was ombudsman at *The Washington Post,* Richard Harwood wrote that he was asked by a much-maligned secretary of the Labor Department, "Who will give me back my good name?" "Not the press," Harwood answered. "That isn't our style." Nor do the news media usually do postmortems on their errors. "Our follies and ineptitudes become family secrets, talked about in barrooms and classrooms but rarely in print."[26]

REDUCING THE NUMBER OF ERRORS

Presstime writer Rolf Rykken tracked down some of the ways news organizations are trying to reduce the number of errors:

- The Sioux City (Iowa) *Journal* requires staffers who make mistakes to write letters of apology to the people involved.
- *The Ledger* of Lakeland, Fla., calls people named in news stories and asks them about the accuracy of those stories. Some papers mail questionnaires to sources to get their reactions to stories about them.
- *Quill* and a few other publications have tried to fine free-lancers whose work contains errors.
- Some papers name the person who made the error in their corrections, although many journalists doubt that public humiliation is an effective way to deal with the problem. (*The Houston Post* once took this form of discipline a step further and required a reporter who got the date of a conference wrong to stand outside the conference hotel holding a sign and passing out corrections.[27])
- *The Plattsburgh* (*N.Y.*) *Press-Republican* and many other papers use their newsroom computers to keep track of the number of mistakes each staffer makes.[28]

Perhaps the most controversial method of preventing mistakes is to call back sources and check the accuracy of stories with them. Some magazines like *Time* and *The New Yorker* regularly read back many articles before they are printed. Some metropolitan dailies like *The Philadelphia Inquirer* and smaller papers like the *Daily Gate City* in Keokuk, Iowa, have similar procedures, especially for lengthy or difficult stories.[29]

But readbacks are taboo in most newsrooms, even though many journalists know how often direct quotes are wrong. One editor of *The Atlanta Journal/The Atlanta Constitution* said he had been interviewed countless times through the years and had been quoted correctly only once.[30] While he may have been exaggerating, studies have found that quotes in the paper do not always jibe with official transcripts of testimony during trials. But the prohibition against letting sources know in advance what information will be in stories is an unwritten law that beginning journalists learn early and most abide by for the rest of their lives.

Jay Matthews, Los Angeles bureau chief for *The Washington Post,* admitted in the *Washington Journalism Review* that after 20 years of newsroom conditioning he broke with custom and read back to a source part of a story he was writing. The readback turned up an error that he was able to correct before the story was published. Matthews argued that it is time for journalists to stop "defending a rotting corpse" and consider readbacks. He wrote:

> Double-checking selected facts is fine. Competent reporters do that. The process catches the vast majority of potential mistakes. What a readback would catch are the unconscious errors, the verbal misunderstandings, the odd misspellings, the mental lapses that occur in communication between human beings.[31]

Reporter Steve Weinberg sees value in readbacks as a way of not only correcting errors but of winning the confidence of sources. He described in a *Quill* article the first time he used the technique:

> I was working on a sensitive project about wrongdoing at a major law firm. My editors at the *Des Moines Register* were giving me plenty of time and resources. But some key sources were reluctant to talk. I understood their reluctance, so I asked them if anything might change their minds.
>
> They said we trust your work, but this project, no matter how carefully reported and written, is bound to have negative fallout for us. We would like to read what you write before it goes into print. Maybe we can minimize our problems by discussing the story at that stage.
>
> Well, why not, I thought. It seemed like a reasonable request under the circumstances. I might have asked for the same courtesy if I had been in their shoes.[32]

Weinberg contended that in the 10 years he has been making read-backs, the practice "had led to more accurate, fair and thorough newspaper pieces, magazine articles and books." He dismissed the argument that readbacks give the sources too much control over the work. He makes it clear to his sources, he said, that he will consider comments they make about the stories but reserves the right to decide what will be changed. If sources claim they are misquoted, he checks the quotes against his tape recordings or his notes. "If the source is incorrect or acting in a self-serving way that obscures rather than illuminates the truth, I change nothing."[33]

After a doctor testifying as an expert witness at a malpractice trial about colon cancer examinations was badly misquoted in *The Virginian-Pilot* and *The Ledger-Star* of Norfolk, Va., the papers' ombudsman, Kerry Sipe, said reporters ought to adopt the practice of contacting sources before publication to confirm what they have written, particularly when the material is technical or complex. He wrote that it was farfetched for reporters to think that reading a few paragraphs of a story back to a source prior to publication constitutes relinquishing control over what is printed."[34]

Who's Watching the Watchdogs?

A responsibility evolving out of the First Amendment that journalists seldom question is the obligation of the news media to be a watchdog of government. Keeping the press free from the government ("Congress shall make no law" etc.) allows the press to help protect citizens from the abuses of government. In modern times this watchdog role has been extended by most journalists to business, education, sports and other important institutions of American life.

Many observers believe that the news media also need scrutiny — a watchdog of the watchdogs. Journalism is too important to be left entirely to journalists. It needs independent and critical monitoring. But journalists have resisted such appraisals on any systematic basis, mostly out of concern that press freedom might be diminished. So the history of U.S. journalism in this century has been only lightly spotted with examples of continuing reviews of journalism's performance.

Some of the instruments that have been suggested over the years to monitor news media performance are news councils, ombudsmen, journalism reviews, reporters regularly covering journalism, and regular crit-

"Hey, Sam! Do something about your damned watchdog!"

ical reviews by schools of journalism and communications. All of these have been tried, and some are being used today, but there is no national or regular audit of news media performance. The only watching most of the watchdogs get comes from their audiences.

OMBUDSMEN

When college official Ferrara-Kerr wanted to complain that she had been mistreated by her local newspaper, she eventually dealt with the newspaper's ombudsman, a person who handles complaints from the public and serves as in-house critic. Although the label "ombudsman" is frequently used, some are known as reader representatives, reader advocates or some similar and more understandable title. There's even an Organization of News Ombudsmen, which they call by its initials ONO ("Oh, no")—said to describe the ombudsman's typical reaction to the paper's latest goof. The idea (and the name) came from Sweden, where a government official with that title represents the public in its dealings with the bureaucracy.

The first news ombudsman in this country was appointed in 1967 by the *Louisville Times* and *The Courier-Journal.* Several newspapers soon followed suit, but most papers shied away from the idea. Editors at *The New York Times* called ombudsmen "gimmicks" and "a cop-out." Many editors still look upon ombudsmen that way. Nearly three-fourths of editors responding to a survey thought they could answer reader complaints just as well as an ombudsman and that the money could be better spent.[35]

Some journalists believe the rationale for having ombudsmen is flawed. *Miami Herald* Executive Editor Douglas Clifton said he considered ombudsmen "a barrier" between readers and journalists, contending that it is good for editors to "feel the wrath of readers" after they have made controversial news decisions.[36] Other papers, like the *St. Petersburg Times,* at first added ombudsmen but then abandoned the concept. Robert Haiman, then executive editor of the *Times,* said that ombudsmen did not get involved with a problem until the paper had printed the story. He compared them to coroners, whose job it is "to do the postmortem on a disaster, to pick through the tatters of flesh after a terrible crash."[37]

Norman Isaacs, the editor who appointed the first ombudsman in Louisville, also became disenchanted with ombudsmen. He said that too often ombudsmen spend too much time writing columns and not enough time responding to readers and criticizing the paper internally. He also noted that at some papers ombudsmen "are purely cosmetic; some guy writing a media column in which all he does is explain the virtues of the newspaper."[38]

However, Lynne Enders Glaser, who writes the ombudsman column for *The Fresno Bee,* said she does not see her job as making the paper popular or beloved by explaining away its problems but regaining the respect of readers by showing that the newspaper cares about readers' reactions and that it is trying to be fair.[39] Lou Gelfand, reader representative of the *Star Tribune* in Minneapolis, has argued that ombudsmen may even help stop the decline in readership by winning back respect for the news media.[40]

Although some ombudsmen do not publicize the media's foibles by writing columns, most do. After reading more than 70 columns by ombudsmen, Richard Salant, former president of CBS News, praised those ombudsmen who "explain just how the subject matter complained about happened—tracing its origins and reasons—thus contributing to public understanding of the news process, and its fallibility." He cited other ombudsmen whose columns question media performance and discuss issues like objectivity and journalistic conflicts of interest.[41]

For ombudsmen to be successful, they must overcome at least three hurdles. They must be accepted by their colleagues. One *Washington Post* ombudsman said the worst part of his job was finding people in the newsroom who would go to lunch with him. However, other ombudsmen have been able to win the respect of reporters and editors. At the Minneapolis *Star Tribune,* reporters have suggested to angry sources that they take their disagreements to the reader representative rather than fight it out themselves.[42]

Second, ombudsmen must win the trust of readers. In Minneapolis, a reader complained that he did not believe an employee of the paper was the proper person to investigate complaints against the paper. Ombudsman Gelfand defended himself in a column, saying that the record showed he was not hesitant to criticize the *Star Tribune.* Of the 57 complaints he had written about in the previous year, he sided with readers 34 times.[43] *The Seattle Times* printed a line at the end of its reader advocate's column indicating that its reader advocate was not a full-time employee of the paper, but a "privately contracted consultant." The paper dropped the position in 1992.

Third, ombudsmen must have the support of their newspapers' management. Many media executives understand that ombudsmen must be free to criticize the organization, but they do not always handle the criticism well. When the ombudsman at Winnipeg's *Free Press* criticized his paper for burying its coverage of the 1992 Los Angeles riots deep in the fourth section, he was fired.[44] Similarly, an ombudsman at KABC in Los Angeles ran into troubles with management when he reported criticisms of KABC by other TV stations. KABC was running a series each night during ratings sweeps week telling how the Nielsen organization conducted ratings. Other stations called the "news segments" a ploy to arouse the curiosity of families with Nielsen monitors attached to their TVs so they would watch KABC. The ombudsman put together a balanced report with comments from station officials. But after the piece was aired, the ombudsman's researchers were fired and his producer reassigned. The ombudsman said he was told that his roles as "investigative reporter, ombudsman and media analyst were terminated."[45]

Fewer than 40 of America's 1,600 dailies have ombudsmen, although the concept is more common in Canada.[46] None of the TV networks had ombudsmen until 1993 when NBC named one. A few months later, ABC appointed its first director of news practices.[47]

Some publications take other steps to inform their readers of major issues in journalism. David Shaw, writing about media issues for the *Los Angeles Times* since 1974, has often been critical of the *Times. The Wall Street Journal, The Washington Post, Chicago Tribune, The New York Times, Newsday, Newsweek* and *Time* all regularly cover the media. But few newspapers do this. Many journalists would agree with a *Sacramento Bee* ombudsman who said, "The press does an abysmal job of explaining itself."[48]

A trend in the early 1990s at newspapers like the *Portland (Maine) Press Herald* and *The Orlando Sentinel* to invite readers to sit in on its editorial meetings may be another way for newspapers to tell the public how they make decisions. The public is invited to offer opinions or listen to the discussions as the editorial writers map out upcoming editorial pages.

The news media are also examined critically by national magazines like *Columbia Journalism Review, American Journalism Review* (formerly *Washington Journalism Review*), *Quill, Nieman Reports* and *Presstime.* These publications are read primarily by journalists. *Journalism Quarterly, Journal of Broadcasting and Electronic Media* and *Newspaper Research Journal* publish reports on research, often by journalism professors, about media issues, and the reports are sometimes critical and evaluative.

But when she was reader advocate of *The Seattle Times,* Colleen Patrick, argued that the media needed to do more. She believed news organizations should criticize one another. "The lack of this self-coverage is considered hypocritical by people who feel the bite of media coverage, but do not see equal scrutiny applied to the media themselves," she wrote. She noted that this call had been made more than 40 years before by the Hutchins Commission on Freedom of the Press (discussed in Chapter 1).[49]

NEWS COUNCILS

For 11 years, the United States had a National News Council charged with the responsibility of monitoring the news media in this country, but it died of neglect in 1984. This council, which grew out of an idea stated by the Hutchins commission, was created in 1973 to investigate complaints against the news media, to listen to the complainant and the journalists involved, and to come to some decision about media conduct in the case. The council had no legal authority and could not assess damages or fines. It hoped that its power would come from publicizing its findings and from the desire of journalists to improve the standards of their trade.

The council was started by grants from the Twentieth Century Fund and the Markle Foundation. Their idea was that media companies would take over the funding of the council once it was functioning. That never happened. Most news organizations failed to support the council with dollars or publicity. Richard Salant, the former head of CBS News who was president of the council when it folded, said he believed media opposition to the council "was rooted in the traditional reluctance of the press to have any outside body . . . looking over its shoulder, and in the conviction of the press that each individual news organization could best solve its own problems and in its own way."[50]

At about the same time the National News Council was founded, local news councils were set up in California, Hawaii, Oregon, Missouri, Illinois, Minnesota and most Canadian provinces. Today, every Canadian province except Saskatchewan has a provincial or regional news council, but the only remaining statewide council in the United States is Minnesota's.[51] The Minnesota council receives funding from many of the state's media companies. Among the issues it investigated in the early 1990s were complaints from an unsuccessful county commission candidate who thought the *Stillwater Evening Gazette* had been unfair in its political coverage[52] and a college professor who said the *Star Tribune* of Minneapolis should have contacted him before reporting that he had lowered the grade of a Native American student who had accused him being prejudiced against Indians.[53]

Although many news councils died in the 1980s, a few journalists would like to see them restarted. Robert W. Chandler, the editor of *The Bulletin* in Bend, Ore., has created a local version of the National News Council for his paper. When someone calls to complain, a staff member meets with the person to discuss the complaint. If the staff member and the complainant can't settle the problem, a panel from the community is asked to investigate the claim. If the panel sides with the paper, the matter is dropped. But if the panel finds against the paper, the paper prints the panel's comments. Few disputes have gone before the panel. "I never expected that very many would," Chandler said. He noted that most people tend to cool off when the paper appears so fair-minded in dealing with their complaints. About 20 other papers have adopted procedures similar to Chandler's.[54]

In 1992, chapters of the Society of Professional Journalists in Oregon and Washington formed the Northwest News Council and planned to rely on volunteers to keep it afloat. Their initial budget was $300, compared with the well-established Ontario Press Council's $185,000 funded by member newspapers.[55] In its first year the council encountered problems getting newspapers to cooperate with its investigations.[56]

Some American universities have attempted news media criticism and monitoring, but their efforts have been spotty and mostly ineffective. One problem is that virtually all universities depend on tax and donated dollars and are reluctant to take on media organizations and their power over public opinion. For that reason alone, we probably should not count on our academic institutions to be major watchdogs of the watchdogs.

What's an Ethical Journalist to Do?

Not all news proprietors would agree with the major thesis of this chapter—that they have an obligation to be accountable to the public. In an earlier day, few newspaper owners thought they had to account to anybody. They saw their papers as private businesses that the public could accept or reject. But more and more media owners today act as if they accept the need to explain at least some aspects of their publications or stations to those who depend on them.

Most newspapers today are conscientious about correcting their errors, but broadcast news organizations seldom admit or correct their mistakes. If the media are committed to truth-telling, correcting the record should be an essential obligation.

A more serious deficiency in the media's obligation to be accountable to the public is the failure of many to do a good job of explaining themselves through columns by editors and ombudsmen and articles about their internal operations. That leaves the public in the unfortunate circumstance of getting most of its insights into journalism in two ways: They watch movies and TV programs that show reporters as insensitive oafs, or they watch news conferences where reporters are shouting questions at public officials, political candidates or their spokespersons. Neither provides an accurate portrayal of the work of most journalists, but many in the public don't know that.

The public is left with no way of knowing why certain events and activities are "newsworthy" and others are not; why their local paper differs so from *The New York Times* and their local TV news from ABC News; how the news staff, whatever its size, is deployed; where all that informational material not produced locally comes from; and how much money the paper or station makes and how much of that profit is reinvested in the local company.

The public would also be better served if it knew more about the ethics policies of the news organizations. The *Wilmington News Journal* publishes its ethics code every year. Not many papers do that, although the relatively few newspapers with ombudsmen usually inform their readers about their ethics guidelines through the ombudsmen's columns. But the huge majority of newspapers and TV news departments, even those with ethics codes, keep their ethics policies to themselves. Many in the public are genuinely surprised to learn that there are codes of ethics and that many of their perceptions about reporters' ethics are wrong.

Most journalism leaders won't accept news councils, ombudsmen and other devices for involving the public in processing news. They have a harder time accepting the idea that some outside agency or group might pass judgment on them and the journalism they produce. That kind of monitoring is an anathema to them.

"Well, I guess if they don't have an ombudsman or news council and the editors won't talk to you, we've got no choice but to sue 'em for all they're worth."

No one who understands our democratic system would want this monitoring to be done by a governmental or even quasi-governmental group. Yet the important role the media play in our society makes it imperative that reporters and editors behave ethically and that the public understand the problems and difficulties of journalists in trying to fulfill their obligations to truth, compassion and democracy.

Perhaps some new instrument through which the public can call journalists into account must be invented. But its invention will be for naught if journalists continue their stubborn resistance against having anyone outside their own organization looking over their shoulders. Some members of the public may have their complaints satisfied by calls or letters to news executives or ombudsmen, or through lawsuits, but the accountability that is needed is broader than that. The public needs to be continually assured that the vital role journalism plays in providing independent information and analysis is not being tainted, abused or handled irresponsibly.

Compassion

A Marine from Colorado was among those taken hostage when Iranians seized the U.S. Embassy in Tehran.

Months later, his family received word that their son might soon be freed. The release of the 52 hostages, coming after months of tense negotiations and a failed rescue attempt by American military forces, was big news. Reporters throughout the state scrambled to be there when the family received word their son was coming home.

Ramon Coronado, a reporter for *The Coloradoan* in Fort Collins, described what happened while the mob of journalists was waiting to capture the joy of Billy Gallegos' parents:

> The media camped in the sloped front yard, an area no bigger than two spaces in a parking lot. Electrical cords, telephones, television sets, radios, tape recorders, microphones, cigarette butts, coffee cups and paper from fast-food restaurants blanketed the ground. In the back, the alley was filled with television news trucks manned with technicians.

About three dozen of the reporters and photographers were allowed inside the small home, but some had to stay outside. As those inside jostled for better positions, one journalist knocked a ceramic plate off a wall, Coronado reported. Photographers stood on furniture, breaking one table. A reporter from Colorado Springs was caught looking at the family's mail.[1]

It's hard not to be appalled by such behavior. When journalists misbehave this badly, it leaves a foul taste in people's mouths and lessens their respect for all journalists. Some news organizations have tried to take steps to avoid these kinds of media circuses. TV stations in several cities, including Milwaukee, Denver and Cleveland, decided to pool interviews with survivors of military personnel killed in the Gulf War in 1991. Each station selected one experienced reporter, and using a rotation system, these reporters interviewed survivors and shared the videotapes.[2]

But what happened in Colorado illustrates a more basic problem for many in journalism: a lack of compassion. Summing up his experience, Coronado wrote that "the press lost sight of the fact the Gallegoses were not just a story but are people. People with feelings and the need for privacy."

Room for Humaneness?

Curiously, this discussion of compassion in journalism would surprise both members of the press and the public — but for much different reasons. Many journalists would be surprised to see compassion considered an important issue for journalists. And about two-thirds of the public would be surprised to find out that journalists even know the meaning of the word.[3]

Journalists, especially the newspaper variety, shun the notion of compassion for many reasons. Some believe it runs counter to objective reporting, which they try to practice despite widespread doubts about its achievability or desirability. A tenet of objective reporting is that reporters are spectators and not participants in what they cover. The discipline of objective reporting, it is said, requires a dispassionate approach to gathering and presenting the facts. Reporters are not supposed to get involved with the people in their stories; they are supposed to be neutral observers. For this reason, Diane Benison, who was a managing editor of the old Worchester, Mass., *Evening Gazette,* thinks compassion may be out of place in news work. "One of the curses of this business," she argued, "is that you're expected to have your pores open, to be able to feel, to be able to empathize with people, and yet to eviscerate yourself to do your job, just as if you were a machine."[4]

A second argument against compassion is the belief that reporters will become weak-willed and forget their obligation to keep the public informed with truthful accounts of the news. Louis Boccardi, president of the AP, recalled that when he was a young reporter covering courts, he was often asked not to put certain things in the paper. He feared that if compassion became too prevalent, reporters would agree to these requests, and legitimate news stories would not be printed.

Competitive pressures are another reason some journalists believe they must suppress compassion. Ginger Casey, when she was a reporter for KQED-TV in San Francisco, was covering a shooting at a playground. Reporters were swarming around the neighborhood looking for angles for stories. She did not want to interview the children who might have seen the attack and make them revisit its horror. But she knew that if one reporter did, she would have to. "You don't want your competition to have any angle you don't have, and crying kids on camera were powerful images," she wrote. "If having your voice heard at a news conference scored points, so did interviewing a child. Your boss would tell you that you 'kicked ass.' Your resume tape would look terrific."[5]

Casey's observation suggests another reason some journalists feel they must shed feelings of compassion: They don't want compassion to get in the way of landing a big story that will impress their editors or news directors. This search for a career-making story may be the reason so many younger reporters advocate questionable reporting tactics. When researchers showed journalists a list of tactics, including badgering sources for information and deceiving people, younger journalists were more likely to believe each could be justified than were their more-seasoned colleagues.[6]

COMPASSION IMPROVES JOURNALISM

Many editors do not believe that compassion lessens the quality of a journalist's work. They believe compassion makes for better reporting. Geneva Overholser, editor of *The Des Moines Register,* argues that the journalist-as-machine notion has made much newspaper writing boring, dull and meaningless. In her view, journalists should write stories that make readers "laugh, weep, sing, hope and wonder how people can go on." That kind of writing can be achieved only if journalists have feelings and are concerned about the people and issues they write about. She said it cannot be done by journalists who spend their time "polishing up their value-free journalism skills."[7]

Journalists often want to write stories that go beyond the bare facts. They want to humanize social problems, even provoke a sympathetic response in their readers. To do this, they must become involved with the people who are experiencing the problem, interview them with sensitivity, and describe their conditions with care and compassion.

Jacqui Banaszynski of the *St. Paul Pioneer Press* wrote a series called "AIDS in the Heartland."[8] The stories portrayed the final months in the life of a man with AIDS. She visited the man and his partner on their farm frequently and interviewed friends and family. Sensing that the relationship was going beyond traditional reporter-source, she started reminding the men that she was a reporter and told her editors to be extra diligent in editing her copy. Because friends and family were so open with her, she read the quotes she planned to use back to them to make sure they were accurate. Her honest and compassionate reporting led to sensitive stories that gave readers a deeper understanding of the AIDS crisis. Her efforts were rewarded with a Pulitzer Prize and a Distinguished Service Award from the Society of Professional Journalists.

"Compassion is basic to good ethics and good journalism," observed Joseph Shoquist, managing editor of *The Milwaukee Journal* for a number of years before becoming journalism dean at the University of South Carolina. He said it is important for journalists to have "a regard for people as human beings, not be so hard-nosed about everything."[9]

Treating People with Respect

Hard-nosed questions don't bother writer Janet Malcolm. It's the way reporters dupe people into talking to them that angers her. In an article for *The New Yorker,* she lambasted Joe McGinniss for the way he gathered information for his book about Dr. Jeffrey MacDonald, who was charged with murdering his wife and two children. The doctor came to regard McGinniss as a friend and supporter who believed in his innocence. He shared his thoughts with McGinniss and allowed him to be with his legal team throughout the trial. But when McGinniss' *Fatal Vision* was published, there was no doubt that McGinniss thought the doctor was a cold-blooded killer. Malcolm accused McGinniss of tricking the doctor into accepting him as a friend so he could get material for his book.[10]

If Malcolm had limited her criticisms to McGinniss, her work probably would not have created much of a stir, but she expanded her observations to journalists in general. Malcolm's article began:

> Every journalist who is not too stupid or too full of himself to notice what is going on knows that what he does is morally indefensible. He is a

kind of confidence man, preying on people's vanity, ignorance, or loneliness, gaining their trust and betraying them without remorse.

That opening paragraph triggered what *Columbia Journalism Review* called "more newsroom and cocktail-party debate, more belligerent editorializing and more honest soul-searching" than almost any other article on journalism ever had.[11] Many journalists began to ask themselves if they tricked their sources into talking and then betrayed them when they wrote their stories.

TRICKS OF THE TRADE

Columbia Journalism Review asked a selection of the nation's top writers and journalists about Malcolm's opening paragraph. Nora Ephron saw little wrong with Malcolm's observations. "Some of the best journalism I've read happened after what Janet is describing as 'betrayal' or as 'immoral.'" Ephron thought the public needed to learn that "journalists are not their friends."[12]

Some journalists acknowledged that there were tricks to getting good interviews. Mike Wallace, known for his hardball interviews on CBS's *60 Minutes,* said, "As a journalist, you do some role playing. You don't turn all your cards face up." To get sources to cooperate, he said, he sometimes uses persuasion. "And as long as it's done honestly, as long as no promises are made which are then broken, then it seems to me perfectly reasonable to 'sell' the object of your scrutiny on the wisdom of cooperation."[13] *New York Daily News* columnist Ken Auletta admitted that he often used a kind of seduction on sources by beginning his interviews with softball questions to get them to relax.[14]

"And when do you want to start the interview, Grandmother?"

Other journalists have written that they are troubled by all this gamesmanship. In an article in the *San Francisco Examiner,* Ginger Casey, a former KQED reporter, wrote: "I knew all the tricks. I had learned to hide my excitement when I found someone naive enough to share their pain with me. And I swallowed the shame of knowing that their tragedy would be a good career move for me."[15]

But many journalists were quick to note that they often went to great pains to make sure they treated people fairly. Long before the tempest over Malcolm's remarks, Bob Greene, the popular columnist for the *Chicago Tribune* (and not to be confused with the former *Newsday* investigative reporter of the same name), wrote about the interviewing style he used for his columns, which often portray the lifestyles of private people and the quirkiness of everyday life. He said he tries "to make an interview subject feel so comfortable and so warm that he cannot conceive of being betrayed by this nice fellow who is asking the questions and making the notes." He continued:

> As often as not, though, the person I'm with has never been interviewed before. He is wary at first; it takes a while to make him understand that this is not a surgical procedure. There are tricks to that, too; I will stumble around in my conversation. I will make my questions sound exceedingly dumb; if he is having a few too many drinks, I will drink right along with him. I may or may not be a likable person in real life, but I can be a likable person in an interview situation; it's just another trick I have learned. . . .
>
> I decided a long time ago in situations like those, I had the obligation to help protect a person even if he didn't know enough to protect himself.[16]

Greene said he has protected interviewees by offering not to use their names, even if he knew they would be willing to be named. He said what the source "doesn't know is that the sight of his words and his world in cold print, in front of hundreds of thousands of strangers, is going to jar him."

Other journalists recognize the problem of dealing with people who are accustomed to being interviewed, but they are not happy with using unnamed sources, particularly if they are writing hard-news stories rather than the more personal columns that Greene often writes. Mike Feinsilber, who was Washington news editor for AP, said he did not want to take advantage of inexperienced interviewees, so he would remind them, "Don't tell me anything you don't want in the newspaper." Feinsilber also gave news sources a chance to collect their thoughts. He would call them, tell them what he wanted to interview them about, and offer to call back in 10 minutes or so. "I find I get better information and better quotes that way, and people appreciate it."[17]

Other reporters take steps throughout the interview to make sure sources know they may be quoted. Barry Michael Cooper, who writes for *The Village Voice* in New York, will stop an interview "when I think subjects could be hurting themselves inadvertently." He'll remind them that the interview is on the record and ask them if they want to continue.[18]

A few editors take this courtesy a step further. If unsophisticated sources call reporters later and say they said something during the interview they don't want printed, reporters are required to remove those comments, even if doing so spoils the story.

SOURCES FEEL BETRAYED

A mother called *The Ann Arbor* (*Mich.*) *News* and told a reporter that he should write a story about the untimely death of her 17-year-old daughter. The woman said her daughter was at a New Year's Eve party where kids were drinking automobile antifreeze to get high. Her daughter drank too much of it and died. The mother hoped the reporter would write a story to alert students and the community to the hazards of drinking antifreeze.

The reporter interviewed the mother, who described her daughter as a good girl who died because of a high school fad. After interviewing the mother, the reporter checked with school authorities, drug experts and police. He found no evidence to back up the mother's belief that drinking antifreeze was common in Ann Arbor. He also talked to people who knew the girl and learned that her life had not been exactly the way her mother described it.

Instead of writing a warning about teens drinking antifreeze, the reporter wrote a story based on what he had discovered about the girl's life and death. When the story appeared, the mother complained that the paper had described her daughter as "wild and crazy," portrayed her as the only kid drinking antifreeze, and hinted she might have committed suicide. The mother said that she had hoped the paper would print "a tribute and a warning." Instead the reporter wrote a news story. "Maybe I was naive to expect anything else," she said. The reporter told the paper's ombudsman that he was not surprised the mother was upset. He recognized during the interview what she wanted and knew he could not write what she had in mind.[19]

That feeling is not uncommon among reporters. John Tierney, a reporter for *The New York Times,* described it as "that common reportorial feeling that I might be exploiting my subjects" because to get them to talk, he has allowed them to believe he will present their ideas favorably when he knows he may not.[20] As in Ann Arbor, people are sometimes hurt and angered when stories about them appear in the paper. "It is natural for a source or subject to feel betrayed when the story comes out and the subject doesn't like everything in it," *Daily News* columnist Ken Auletta said. "But that doesn't mean the accusation of betrayal is justified. In journalism your loyalty is to the truth as you perceive it, not necessarily to your subject."[21]

Although most journalists would probably agree with Auletta, many believe that journalists should remain sensitive to the feelings of their inexperienced sources and perhaps remind them how the news game is played. When the Ann Arbor paper's ombudsman wrote about the mother's complaint, he did not criticize the reporter's story, but he did sympathize with the mother's plight. "Reporters do not write tributes." But the girl's mother "did not understand that when she called the *News*. I wish someone would have told her."[22]

A more sensitive reporter might have been more frank with the woman. He might have explained that he could not write a tribute and that before he wrote the story he would check with other people and include in his story what they had to say. The mother might then have understood the procedures. And as it became clear that the woman's fears of an antifreeze craze in the high schools were unfounded, the reporter might have called and explained that.

Some might wonder, if the reporter had explained how he would handle the story, would the mother have backed out of the interview? She might have. The newspaper would have lost a story about an isolated event and an apparently troubled young woman, a story that served only to satisfy the curiosity of readers and unintentionally caused pain to the mother. If the story had been about a real threat to the community, the reporter would have had to temper his compassion with the need to get the news out. But even then he could have attempted to explain to the mother why the story was important before it was printed.

As Joann Byrd, ombudsman at *The Washington Post,* has said, if reporters and photographers would take the time to call people involved in their stories and pictures, the hurt would be less when the stories appear. She told *Quill* that those phone calls are essential and compassionate and might help the journalist sleep at night.[23]

When Compassion and News Values Clash

Most editors in recent years have been willing to cooperate with police when asked to delay publicity that might put lives in danger. When Patty Hearst of the famous newspaper family was kidnapped in 1974, police asked the news media in the San Francisco Bay area to hold the story for 12 and a half hours. Only *The Oakland Tribune* did not. Its publisher insisted on publishing the story because, he said, it was no ordinary kidnapping, many heard the gunfire when she was abducted, and a story that big could not be kept quiet.[24]

Afterward, most journalists joined police in condemning the *Tribune,* but not all. The AP decision to hold the Hearst story was protested by Robert Haiman, then executive editor of the *St. Petersburg Times.* Haiman argued that when the media keep secrets for the government, the result rarely benefits the government or the media. AP President Boccardi defended AP's conduct. He said that not using the Hearst story was "the ethical, responsible thing to do. To have rushed out in a life-be-damned headline splurge would have been in my view, nothing short of irresponsibility on our part." When the APME Professional Standards Committee asked 328 editors if they agreed that the story should have been held, 260 said yes, 40 disagreed and 28 were not sure.[25]

Several news organizations in Florida also wrestled with such a request when police asked them not to report the kidnapping of a young boy for fear the stories might spook the kidnapper and cause him to kill the boy and run. All the news media agreed. On the second day, reporters were able to get some details of the abduction and learn that the boy's father was a prominent local doctor. The FBI added to what was known by releasing a photograph of the child but asked that his name not be used. Being asked to publicize a photo without a name was tough, but authorities convinced editors and TV news directors that if the name was publicized, every "kook and crazy" in South Florida would make crank calls to the family and interfere with ransom instructions from the kidnapper. Going along with the embargo "was the responsible thing to do," said Bill Dunn, then managing editor of *The Orlando Sentinel;* printing the name would not serve the public. Police eventually arrested the kidnapper, and the boy was found unharmed.[26]

An even tougher embargo was asked of news media in El Paso, Texas, when two small boys were abducted from their town house. Because the kidnappers told the family they would kill their children if

Sometimes not blowing the whistle is the right thing to do.

stories about them were printed or broadcast in the first 36 hours, the media agreed to hold the story that long. They also held the story when the FBI asked for an extension of the blackout. Two and a half days after the kidnapping, the embargo was lifted when the kidnappers told the family they could find the boys in an abandoned car across the river in Juarez, Mexico. The boys were safe.

"With the FBI telling us that two lives were at stake, it was an easy decision not to run the story," Paula Moore, co–managing editor of the *El Paso Times,* told readers in an article about the media blackout. "We're not accustomed to withholding news from the community for any reason, but people's lives are certainly more important than an immediate story. We knew we could tell the full story later."[27]

PERSONAL TRAGEDIES

Decisions may be easy when police argue that people may die if the story is published. But not all choices between showing compassion and getting the story are that clear-cut. Former *Minneapolis Tribune* ombudsman Richard Cunningham wrote about such an incident involving sportswriters at *The Sacramento Bee.*[28] The brother of a freshman on the nearby University of California-Davis basketball team was killed in a plane crash. The student was crushed by the loss of his brother, who had played with the Phoenix Suns in the NBA. When the season started, the player continued to have problems dealing with his brother's death, was hesitant to board airplanes, and found it difficult to talk about his problems.

At first, writers at the *Bee* decided not to interview him, "recognizing that he was still in grief and shock." Then the sports information officer at the school sent a memo to reporters who cover the team asking them not to interview "the young man relative to the recent tragedy in his life," adding that after-game interviews with him about that night's game could be arranged. When *Bee* sportswriters got the memo, one of them asked team officials if the player had been asked whether he minded discussing his brother's death with reporters. The sports information officer acknowledged that they had not directly asked him, so a *Bee* reporter contacted the player, asked him for an interview, and pointed out that he could say no. The player agreed to be interviewed but broke down when the subject of his brother came up. The reporter later acknowledged that the interview revealed only that the player was not handling his brother's death well.

After the story ran, the player's family, team officials and fans scolded the paper for its conduct. Team officials said his play suffered after the interview. The information officer said he thought the story could have waited until at least the end of the season. Another person charged that the paper "seemed intent on proving that no one can tell *The Sacramento Bee* what to do, and if it hurts people and causes them anguish, what the hell."

The paper's ombudsman thought the paper deserved the criticism. He noted that coaches and team officials were supposed to know their players' feelings. "I could discern no urgency to the story. It could indeed have kept. As it was, because [the young man] apparently could not bring himself to articulate his personal pain, the finished story was thin gruel containing only one quote from him, the rest from three teammates and a coach." The ombudsman concluded his column: "A great newspaper is known for many things, among them insight, vigor and courage. But also for its ability to see clearly where the line between privacy and public interest should be drawn. It's called compassion."

Editors at the old *Dallas Times Herald* took the compassion test when they got a call from a 69-year-old retired oil engineer, Norman John Rees, who had lived for a while in Dallas but was then living in Connecticut. The editors were about to publish an article revealing that Rees had been a Soviet spy for 30 years, during the last four a double agent also spying for the FBI. Reporters had spent three months gathering information for the story, and after they had nailed down the details, they asked the man to comment. He admitted having spied for the Soviets, a fact that was verified by the FBI.

But the Saturday night before the story was to run, he called the paper and asked editors if he would be named in the story. "When he was told that he would be identified, he said that such a disclosure left him no choice but to commit suicide," Kenneth P. Johnson, then executive editor, reported. "In this instance, it was decided that the story could not be suppressed even in the face of Mr. Rees's threat." The next day his wife found his body. Rees had shot himself in the head.[29]

Few would argue that the news media should blindly yield when the subject of a story threatens suicide, but other papers have decided to delay printing stories long enough to contact family members in hopes that they can encourage these people to seek help. They decided that holding a story for a day or two was worth the chance to save a life.

GETTING INVOLVED IN THE STORY

One of the traditional dictates of journalism is that reporters are not to get involved in their stories. They are supposed to watch the fortunes and misfortunes of others, write about them, and move on to their next story. But Michael Nicholson, a journalist for Britain's Independent Television News, decided he could not do that. Assigned to cover the civil war in Bosnia, he became attached to a 9-year-old girl in Sarajevo, a city then under constant shelling. Wanting to get her out of the war zone, he illegally added her name to his passport. She was then able to travel to London, where his wife was waiting to meet her.

Some journalists applauded his conduct. "It's ridiculous to say journalists don't have feelings. You can't expect journalists to be machines," Robin Knight, *U.S. News & World Report* senior European editor, told *Columbia Journalism Review*. *Los Angeles Times* European correspondent William Tuohy agreed. He said he appreciates objectivity, but "one must do what has to be done." But Nicholson's action horrified other journalists. Some said he had sacrificed his impartiality. "By revealing his cards, he is blaming the Serbs for ruining this girl's life, for invading her country," Ian Bremner, news desk assistant at ABC News in London, said. Others thought his conduct would tarnish all journalists. "If you get that involved personally, it affects your judgment and it allows people to dismiss journalists, to dismiss their objectivity," explained ABC News' Paul Cleveland. Some argued that Nicholson should decide whether he wants to be a journalist covering the civil war or a social worker trying to save children from the war.

Nicholson said he understood the complaints but contended that saving a child's life was not taking sides. "To be partial politically is wrong. But if you act as any decent person would act, then it is okay."[30]

Doing what he thought was the right thing created professional problems for a police reporter at the Rochester *Times-Union*. He was covering a hostage taking after a robbery attempt when the robber made an unusual request. He would kill his hostage unless he could talk to a reporter. Police negotiators were able to sweeten the deal: The man would release the woman if he could talk to a reporter. So the *Times-Union* police reporter exchanged himself for the hostage. Eventually he found a way to escape and after learning that the robber killed himself, headed back to the newsroom. If the reporter expected a pat on the back from his editor, he was mistaken. The reporter was reprimanded because "he became part of the story," and the editor put out a memo warning other staff members that if they tried anything like that, he would fire them.[31]

Many editors would have reacted differently.

Reporter Christine Wolff was driving back to the newsroom of *The Bradenton (Fla.) Herald* when she saw a van stopped on the high center peak of the five-mile Sunshine Skyway Bridge over Tampa Bay, a platform for some 40 suicide tries. So she turned her car around and returned to the van to find a tollgate supervisor restraining the van's driver, who was threatening to jump. Wolff and the supervisor talked to the driver for 32 minutes until a state trooper arrived. When the supervisor saw the trooper, he released his grip on the man, who promptly lunged out of the van and started for the railing.

Wolff grabbed him just as he threw one leg over the railing. She was able to hold him long enough for the trooper to get there and pull the man away from the 150-foot drop. She stayed with the man until more police officers and an ambulance arrived 20 minutes later. She said later that in general "reporters should stay as objective as possible" but that "in this situation, I became a person, a citizen responding." Her editors agreed. She was given a bonus, and city editor Dan Stober told her that if she hadn't helped, he would not want her on his staff.[32]

ON SAVING JANET'S JIMMY

Jimmy lived for almost seven months. He was created on the front page of *The Washington Post* by Janet Cooke — "Jimmy" was what she called the 8-year-old heroin addict she wrote about — and he died almost seven months later when she confessed she had made him up. (An account of this fakery and its aftermath appeared in Chapter 9.) The most compelling of the many ethical issues raised by the fabrication, in the minds of some observers, was whether the *Post* should have tried to help poor Jimmy instead of turning him into a front-page tearjerker.

The two ethical issues that received the most attention right after the fakery was disclosed related to the deception and the use of anonymous sources. But to Charles Seib, retired ombudsman for the *Post,* the more serious question was "Why were the *Post* editors so willing to let Jimmy die?" Seib noted that the massive postmortem *Post* ombudsman William L. Green Jr. wrote after the fraud was exposed in 1981 mentioned no concern for Jimmy. Green's report had lots to say about "the editors' enthusiasm over the story," Seib wrote in *Presstime.* "There was deep concern for Cooke's safety" after she claimed that Jimmy's dope-dealing guardian had threatened her life. "But not a thought for Jimmy."[33]

Seib said that before Cooke admitted the story was phony, a *Post* editor told him privately that if he had it to do over again, he would handle the story differently. "Before publishing the story, he would put pressure on Jimmy's mother to get the child into treatment," the editor told him. "The *Post* could have footed the bill, he said. There would have been no need to bring in the authorities." If the *Post* editor had done that, "if he had allowed a humanitarian instinct to rise briefly above his enthusiasm for a smashing story, there is a good possibility that he would have uncovered the deception and the story would have died aborning."

Seib was not alone in feeling that the *Post* should have tried to help Jimmy. Thomas J. Bray, then associate editor of the editorial page of *The Wall Street Journal,* asked, "Why didn't the *Post* scrap the story and insist that the reporter report this pathetic case to the authorities? Was the story in this instance really more important than 'Jimmy'?"[34] John Troan, retired editor of the *Pittsburgh Press,* wondered why somebody at the *Post* had not said, "Hey, let's get this kid out of his horrible predicament, get him the help he needs — and then run the story. That way we might not only win a prize but — even more important — save a life."[35] John Bull, assistant to the executive editor of *The Philadelphia Inquirer,* believed that "the real problem with the Janet Cooke story was the *Post*'s insensitivity to the life of the child. When everybody said please tell us who he is, we want to save his life, the *Post* arrogantly went into its bunker of confidential sources and First Amendment, and . . . the poor kid . . . could have died for all anybody at the *Post* cared."[36]

Bill Green, who served that year as *Post* ombudsman, claimed the *Post* "was under siege for four or five days after 'Jimmy's World' was published. It was under siege not because the story was challenged, but because the community was convulsed with feeling about the boy himself. 'Let's save the boy! How dare you play God!' they shouted at us." Green said he tried to explain in a column why the *Post* felt it could not name the boy, why Janet Cooke's promise of anonymity had to be kept.[37]

Benjamin Bradlee, then executive editor of the *Post,* acknowledged the legitimacy of the question Seib and others raised, but "we talked ourselves into the position that we were focusing on a social problem and

"Shame! Shame! What about poor Jimmy?"

would do the community more good by focusing on it than by going to the cops with a story we thought would put our reporter in physical jeopardy." Bradlee admitted he was uncomfortable with case-by-case ethics on when journalists should report crimes to the police.[38]

In its overall investigation of the *Post*'s counterfeit, the late National News Council looked into whether authorities should or should not have been told who "Jimmy" was. The council report quoted Robert Woodward, one of the Watergate reporters who then was assistant managing editor in charge of the metro staff, as saying that the *Post* had been wrong in deciding to go with the Jimmy story instead of telling authorities about him. The *Post* was in a "morally untenable position," having witnessed a crime and saying "to hell with" the 8-year-old victim, said Woodward. The council report said:

> Neither the complaint nor the ombudsman's report addressed what the Council believes to be a pivotal issue in this case: the human concern that a journalist as citizen ought to have for an 8-year-old child whose life is being criminally endangered. The Council's investigation shows that there was no adequate discussion among *Post* editors of a question that admittedly presents an uncomfortable dilemma for news organizations — whether to fulfill their obligations as citizens and report the crime to the police or to stand on the principle that it is the journalist's obligation to publish the story to call attention to a social problem. The Council regrets that even after the story was published, the *Post*'s editors failed to try to help the mortally endangered child they believed to exist.[39]

Journalists seem to have learned many lessons from the Janet Cooke case. It may be hoped that one of them is the lesson of compassion—that it is all right to act like a human being even in a business that worships independence, noninvolvement and dispassion.

GIVE THE KID A BREAK!

Compassion, or lack of compassion, among journalists is tested when juveniles are in trouble with the law. The ethical issue is whether to name offending juveniles in news reports. The traditional argument against publicizing the names is that the publicity might hinder their rehabilitation: If we give kids a second chance, they may grow up to be law-abiding citizens. But journalists, and many in the public and the judicial system, have grown concerned in recent years about the increased incidence of juveniles committing major crimes such as murder, rape, mugging and armed robbery. So when juveniles are charged with major crimes, they are usually identified fully in news reports. The argument for naming the juveniles is that the public needs to know the identities of people who threaten the peace and civility of the community, regardless of age.

But how do you decide when a juvenile who did something illegal is a threat or just another dumb kid? And how do you define "major crimes"? Murder and rape are surely major. But some kid who makes a smoke bomb and ignites it in his school, is that the kind of offense that makes him a threat to the community?

The major newspapers covering the New Jersey suburbs of Philadelphia fully identified a 16-year-old boy who set off his homemade bomb in his locker at a Cherry Hill, N.J., high school in the early 1980s. The boy was arrested and charged with criminal intent and causing and risking injury or damage. None of the journalists who made the decision to identify the 16-year-old seemed to see him as a threat, but they justified their decision by some special circumstances. First, when the bomb was discovered, school officials evacuated all 2,800 students. Second, the Philadelphia police bomb squad that removed the bomb said it had the destructive force of a hand grenade (but later they found it was only a badly designed harmless smoke bomb). Finally, the boy was the son of the editor of the editorial page of a major daily newspaper in the area, which made the father a public figure, at least in the eyes of the decision-making editors.

The boy was put on probation for a year after explaining to the juvenile court that he made the smoke bomb and ignited it because "it was getting near the end of the year; things were getting monotonous and I thought I'd break up the monotony."[40] His editor father did not argue with the view that he was a public figure, but he regretted that his son "got penalized for that." The father said the whole experience changed his attitude about publicity for juvenile offenders:

> I am a hell of a lot more circumspect about what I publish. My feeling about the public's right and need to know has not been changed, but now I weigh that against other factors such as: Does this child have a chance to be rehabilitated, and by publishing his name, am I going to impair that chance? Does the community really need to know the child's name? I think I may have considered those questions before, but not with the understanding I have now.[41]

It is hoped that all journalists will not have to go through what the Philadelphia editor experienced before they develop a more compassionate view of juvenile offenders and others who become temporarily newsworthy.

Pity the Shooters

News photographers for print and TV frequently get into ethical difficulties because they so often arrive at scenes of tragedy before the authorities. They have been trained to move fast, apparently to get their photos before the authorities change the scene by rescuing and treating the victims or cordoning off the area.

Another ethical problem for news photographers — "shooters," as they are sometimes called — arises from the convention that directs them to shoot first, think later. Not all photographers are enslaved by this convention, but many still see their job as "get the pictures, let the editors decide what to do with them later." If photographers worry too much about the ethics or propriety of taking this or that picture, they're apt to come back with no pictures, this convention holds.

A classic case illustrates both of the major ethical problems photographers face. It involved a photographer for the old *Oregon Journal,* William T. Murphy Jr., who was driving across a Columbia River bridge when he spotted a man and a woman struggling near the railing. He stopped his car and instinctively grabbed his camera. By then, the man was standing on the outside of the bridge railing and the woman, who turned out to be the man's wife, was on the inside desperately trying to stop the man from jumping into the swirling river 100 feet below. "At first they didn't notice me," Murphy said. The wife was screaming and pleading with the man. Murphy took one picture, then another just as a boy on a bike pedaled within a few feet of the woman. Cars on the bridge slowed when they saw what was going on, but none stopped.[42]

Murphy tried to remember how suicide-prevention experts dealt with jumpers. "One thing was for certain," Murphy said. "I didn't want to try to rush the guy because I thought he'd jump for sure. I got within 10 feet when he noticed me." Murphy started talking to the man, and when a van stopped, he told the driver to go to the police at the end of the bridge. But time ran out. The man "leaned out and was gone." Murphy photographed the man falling away from the bridge. (He took a total of only five pictures.) About then, he noticed that the van driver had gotten out and was standing about 50 feet away watching the man jump.

After his pictures were published in his paper and were carried by a wire service to other papers around the nation, angry letters and phone calls started coming in. "Don't the ethics of journalism insist that preservation of human life comes first, news second?" asked a woman in Philadelphia. "He let a man die for the sake of a good photograph," a New Yorker wrote.

Murphy was in agony. He had taken his pictures, but he had also tried to help the man. "Why didn't someone else stop?" he asked. "I don't know what I could have done differently. I am a photographer and I did what I have been trained to do. I did all I could."[43]

It is difficult to assess Murphy's actions. No one can be sure how a distraught man might react if he saw Murphy photographing him or saw Murphy approaching him with cameras around his neck. Some have suggested that Murphy should have gone for the police and then photographed the scene with a long lens. Others contend that if he believed he could talk the man out of jumping, he should have left the cameras behind.

But the point in telling Bill Murphy's story is not to imply that he should have done anything differently or that anyone else would have been able to handle the bridge suicide better. His experience illustrates the frustrations that journalists face when they have to decide whether to help people or go for the story or picture—or to put it another way, when they have to decide whether to substitute compassion for dispassion.

MURPHY CASE SPARKS CHANGE

The case described above had a major impact on news photography in this country. Many editors and photographers began to worry about being thought of as cold-hearted and uncaring. They didn't like the

A suicide leap. This is the scene photojournalist William T. Murphy Jr. found when he stopped his car on a bridge connecting Washington and Oregon.

"That's not the right thing to do, pal," Murphy said he shouted at the man struggling to free himself from his wife's weakening grip. The unidentified bicyclist did not stop.

The man jumped to his death in the swirling Columbia River nearly 100 feet below. Murphy then noticed that the young woman he had asked to go for the police was still on the bridge watching the suicide. (Photos courtesy of William T. Murphy Jr., Portland *Oregonian*.)

image of putting pictures above human life. Murphy told of two occasions after the bridge tragedy when he used his first-aid training to help accident victims. After a two-car collision near Sandy, Ore., Murphy pulled an older man out of his car and turned off the engine. He bandaged another victim in that crash, using a first-aid kit he carried in his car, then wrapped her in his coat because she seemed to be going into shock. He took no pictures until the ambulance crew arrived. Another time, when he was in a rented car and came upon an accident, Murphy flagged down a passing car to get bandages to wrap around an injured man's head. Again he took no pictures until the man was OK.[44]

A more recent case, which occurred 14 years after Murphy's bridge photos were taken, gives hope that photographers and editors are developing a more compassionate attitude toward newsworthy victims. Bill Perry, photo editor for Gannett News Service, was on assignment in Yosemite National Park waiting for the sun to rise so he could take early-light photos for a series on our national parks. Suddenly a woman rushed toward him screaming that a car with children in it had gone into the river. Perry drove quickly to the scene to find a partially submerged car jammed against a tree trunk out in the icy Merced River. Two women and three young children about 7, 5 and 3 were perched, terrified, on the car's roof.

A nonswimmer with no emergency gear in his car, Perry shouted to the stranded five that he would go for help. He raced to the nearest campground office where he called for help and was assured that park rangers were on the way. After speeding back to the desperate scene, Perry for the first time pulled out his cameras and reloaded them with faster film. Shooting with a long lens, he could see not five people but only the older of the two women, who was squeezed between the partially opened driver's door and the car, a rope tied around her waist. The woman, Pearl Jordan, 62, was soon rescued by a park ranger in a wetsuit who attached himself by rope to a tree on the bank and went into the raging waters to bring her ashore.

After photographing the rescue, Perry learned what had happened. While he was off calling for help, some young men came upon the scene and tossed out a rope. The 7-year-old girl grabbed the rope, jumped into the current, and was pulled ashore. But her two younger brothers leaped into the icy waters right after their sister and were instantly swallowed by the current, as was their great-aunt, who jumped in to save them. She and the two boys drowned.

"I know I couldn't have found help any faster than I did," Perry said afterward. "I know the rangers got there as fast as they could. I know that three people would still be alive if they had waited for profes-

Rescued from flood. The news photographer who
took this photo first went for help. (Photo courtesy of
Bill Perry, photo editor, Gannett News Service.)

sional help. I don't think I'll ever forget those five terrified faces."[45] Bill
Perry apparently would agree with his colleague William Sanders,
former president of the National Press Photographers Association, who
said he "would give up a picture to help somebody in trouble" because
"you're a member of the human race first and a journalist second."[46]

OTHER PHOTOS NEVER TAKEN

Photographers covering wars are often witnesses to bloody horrors,
many of which they photograph, bringing back pictures that ought to,
but don't seem to, end war forever. The best of these visual chroniclers
are not without humaneness, however. Liz Nakahara, in a remarkable
article in *The Washington Post,* told of pictures that some of the top
photographers in journalism didn't take. One of these, Eddie Adams,
who covered the Vietnam War for AP, recalled pulling his camera away
from the face of an 18-year-old Marine whose "wide, glassy eyes"
showed his intense fear. "I'll never forget what was going through my
mind—that my face looked exactly like his," Adams said, explaining
why he could not bring himself to push his shutter button. "I was just

too embarrassed for his sake and mine, plus the picture could have labeled that kid for the rest of his life. I always try to put myself in the other person's place."

Robin Moyer of the Black Star agency told Nakahara of the time he accompanied 150,000 malnourished Cambodian refugees as they listlessly staggered across the Thai border. "I saw people die of malaria in front of my camera," Moyer said. "Bullets killing people is one thing. But watching people die of malnutrition is much more terrible." At one point Moyer put aside his camera to help carry people out of the hills.

Don McCullin of the *Sunday Times* in London did the same thing when he was photographing guerrilla fighters in El Salvador. He and a *Newsweek* reporter asked guerrilla leaders, victorious for the moment, for permission to carry wounded enemy soldiers to a hospital truck. McCullin said he'll never forget the last soldier he picked up that day, bloody and horrendously wounded by a bullet that had shattered his mouth and jaw. The photographer went on the truck with this wounded man and carried him into the hospital when orderlies refused to touch him.

Patrick Chauvel, French free-lancer, described photographers in Beirut when Israel invaded Lebanon in 1982. "One guy would cry, another would open his camera and throw out his film, another would go on working and still another would walk away." Chauvel said he was not sure he agreed with the contention that "the professional [photographer] is the guy who works. . . . I know I prefer to have as a friend the guy who walks away."[47]

SHOOT-OUT IN ALABAMA

Someone once described progress as two steps forward, one step back. One step back was the way most ethics observers felt a few years ago after an incident involving two photographers for a small television station in Alabama. The photographers for WHMA-TV in Anniston were dispatched to nearby Jacksonville, Ala., after a man had called the station four times late one evening to say that he was going to set himself on fire to protest unemployment. The station notified Jacksonville police. The caller, who turned out to be a 37-year-old unemployed roofer who had apparently been drinking, asked for a reporter and photographer to come to the town square. WHMA news director Phillip D. Cox sent two photographers instead because none of the station's three full-time reporters was working when the calls came in. One of the photographers was an 18-year-old college student who worked part-time for the station.

Once the photographers were in the square and had their cameras ready, the man doused himself with charcoal starter fluid and applied a lighted match. One of the photographers filmed the horror for several seconds before his young partner rushed forward and tried to beat out the flames with his small notebook. But the flames got stronger and were not put out until the burning man raced across the square to a volunteer firefighter who smothered the fire with an extinguisher. The man survived but spent eight painful weeks in a hospital.

Interviewed after the incident, Cox contended that many people misunderstood the actions of his crew. For one thing, his photographers tried to stop the apparently drunken man from setting himself afire, but he warned them off. "He said 'Stay back!' several times," Cox explained. Cox was miffed that the station had been so heavily criticized by people who assumed the station broadcast the full tape that night. Actually, no scenes of the man on fire were shown on WHMA, he said, only the aftermath.[48]

The question whether a TV station should show such shocking scenes is an important one, of course, but it is a small ethical question compared to whether the photographers should have done more to stop the self-immolation, even if that meant not getting their pictures. If they had refused his request to film him and put their cameras away, might he have delayed setting himself on fire long enough for police to arrive? Should the crew have been sent there in the first place, "creating the news," as *The New York Times* put it in a critical editorial?[49]

Cox was satisfied with the behavior of his photographers. "Our people did what was expected of them." And he did not regret sending them to the scene. However, he said, the incident prompted some discussions of ethics, and the station circulated copies of the codes of ethics of CBS and two professional groups to the news staff.

All three TV networks picked up copies of WHMA's tapes and telecast footage of the man torching himself. Their stories, as well as those in other national news media, were not about the torching incident so much as the ethics of what the Alabama station did that night.

Some good came out of this awful Alabama incident. A photographer in Middletown, Ohio, specifically mentioned the Alabama case after he helped save the life of a burning man. When an explosion at an auto body shop set a worker on fire, he ignored his camera, grabbed a coat, and tried to smother the flames. He said later, "I don't know how you could continue filming. . . . That's what ethics are—you don't just stand by."[50] And after a Santa Fe *New Mexican* photographer helped rescue a family from a burning semitrailer before he took a single shot, he said his actions were more typical than the stereotype of a news photographer ignoring victims to get a good shot. "I think that's a stigma we're kind of stuck with," he said.[51]

What those two Alabama TV photographers did reminded some of the shocking photos that came out of the Vietnam War in 1963 — photos of Buddhist monks burning themselves to death as a protest on the streets of Saigon. Two of the photographers who took those photos have defended what they did. Malcolm Browne, then with the AP, said shortly after taking the pictures that it never occurred to him to try to stop the immolations: "I have always felt that a newsman's duty is to observe and report the news, not try to change it." He explained that he photographed "the whole horrible sequence" because "it is difficult to conceive of any newsman acting otherwise."[52] Browne's then AP colleague Peter Arnett admitted years later that he "could have prevented that immolation by rushing at him and kicking the gasoline away." He added, "As a human being I wanted to, as a reporter I couldn't."[53]

Virtually no one argued with Browne or Arnett back in the 1960s. Photos of monks committing suicide by fire were widely used in American news media. But that was part of a war, and the photos were perhaps important in explaining that terrible conflict. The attitude toward taking and using such photos seems to be changing, however. Today most journalists would probably question Browne and Arnett about whether the presence of their cameras inspired the protest suicides and whether they should have tried to stop them. Slowly, American journalism is moving away from pure dispassion to an admission of compassion as a basis of journalistic behavior.

What's an Ethical Journalist to Do?

We've all seen this a time or two. We've been in electronics stores or on used-car lots and watched as salespeople turn up the charm and turn down the honesty in hopes of getting some naive couple to part with their hard-earned cash. Some of us have been disgusted by the unctuous conduct of these salespeople; others have chuckled at their blatant devotion to greed. But we should keep in mind that many believe that those salespeople live by higher ethical standards than those of most journalists.

Many see journalists as vultures floating over the land, looking for someone suffering a misfortune so they can scoop down and snag a front-page story. Getting that story and advancing their careers are their motivations. The First Amendment is just a tool they use to help them win prizes.

It's not hard to understand why many have that attitude. They read stories like the one that opened this chapter, about reporters in Colorado who showed total disrespect for the family of the hostage and trashed their home. And they hear of reporters and editors like those at *The Washington Post* who valued a story about the 8-year-old heroin addict more than helping the child out of that environment. They see pictures of people mourning the death of kin, trying to commit suicide, or even setting themselves afire, and they rightfully wonder why those photographers didn't drop their cameras and help the poor people.

Their impressions of reporters are also formed by other incidents, the small ones they hear about in their own communities. They empathize with the mourning mother who wanted the paper to print a tribute to her daughter and instead read an account of her daughter's wild ways and possible suicide. They don't understand the bravado that would drive a sportswriter to question a college student who hasn't been able to come to terms with the death of an idolized brother any more than they can understand a reporter forcing Arthur Ashe to announce he had AIDS. These incidents reinforce the image of the journalist as a callous brute intent on getting the story — any story — no matter who gets hurt.

Fortunately, not all journalists behave this way. And many owe their success to dealing with people honestly and honorably. They have found that these traits often win the respect of sources and readers alike.

As news organizations broaden their definitions of news, reporters are no longer concentrating on city hall and the police station. They are covering subjects and issues that have an impact on their communities. These stories often demand that reporters deal with a variety of people and deal with them compassionately.

As Geneva Overholser of *The Des Moines Register* explained, journalists who have trained themselves to be devoid of emotion and feeling all too often have produced a journalism that was equally emotionless and frequently dull. Journalists who demand "only the facts, ma'am" miss the nuances of stories that more sensitive reporters include.

None of this is to say that journalists should become weak-kneed fawns allowing themselves to be pushed around by sources. As long as there are stories people do not want to see reported, journalists will have to ask tough questions and push to get information. But it is not too much to ask that the motive for producing stories that cause harm be something more than an opportunity for a byline or a front-page story.

No one wants a complaisant press that avoids controversy and ignores wrongdoing, but that does not mean we cannot have a compassionate press that shows respect for people and avoids causing needless pain.

NOTES

1. THE SEARCH FOR PRINCIPLES

1. David Shaw, "Media: High Ratings Are Tempered," *Los Angeles Times,* Aug. 11, 1985.

2. Times Mirror survey in 1989, cited by Peter Brown, "Squires is right — we are out of touch with voters and their concerns," *ASNE Bulletin,* Nov. 1992, p. 8.

3. Gerald Stone and John Less, "Portrayal of Journalists on Prime Time Television," *Journalism Quarterly,* Winter 1990, p. 707.

4. Bill Mahon's findings in his master's thesis at Penn State University are cited in Chip Rowe, "Hacks on Film," *Washington Journalism Review,* November 1992, p. 27. A study of the newspaper industry's efforts in the 1930s and 1940s to have journalists shown in a more favorable light can be found in Stephen Vaughn and Bruce Evensen, "Democracy's Guardians: Hollywood's Portrait of Reporters, 1930–1945," *Journalism Quarterly,* Winter 1991, pp. 829–837.

5. Debra Gersh, "Stereotyping Journalists," *Editor & Publisher,* Oct. 5, 1991, p. 18. The movie, which starred Kirk Douglas, was originally titled *Ace in the Hole* but was reissued as *The Big Carnival.*

6. Glenn Garelik, "Stop the Presses! Movies Blast Media. Viewers Cheer," *The New York Times,* Jan. 31, 1993, national edition, pp. H11, H18.

7. An interesting discussion of the origins of objectivity can be found in Dan Schiller, *Objectivity and the News,* Philadelphia: University of Pennsylvania Press, 1981. A short history of reporting philosophy and the development of the idea of the reporter as interviewer can be found in Bernard Roshco, *Newsmaking,* Chicago: University of Chicago Press, 1975, pp. 23–37, 39–57.

8. Wm. David Sloan, James G. Stovall, and James D. Startt, editors, *The Media in America: A History,* Worthington, Ohio: Publishing Horizons, Inc., 1989, p. 71.

9. James W. Carey, "The Press and the Public Discourse," *Kettering Review,* Winter 1992, p. 19.

10. Theodore Peterson, "The Social Responsibility Theory of the Press" in Fred Siebert, Theodore Peterson and Wilbur Schramm, *Four Theories of the Press,* Urbana: University of Illinois Press, 1956, (paperback edition, 1973) p.88.

11. Interview by author, Oct. 8, 1981.

12. David Halberstam, *The Powers That Be,* New York: Alfred A. Knopf, 1979, p.194.

13. Halberstam, p. 446.

14. Sloan, Stovall, Startt, p. 409.

15. Daniel C. Hallin, "Whose Campaign Is It, Anyway?" *Columbia Journalism Review,* January/February 1991, p. 44. Details of the incident are taken from his article.

16. See S. Robert Lichter, Stanley Rothman and Linda S.Lichter, *The Media Elite,* Bethesda: Adler & Adler, 1986, pp. 54–71. They contend that journalists tend to be liberal, and although they may call conservative sources, they are more likely to call sources who will give a liberal interpretation of the news.

17. An interesting account of the news coverage of the early medical findings about cancer and tobacco can be found in Karen Miller, "Smoking Up a Storm," *Journalism Monographs,* Dec. 1992.

18. Dr. Henry Kendall, speech to the national convention of the Society of Professional Journalists, Baltimore, Nov. 1992.

19. "Environmental Coverage Earns Low Marks," *Quill,* May 1993, p. 4.

20. *A Free and Responsible Press: Report of the Commission on Freedom of the Press,* Chicago: University of Chicago Press, 1947, (Midway reprint, 1974), 20–29. Also see Peterson, "Social Responsibility Theory of the Press," pp. 73–104.

21. John Vivian, *The Media of Mass Communication,* Boston: Allyn and Bacon, 1991, p. 338.

22. Peterson, pp. 74–78.

23. Peterson, p. 77.

24. David Weaver and G. Cleveland Wilhoit, "The American Journalist in the 1990s," preliminary report, Arlington:Freedom Forum, 1992, p. 5.

25. William Glaberson, "Gay Journalists Leading a Revolution," *The New York Times,* Sept. 10, 1993, p. A20.

26. See Jim Strader, "Black on Black," *Washington Journalism Review,* March 1992, pp. 33–36, and Christine Reid Vernois, "Black Press Comeback?" *Presstime,* July 1989, 20–22. In Stephen Lacy, James M. Stephens and Stan Soffin, "The Future of the African-American Press: A Survey of African-American Newspaper Managers," *Newspaper Research Journal,* Summer 1991, pp. 8–19, it is reported that some editors reported considerable competition from mainstream publications while others did not see it as a problem.

27. Quoted in Strader, p. 36.

28. Stephen J. Simurda, "Living With Diversity," *Columbia Journalism Review,* January/February 1992, p. 21.

29. Carolyn Phillips, "Evaluating & Valuing Newsroom Diversity," *Newspaper Research Journal,* Spring 1991, pp. 28–37.

30. Andy Newman, "Is It Opinion, or Is It Expertise?" *American Journalism Review,* March 1993, pp. 12–13.

31. Remarks made by her in the 13th annual Otis Chandler lecture at the University of Southern California School of Journalism, quoted in M.L. Stein, "Here We Go Again!" *Editor & Publisher,* Nov. 28, 1992, p. 11.

32. Carl Sessions Stepp, "Ten Ways to Keep Your Readers," *American Journalism Review,* April 1993, p. 23.

33. David Shaw, "How Media Gives Stories Same 'Spin,' " *Los Angeles Times,* Aug. 25, 1989, p. A1.

34. Katrin Schumann, "The Gulf," *News Inc.,* Nov. 1992, p. 30. Her article includes parts of stories to illustrate the differences.

35. Shaw.

36. Weaver and Wilhoit, "The American Journalist in the 1990s," p. 12.

37. Eleanor Randolph, "The Other Side of the Pen: Reporters in the News," *Messages: The Washington Post Media Companion,* Boston: Allyn and Bacon, 1991, p. 351.

38. Randolph, p. 350.

39. Shaw, "Press Turns the Mirror on Itself," *Los Angeles Times,* June 19, 1988, p. 1.

40. *The People & the Press,* Los Angeles: Times Mirror, 1986.

41. David Shaw, "Poll Delivers Bad News to the Media," *Los Angeles Times,* March 31, 1993, p. A16.

42. How Are We Doing?" *Columbia Journalism Review,* January/February 1992, p. 15.

43. David Shaw, "Trust in Media Is on Decline," *Los Angeles Times,* March 31, 1993, p. A1.

44. David Shaw, "Media: High Ratings Are Tempered," *Los Angeles Times,* Aug. 11, 1985. Also see William Schneider and I.A. Lewis, "Views on the News," *Public Opinion,* August/September 1985, pp. 6–11, 58–59.

45. George Garneau, "Press Freedom in Deep Trouble," *Editor & Publisher,* April 20, 1991, p. 11. Wyatt's report, "Free Expression and the American Public," was commissioned by the American Society of Newspaper Editors.

46. Interview by author, Nov. 25, 1980.

47. Gary Hoenig, "What's the Objective?" *News Inc.,* Nov. 1992, p. 4.

48. Interview by author, April 8, 1981.

49. See Sloan, Stovall and Startt, pp. 91–120, for an interesting account of the editors of this era.

50. Sloan, Stovall and Startt, p. 104.

51. The first is reported in John W.C. Johnstone, Edward J. Slawski and William W. Bowman, *The News People: A Sociological Profile of American Journalists and Their Work,* Urbana: University of Illinois Press, 1976. David H. Weaver and Cleveland Wilhoit have replicated and expanded on their research three times. See their *The American Journalist: A Portrait of U.S. News People and Their Work,* Bloomington: Indiana University Press, First Edition, 1986, Second Edition, 1991, and their report "The American Journalist in the 1990s: A Preliminary Report of Key Findings From a 1992 National Survey of U.S. Journalists," Arlington: Freedom Forum, 1992.

52. Weaver and Wilhoit, Second Edition, pp. 112–127.

2. CODES AND PROFESSIONAL STATUS

1. Gary A. Hogge, M.D., "You Can Fight City Hall: Even When It's a Newspaper," *Medical Economics,* July 21, 1980, pp. 69–72.

2. See AP Report, Nov. 4, 1993; Allan Freedman, "The Overtime Wars," *Columbia Journalism Review,* July/August 1992, 55–56, and Lou Prato, "Pay Ruling Upsets Newsroom Budgets," *Washington Journalism Review,* July/Aug. 1991, p. 38. Note that newspapers with small circulations may not be required to pay overtime. See "Overtime Ruling Sets Precedent for Groups," *Presstime,* Dec. 1992, p. 34.

3. Edmund B. Lambeth, *Committed Journalism: An Ethic for the Profession,* Bloomington: Indiana University Press, 1986, p. 83.

4. *Problems of Journalism: Proceedings of the ASNE 1923,* Washington, D.C.: ASNE, pp. 39–52, 118–125.

5. Karen Schneider and Marc Gunther, "Those Newsroom Ethics Codes," *Columbia Journalism Review,* July/August 1985, p. 55. A more recent survey found that about 43 percent of American dailies had codes with enforcement procedures. See Jay Black and Bob Steele, *The SPJ Ethics Handbook,* Society of Professional Journalists, 1992, p. 206, or Jay Black, "Taking the Pulse of the Nation's News Media," *Quill,* Nov. 1992, p. 32.

6. Douglas A. Anderson and Frederic A. Leigh, "How Newspaper Editors and Broadcast News Directors View Media Ethics," *Newspaper Research Journal,* Winter/Spring 1992, p. 115.

7. See Steele and Black, *SPJ Ethics Handbook,* or Black, "Taking the Pulse."

8. Interview by author, Sept. 2, 1981.

9. Comments made on CBS-TV's *60 Minutes,* Sept. 27, 1981.

10. Interview by author, Oct. 7, 1981.

11. Interview by author, March 14, 1986.

12. Jean Chance and Connie Bouchard, "The Gainesville Slayings: A Study in Media Responsibility and Unnamed Sources," a paper presented at the AEJMC Southeast Colloquium, 1993.

13. David Pritchard and Madelyn Morgan, "Impact of Ethics Codes on Judgments by Journalists: A Natural Experiment," *Journalism Quarterly,* Winter 1989, pp. 934–941.

14. Philip Meyer, *Ethical Journalism,* New York: Longman, 1987, p.18.

15. Clifford Christians, "Enforcing Media Codes," *Journal of Mass Media Ethics,* Fall/Winter 1985–86, pp. 14–21.

16. Frank Sutherland, "Headquarters Stays in Chicago; Quill Editor Named," *Quill,* June 1985, p. 42.

17. Jay Black, "Taking the Pulse."

18. "Newsroom Ethics: How Tough Is Enforcement?" *ASNE Ethics Committee Report,* 1986.

19. Interview of Gene Foreman by author, Oct. 7, 1981.

20. Interview of Joseph W. Shoquist by author, Oct. 19, 1981.
21. Interview by author, Oct. 14, 1981.

3. THE NEWS BUSINESS

1. Dale Nelson, "Riding Out the Storm," *Quill,* April 1991, p. 15.
2. Quoted in Karen Rothmyer, "The Media and the Recession: How Bad Is it — and Who's Really Getting Hurt?" *Columbia Journalism Review,* September/October 1991, p. 27.
3. Jon Katz, "Memo to Local News Directors, Re: Improving the Product," *Columbia Journalism Review,* May/June 1990, p. 45.
4. "Journalistic ethics: Some Probings by a Media Keeper," *Nieman Reports,* Winter/Spring 1978, pp. 9–10.
5. Robert P. Clark, "Greed Is Dangerous," *ASNE Bulletin,* July/August 1990, p. 27.
6. Christopher H. Sterling and Timothy R. Haight, *The Mass Media: Apsen Institute to Communication Industry Trends,* New York: Praeger, 1978, p. 83.
7. Interview by author, June 4, 1981.
8. Clark, p. 24.
9. John L. Hulteng, *The Messenger's Motives: Ethical Problems of the News Media,* Englewood Cliffs: Prentice-Hall, 1976, pp. 214–220.
10. See Ben H. Bagdikian, *The Media Monopoly,* Third Edition, Boston: Beacon Press, 1990, pp. 226–227.
11. Quoted by Clark, p. 27.
12. Mary Anderson, "Ranks of Independent Newspapers Continue to Fade," *Presstime,* August 1987, p. 22.
13. Anderson, pp. 16–23.
14. Alex Ben Block, "Communications Media," *Forbes,* Jan. 12, 1987, p. 99.
15. Block, p. 99.
16. Anderson, p. 20.
17. William Glaberson, "Times Co. Acquiring Boston Globe for $1.1 Billion," *The New York Times,* June 11, 1993, p. 1.
18. See Bagdikian, *The Media Monopoly,* p. 5.
19. The new rules also prevented one owner from having stations that reached more than 25 percent of the population. Some FCC officials have made efforts to drop the ownership rules altogether.
20. For a review of some research in this area, see F. Dennis Hale, "The Influence of Chain Ownership on News Service Subscribing," *Newspaper Research Journal,* Fall 1991, pp. 34–46.
21. Interviews by author, May 28, Sept. 18, 1981.
22. Stephan Barr, "Personal Best," *News Inc.,* Nov. 1992, p. 25.
23. Interview by author, Sept. 18, 1981.
24. Barr, p. 26.
25. Gannett owned 81 daily newspapers in 1991 according to *'93 Facts About Newspapers,* Reston, Va: Newspaper Association of America, 1993, p. 6. Number of papers owned and circulation figures for Gannett, Thomson, and Knight-Ridder come from this booklet.
26. Interview by author, Oct. 15, 1981.
27. John Morton, "Newspapers Are Losing Their Grip," *Washington Journalism Review,* May 1987, p. 52.
28. Kay Lazar, "Provincial Profits," *News Inc.,* March 1990, p. 25.
29. Interview by author, Oct. 21, 1981.
30. Quoted in Lazar, p. 23.
31. Rothmyer, pp. 23–28.
32. Donald E. Lippincott, "Investigative Reporting: Tighter Newsroom Budgets Are

Forcing Editors to Be More Selective in Initiating Long-term Projects," *Presstime,"* Feb. 1991, p. 15.

33. Quoted in Lippincott, p. 15.

34. Morton, "Newspapers Are Losing Their Grip," p. 52.

35. Stephen Lacy and Frederick Fico, "The Link Between Newspaper Content Quality & Circulation," *Newspaper Research Journal,* Spring 1991, pp. 46–57.

36. Andrew Schwartzman, executive director of Media Access Project, quoted in Dillon Smith, "Budget Ax Hits Television Editorials," *Washington Journalism Review,* April 1991, p. 46.

37. Michael L. McKean and Vernon A. Stone, "Deregulation and Competition: Explaining the Absence of Local Broadcast News Operations," *Journalism Quarterly,* Autumn 1992, p. 722.

38. Katz, p. 42.

39. Smith, p. 46.

40. Douglas A. Anderson and Frederic A. Leigh, "How Newspaper Editors and Broadcast News Directors View Media Ethics," *Newspaper Research Journal,* Winter/Spring 1992, p. 118.

41. Robert Rutherford Smith, "Mystical Elements in Television News," *Journal of Communication,* Fall 1979, pp. 75–82.

42. Randall Rothenberg, "Playing the B-Roll Bop," *Quill,* Sept. 1990, pp. 27–31.

43. Bob Sonenclar, "The VNR Top Ten: How Much Video PR Gets on the Evening News," *Columbia Journalism Review,* March/April 1991, p. 14.

44. Rothenberg, p. 29.

45. Ken Auletta, *Three Blind Mice: How the TV Networks Lost Their Way,* New York: Random House, 1991, pp. 331–335.

46. Dan Rather, "From Murrow to Mediocrity?" *New York Times,* March 10, 1987; reprinted in Auletta.

47. Newspaper and Guild averages are taken from Heidi Evans, "Working for Peanuts," and Russell Frank and Martha Freeman, "Financial Clinic: Tips on How to Divvy Up That Paycheck," both in *Quill,* April 1991.

48. Median salaries for newspaper and television journalists were taken from David Weaver and G. Cleveland Wilhoit, "The American Journalist in the 1990s: A Preliminary Report of Key Findings from a 1992 National Survey of U.S. Journalists," presented to the national convention of the Society of Professional Journalists, Baltimore, Nov. 1992.

49. "J-School Grads' Pay Stays Poor," *Presstime,* Jan. 1993, p. 54.

50. Steve Nash, "With an Efficiency, Used Car, Peanut Butter and Byline, What More Could One Want," *Presstime,* April 1985.

51. Evans, "Working for Peanuts," pp. 11–13.

52. Statistics cited in Mary Alice Bagby, "Transforming Newspapers for Readers," *Presstime,* April 1991, p. 20.

53. John P. Robinson, "Thanks for Reading This," *American Demographics,* May 1990, p. 6.

54. "Times Mirror Studies Find Lagging Interest in News," *Presstime,* Aug. 1990, p. 40.

55. Robinson, p. 6.

56. Nelson, p. 15.

57. David Shaw, "Trust in Media Is on Decline," *Los Angeles Times,* March 31, 1993, p. A1.

58. "Times Mirror Studies."

59. "Times Mirror Studies."

60. Richard Oppel, "Newspapers, Television News and Voters Gain From Cooperative Campaign Ventures," *ASNE Bulletin,* Nov. 1992, p. 11.

61. Peter Mitchell and Mike Oliver, "Looking for Local Political News on TV? It's Tough to Find," *The Orlando Sentinel,* Sept. 28, 1992, p. B6.

62. Mitchell and Oliver, p. B-1. Also see "Different Media, Different Results," *Poynter Report,* Summer 1992, p. 17.

63. Ben Bagdikian, "Fast-Food News: A Week's Diet," *Columbia Journalism Review,* March/April 1982, pp. 32–33.

64. Weaver and Wilhoit. Also see their book *The American Journalist: A Portrait of U.S. News People and Their Work,* Third Edition, Bloomington: Indiana University Press, 1991, p. 114.

65. Doug Underwood and Keith Stamm, "Balancing Business With Journalism: Newsroom Policies at 12 West Coast Newspapers," *Journalism Quarterly,* Summer 1992, p. 317.

66. Carl Sessions Stepp, "When Readers Design the News," *Washington Journalism Review,* April 1991, p. 24.

67. "Darts and Laurels," *Columbia Journalism Review,* July/August 1992, p. 22.

68. Donald E. Lippincott, "Investigative Reporting: Tighter Newsroom Budgets Are Forcing Editors to Be More Selective in Initiating Long-Term Projects," *Presstime,* February 1991, p. 16. Editors from *The News* made similar comments when speaking to the Central Florida chapter of the Society of Professional Journalists Spring 1991 meeting.

69. Stepp, p. 24.

70. Michael Hoyt, "The Wichita Experiment," *Columbia Journalism Review,* July/August 1992, pp. 43–47.

71. Mary Alice Bagby, "Transforming Newspapers for Readers," *Presstime,* April 1991, p. 21.

72. Lou Ureneck, "Newsroom Juggling in Portland, Maine," *1992 ASNE Special Report: Crisis Management,* p. 20.

73. "Occasional Readers Might Read More If Newspapers Targeted Their Needs, Study Says," *Presstime,* April 1991, p. 58.

74. Bagby, pp. 20–22.

75. See M.L. Stein, *"USA Today* Is Called a Formidable Influence," *Editor & Publisher,* May 28, 1983, p. 16.

76. George Albert Gladney, "The McPaper Revolution? *USA Today*–Style Innovation at Large U.S. Dailies," *Newspaper Research Journal,* Winter/Spring 1992, pp. 54–71.

77. Robert Greene, speech reprinted in George A. Hough, *Practice Exercises in News Writing,* Third Edition, Boston: Houghton Mifflin, 1984.

78. See John L. Hulteng and Roy Paul Nelson, *The Fourth Estate: An Informal Appraisal of the News and Opinion Media,* Second Edition, New York: Harper & Row, 1983, p. 104.

79. "Some Industry Averages," *Presstime,* January 1993, p. 15.

80. Anderson and Leigh, 118–119.

81. Interview of James A. Dunlap of *Sharon Herald* by author, Oct. 28, 1981.

82. Interview by author, June 25, 1980.

83. Quoted in Charles Brewer, "Automobile Dealer Boycotts: How Widespread?" unpublished student paper, Penn State University, in possession of author.

84. Elizabeth Lesly, "Realtors and Builders Demand Happy News and Often Get It," *Washington Journalism Review,* Nov. 1991, p. 21.

85. Doug Underwood, "Retail Stores and Big-City Papers," *Columbia Journalism Review,* September/October 1990, pp. 33–35.

86. G. Pascal Zachary, "Many Journalists See a Growing Reluctance to Criticize Advertisers," *The Wall Street Journal,* Feb. 6, 1992, p. A9.

87. "Darts and Laurels," *Columbia Journalism Review,* May/June 1993, p. 23.

88. Zachary, p. A9.

89. Wendy Swallow Williams, "Two New Surveys Show the Industry's Reach," *Washington Journalism Review,* November 1991, p. 24. Also see Wendy Swallow Williams. "For Sale! Real Estate Advertising & Editorial Decisions About Real Estate News," *Newspaper Research Journal,* Winter/Spring 1992, pp. 160–168.

90. Williams, p. 22.

91. Lisa Benenson, "Tougher Coverage Isn't Always a Tougher Sell," *News Inc.,* Jan. 1993, p. 35.

92. Steve Singer, "When Auto Dealers Muscle the Newsroom," *Washington Journalism Review,* Sept. 1991, pp. 25–28.

93. "Darts and Laurels," *Columbia Journalism Review,* July/August 1990, p. 14.

94. Jonathan Friendly, *"Trenton Times* Journalists Quit Over New Policies," *The New York Times,* Feb. 21, 1982, p. 39.

95. "F.Y.I.," *Washington Journalism Review,* Nov. 1992, p. 11.

96. "Cartoon Sparks Boycott, Letters," *Presstime,* March 1992, p. 43.

97. Adam Platt, "Angry Dealers Pull TV Ads," *Washington Journalism Review,* Sept. 1991, p. 27.

98. Underwood, pp. 33–35.

99. Philip Meyer, *Ethical Journalism,* New York: Longman, 1987, p. 39.

100. Ann Marie Kerwin, "Advertiser Pressure on Newspapers Is Common: Survey," *Editor & Publisher,* Jan. 16, 1993, pp. 28–29, 39.

101. *ASNE Ethics Committee Report* cited by Gil Cranberg, "Newspapers Face More Advertising Pressure Than They Report," *Editor & Publisher,* May 15, 1993, p. 52.

102. Stephen Rynkiewicz, "Can Editorial and Advertising Departments Exist in Piece?" *Solutions Today for Ethics Problems Tomorrow: A Special Report by the Ethics Committee of the Society of Professional Journalists, 1989,* p. 18.

103. Quoted by Lesly, p. 28.

104. Zachary, p. A9.

105. Singer, p. 25.

106. Both were quoted anonymously in Anderson and Leigh, p. 118.

107. Rothmyer, pp. 23–28.

108. Katz, p. 43.

109. Katz, p. 49.

110. John Morton, "Shed No Tears for the Newspaper Industry," *Washington Journalism Review,* Oct. 1992, p. 64.

4. CONFLICTS OF INTEREST

1. Quoted in Eleanor Randolph, "The Media and the March," in *Messages: The Washington Post Media Companion,* Boston: Allyn and Bacon, 1991, p. 341.

2. Randolph, p. 342.

3. Quoted by David Shaw in "Can Women Reporters Write Objectively on Abortion Issue?" *Press Woman,* April 1991, p. 14.

4. Shaw, p. 14.

5. Laurence Zuckerman, "To March or Not to March," *Time,* Aug. 14, 1989, p. 45.

6. Zuckerman.

7. Elizabeth Kolbert, "Covering Gay Rights: Can Journalists Be Marchers?" *The New York Times,* April 24, 1993, Sec. 1, p. 10.

8. "May Reporters Speak Out on Topics They Cover?" *Quill,* March 1991, p. 37.

9. *The Washington Post*'s code on conflicts of interest is excerpted in Kim Mills, "Taking It to the Streets," *American Journalism Review,* July/August 1993, pp. 22–26.

10. Zuckerman.

11. "Journalists Vote on War: 4 Yes, 2 No," *Washington Journalism Review,* March 1991, p. 14.

12. Mills.

13. Zuckerman.

14. "No Cheering in the Press Box," *Newsweek,* July 19, 1993.

15. Quoted in Shaw, p. 12.

16. Shaw, p. 13.

17. Shaw, p. 12.

18. Shaw, pp. 12–13. The study was done by the Center for Media and Public Affairs in Washington.

19. Shaw, p. 13.
20. "No Cheering in the Press Box."
21. His remarks were made to the Association for Education in Journalism and Mass Communication in Washington, Aug. 1989.
22. Nancy Monaghan, "Journalists Don't Do Marches," *The Professional Communicator* (publication of Women in Communication Inc.), Fall 1989.
23. "Journalists Vote on War: 4 Yes, 2 No," p. 14.
24. The incidents at the Norfolk papers were reported by Richard Cunningham, "Reporters Op/ed Pieces Muddy the Fairness Line," *Quill,* June 1991, pp. 6–7.
25. Cunningham, "Reporters' Op/Ed Pieces Muddy the Fairness Line."
26. Kolbert.
27. Cited in "To March or Not to March."
28. Hammer's experience and his reactions are reported by Sandy Petykiewicz in "Many Editors Willing to Join Community Groups," *ASNE Bulletin,* Sept. 1992, p. 8.
29. Quoted in Sandy Petykiewicz.
30. Mills.
31. Henry McNulty, "Let Landers Be Landers Every Day," *The Hartford Courant,* May 24, 1992, p. E3.
32. Interview by author, March 19, 1986.
33. "Arbiter Reinstates Reporter," *Presstime,* May 1984, p. 73; "Reporter Dismissed After Election to School Board," *The New York Times,* June 15, 1983, p. A16.
34. The paper's code is exerpted in Mills.
35. The *Times'* policy is excerpted in Mills.
36. "The Editorial Candidate," *Presstime,* Oct. 1992, p. 6.
37. "Councilman's Dual Hats Are Front-page News in Tyrone," Johnstown (Pa.) *Tribune-Democrat,* July 1, 1985.
38. "An Editorial Leads to Two Newsmen's Resignations From Public Office," *Quill,* May 1980, p. 6.
39. Alan Horton, "Survey Finds Editors Split on Staffers' Community Involvement," *ASNE Bulletin,* Sept. 1992, p. 8.
40. MacCluggage's discussion of *The Day*'s activities is in "Squaring With the Reader," *Kettering Review,* Winter 1992, pp. 33–51.
41. "Squaring With the Reader."
42. Michael Moore, "How to Keep Them Happy in Flint," *Columbia Journalism Review,* September/October 1985, pp. 40–43.
43. "Squaring With the Reader."
44. "The Reporter," *Philadelphia Magazine,* April 1967, pp. 42–45, 92.
45. "Dirty Linen," *The Wall Street Journal,* April 2, 1984, p. 32.
46. Howard Kurtz, "Firings Cause Stir in St. Petersburg," *The Washington Post,* Oct. 13, 1990, p. D1.
47. "Columnist Resigns After Paper Learns of His Outside PR Work," *Editor & Publisher,* Nov. 9, 1985, p. 12.
48. Richard B. Tuttle, "Invitation Led to Dispute," 1980 report of APME Professional Standards Committee, pp. 9–10.
49. Randell Beck, "TV Reporter Covers TVA—and Free-lances for It," 1985–86 report of SPJ-SDX Ethics Committee, p. 22.
50. Interview by author, April 17, 1981.
51. Thomas Collins, "Newspeople Shouldn't Sell More Than the News," *The Orlando Sentinel,* May 30, 1989, p. A7. Collins is the media writer for *Newsday.*
52. "National and International Journalism Competitions," *Editor & Publisher,* Dec. 28, 1985, p. 10J.
53. Interview by author, April 8, 1981.
54. Richard P. Cunningham, "Of Mice and Mysids," *Quill,* June 1986, p. 10.
55. "Contests: Which Programs Qualify Under Codes of Ethics?" 1984–85 report of SPJ Ethics Committee.
56. "Can Marriage and Ethics Mix?" 1983–84 report of SPJ-SDX Ethics Committee.

57. Charles Bailey, *Conflicts of Interest: A Matter of Journalistic Ethics,* a report to the National News Council, 1984, p. 10.

58. Interview by author, Oct. 22, 1981.

59. "Appearances Are Deceiving, or So Some Editors Think," *Feed/back,* Summer 1985, p. 1.

60. "When Is a Reporter in Conflict of Interest?" *Editor & Publisher,* Feb. 9, 1985, p. 14.

61. Susan Page, " 'Till Death Do Us Part," *Washington Journalism Review,* March 1985, pp. 45–48.

62. Katie Hickok, "Married With Bylines," *American Journalism Review,* Oct. 1993, p. 31.

63. Interview by author, May 28, 1981.

64. "Auburn Aflame Over Critical Sports Reporting," *Presstime,* Dec. 1991, p. 43.

65. Michael York, "Causing a Hoopla in Kentucky," *Washington Journalism Review,* Jan. 1986, pp. 46–49.

66. A discussion of the APSE debate is in Jack Romanelli, "Ethical Questions Divide Journalists," *The (Montreal) Gazette,* Jan. 11, 1993.

67. Lawrence Grossman, "Regulate the Medium, Liberate the Message," *Columbia Journalism Review,* November/December 1991, pp. 72–73.

68. "Darts and Laurels," *Columbia Journalism Review,* January/February 1990, p. 24.

69. Interview by author, Feb. 10, 1986.

70. Ron Dorfman, "Editors, Publishers and Entangling Alliances," *Quill,* Sept. 1985, pp. 11–12.

71. Tony Case, "Can Journalists Be Joiners?" *Editor & Publisher,* Jan. 30, 1993, p. 43.

72. *In the Public Interest—II: A Report by the National News Council, 1975–1978,* New York: National News Council, 1979, pp. 393–414.

73. Bailey, *Conflicts of Interest,* p. 38.

5. THE SEDUCERS

1. Interview by author, Oct. 23, 1981.

2. Rick Alm, "Merchants Woo Writers With 'Freebie' Feasts," *Kansas City Star and Times,* Feb. 17, 1980; Bill Norton, "Some Outdoor Writers Accept Gifts, Discounts," ibid.

3. Interview by author, Oct. 14, 1981.

4. Tamara Jones, "Reporters in Germany Open Wallets for Stories," *Los Angeles Times,* March 26, 1991.

5. Interview by author, June 2, 1981.

6. Rhoda Koenig, "Diary of a Freeloader," *Harper's,* June 1982, pp. 20–26.

7. Quoted in George E. Osgood Jr., "Ethics and the One-Reporter, Rural Bureau" (master's thesis, Pennsylvania State University, July 1981), pp. 22–23.

8. Ibid., p. 25.

9. Interview by author, June 3, 1981.

10. Interview of Rick Starr, sports editor of the New Kensington, Pa., *Valley News Dispatch,* Nov. 14, 1981.

11. Tom Goldstein, *The News at Any Cost: How Journalists Compromise Their Ethics to Shape the News,* New York: Simon and Schuster, 1985, pp. 169–171.

12. M.L. Stein, "The Press Takes Advantage of Media Freebies," *Editor & Publisher,* Aug. 18, 1984, p. 15.

13. Jack Romanelli, "Ethical Questions Divide Journalists," *The (Montreal) Gazette,* Jan. 11, 1993.

14. Ed Avis, "Have Subsidy, Will Travel," *Quill,* March 1991, p. 24.

15. Eric Hubler, "Freebies on the Tube," *Quill,* March 1991, p. 27.

16. Interview by author, Oct. 6, 1981.

17. Avis, p. 21.

18. Avis, p. 25.

19. Hubler, p. 27.

20. Avis, p. 23.

21. Interview by author, Sept. 10, 1981.

22. "Taking Long Trips on a Short Budget," *Quill,* March 1991, p. 24.

23. Jay Boyar, "From studios: A Few Good Doodads," *The Orlando Sentinel,* March 5, 1993, Calendar section, p. 17.

24. Report of 1979 ASNE Ethics Committee.

25. John Harwood and David Finkel, "Disney Birthday a Hit With Media," *St.Petersburg Times,* Oct. 5, 1986, pp. A1, A4; "Journalists Flock to Birthday Party at Disney World," *The New York Times,* October 8, 1986, p. A34.

26. George Garneau, "Ethics Debate Reprised," *Editor & Publisher,* Oct. 19, 1991, pp. 14–15.

6. REPORTERS AND THEIR SOURCES

1. Details of the Foreman story are taken from "Inquirer Conflict in Cianfrani Case," *The Philadelphia Inquirer,* Aug. 27, 1977, p. 1; "Reporter Linked to a Senator's Gifts," *The New York Times,* Aug. 28, 1977, p. 4; Donald L. Barlett and James B. Steele, "The Full Story of Cianfrani and the Reporter," *The Philadelphia Inquirer,* Oct. 16, 1977.

2. Interview by author, Oct. 7, 1981.

3. Interview by author, Oct. 8, 1981.

4. Quoted in Eleanor Randolph, "Conflict of Interest: A Growing Problem for Couples," *Esquire,* Feb. 1978, pp. 55–59, 124–129.

5. Richard Cohen, "For Notorious Woman, 'It Just Ain't Fair,'" *The Washington Post,* Oct. 2, 1977.

6. Randolph.

7. Interview by author, Sept. 23, 1981.

8. Jack W. Germond and Jules Witcover, *Blue Smoke and Mirrors,* New York: Viking, 1981, pp. 55–75, 77–78.

9. Interview by author, June 5, 1981.

10. Interview by author, Feb. 15, 1981.

11. James J. Kilpatrick, "800-Pound Gorillas, Yes – News People No," *The Orlando Sentinel,* Nov. 27, 1992. Kilpatrick's column is widely published.

12. Interview by author, Nov. 4, 1981.

13. Quoted from his essay in "Dangerous Liaisons," *Columbia Journalism Review,* July/August 1989, pp. 23–24.

14. Halberstam essay in "Dangerous Liaisons," p. 31.

15. Tamara Jones, "Reporters in Germany Open Wallets for Stories," *Los Angeles Times,* March 26, 1991.

16. Michael Dobbs, "Psst! Kremlin News for Sale: Hard Cash Only," *The Washington Post,* Feb. 5, 1992, p. A21.

17. Anthony Lewis, "Hire and Salary," *The New York Times,* Jan. 26, 1978, p. A29; John Herbers, "Former Aide Interviews Nixon," *New York Times,* April 9, 1984, p. C18.

18. Interview by author, Nov. 2, 1981.

19. Ann Hodges, "Cult Interviews Worth Big Bucks to News Shows," *The Houston Chronicle,* April 24, 1993, p. 6.

20. Michael Hedges, "Media Mull the Ethics of Buying Tawdry Tales," *The Washington Times,* Jan. 29, 1992, p. A1.

21. April Lynch, "Newsweek Paid Hooker After Photo, Interview," *The San Francisco Chronicle,* July 19, 1990, p. A6.

22. Kenneth Jost, "The Dawn of Big-Bucks Juror Journalism," *Legal Times,* July 20, 1987, p. 15.

23. See Jost's article for a detailed discussion of these arguments.

24. Renee Montage, *Morning Edition,* National Public Radio, June 1, 1993.

25. *Morning Edition.*

26. Charles Walston, "Tabloid TV Has Changed the Rules," *The Atlanta Journal and Constitution,* Nov. 17, 1991, p. G1.

27. *Morning Edition.*

28. "Newspaper Suspends 2 for Ethics Violations," *Chicago Tribune,* Nov. 13, 1989, p. 3.

29. Walston.

30. John Tierney, "Cash on Delivery," *The New York Times,* April 18, 1993, Sec. 6, p. 64.

31. *Nightline,* ABC, April 8, 1993. On this program, Donahue said his show had not paid for interviews, but he said he would not rule out paying for them. About two weeks later, *New York Daily News* and National Public Radio reported his show had paid for appearances by two of the police officers in the Rodney King incident in Los Angeles.

32. Interview by author, Sept. 21, 1981.

33. ASNE poll cited in Julie Dodd and Leonard Tipton, "Shifting Views of High School Students About Journalism Careers," *Newspaper Research Journal,* Fall 1992/ Winter 1993, pp. 111–119.

34. David Weaver and LeAnne Davis, "Public Opinion on Investigative Reporting in the 1980s," *Journalism Quarterly,* Spring 1992, pp. 146–155.

35. The case was widely reported. Details here were taken from Alex S. Jones, "Weighing the Thorny Issue of Anonymous Sources," *The New York Times,* March 3, 1992, p. A14; Frank Green, "Adams Case Spurs Debate on Use of Unnamed Sources," *San Diego Union-Tribune,* March 4, 1992, p. A2. Also see Cheryl Reid, "Anonymous Sources Bring Down a Senator," *Washington Journalism Review,* April 1992, p. 10.

36. Green.

37. Gina Lubrano, "Anonymous Sources Test a Newspaper," *San Diego Union-Tribune,* March 9, 1992, p. B7.

38. Quoted by Alex S. Jones, "Anonymity: A Tool Used and Abused," *The New York Times,* June 25, 1991, p. A20.

39. Alex Jones.

40. Interview by author, Nov. 4, 1981.

41. William Blankenburg, "The Utility of Anonymous Attribution," *Newspaper Research Journal,* Winter/Spring 1992, pp. 10–23.

42. Jean C. Chance and Connie Bouchard, "The Gainesville Slayings: A Study in Media Responsibility and Unnamed Sources," a paper presented at the AEJMC Southeast Colloquium at the University of Alabama, March 25–27, 1993.

43. Interview by author, Oct. 7, 1981.

44. Interview by author, Oct. 5, 1981.

45. Interview by author, Oct. 16, 1981.

46. Interview by author, Oct. 6, 1981.

47. Chance and Bouchard, p. 14.

48. See F. Dennis Hale, "Unnamed News Sources: Their Impact on the Perceptions of Stories," *Newspaper Research Journal,* Winter 1983, pp. 49–56.

49. Results of four opinion polls are reported in Weaver and Daniels.

50. "Editor's Note," *The New York Times,* Jan. 23, 1991, p. A3.

51. Chance and Bouchard, p. 14.

52. Jeff Testerman, "Media Firestorm," *St. Petersburg Times,* April 12, 1992, Perspective section, p. 10.

53. Howard Kurtz, "Sez Who? How Sources and Reporters Play the Leak Game," *The Washington Post,* March 7, 1993, p. C5. References to Kurtz in this section are from this article.

54. Andrew Rosenthal, "Inquiry Raises Questions on Anonymous Sources," *The New York Times,* June 27, 1988, p. A13.

55. Eleanor Randolph, "Journalists Face Troubling Questions About Leaks From Criminal Probes," *The Washington Post,* Aug. 12, 1989, p. A4.

56. For an example of this, see Rosenthal or Randolph, "Journalists Face Troubling Questions About Leaks From Criminal Probes."

57. David Heckler, "Danger Ahead: Sex Abuse Cases," *Washington Journalism Review,* Sept. 1991, p. 38.

58. Kurtz.

59. David Rosenbaum, "The House, the Press and Bad Feelings," *The New York Times,* June 7, 1989, p. A25.

60. Doris Graber, *Mass Media and American Politics,* Washington: CQ Press, 1989, p. 254.

61. "Administration Is Accused of Deceiving Press on Libya," "Schultz Justifies Scaring Qaddafi by Use of Press," and "News Executives Express Outrage," *The New York Times,* Oct. 3, 1986, pp. A1, 6, 7.

62. Randolph.

63. Graber, 248–249.

64. "Lesson on Flacking for Government," *The New York Times,* Aug. 30, 1984, p. B10.

65. Quoted by Kurtz.

66. Randolph.

67. Frank Smyth, " 'Official Sources,' 'Western Diplomats,' and Other Voices From the Mission," *Columbia Journalism Review,* January/February 1993, p. 35.

68. Quoted by Kurtz.

69. James McCartney, "Perhaps Every Reporter Should Take an Oath to Walk Out on Officials Who Insist on Talking 'Off the Record,' " *ASNE Bulletin,* Oct. 1984, pp. 14–15.

70. Interview by author, Oct. 7, 1981.

71. Gary Ruderman, "Off-the-Record Comments Should Be Just That," *Solutions Today for Tomorrow's Ethical Problems,* Chicago: Society of Professional Journalists, October 1989, p. 8.

72. Walter Isaacson, "The 'Senior Official,' " *Washington Journalism Review,* Nov. 1992, pp. 30–34.

73. Alex Jones.

74. Carl Bernstein and Bob Woodward, *All the President's Men,* New York: Simon and Schuster, 1974, p. 71.

75. Ruderman.

76. Laurence Zuckerman, "Breaking a Confidence," *Time,* Aug. 3, 1987, p. 61; Eleanor Randolph, "Managing Confidential Sources," *Messages: The Washington Post Media Companion,* Boston: Allyn and Bacon, 1991, pp. 347–349.

77. Milton Coleman, "A Reporter's Story: 18 Words, Seven Weeks Later," *The Washington Post,* April 8, 1984.

78. Coleman.

79. Interview by author, Feb. 25, 1986.

80. See Bill Salisbury, "Burning the Source," *Washington Journalism Review,* Sept. 1991, pp. 18–22; "No Way to Treat a Tipster," *Columbia Journalism Review,* January/February 1986, pp. 10–11.

81. Alex Jones.

82. Alex Jones.

83. Rita Ciolli, "Newsrooms More Cautious," *Newsday,* March 24, 1991, p. 15.

84. Interview by author, Nov. 4, 1981.

85. William Blankenburg, "The Utility of Anonymous Attribution," *Newspaper Research Journal,* Winter/Spring 1992, p. 11.

86. Hugh Culbertson, *ANPA News Research Bulletin,* May 14, 1975 and May 19, 1976, cited in Herbert Strentz, *News Reporters and Their Sources,* Ames: Iowa State University Press, 1978, p. 88.

87. "Reporter Decides to Serve Jail Time," *St. Petersburg Times,* March 11, 1993, p. A1; "Protecting a Principle," *St. Petersburg Times,* March 11, 1993, p. A18. Background to the case is in Bruce Sanford and Anne Noble, "Threats Escalate to Strip Confidential

Sources From the Reporter's Tool Kit," *Quill,* April 1992, pp. 10–11.

88. "I'll Shield Sources, Reporter Vows," *Newsday,* Feb. 14, 1992, p. 17; "NPR Reporter Won't Reveal Sources," *The Washington Post,* Feb. 25, 1992.

89. "Source Saves Reporter From Jail Term," *News Media & the Law,* Summer 1985, pp. 26–27.

90. Ralph Holsinger, *Media Law,* New York: Random House, 1987, pp. 270–271.

91. *Facts About Newspapers '93,* Reston, Va.: Newspaper Association of America, p. 27.

92. "Confidential Sources," *Freedom of Information Annual Report 1979,* APME, pp. 4–5.

93. David Shaw, "The Press and Sex: Why Editors Lean to Dots, Dashes, Euphemisms," *Los Angeles Times,* Aug. 19, 1991, p. A19.

94. Mitchell Stephens and Eliot Frankel, "All the Obscenity That's Fit to Print," *Washington Journalism Review,* April 1981, pp. 15–19.

95. "There He Goes: Reagan's Mike Tattles on Him," AP dispatch in *The Orlando Sentinel,* March 1, 1986.

96. Interview by author, May 28, 1981.

97. Shaw.

98. Thomas Collins, "When News Gets Explicit," *Newsday,* Aug. 13, 1990.

99. Chip Rowe, " 'Maledicta' Favors The Whole F—ing Truth," *Washington Journalism Review,* January/February 1992, pp. 14–16.

100. Shaw.

101. Shaw.

102. Dick Haws, "#!½* YOU, TOO!" *Columbia Journalism Review,* July/August 1991, p. 16.

103. Rowe.

104. John Dean, "Rituals of the Herd," *Rolling Stone,* Oct. 7, 1976.

105. Tony Schwartz, "The Insider," *New Times,* Oct. 15, 1976, p. 27.

106. "Most Papers Bleeped Out Butz's Punch Line," *Editor & Publisher,* Oct. 16, 1976, p. 13.

107. Ibid.

108. Ibid.

109. See Jerry Nachman, "Beyond the Blotter," *Columbia Journalism Review,* May/June 1993, pp. 76–77. He reviews Robert Blau's *The Cop Shop: True Crime on the Streets of Chicago.*

7. THE GOVERNMENT WATCH

1. Interview by author, Feb. 24, 1986; Cliff Brown, "The Public's Right to Know Can Kill You," unpublished paper in possession of author.

2. "The *American* Did Not Take Part in Hoax," *Hattiesburg (Miss.) American,* Dec. 11, 1984.

3. Duane McAllister, "Publisher Goes on Donahue Show to Defend a Tough Ethics Decision," *Gannetteer,* March 1985, pp. 6–7.

4. Janet Braswell, "Police Stage Hoax to Stop Contract 'Hit,' " *Hattiesburg (Miss.) American,* Dec. 10, 1984.

5. Frank Sutherland, "A Man Threatens Murder in Hattiesburg—And Debate Rages on Using False Stories," "Editorially Speaking" section, *Gannetteer,* Aug. 1986, pp. 4–8.

6. Interview by author, March 19, 1986.

7. Sutherland, p. 8.

8. Peter Braestrup, "Duty, Honor, Country," *Quill,* Sept. 1985, pp. 15–21.

9. Interview by author, Feb. 10, 1986.

10. Interview by author, Feb. 21, 1986.

11. Phillip Knightly, *The First Casualty: From the Crimea to Vietnam—The War Correspondent as Hero, Propagandist, and Myth Maker,* New York: Harvest, Harcourt Brace Jovanovich, 1975, p. 376.

12. Michael Schudson, *Discovering the News: A Social History of American Newspapers,* New York: Basic Books, 1978, pp. 171–172.

13. Interview by author, March 14, 1986.

14. Charles W. Bailey, *Conflict of Interest: A Matter of Journalistic Ethics,* report to the National News Council, 1984; George F. Will, "A Journalist Is a Citizen Also," *ASNE Bulletin,* Nov. 1983; "N.Y. Daily News Drops Will Column," *Editor & Publisher,* July 16, 1983, p. 33.

15. Interview by author, Nov. 2, 1981.

16. Interview by author, Oct. 6, 1981.

17. Interview by author, Sept. 9, 1981.

18. Interview by author, Sept. 8, 1981.

19. Interview by author, Oct. 8, 1981.

20. Interview by author, Oct. 5, 1981.

21. Jonathan Friendly, "Just When Is Pretrial Publicity Unfair?" *The New York Times,* Oct. 30, 1983; Lyle Denniston, "How Flynt Hustled CBS," *Washington Journalism Review,* January/February 1984, p. 14.

22. Sissela Bok, *Secrets: On the Ethics of Concealment and Revelation,* New York: Vintage, 1984, p. 177.

23. Howard Simons, "Government and National Security," excerpt from talk to 1986 ASNE convention in *Editor & Publisher,* April 26, 1986, pp. 80–89.

24. Bok, *Secrets,* p. 208.

25. Malcolm W. Browne, "The Fighting Words of Homer Bigart: A War Correspondent Is Never a Cheerleader," *New York Times Book Review,* April 11, 1993, p. 13.

26. Anthony Marro, "When the Government Tells Lies," *Columbia Journalism Review,* March/April 1985, pp. 29–39; Drew Middleton, "Barring Reporters from the Battlefield," *New York Times Magazine,* Feb. 5, 1984, pp. 36–37, 61, 69, 92; "Coverage Efforts Thwarted," *News Media and the Law,* January/February 1984, p. 6.

27. "Pentagon Activates Press Pool to Cover Libya Bombing," *Presstime,* May 1986, p. 69.

28. William Boot, "Wading Around in the Panama Pool," *Columbia Journalism Review,* March/April 1990, pp. 18–20.

29. Pete Yost, "U.S. Sharply Distorts War News, Study Says," *Chicago Tribune,* Jan. 19, 1992.

30. Stanley W. Cloud, "Covering the Next War," *The New York Times,* Aug. 4, 1992, p. A19.

31. Chris Hedges, "The Unilaterals," *Columbia Journalism Review,* May/June 1991, pp. 27–29.

32. Walter Goodman, "Arnett," *Columbia Journalism Review,* May/June 1991, pp. 29–31.

33. David Shaw, "How Media Gives Stories Same 'Spin,' " *Los Angeles Times,* Aug. 25, 1989, pp. 32–34; "Opinion Leaders Dictate the Conventional Leaders," part 2, *Los Angeles Times,* Aug. 26, 1989, pp. 24–26.

34. Shaw, "How Media Gives Stories," p. 33.

35. Shaw, "Opinion Leaders," pp. 24–25.

36. Times Mirror poll cited in "How Are We Doing?" *Columbia Journalism Review,* January/February 1992, p. 15, and in Peter A. Brown, "Squires Is Right — We Are Out of Touch with Voters and Their Concerns," *ASNE Bulletin,* Nov. 1992, p. 8.

37. William Schneider and I. A. Lewis, "Views on the News," *Public Opinion,* August/September 1985, pp. 6–11, 58–59.

38. Brown, p. 8.

39. *The Public & The Press,* Los Angeles: Times Mirror, 1986, p. 30.

40. The results of this survey were reported in David Shaw, "Public and Press — Two Viewpoints," *Los Angeles Times,* Aug. 11, 1985, and William Schneider and I. A. Lewis, "Views on the News," *Public Opinion,* August/September, 1985, pp. 6–11, 58–59. Unless otherwise indicated, subsequent references in this chapter to the *Times* poll are taken from these sources.

41. David Weaver and G. Cleveland Wilhoit, *The American Journalist;* Second Edition, Bloomington: Indiana University Press, 1991, p. 24.

42. Schneider and Lewis, p. 7.

43. Times Mirror Center for the People and the Press, "The Campaign and the Press at Halftime," supplement to *Columbia Journalism Review,* July/August 1992.

44. Weaver and Wilhoit, "The American Journalists in the 1990s: A Preliminary Report of Key Findings From a 1992 National Survey of U.S. Journalists," Arlington: Freedom Forum, 1992, p. 7.

45. See S. Robert Lichter, Stanley Rothman, and Linda S. Lichter, *The Media Elite,* Bethesda: Adler & Adler, 1986. Weaver and Wilhoit also found journalists at prestigious organizations more liberal, but not to the extent that Lichter, Rothman, and Lichter did.

46. Todd Gitlin, "Media Lemmings Run Amok!" *Washington Journalism Review,* April 1992, p. 31.

47. N. Thimmesch, "The Editorial Endorsement Game," *Public Opinion,* October/ November 1984, pp. 10–13. He used aggregate circulation figures to measure the penetration of endorsements rather than count numbers of papers.

48. George Garneau, "Clinton's the Choice," *Editor & Publisher,* Oct. 24, 1992, p. 9; "Endorsement Addendum," *Editor & Publisher,* Nov. 7, 1992. He reported numbers of endorsements and noted that the Republicans had received more endorsements since 1940, with the two exceptions.

49. Byron St. Dizier, "Editorial Page Editors and Endorsements: Chain-Owned vs. Independent Newspapers," *Newspaper Research Journal,* Spring 1987, pp. 63–68.

50. David Shaw, "Of Isms and Prisms," *Columbia Journalism Review,* January/ February 1991, pp. 56–57.

51. Michael Robinson and Maura E. Clancey, "Network News, 15 Years After Agnew," *Channels,* January/February 1986, p. 34.

52. Robinson and Clancey, p. 34.

53. Robinson and Clancey, p. 38.

54. Doris A. Graber, "Kind Pictures and Harsh Words: How Television Presents the Candidates," in Kay Schlozman, *Elections in America,* Boston: Allen & Unwin, 1987, pp. 115–141.

55. See L. Brent Bozell III and Brent H. Baker, eds., *And That's the Way It Isn't,* Alexandria, Va.: Media Research Center, 1990.

56. John Robinson, "Just How Liberal Is the News? 1980 Revisited," *Public Opinion,* February/March 1983, pp. 55–60.

57. Robinson and Clancey, p. 38.

58. Quoted in Shaw, "Press Turns the Mirror on Itself," *Los Angeles Times,* June 19, 1988, p. 1.

59. Shaw, "Of Isms and Prisms," p. 56.

60. Quoted in William A. Henry III, "Are the Media Too Liberal?" *Time,* Oct. 19, 1992, p. 47.

61. Thomas Palmer Jr., "Reputation For Bias Seems Well Earned," *The Boston Globe,* Jan. 3, 1993, p. 65.

62. Henry.

63. ASNE poll cited in Schneider and Lewis, p. 11.

64. Jeffrey Katz, "Tilt?" *Washington Journalism Review,* Feb. 1993, p. 26.

65. Richard Harwood, "Bill Clinton and the Press," *Centre Daily Times,* State College, Pa., June 22, 1993. His column appears in *The Washington Post* and other papers.

66. Quoted in William Glaberson, "The Capitol Press vs. the President: Fair Coverage or Unreined Adversity," *The New York Times,* June 17, 1993, p. A22.

8. DECEPTION

1. Ben H. Bagdikian, "No. 50061, Inside Maximum Security," *The Washington Post,* Jan. 31, 1972.

2. Letter to author, Nov. 14, 1981.

3. David Shaw, "Deception — Honest Tool of Reporting?" *Los Angeles Times,* Sept. 20, 1979.

4. *60 Minutes,* Sept. 27, 1981.

5. William J. Coughlin, "Tell It to the Marines," *Washington Journalism Review,* July/August 1984, pp. 54–55.

6. Neil Henry, "The Black Dispatch," *The Washington Post,* Oct. 9–14, 1983.

7. Interview by Donna Shaub in "Undercover Reporting: Is It Always Ethical?" Unpublished paper on file with author.

8. Interview by author, Feb. 19, 1986.

9. Michael Salwen, "Getting the Story by Hook or Crook," *Quill,* Jan. 1981, pp. 12–14.

10. Daniel Anderson and Peter Benjaminson, *Investigative Reporting,* Bloomington: Indiana University Press, 1976, p. 109.

11. Steven Stark, "Investigating Bob Greene," *Quill,* June 1993, p. 12.

12. Tony Case, "In Disguise," *Editor & Publisher,* Nov. 14, 1992, p. 14; Richard Harwood, "Knights of the Fourth Estate," *The Washington Post,* Dec. 5, 1992, p. A23.

13. Interview by author, Nov. 4, 1981.

14. David Halberstam in "Dangerous Liaisons," *Columbia Journalism Review,* July/August 1989, p. 31.

15. David Weaver and LeAnne Daniels, "Public Opinion on Investigative Reporting in the 1980s," *Journalism Quarterly,* Spring 1992, p. 151.

16. ASNE poll cited in Julie Dodd and Leonard Tipton, "Shifting Views of High School Students About Journalism Careers," *Newspaper Research Journal,* Fall 1992/Winter 1993, p. 117.

17. Weaver and Daniels.

18. Details are taken from Beth Nissen, "An Inside View," *The Wall Street Journal,* July 28, 1978; interviews by author with Lawrence O'Donnell, *Journal* associate editor, Feb. 22, 1982, and Ed Cony, then publisher of the *Journal,* Oct. 20, 1981.

19. Leslie Linthicum, "When to Go Undercover? As Last Resort to Get Story," 1983–84 report of the SPJ-SDX Ethics Committee, p. 20; Leslie Linthicum, "Undercover Student" series, *Albuquerque Tribune,* March 7–14, 1983; Deni Elliott, "End vs. Means: Comparing Two Cases of Deceptive Practices," a 1985 report of SPJ-SDX Ethics Committee, pp. 15–16.

20. Richard Cunningham, "Using Deception to Get at the Truth," *Quill,* Jan. 1987, pp. 8–9.

21. Howard Kurtz, "Hidden Network Cameras: A Troubling Trend," *The Washington Post,* Nov. 30, 1992, p. A1.

22. Letter to author, Nov. 14, 1981.

23. Linda Mainiero, ed., *American Women Writers from Colonial Times to the Present: A Critical Reference Guide,* New York: Frederick Ungar, 1979, pp. 381–383.

24. Silas Bent, *Newspaper Crusaders: A Neglected Story,* New York: Whittlesey House, 1939, p. 198.

25. Frank Luther Mott, *News Stories of 1934,* Iowa City: Clio Press, 1935, pp. 258–260, 264–71.

26. Doug Struck, "Inside Crownsville," *Annapolis Evening Capital,* Oct. 6–25, 1975.

27. Interview by author, Sept. 9, 1981.

28. "Undercover," research report of the Times Publishing Co., St. Petersburg, Fla., and the Department of Mass Communication, University of South Florida, Summer 1981.

29. Kurtz, p. A1.

30. Details are taken from Kurtz, p. A1; "Another Missing Union Label at ABC," *The Washington Times,* April 27, 1993, p. F2; Diane Kunde, "Food Lion Roars Back at Critics in Ad Blitz," *The Dallas Morning News,* Nov. 5, 1992, p. D1.

31. Details of this incident are taken from Jennifer Stevenson, "Navigating the Ethical Edge," *St. Petersburg Times,* May 12, 1993, p. B8.

32. Kenneth Clark, "Hidden Meanings: Increasing Use of Secret Cameras and Micro-

phones Raises Ethical Questions About TV Journalism," *Chicago Tribune,* June 30, 1992, p. C1.

33. Quoted by Colman McCarthy, "Getting the Truth Untruthfully," *The Washington Post,* Dec. 22, 1992, p. D21.

34. Interview by author, Feb. 24, 1986.

35. Kurtz.

36. Kurtz.

37. Shaw.

38. Quoted by Stevenson.

39. McCarthy.

40. Clark.

41. Kurtz.

42. McCarthy.

43. Interview by author, Sept. 8, 1981.

44. Clark.

45. Clark.

46. "Undercover."

47. McCarthy.

48. Pat Widder, "Playing With Fire: Blur of Fact and Fiction Costs NBC," *Chicago Tribune,* Feb. 11, 1993, p. 1.

49. Russ W. Baker, "Truth, Lies and Videotape," *Columbia Journalism Review,* July/August 1993, pp. 25–28.

50. Kurtz.

51. Kenneth Kobre, *Photojournalism: The Professionals' Approach,* Second Edition, Boston: Focus Press, 1991, pp. 328–329.

52. Clark.

53. David Zurawik and Christina Stoehr, "Money Changes Everything," *American Journalism Review,* April 1993, p. 29.

54. Thomas Rosenstiel, "TV News: Is Seeing Believing?" *Los Angeles Times,* Nov. 5, 1989, p. A1.

55. Zurawik and Stoehr.

56. Clark.

57. Kurtz.

58. Details are taken from Paul Shannon, "For Rent or Not for Rent," *IRE Journal,* Fall 1985, pp. 21–22, and an interview by author of Heath Meriwether, Feb. 21, 1986.

59. Marcel Dufresne, "To Sting or Not to Sting?" *Columbia Journalism Review,* May/June 1991, pp. 49–51. Details of the *Newsday* project are from this article.

60. These criteria came from participants in an ethical decision-making seminar at the Poynter Institute for Media Studies, reported in Jay Black, Bob Steele, and Ralph Barney, *Doing Ethics in Journalism,* Greencastle, Ind.: Sigma Delta Chi Foundation, Society of Professional Journalists, 1993, pp. 112, 113.

9. FAKERY

1. AP Los Angeles Bureau, Sept. 21, 1981.

2. Interview by author, Oct. 8, 1981.

3. See Wm. David Sloan and James G. Stovall, editors, *The Media in America: A History,* Worthington: Publishing Horizons, 1989, p. 125; Fred Fedler, *Media Hoaxes,* Ames: Iowa State University Press, 1989, pp. 55–68.

4. Mark Fitzgerald, "Hoax in Chicago," *Editor & Publisher,* Dec. 7, 1985, pp. 22, 33.

5. Jessica Savitch, *Anchorwoman,* New York: G.P. Putnam's Sons, 1982, pp. 172–173.

6. Janet Cooke, "Jimmy's World," *The Washington Post,* Sept. 28, 1980.

7. *After Jimmy's World,* report by the National News Council, New York, 1981, pp. 16–22.

8. William Green, "The Confession," *The Washington Post,* April 19, 1981.

9. NBC's *Today,* Feb. 1, 2, 1982.

10. Gail Sheehy, "Wide Open City/Part 1: The New Breed," *New York,* July 26, 1971, pp. 22–25; "Wide Open City/Part II: Redpants and Sugarman," *New York,* Aug. 2, 1971, pp. 26–36.

11. Michiko Kakutani, "Blurring the Lines Between Fiction and Nonfiction," *ASNE Bulletin,* July/August 1981, p. 16.

12. For two views on Woodward's books, see Stephen Banker, "In Bob We Trust," *Washington Journalism Review,* June 1991, p. 33; Bill Monroe, "Woodward Reporting Yields Inside Grit," *Washington Journalism Review,* July/August 1991, p. 6.

13. Interview by author, June 4, 1981.

14. See Tal Sanit, "The New Unreality," *Columbia Journalism Review,* May/June 1992, pp. 17–18.

15. Tal Sanit, "Stand and Deliver," *Columbia Journalism Review,* July/August 1992, pp. 15–16.

16. *Dateline: NBC,* Feb. 9, 1993. A detailed account of NBC's story can be found in "TV's Credibility Crunch," *The Washington Post National Weekly Edition,* March 8–14, 1993, p. 6.

17. Jonathan Adler, "On the Ropes at NBC News," *Newsweek,* March 8, 1993.

18. Interview by author, Nov. 10, 1981.

19. "2 Plead Guilty to Buying Beer for Teens for TV Story," *The Orlando Sentinel,* Feb. 24, 1993, p. A6; "TV News Pair Get Jail Time for Buying Beer for Teens," *The Orlando Sentinel,* March 24, 1993, p. A10.

20. "TV Reporter on Trial for Staging Dog Fights," United Press International, July 23, 1991; "Reporter Convicted in Pit Bull Trial," United Press International, Aug. 7, 1991.

21. Quoted by John Leo, "Image-based Truth as Reality: No Apology Necessary, or Is It?" *The Orlando Sentinel,* March 3, 1993, p. A19.

22. David Shaw, "Poll Delivers Bad News to the Media," *Los Angeles Times,* March 31, 1993, p. A16.

23. Interviews by author of Lovelady and *Inquirer* executive editor Eugene Roberts, May 28, Sept. 15, Sept. 16, 1981.

24. Roy Peter Clark, "The Unoriginal Sin: How Plagiarism Poisons the Press," *Washington Journalism Review,* March 1983, pp. 43–47.

25. Larry Tye, "Plagiarism Seen as Common but Little Discussed," *The Boston Globe,* July 16, 1991, metro section, p. 1.

26. Mark Fitzgerald, *"Sun-Times* Drops Columnist Over Plagiarism," *Editor & Publisher,* June 27, 1990, p. 17.

27. Eleanor Randolph, "Plagiarism and News," in *Messages: The Washington Post Media Companion,* Boston: Allyn and Bacon, 1991, p. 344.

28. Tye.

29. Peter Johnson, "CNN Owns Up to Copying Story From *Newsweek,*" *USA Today,* Aug. 14, 1991.

30. Steve Polilli, "More Plagiarism Incidents Plague Texas Daily," *Editor & Publisher,* Jan. 19, 1992, p. 11.

31. William Henry III, "Recycling the News," *Time,* July 29, 1991, p. 59.

32. Randolph, "Plagiarism and News," p. 345.

33. Kevin McManus, "The, Uh, Quotation Quandary," *Columbia Journalism Review,* May/June 1990, pp. 54–56.

34. Jacques Leslie, "The Pros and Cons of Cleaning Up Quotes," *Washington Journalism Review,* May 1986, pp. 44–46.

35. Quoted by McManus, p. 54.

36. John Drury, "Should Reporter Quote What They Say, or What They Mean?" *Solutions Today for Ethics Problems Tomorrow,* Chicago: Society of Professional Journalists, Oct. 1989, pp. 11, 21.

37. Ronald Turovsky, "Did He Really Say That?" *Columbia Journalism Review,* July/August 1980.

38. McManus, pp. 55–56.

39. Ron Lovell, "Wrong Way Stretch: Scoops Vanish, Credibility Remains — As One Reporter Learned After Re-creating Quotes," *Washington Journalism Review,* May 1986, pp. 44–46.

40. The Malcolm case was widely reported. See "The Jeff and Janet Show," *Newsweek,* May 31, 1993, p. 59; "Two Media Cases Remanded," *Presstime,* July 1991, p. 48; "The Malcolm Case," *Columbia Journalism Review,* May/June 1990, p. 56; "Ruling Slices Into Libel Defenses," *Presstime,* June 1992, p. 52; Lyle Denniston, "New Yorker Libel Case Threatens the Press," *Washington Journalism Review,* March 1991, p. 54.

41. Jane Gross, "Impasse Over Damages in New Yorker Libel Case," *The New York Times,* June 4, 1993, p. A1.

42. Thomas Collins (of *Newsday*), "News Photographers Under Fire," *The Orlando Sentinel,* Dec. 12, 1981.

43. Quoted in Don E. Tomlinson, "Legal and Ethical Ramifications of Computer-Assisted Photograph Manipulation," in *Protocol,* Washington: National Press Photographs Association, 1991, p. 5.

44. "The Trouble With Harry," *Columbia Journalism Review,* January/February 1990, 4–5.

45. David Zurawik and Christina Stoehr, "Money Changes Everything," *American Journalism Review,* April 1993, p. 30.

46. Nancy M. Davis, "Electronic Photo Manipulation: Many Are Doing It, and Editors, Photojournalists Urge Strict Guidelines to Protect Credibility," *Presstime,* Feb. 1992, pp. 22–23.

47. Deni Elliott, "Deception and Imagery," in *Protocol,* Washington: National Press Photographers Association, 1991, p. 3.

48. Davis.

49. Lou Hodges, "The Moral Imperative for Photojournalists," in *Protocol,* Washington: National Press Photographs Association, 1991, pp. 7–8.

50. Shiela Reeves, "What's Wrong With This Picture? Daily Newspaper Photo Editors' Attitudes and Their Tolerance Toward Digital Manipulation," *Newspaper Research Journal,* Fall 1992/Winter 1993, pp. 131–155.

51. Patrick Boyle, "Standards for Photography's Cutting Edge," *Washington Journalism Review,* Nov. 1992, p. 12.

52. Clark DeLeon, "The Scene," *The Philadelphia Inquirer,* May 1, 1981.

53. Rich Stim, "Was Randy Mantooth Ever in the Service?" *Columbia Journalism Review,* November/December 1989, pp. 38–40.

54. "Darts and Laurels," *Columbia Journalism Review,* January/February 1993, p. 23.

55. James Cox, "A Plague of Plagiarism," *USA Today,* July 25, 1991, p. 1B.

10. PRIVACY

1. Charles B. Seib, "How the Papers Covered the Cinema Follies Fire," *The Washington Post,* Oct. 30, 1977. Subsequent references to Seib about the fire are from this column.

2. George Beveridge, "Identifying the Movie-Fire Victims," *Washington Star,* Oct. 31, 1977. Subsequent references to Beveridge about the fire are from this column.

3. Bruce DeSilva, "Views of Newspaper Gatekeepers on Rape and Rape Coverage," unpublished paper presented at Association for Education in Journalism and Mass Communication convention, Corvallis, Oregon, 1983.

4. D.D. Guttenplan, "Not Naming Names," *Newsday,* May 3, 1989, p. 2.

5. Dershowitz made similar observations about the New Bedford and William Smith trials. His comments are widely quoted, including Robin Benedict, *Virgin or Vamp: How the Press Covers Sex Crimes,* New York: Oxford University Press, 1992, p. 253, and

Rita Ciolli, "Naming Rape Accusers: A Policy Under Review," *Newsday,* May 5, 1991, p. 6.

6. Eleanor Randolph, "Naming Rape Victims," in *Messages: The Washington Post Media Companion,* Boston: Allyn and Bacon, 1991, p. 361.

7. Ciolli, p. 6.

8. Benedict, p. 254.

9. James Warren, "Parasites vs. Privacy," *Chicago Tribune,* Feb. 24, 1991, p. C2.

10. Jane Schorer, "The Story Behind a Landmark Story of Rape," *Washington Journalism Review,* June 1991, pp. 20–26.

11. Benedict, pp. 252–253.

12. Quoted by Ciolli.

13. Cited by Elizabeth Culotta, "Naming Alleged Rape Victims: Two Policies Within 30 Miles," *Washington Journalism Review,* July/August 1992, p. 14.

14. Ciolli.

15. Christine Spolar, "Privacy for Public Figures?" *Washington Journalism Review,* June 1992, pp. 20–22.

16. See Kenny Moore, "The Eternal Example," *Sports Illustrated,* Dec. 21, 1992, pp. 16–27.

17. Quoted in "Arthur Ashe AIDS Story Scrutinized by Editors, Columnists," *Quill,* June 1992, p. 17.

18. "Arthur Ashe AIDS Story Scrutinized by Editors."

19. Christine Spolar, "Privacy for Public Figures?" *Washington Journalism Review,* June 1992, pp. 20–22.

20. "Arthur Ashe Story Scrutinized."

21. Ibid.

22. Ibid.

23. Victor Zonana, "Ashe Case Raises Fame vs. Privacy Case," *Los Angeles Times,* April 10, 1992.

24. Spolar, p. 22.

25. "Arthur Ashe Story Scrutinized."

26. Spolar, p. 21.

27. Marlene Cimons, "Ashe Calls for Sensitivity From the Media," *Los Angeles Times,* May 27, 1992, p. C2.

28. Interview by author, Jan. 8, 1982.

29. Richard P. Cunningham, "Child Photos: Drawing the Line," *Quill,* February 1986, pp. 8–9.

30. "Graphic Excess," *Washington Journalism Review,* Jan. 1986, pp. 10–11.

31. Richard Harwood, "Sometimes Compassion," *The Washington Post,* April 28, 1991, p. C5.

32. Lewis Regelman is the man who tried to help save the woman's life and then took photographs as firefighters and an ambulance crew worked on her before taking her to the hospital. He gave permission to reproduce his photographs and asked that he be credited only in this way.

33. Interview by author, Oct. 16, 1981.

34. George Padgett, "Let Grief Be a Private Affair," *Quill,* Feb. 1988, p. 13.

35. "Privacy and the Need to Know," *Presstime,* Oct. 1992, p. 24.

36. Robert Bentley, "Lessons Sought From Tragic Events," Bakersfield *Californian,* Aug. 4, 1985.

37. Bob Greene, "News Business and Right to Privacy Can Be at Odds," 1985–86 report of the SPJ-SDX Ethics Committee, p. 15.

38. Quoted in Richard Cunningham, "Seeking a Time-out on Prurience," *Quill,* March 1992, p. 6.

39. Fred Friendly, "Gays, Privacy and a Free Press," *The Washington Post,* April 8, 1990, p. B7.

40. Pat Murphy, "Ford Hero's Mother Has Misgivings," *The Detroit News,* Sept. 26, 1975.

41. For a discussion of outing, see Randy Shilts, "Is 'Outing' Gays Ethical?" *The New York Times,* April 12, 1990, p. A23.

42. Deni Elliott, *St. Petersburg Times,* March 26, 1989.

43. Friendly, p. B7.

44. William A. Henry III, "To 'Out' or Not to 'Out,' " *Time,* Aug. 19, 1991, p. 17.

45. Mitchell Hartman, "When to Say Someone Is Gay," *Quill,* November/December 1990, p. 7.

46. Joseph L. Bernt and Marilyn S. Greenwald, "Differing Views of Senior Editors and Gay/Lesbian Journalists Regarding Newspaper Coverage of the Gay and Lesbian Community," *Newspaper Research Journal,* Fall 1992/Winter 1993, pp. 99–110.

47. Richard P. Cunningham, "Names Make News, but Not Always," *Quill,* Feb. 1985, p. 5.

48. Warren.

49. Daniel Lynch, "AIDS: The Number 11 Killer," *Washington Journalism Review,* January/February 1992, pp. 19–21.

50. Thomas Collins, "When News Gets Explicit," *Newsday,* Aug. 13, 1990, Sec. II, p. 4.

51. "Mama Mia! Breast Pic Offends Readers," *Quill,* April 1992, p. 5.

52. Thomas Oliphant, "Invaded – by the Press," *The Boston Globe,* April 19, 1991, p. 19.

53. "Privacy and the Need to Know."

54. Collins.

55. Collins.

56. Interview by author, Sept. 25, 1981.

57. Warren, p. 2.

58. Interview by author, May 27, 1993.

59. Warren.

60. C. Fraser Smith, "Reporting Grief," *Washington Journalism Review,* March 1984, pp. 21–22, 58.

61. Pamela Terrell, "Full Name, Age and Address – or Not?" *Presstime,* Dec. 1990, pp. 30–33.

62. Greg Ring, "Are Exact Addresses Always Part of the News?" *ASNE Bulletin,* Feb. 1985, p. 5.

63. Terrell.

64. Terrell.

65. Larry J. Sabato, *Feeding Frenzy: How Attack Journalism Has Transformed American Politics,* New York: The Free Press, 1991, p. 27.

66. John Seigenthaler, "The First Amendment: The First 200 Years," *Presstime,* Feb. 1991, pp. 24–30.

67. Seigenthaler.

68. Seigenthaler, p. 29.

69. Details taken from David Shaw, "Stumbling Over Sex in the Press," *Los Angeles Times,* Aug. 18, 1991, p. A1; Seigenthaler; Sabato.

70. Details of the 1884 campaigns are reported by Sabato, pp. 25–51, and Seigenthaler, p. 30.

71. See Gloria Borger, "Private Lives, Public Figures," *U.S. News & World Report,* May 18, 1987, p. 20; Sabato, pp. 25–52.

72. Sabato, p. 30.

73. That FDR had a mistress is widely reported. See Borger, Seigenthaler, or Sabato.

74. Sabato, p. 30.

75. Sabato, p. 31.

76. Sabato, p. 40.

77. See Sabato or Borger.

78. Seigenthaler, p. 24.

79. David Shaw, "Trust in Media Is on Decline," *Los Angeles Times,* March 31, 1993, p. A1.

80. Sabato, p. 46.

81. Harry F. Waters, "Public or Private Lives?" *Newsweek,* Feb. 17, 1975, p. 83.

82. Interview with author, Oct. 7, 1981.

83. Waters.

84. Waters.

85. The Hart-Rice story was widely told. Borger has a good discussion.

86. Sabato, p. 36.

87. Shaw.

88. Martin Schram, "What Ever Happened to Journalistic Standards," *Newsday,* Jan. 30, 1992, p. 94.

89. Shaw, "Trust in Media Is on Decline."

90. Gregory Gordon, "Some Critics Say Press Goes Too Far," *The Detroit News,* Aug. 13, 1992.

91. Shaw, "Trust in Media Is on Decline."

92. Gordon.

93. Quoted in "So, When Is Sleaze News?" *Washington Journalism Review,* April 1992, p. 30.

94. Phil Donahue, "Infidelity Is a Valid Campaign Issue," *The New York Times,* Aug. 26, 1992, p. A21.

95. Quoted in "Why Must Our Candidates Be Choirboys?" *Newsday,* Jan. 29, 1992, p. 77. Reeves' book is *A Question of Character: A Life of John F. Kennedy,* published by Free Press.

96. From her 1992 Press-Enterprise lecture at the University of California, Riverside. Quote from "So, When Is Sleaze News?"

97. Shaw, "Trust in Media Is on Decline."

98. Mona Charon, "Parents Are Fair Game, but Leave Chelsea Alone," *The Atlanta Constitution,* Nov. 17, 1992, p. A23.

99. "Privacy and the Need to Know," p. 24.

100. Ellen Karasik, "Sen. Scott's Daughter Is Arrested," *Philadelphia Inquirer,* July 31, 1975.

101. Interview by author, Oct. 10, 1981.

102. Interview by author, Nov. 4, 1981.

103. Eric Schmitt, "Absence of Pity," *Quill,* July/August 1984, pp. 10–11.

104. California, Florida, Illinois, Maryland, Massachusetts, Montana, New Hampshire, Oregon, Pennsylvania and Washington had laws requiring notification in 1992, according to Brian Gallagher, "Permission Required," *Quill,* March 1992, p. 5.

105. S. Elizabeth Bird, "Newspaper Editor's Attitudes Reflect Ethical Doubt on Surreptitious Recording," *Journalism Quarterly,* Summer 1985, pp. 284–88.

106. Alan R. Ginsberg, "Secret Taping: A No-no for Nixon—but Okay for Reporters?" *Columbia Journalism Review,* July/August 1984, pp. 16–19.

107. Michael York, "Causing a Hoopla in Kentucky," *Washington Journalism Review,* Jan. 1986, pp. 46–49.

108. Interviews by author, Feb. 24, 1986 (Sanders), Sept. 24, 1981 (Wheeler).

109. Ann Zimmerman, "By Any Other Name . . ." *Washington Journalism Review,* November/December 1979, pp. 43–45.

110. Interview by author, Oct. 15, 1981.

111. "Long Ears in Louisville," *Time,* Oct. 14, 1974.

112. Interview with author, Oct. 23, 1981.

113. Meyer, p. 83.

114. Meyer, p. 203.

115. Frank Sutherland, "Jerry Thompson: Before and After the Klan Series," *Gannetteer,* April 1981, pp. 10–11.

116. Interviews by author of Larry Beaupre and Robert Giles, then editors at the *Times-Union,* Oct. 15, 1981.

117. "Digging Out the News," *Washington Journalism Review,* September 1985, pp. 12–13.

118. Interview with author, Sept. 2, 1981.

119. Interview of William Deibler, managing editor of the *Pittsburgh Post-Gazette,* by the author, Oct. 22, 1981.

120. "Privacy and the Need to Know."

121. "Shattering the Illusion of Privacy," *Macworld,* July 1993, p. 128.

122. "Privacy and the Need to Know."

123. Sigman L. Splichal, "How Florida Newspapers Are Dealing With Access to Computerized Government Information," *Newspaper Research Journal,* Fall 1992/Winter 1993, pp. 73–83.

124. Harwood, "Sometimes Compassion."

125. "Privacy and the Need to Know."

11. ERRORS AND ACCOUNTABILITY

1. The original story was "Dean Probes Sexism Issue," *Calgary Herald,* Nov. 15, 1991, p. B1. The correction was printed the next day. The newspaper's ombudsman, Jim Stott, discussed the incident in "More Flexible Error Correction Policy Would Serve All," *Calgary Herald,* Dec. 8, 1991, p. A7.

2. Michael Singletary and Richard Lipsky, "Accuracy in Local TV News," *Journalism Quarterly,* Summer 1977, pp. 363–364.

3. David Shaw, "Press Turns the Mirror on Itself," *Los Angeles Times,* June 19, 1988, p. 1.

4. Reprinted in "The Lower Case," *Columbia Journalism Review,* November/December 1990, p. 65.

5. Richard P. Cunningham, "Gov. Lamm and the 'Duty to Die,' " *Editor & Publisher,* May 19, 1986, p. 7.

6. *After "Jimmy's World": Tightening Up in Editing,* New York: National News Council, 1981, p. 114.

7. Letter to Professor R. Thomas Berner, Pennsylvania State University, Nov. 30, 1981, excerpted with letter writer's permission.

8. H.L. Mencken, *Promises: Sixth Series,* New York: Knopf, 1927, p. 15.

9. David Shaw, "Legal Issues: Press Still Falls Short," *Los Angeles Times,* Nov. 11, 1981.

10. A. Kent MacDougall, "Flaws in Press Coverage Plus Business Sensitivity Stir Bitter Debate," *Los Angeles Times,* Feb. 3, 1980.

11. "F.Y.I." *Washington Journalism Review,* January/February 1993, p. 13.

12. Cortland Anderson, remarks to APME Convention, Toronto, Oct. 21, 1981.

13. Interview by author, Nov. 25, 1980.

14. David Weaver and G. Cleveland Wilhoit, *The American Journalist in the 1990s: A Preliminary Report,* Arlington: The Freedom Forum, 1992, p. 7.

15. Seymour Topping, " 'Expert Journalism' Requires a Broad Education," *ASNE Bulletin,* Nov. 1992, p. 2.

16. Rolf Rykken, "New Tactics Mark the Push for Accuracy," *Presstime,* July 1991, p. 6.

17. Howard Kurtz, "Why the Press Is Always Right," *Columbia Journalism Review,* May/June 1993, pp. 34–35.

18. Steve Brill, "NBC Fraud Shows Media Double Standard," *Chicago Tribune,* April 25, 1993, p. C1.

19. Kurtz, p. 33.

20. Brill.

21. Michael Cremedas, "Corrections Policies in Local Television News: A Survey," *Journalism Quarterly,* Spring 1992, pp. 166–172.

22. Ralph Holsinger, *Media Law,* New York: Random House, 1987, p. 119.

23. "So There: Editor's Apology in No Uncertain Terms," AP unpublished file copy, Dec. 22, 1980.

24. Stott.
25. Stott.
26. Quoted in Richard Cunningham, "Speak Softly and Carry an Ombudsman," *Quill,* April 1992, p. 4.
27. "Darts and Laurels," *Columbia Journalism Review,* March/May 1993, p. 22.
28. Rykken, pp. 6–8.
29. Ibid.
30. Eleanor Randolph, "The Other Side of the Pen," in *Messages: The Washington Post Media Companion,* Boston: Allyn and Bacon, 1991, p. 351.
31. Jay Matthews, "When in Doubt, Read It Back," *Washington Journalism Review,* Sept. 1985, pp. 33–35.
32. Steve Weinberg, "So What's Wrong With Pre-Publication Review?" *Quill,* May 1990, pp. 26–28.
33. Weinberg, p. 27.
34. Quoted in Richard P. Cunningham, "Why Not Check Quotes With Sources?" *Quill,* April 1988, p. 9.
35. Frank Wetzel, "Listening to Readers Through an Ombudsman," *Presstime,* June 1990, p. 32.
36. Kate McKenna, "The Loneliest Job in the Newsroom," *American Journalism Review,* March 1993, pp. 41–44.
37. Robert Haiman, talk prepared for convention of ASNE, April 22, 1981.
38. Interview by author, Oct. 7, 1981.
39. Richard Salant, "Ombudsmen—Worth Saving?" *Nieman Reports,* Fall 1992, p. 75.
40. Lou Gelfand, "Newspaper Ombudsmen Can Help to Retain Readers," *Presstime,* April 1992, p. 35.
41. Salant, p. 84.
42. Cunningham, "Speak Softly."
43. Lou Gelfand, "Readers Can Judge for Themselves How I'm Doing," Minneapolis *Star Tribune,* April 28, 1992, p. 19A.
44. "Darts and Laurels," *Columbia Journalism Review,* July/August 1992, p. 22.
45. Charles Fountain, "The Ombudsman Who Went Too Fair," *Columbia Journalism Review,* November/December 1987, p. 48.
46. Gelfand.
47. "Ethics Police," *American Journalism Review,* June 1993, p. 9.
48. Interview by author, Nov. 2, 1981.
49. Colleen Patrick, "The Value of Self-Coverage in the Media Age," *The Seattle Times,* Sept. 14, 1991.
50. "News Council Closes, Gives Files to Minnesota," *Quill,* May 1984, p. 44.
51. William MacPherson, "Sole Newspaper Watchdog in U.S. Finally Gets Some Company," *The Ottawa Citizen,* Sept. 18, 1992, p. A11.
52. "Panel Says Stillwater Paper Unfair to County Official," Minneapolis *Star Tribune,* Dec. 12, 1992, p. 2B.
53. "Star Tribune Apologizes to Mankato Professor," Minneapolis *Star Tribune,* April 15, 1992, p. 38.
54. Chandler's plan is outlined in William L. Winter, "How Publishers Can Calm Angry Readers," *Presstime,* May 1990, pp. 14–15.
55. MacPherson, p. A11.
56. M.L. Stein, "Editors Stiff Regional Press Council," *Editor & Publisher,* March 13, 1993, p. 9.

12. COMPASSION

1. Ramon Coronado, "Broken Goblet, Broken Table: The Media Cover a Hostage Family," and "How Far Should the Media Go to Get a Story?" in "Editorially Speaking," *Gannetteer,* May 1981, pp. 2, 4.

2. James Warren, "Parasites vs. Privacy," *Chicago Tribune,* Feb. 24, 1991, p. C-2.

3. *The People & the Press,"* Los Angeles: Times Mirror, 1986.

4. Interview by author, Oct. 19, 1981.

5. Ginger Casey, "Playground Vultures," *Quill,* November/December 1992, p. 27. The *Quill* piece is an excerpt from an article she wrote for the San Francisco *Examiner.*

6. David Pritchard, "The Impact of Newspaper Ombudsmen on Journalists' Attitudes," *Journalism Quarterly,* Spring 1993, pp. 77–86.

7. Remarks made in the 13th annual Otis Chandler lecture at the University of Southern California School of Journalism, quoted in M.L. Stein, "Here We Go Again!" *Editor & Publisher,* Nov. 28, 1992, p. 11.

8. A thorough discussion of the ethical issues involved in these stories can be found in Bob Steele, "Doing Ethics: How a Minneapolis Journalist Turned a Difficult Situation Into a Human Triumph," *Quill,* November/December 1992, pp. 28–30.

9. Interview by author, Oct. 19, 1981.

10. Janet Malcolm, "Reflections: The Journalist and the Murderer," *The New Yorker,* March 13, 20, 1989. The article also appeared in Malcolm's *The Journalist and the Murderer,* New York: Knopf, 1991.

11. Editor's Note to "Dangerous Liaisons," *Columbia Journalism Review,* July/August 1989, pp. 21–35. This article is a collection of short essays. Quotes from writers and journalists in this section are taken from this collection.

12. "Dangerous Liaisons."

13. "Dangerous Liaisons."

14. "Dangerous Liaisons."

15. Casey.

16. Bob Greene, "By Any Other Name," *Esquire,* Sept. 1981, pp. 23–24.

17. Interview by author, Sept. 23, 1981.

18. Quoted in "Dangerous Liaisons."

19. Richard Cunningham, "When News Features Hurt the Innocent," *Quill,* March 1987, p. 7. Details of this incident are taken from this article.

20. John Tierney, "Cash on Delivery," *The New York Times,* April 18, 1993, Sec. 6, p. 64.

21. "Dangerous Liaisons."

22. Cunningham, "When News Features Hurt the Innocent."

23. Richard Cunningham, "A Byrd's-eye View of Ethics Inside *The Washington Post,"* *Quill,* November/December 1992, p. 10.

24. Bill Boyarsky, "Motives Sought in Suicide of Oakland Publisher Knowland," *Los Angeles Times,* Feb. 25, 1974.

25. Joe Shoquist, "When Not to Print the News," 1974 report of APME Professional Standards Committee.

26. Thomas Collins, "When the Press Restrains Itself," *Newsday,* March 30, 1983.

27. Paula Moore, "Two Boys Are Kidnapped in El Paso — and the Media Weigh Withholding the Story," "Editorially Speaking," *Gannetteer,* Aug. 1986, pp. 2–3.

28. Richard P. Cunningham, "Aside From That, How Was the Play, Mrs. Lincoln?" *Quill,* April 1988, pp. 8–9. Details and quotes about this incident are taken from this article.

29. "Soviet Spy Worked for 4 Years in Dallas," *Dallas Times Herald,* March 2, 1976.

30. Anna Shaw, "Natasha's Story: Judgment Call in Sarajevo," *Columbia Journalism Review,* September/October 1992, p. 22.

31. Interview with Anthony Casale of *USA Today* by author, Oct. 16, 1981.

32. Interview by author, Jan. 17, 1983.

33. Charles B. Seib, "Could a Little Caring Have Prevented Hoax?" *Presstime,* June 1981, p. 35.

34. Thomas Bray, "What If the 'Jimmy' Story Had Been True?" *The Wall Street Journal,* April 17, 1981.

35. John Troan, "The Lesson in the Janet Cooke Case," *Pittsburgh Press,* May 3, 1981.

36. Interview by author, May 27, 1981.

37. Interview by author, June 3, 1981.

38. Interview by author, June 5, 1981.

39. *After "Jimmy's World": Tightening Up in Editing,* New York: National News Council, 1981, p. 61.

40. Julia Cass, "Smoke Bomb Puts Student on Probation," *The Philadelphia Inquirer,* Aug. 6, 1981.

41. Interview of Jerry Bellune by author, Nov. 3, 1981.

42. Interview by author, March 27, 1982.

43. H.L. Stevenson, "Bill Murphy and the Bridge Jumper," *Editor & Publisher,* Nov. 12, 1977, p. 34.

44. Interview.

45. Gannett News Service, *News Watch,* June 2, 1991.

46. Interview by author, Feb. 24, 1986.

47. Liz Nakahara, "In the Eye of the Story," *The Washington Post,* Nov. 6, 1983, pp. K1, 6, 7.

48. Interview by author, July 27, 1983.

49. "The Double Fire," *The New York Times,* March 13, 1983.

50. "Ethics Led Photog to Miss News Shot," *Editor & Publisher,* Aug. 3, 1985, p. 44.

51. "Photographer Helps Rescue Family—Then Snaps His Pictures," *Editor & Publisher,* Aug. 3, 1985, p. 55.

52. John Hohenberg, *The News Media: A Journalist Looks at His Profession,* New York: Holt, Rinehart and Winston, 1968, pp. 214–15.

53. Phillip Knightley, *The First Casualty: From the Crimea to Vietnam, The War Correspondent as Hero, Propagandist and Myth Maker,* New York: Harcourt Brace Jovanovich, 1975, p. 406.

SELECTED BIBLIOGRAPHY

Bagdikian, Ben. *The Media Monopoly.* 3rd ed. Boston: Beacon Press, 1990.

Bailey, Charles W. *Conflicts of Interest: A Matter of Journalistic Ethics.* New York: National News Council, 1984.

Bayley, Edwin R. *Joe McCarthy and the Press.* Madison: University of Wisconsin Press, 1981.

Bernstein, Carl, and Bob Woodward. *All the President's Men.* New York: Simon and Schuster, 1974.

Benedict, Robin. *Virgin or Vamp: How the Press Covers Sex Crimes.* New York: Oxford University Press, 1992.

Black, Jay, Bob Steele, and Ralph Barney. *Doing Ethics in Journalism.* Greencastle, Ind.: Sigma Delta Chi Foundation, Society of Professional Journalists, 1993.

Bok, Sissela. *Lying: Moral Choice in Public and Private Life.* New York: Vintage, Random House, 1984.

Christians, Clifford G., William L. Rivers, and Wilbur Schramm. *Responsibility in Mass Communication.* 3rd ed. New York: Harper and Row, 1980.

Christians, Clifford G., Kim B. Rotzoll, and Mark Fackler. *Media Ethics: Cases and Moral Reasoning.* 3rd ed. New York: Longman, 1991.

Commission on Freedom of the Press. *A Free and Responsible Press.* Chicago: University of Chicago Press, 1947.

Crawford, Nelson A. *The Ethics of Journalism.* New York: Knopf, 1924.

Fedler, Fred. *Media Hoaxes.* Ames: Iowa State University Press, 1989.

Goldstein, Tom. *The News at Any Cost: How Journalists Compromise Their Ethics to Shape the News.* New York: Simon and Schuster, 1985.

Halberstam, David. *The Powers That Be.* New York: Knopf, 1979.

Hohenberg, John. *The News Media: A Journalist Looks at His Profession.* New York: Holt, Rinehart and Winston, 1968.

———. *The Professional Journalist.* New York: Holt, Rinehart and Winston, 1983.

Isaacs, Norman E. *Untended Gates: The Mismanaged Press.* New York: Columbia University Press, 1986.

Johnstone, John W. C., Edward J. Slawski, and William W. Bowman. *The News People: A Sociological Portrait of American Journalists and Their Work.* Urbana: University of Illinois Press, 1976.

Knightly, Phillip. *The First Casualty: From the Crimea to Vietnam, The War Correspondent as Hero, Propagandist and Myth Maker.* New York: Harvest, Harcourt Brace Jovanovich, 1975.

Lambeth, Edmund B. *Committed Journalism: An Ethic for the Profession.* 2nd ed. Bloomington: Indiana University Press, 1991.

Malcolm, Janet. *The Journalist and the Murderer.* New York: Vintage, Random House, 1990.

Merrill, John C. *Existential Journalism*. New York: Hastings House, 1977.

―――. *The Dialectic in Journalism*. Baton Rouge: Louisiana State University Press, 1989.

Merrill, John C., and S. Jack Odell. *Philosophy and Journalism*. New York: Longman, 1983.

Meyer, Philip. *Editors, Publishers and Newspaper Ethics: A Report to the American Society of Newspaper Editors*. Washington, D.C.: American Society of Newspaper Editors, 1983.

―――. *Ethical Journalism: A Guide for Students, Practitioners and Consumers*. New York: Longman, 1987.

Sabato, Larry J. *Feeding Frenzy: How Attack Journalism Has Transformed American Politics*. New York: Free Press, 1991.

Schudson, Michael. *Discovering the News: A Social History of American Newspapers*. New York: Basic Books, 1978.

Siebert, Fred S., Theodore Peterson, and Wilbur Schramm. *Four Theories of the Press*. Urbana: University of Illinois Press, 1963.

Swain, Bruce M. *Reporters' Ethics*. Ames: Iowa State University Press, 1978.

Thayer, Lee, ed. *Ethics, Morality and the Media*. New York: Hastings House, 1980.

Weaver, David H., and G. Cleveland Wilhoit. *The American Journalist: A Portrait of U.S. News People and Their Work*. Bloomington: Indiana University Press, 1986.

―――. *The American Journalist in the 1990s*. Arlington, Va.: Freedom Forum, 1992.

Wicker, Tom. *On Press: A Top Reporter's Life in and Reflections on American Journalism*. New York: Viking, 1978.

INDEX

Gene Goodwin, professor emeritus of journalism at Pennsylvania State University, can look back on 12 years as a practicing journalist and 30 years as journalism teacher and administrator. His professional newspaper experience began in Iowa and included reporting and editing jobs on the Baltimore *Sun,* the Associated Press and the old *Washington Star.*

Goodwin served as director of the Penn State School of Journalism for 12 years. He also taught journalism ethics, reporting, editing and other subjects, winning an Amoco Foundation award for excellence in teaching in 1980. During World War II, 1st Lt. Goodwin was a B-17 navigator in the 8th Air Force in England, earning the Distinguished Flying Cross and Air Medal. In retirement, he writes a column for the weekly newspaper where he now lives in Mount Dora, Florida.

For the first edition of this book, Goodwin received the Kappa Tau Alpha national research award for the best book about journalism published in 1983.

Ron F. Smith, associate professor of journalism at the University of Central Florida, Orlando, has worked as a reporter for newspapers in Indiana, Ohio and Florida. His journalistic experience began as a summer intern subbing for the police reporter and has included stints as court reporter, sports copy editor, wire editor and news editor.

At Orlando, Smith has taught ethics, editorial writing, copy editing, writing for public relations and reporting. He has served on the faculty senate for four years and is adviser to the student chapter of the Society of Professional Journalists. Among his numerous publications are articles in *Journalism Quarterly, Newspaper Research Journal, Public Relations Review, Quill* and *Journalism Educator.*